TRADE UNIONS IN BRITAIN

KEN COATES is Reader in Adult Education at the University of Nottingham.

TONY TOPHAM is Senior Lecturer in Industrial Studies, Adult Education Department, at the University of Hull.

They are the co-authors of *Industrial Democracy in Britain* (1967), *The New Unionism: the Case for Workers' Control* (1972), *The Shop Steward's Guide to the Bullock Report* (1977) and *Trade Unions and Politics* (1986), and they are currently engaged in a major study of the history of the TGWU.

'Of the hundreds of books published on the trade union movement, this is the one to read first, if you wish to steer your way into this complicated territory.'

WALTER GREENDALE, General Council of the Trades Union Congress Education Committee

'Enormous value . . . fills a major need and deserves to be read throughout the Labour movement and way beyond it . . . detailed and scholarly, presenting all points of view and examining all the relevant literature . . . A mine of useful information, cautious in its judgements and clear in its expression, it will be essential reading for everybody who wishes to appreciate the central importance of unions in the nation's affairs.'

BEN PIMLOTT, *Labour Weekly*

'In *Trade Unions in Britain* is all the information which you wanted to know and didn't know where to find, written in clear, straightforward prose. It is a best buy, both for its content and because it is cheap for a major book these days.'

DAVID RUBINSTEIN, *Labour Leader*

TRADE UNIONS IN BRITAIN

Ken Coates and Tony Topham

Fontana Press

First and second editions published by Spokesman, 1980 and 1982
This third edition first published in 1988 by Fontana Press,
an imprint of Fontana Paperbacks,
part of the Collins Publishing Group,
8 Grafton Street, London W1X 3LA

Set in 10½/12 Linotron Baskerville by
The Word Factory Ltd, Rossendale, Lancashire

Made and printed in Great Britain by
William Collins Sons & Co. Ltd, Glasgow

This book is gratefully dedicated to
BILL JONES

CONTENTS

LIST OF TABLES

LIST OF TABLES

INTRODUCTORY NOTE

When we first published *Trade Unions in Britain*, long ago in 1980, we knew that the political and economic order in Britain was changing convulsively, and we did not expect that the trade union movement would escape important changes itself. But in the intervening years between the publication of that first edition and the preparation of this new Fontana Press version, the whole landscape has altered. The result is that large parts of this work are completely new.

We have tried to provide a straightforward introduction to Britain's unions, and to allow the facts to speak for themselves.

Any book on industrial relations is bound to be stiff with initials. Not only do the trade unions themselves delight in acronyms which make a complicated puzzle, but they also multiply joint bodies, confederations and alliances, each of which is normally known by some abbreviation or other.

A list of all the unions which are named in this book (and some which are not) will be found in the index of trade unions on page 427. Each acronym commonly used by such unions is decoded in that index, which is cross-referenced.

A variety of other industrial relations bodies are also normally referred to by their initials. A list of these bodies will be found on page 407.

CHAPTER 1

Trade Unions and Their Setting

Some Definitions

'A trade union, as we understand the term, is a continuous association of wage-earners for the purpose of maintaining or improving the conditions of their employment.' It was in this way, back in 1894, that Sidney and Beatrice Webb opened their classic work on the *History of Trade Unionism.*[1]

In commonsense terms, there is still merit in this definition. But in 1920, when they re-edited the work for students of the Workers' Educational Association, the Webbs deleted the word 'employment', and added the wider term 'working lives'. They made this change, they insisted, because they had been accused of assuming that unions had 'always contemplated a perpetual continuance of the capitalist or wage-system'. 'No such implication', they sternly added, 'was intended.'

More recently, critics have objected to even the modified formula, on the grounds that it places too much emphasis on the continuity of association.[2] In truth, many working-class initiatives are spontaneous, and only take on 'continuity' by accident. The TUC itself began as an ad hoc conference on threatened legal changes, and could easily have finished its career as a one-off event, like innumerable other union conferences.[3] Many trade unions may trace their original formation to a particular dispute, or trauma, out of which developed a permanent organization. Such development does look a bit haphazard to any outside observer. What is it that turns one indignant demonstration, or strike, into the root of a new organization, while a seemingly identical event next day, or in the next town, provokes no such continuity? These questions recur in every generation. During the extraordinary upsurge of factory occupations in 1971 and the following years, there were more than two hundred 'work-ins' or 'sit-ins'.[4] Of these, perhaps half a dozen evolved into permanent workers' producer co-operatives, of which a few survived.[5] Is the history of 'continuous associations' of self-management organizations to be written about the survivors only? But some of the failures are as interesting as the successes. Is our concern to be restricted, in this case, to people who sought 'continuity' for their initiative? But the handful of co-ops were part of a wider movement in which co-operative objectives played a relatively minor role. Whatever we think about these questions, it is difficult to understand trade unionism as a living movement in terms of its continuity alone.

This was, mercifully, adequately recognized in the law governing trade unions from 1871 onwards. Consolidating various laws of 1871, 1876 and 1913, we arrived at a legal definition of a trade union which said it was:

> any combination, whether temporary or permanent, the principal objects of which are under its constitution statutory objects, namely the regulation of the relations between workmen and masters or between workmen and workmen, or between masters and masters, or the imposing of restrictive conditions on the conduct of any trade or business, and also the provision of benefits to members, whether such combination would or would not, if the Trade Union Act, 1871, had not been passed, have been deemed to be an unlawful combination by reason of some one or more of its purposes being in restraint of trade.[6]

Although the recognition that temporary associations could be regarded as trade unions was vital for the protection of strikes, and much to be preferred as a legal provision to any attempt to limit legal protection to permanent bodies, this definition was generally felt to have been outdated, long before it was at last revised.

The official Donovan Report which was published in 1968[7] suggested that it was also too wide, since it dealt with employers' organizations under the same framework as unions themselves, which does not accord with any commonsense view. The Royal Commission also disliked the imprecision of the term 'workmen'. They wished to have it replaced by the word 'employee', and they suggested revisions of the provisions concerning 'restrictive conditions'. After a long debate and after the volcanic upheaval of the Industrial Relations Act of 1971, trade union law was finally resolved in the Trade Union and Labour Relations Act of 1974, which offers the following definition of a trade union:

> 28.—(1) In this Act, except so far as the context otherwise requires, 'trade union' means an organization (whether permanent or temporary) which either—
>
> (*a*) consists wholly or mainly of workers of one or more descriptions and is an organization whose principal purposes include the regulation of relations between workers of that description or those descriptions and employers or employers' associations: or
>
> (*b*) consists wholly or mainly of—
>
> (i) constituent or affiliated organizations which fulfil the conditions specified in paragraph (*a*) above (or themselves consist wholly or mainly of constituent or affiliated organizations which fulfil those conditions), or
>
> (ii) representatives of such constituent or affiliated organizations:
>
> and in either case is an organization whose principal purposes include the regulation of relations between workers and employers or between workers and employers' associations, or include the regulation of relations between its constituent or affiliated organizations.

As we have just said, employers' organizations had been defined (somewhat paradoxically) as trade unions in the earlier legislation, but from 1974 onwards their role has been treated separately, no doubt in part because of the Royal Commission's recommendation. We pass over this complex issue since it is outside the area of our concern in this book. Returning to the unions, we should note that the current legal meaning of the words 'trade union' still preserves any element of protection which spontaneous organizations (however ephemeral these might have been) have traditionally been able to derive from the archaic working of the Act of 1871 and its successors. Otherwise, it is considerably closer to normal usage. Nonetheless, it remains a legal formula, rather than a sociological description. If we are to approach closer to an appreciation of what unions are about, we must look elsewhere.

Refreshingly direct, and free from the common jargon of bureaucracy, is the long statement put in by the TUC itself to Lord Donovan's Commission: this sets out some of the basic reasons why it is right for a democratic state to safeguard the rights of independent trade unions.

> The status of the employed person in an industrial economy is one of dependence on earnings with little or no individual power of direct decision. The individual contract between an employee and an employer does not reflect a position of equal strength on the two sides. Equality before the law is only relevant to the observance of the contract and not to its terms or the procedure by which it is made. In these circumstances the economic freedom of the individual employee is very small. This must be the starting point of any objective examination of the rights and needs of employed persons. These fundamental rights and needs deriving from the nature of the employment relationship are in essence permanent and enduring, though they lead to changes in substantive terms, for example in the level of wages, as the years go by.
>
> It would be generally recognized that employed persons can justly claim the right to have their interests taken into account . . .
>
> Trade unions are the unique means whereby men and women in employment can themselves decide how their interests can best be furthered. Workpeople have the right to combine to form their own organizations and through this means to advance and protect their interests.

> Thus the essential characteristic of free trade unions is that they are responsible to the workpeople themselves who comprise their membership and cannot be directed by any outside agency . . .
>
> Recognition of the fact that the interests and preferences of individuals and groups are different, according to the perspective of each of them, is embodied in the structure of individual trade unions and in the trade union movement as a whole. Recognition of the legitimacy of distinct and often diverging interests is also the basis of bargaining between trade unions and employers.[8]

The TUC was compelled to pay special attention to the problems which are involved in the very idea of an 'employee'. Not so long ago, British laws referred to all employees as 'servants'. This reflects a distasteful relationship because it implies that employers are 'masters', as the 1871 legislation still specified. We should remember that this fundamental attitude dates from a time when 'democracy' itself was a most controversial concept, linked in the minds of the Establishment with anarchy and mob-rule.

Indeed, it is remarkable how modern sound some of the very earliest writings of political economy when they consider this question. Adam Smith, for instance, writing in *The Wealth of Nations*, which founded modern economics in 1776, says 'we rarely hear . . . of the combinations of masters, though frequently of those of workmen. But whoever imagines, upon this account, that masters rarely combine, is as ignorant of the world as of the subject. Masters are always and everywhere in a sort of tacit, but constant and uniform combination, not to raise the wages of labour above their actual rate . . . Masters, too, sometimes enter into particular combinations to sink the wages of labour even below this rate. These are always conducted with the utmost silence and secrecy, till the moment of execution . . .' On the other hand, even two hundred years ago, when labourers combined 'whether their combinations be offensive or defensive, they are always abundantly heard of'.[9]

Recognizing this fact, which is still very much a part of contemporary life, the Trades Union Congress added to its Royal Commission statement these cautiously defensive remarks:

> Arising out of their status as employed persons, dependent on earnings, dependent on securing and retaining employment, workpeople know that to exercise their rights they must find a means to redress the balance of unequal strength vis-à-vis their employers. Whilst the position of the individual employee, both in law and in practice, is one of subordination, individual employees together recognize that it is through combination that they can develop a means, the essential means which they possess, to harness their own potential strength. It is in the nature of the employment situation that working people readily identify themselves with their fellows in groups. This feeling of collective identity enhances the economic freedom of the individual, a freedom which rests on the knowledge that unity is strength.
>
> Just as the bargaining strength of the individual is enhanced when he combines with his fellow workers in a group at a place of employment, so on a wider plane trade unions grow in size and extent to become whatever may be the most effective combination of workpeople to advance and protect those interests, arising from their employment, which they have in common.[10]

The Components of Trade Unionism

Sociologists, who do not always write as clearly as the TUC, have offered a variety of divergent efforts to bend the efforts of science in order to determine what constitutes a trade union. R. M. Blackburn, for instance, employs the concept of 'unionateness', which braids seven distinct strands:

1. It regards collective bargaining and the protection of the interests of members, as employees, as its main function, rather than, say, professional activities or welfare schemes.
2. It is independent of employers for purposes of negotiation.
3. It is prepared to be militant, using all forms of industrial action which may be effective.

4. It declares itself to be a trade union.
5. It is registered as a trade union.
6. It is affiliated to the Trades Union Congress.
7. It is affiliated to the Labour Party.[11]

As Blackburn points out, these seven strands are not equally internally consistent. The first few can be a matter of degree, while the last four are clear characteristics which an organization 'either has or does not have'. Within such a view, different unions may be more, or less, 'unionate' when contrasted at the same time; while the same union may become increasingly 'unionate' as it develops. NALGO, the Local Government Officers' Association, and the NUT (Teachers' Union) both resisted affiliation to the TUC over a long period of time, and even, at one moment, struggled to set up an alternative national centre for Professional Workers. When they finally took the plunge, their identification with traditional unionism was obviously the more complete for so doing. If they were tomorrow to follow the Colliery Officials into the Labour Party, their 'unionateness' would be even firmer in its consistency. (Blackburn was aware of the grey areas on the margins of his subject, because he was involved in a study of the Bank Employees, who subsequently so far forgot their unionate manners as to allow themselves to be suspended from membership of the TUC, after they had refused to implement its policies on the 1971 Industrial Relations Act.) Unions which would never have contemplated the thought, a few years ago, have recently been greatly more prone to link up with the TUC: which now includes not only the two mass professional associations just named, but also the Association of University Teachers, the British Association of Colliery Managers, the Institute of Professional Civil Servants, and a number of other representatives of the higher salariat. 'Unionateness', here, must still, surely, be rather evidently in the balance.

Nonetheless, when Mr Wilfred Miron, of the National Coal Board, was preparing his contingency plans for the handling of mining trade unions with entirely practical objectives in view, his analysis dovetailed quite precisely into that of Blackburn, including a careful estimate of the commitment of the colliery managers. In a private memorandum to Sir Derek Ezra, then Chairman of the National Coal Board, Mr Miron argued, on 6 December 1973, that:

> The position of NACODS vis-à-vis BACM must be considered in the total context. The more supervisory staff who can be channelled into BACM the better. NACODS is a member of the TUC: BACM is not. NACODS have demonstrated recently that they are less and less a real part of management – they want the status and the money but not the responsibility or the risk. This is not surprising because they are basically still 'industrial' grades and identify themselves community-wise and socially inevitably with NUM membership.

Until 1979, 'unionate' organizations were growing in a most spectacular fashion, and the result was a dramatic influence in that proportion of the workforce belonging to unions. In 1969, 44 per cent of the labour force were enrolled in appropriate unions, and this proportion grew steadily until 1972, when it began to see-saw around 50 per cent. The re-election of a Labour government in 1974 established a new rising trend, reaching 54½ per cent in 1979. Thereafter, decline set in, as unemployment figures soared away out of sight.[12] By 1984, the proportion of the workforce belonging to unions was down to 45.7 per cent, or a figure very close to that of 1969.

Mass unemployment has always undermined trade unions. During the great lay-offs of the 1980s this remained true. Employment in production and construction declined by one-fifth between 1980 and 1984: but union membership in those sectors went down by very nearly one-third. Employment in services was more or less maintained (with a decline of only 0.5 per cent), but even there, union membership declined by 6.4 per cent. Taking the overall economy, between 1980 and 1984, employment diminished by 7.9 per cent but union membership by 14.4 per cent.

The total number of trade union members peaked in 1979,

when 13.3 million people were enrolled. Then decline set in. By 1984, 371 unions shared between them 11,086,000 members.

Of course, old-established and better organized industries have been among the worst hit by industrial decline. Such employment growth as there has been, in services and small firms, has brought a marked increase in part-time jobs, especially for women. But small enterprises have always been difficult to organize, and part-time employees even more so.

We shall return to this question: here it is enough to note that British trade unions retain a strong representative character even though they have lost much influence.

Table 1.1

Percentage of trade unionists in total labour force, 1969–84

	(a) Labour force 000s	(b) Trade union members, 000s	% (b) of (a)
1969	23,603	10,472	44.4
1970	23,446	11,179	47.7
1971	23,231	11,127	47.9
1972	23,303	11,349	48.7
1973	23,592	11,444	48.5
1974	23,689	11,755	49.6
1975	23,553	12,026	51.1
1976	23,713	12,386	52.2
1977	23,920	12,846	53.7
1978	24,061	13,112	54.5
1979	24,365	13,289	54.5
1980	24,511	12,947	52.8
1981	24,265	12,106	49.9
1982	24,166	11,593	48.0
1983	23,996	11,337	47.2
1984	24,264	11,086	45.7

When the Royal Commission on Trade Unions sat, under Lord Donovan's chairmanship, during the mid-1960s, it circulated unions with a booklet which spelt out the areas upon which it was seeking information. This included a suggested classification of types of organization: and it provoked an interesting reply from the Transport and General Workers' Union, which was entered into the evidence it offered the Commission.

> It is our view that the classification of types of trade union quoted in the Commission's booklet, i.e., 'craft', 'general', 'industrial' and 'white-collar' is not really appropriate to the present pattern of industry.
>
> With one or two exceptions, it is impossible to isolate a 'craft' today. New skills are constantly developing and entry to them is by a variety of methods, sometimes in maturity. Apprenticeship itself – the traditional way into the 'craft' – is steadily becoming more liberal in the education and training it offers, and may equip a youngster with more than one skill.
>
> The attempt to define an industry is even more frustrating. What is the Engineering Industry? Or the Chemical Industry? Or plastics? Or food?
>
> We consider it wrong, socially and industrially, to separate 'white-collar' employees from others, since their problems are identical in essence, and increasingly so in detail.
>
> It seems to us, therefore, that the modern union is bound to become a 'general' one.[13]

We shall consider these traditional typologies ('craft', 'industrial', 'general' and so on) in detail in our next chapter: but it is appropriate to note this response as one successful answer to the shifting stresses of the changing labour market. Here we find an explicit recognition of these pressures, and a deliberate strategy for dealing with them. Sometimes, it is true, less foresight is shown by unions: but once one organization adapts to meet new challenges, others will not only follow very quickly, but also profit from any previous example by avoiding its mistakes. If unions develop at an uneven rate, and are 'unionate' to different degrees, they also tend to learn from each other. This sometimes enables them to *combine* features of development which were previously evolved separately, leapfrogging whole stages of transition which were necessary to the first innovators. New initiatives may sometimes be diffused at the speed of television transmission, speedily and cleanly.

Social historians have often noted the contextual limits of union organization: how, in many countries, unions have grown through similar successive phases. First, spontaneous uprisings, outbreaks of rioting or machine breaking; then, local associations of craftsmen; later, national organizations, industrial movements inolving semi-skilled along with the skilled. Stages like these are not neatly sealed off from each other like geological sediments, though: if a metaphor from the earth sciences applies to unions, we are bound to see that such deposits are jumbled by successive earth-movements which bend and shear the strata, and yet allow all kinds of otherwise anachronistic bodies to live on, in little time-capsules of their own. In Britain, these processes have left us with an exceptionally complicated trade union legacy. This complexity is being reduced, by force of new circumstances, as we shall see in Chapter 2.

The Conditioning Social Context

What is quite plain is that the unions never develop in a vacuum, and that the social and economic environment in which they grow exercises a continuously changing influence upon that growth. In the year of Robert Owen's Grand National Consolidated Trade Union (1834) there were 298 miles of railways. By 1848, the year of Chartism's last great upheaval, about 5,000 miles existed. In 1868, there were, by the time of the birth of the TUC, 12,319 miles.[14] Legislation bringing limited liability companies into being was approved in 1855, partly because of the pressures of scale involved in these developing railway networks: no traditional commercial partnership accepting full, conventional responsibility for its deeds could possibly extend its operations over a national modern railway system. (Neither could the vast capital commitments of the necessary related steel industry be undertaken by old-style entrepreneurs.) We shall return to the question of the effects of successive developments of new forms of company structure: it is enough here to note that in this complex skein, the type of trade union which had been just imaginable in 1834 had become perfectly physically possible by 1868.

The closer linkages of modern communications (newspapers, as well as transportation systems) not merely brought hitherto separate areas and trades within reach of one another, but at the same time integrated their economic experience, and intensified the need for their co-operation. Karl Marx pithily summarized the growth processes of modern capitalism:

> The battle of competition is fought by cheapening commodities. The cheapness of commodities depends, *ceteris paribus*, on the productivity of labour, and this again on the scale of production. Therefore, the larger capitals beat the smaller . . . The credit system becomes a new and formidable weapon in the competitive struggle, and finally it transforms itself into an immense social mechanism for the concentration of capitals . . . Centralization completes the work of accumulation by enabling the industrial capitalists to expand the scale of their operations.[15]

National trade unions grow up as an answering response at a certain point in this evolution, and national centres like the TUC emerge at another. Yet, if these are experiences which are in some degree common to a variety of national movements, it should be re-emphasized that such movements may, each, learn from all the others, thus foreshortening the perspective of development as one lesson follows another. Because unions develop consciously, they need not passively reflect what happens to them, but may, in some circumstances, initiate actions which can control, or even determine, to a greater or lesser extent, the environment in which they have to operate. For all that, it seems clear that, over the century, trade union history does undoubtedly involve a great deal of purely defensive response.

Defence, however, can be more or less effective. To weigh its full weight, it needs to protect its protagonists at an appropriate level. While in the early years of industrialism it could be quite local and still competent, yesterday it already had to be fully national. Today, as we shall see, it will not be adequate unless it becomes international, which means that every modern union faces major problems of adjustment.

Concentration of Capital and Power

In the most recent phase of capital concentration, the great postwar economic explosion has meant that a relatively small number of transnational companies have come to dominate the major markets of the world. The vast scale of much modern production, the prodigious costs involved in high technology, the close protective association of big industry with governments, the nervous alignments which partition access to raw materials as well as capital: none of these is entirely a new phenomenon. What has been new has been the rapid growth of explicitly multinational operations, institutionalizing all these processes into a tiny handful of nuclei, each operating on a truly universal scale. Since the mid-1960s at least half the American companies with annual sales of a billion dollars or more have either owned a quarter or more of their assets abroad, or secured a quarter or more of their sales abroad, or both. In Britain, by 1970 'the top hundred manufacturing firms in Britain had controlled some half of manufacturing output. In 1950 they had controlled only a fifth, and in 1910 only 15 per cent.'[16] If the big companies get bigger, however, this does not necessarily increase their share of domestic production or employment, because, in the nature of things, much of this expansion will take place abroad. As Stuart Holland explains, this has serious implications for conventional economic theory: 'Such companies span the previous gap between micro- and macro-economic theory. The competitive firm of micro-economical theory was too small to influence macro-economic aggregates such as national investment, trade and employment. Even in collusion, it was generally held, they could not seriously influence the price level set by sovereign consumers. Such theory still has relevance to the thousands of small companies which the giants are squeezing into the bottom half of the industry. But *in between* these micro-economic firms and the macro-economic level of government policy, the new giants have introduced an intermediate or *meso*-economic sector. Put more simply, these are the big league firms which now command the heights of British industry and dominate the thousands of small league firms.'[17]

Throughout the 1950s and 1960s the fastest growth tended to occur in the overseas subsidiaries of such companies. Banks have joined and stimulated these processes. A key constituent in them has been the growth of military-based orders and research, which have both stimulated, in particular, aircraft, motors and electronics industries. As the benefits of governmental finance of research and development are converted to profitable private investment, so growth has simultaneously facilitated the evasion of obligations to governments: taxes in particular. The device of transfer pricing, in which a company's subsidiaries exchange products at purely fictional prices in order to rearrange surpluses in the most beneficial areas from a taxation point of view, has become both widespread and sophisticated. Dr Penrose cites one multinational company which, 'to her knowledge, prepares "three sets of accounts, one for internal accounting purposes, using cost prices, one for the internal revenue authorities, and one for shareholders"'.[18]

Michael Barratt Brown cites, from *Fortune* magazine, a classic case of the manipulation of cross-frontier cash payments:

> 'One of our Danish subsidiaries,' it said, 'had excess cash which it lent to another Danish subsidiary that was receiving goods from the Swedish subsidiary. The Danish company prepaid its account with the Swedish subsidiary, and this money financed the movement of Swedish products into the Finnish subsidiary. What did the manoeuvre

accomplish? If Finland had been required to pay for the goods, it would have had to borrow at 15 per cent, the going Finnish rate. If the Swedish subsidiary had financed the sale, it would have had to borrow at about 9 per cent. But cash in Denmark was worth only 5 per cent to 6 per cent. Moreover, Danish currency was weak in relation to the Swedish: by speeding up payments to Sweden we not only obtained cheaper credit, we hedged our position in Danish kroner as well.'[19]

Such movements of capital not only threaten the national management of economic affairs, a question which has been elaborately treated elsewhere, they also are a major weapon against effective trade union bargaining, as Stuart Holland has cogently insisted:

Such transfer pricing in multinational trade weakens union wage bargaining power by understating real profits made in the UK.[20]

All this argues the necessity of a new style of international trade union organization, and of a system of combine union committees, to which we will return in later sections of this book. Here it is sufficient to note the extent of the challenge, and to note the shape of the terrain it occupies. This was carefully documented in the report of the Bullock Committee which enquired into the question of industrial democracy, and produced the following analysis of the structure of British industry.[21]

In Table 1.2, the figures given in brackets report the numbers of subsidiaries of overseas-based transnational companies. We see that some 2,100 companies employed 200 or more people in the UK at the time of the enquiry: of these, a third (738 enterprises) employ 2,000-plus people. One hundred of these firms are foreign-based transnationals. Another table from the same source reveals an even greater degree of concentration: 155 enterprises employ 10,000 or more UK employees apiece. Thus, more than a quarter of the British workforce, or more than 7 million people, were at that time employed in large firms in the private sector, many of which were multinational. An equivalent

Table 1.2

United Kingdom enterprises with over 200 employees in the United Kingdom

ANALYSIS BY INDUSTRY AND NUMBER OF EMPLOYEES

Standard Industrial Classification order	Sector	No. of UK employees							
		201–500	501–1,000	1,001–2,000	2,001–5,000	5,001–10,000	Over 10,000	Total over 2,000	TOTAL
		Number of enterprises (of which controlled from overseas)							
I–III	Food, drink and tobacco	21 (3)	30 (7)	28 (4)	20 (4)	9 (3)	22 (1)	51 (8)	130 (22)
IV–V	Petroleum products etc. and chemicals etc.	34 (18)	31 (19)	24 (11)	21 (9)	8 (3)	7 (1)	36 (13)	125 (61)
VI–XII	Metal manufacturing, engineering, shipbuilding, vehicles	55 (17)	140 (30)	138 (31)	125 (34)	45 (9)	48 (10)	218 (53)	551 (131)
XIII–XV	Textiles and clothing	11 (1)	44 (4)	44 (2)	37 (3)	8 (—)	10 (—)	55 (3)	154 (10)
XVI–XIX	Other manufacturing	32 (5)	78 (5)	62 (8)	57 (7)	35 (1)	17 (3)	109 (11)	281 (29)
XX and XXII	Construction, transport and communications	32 (2)	44 (3)	55 (2)	40 (1)	16 (—)	11 (—)	67 (1)	198 (8)
XXIII	Wholesale and retail distribution	43 (10)	65 (4)	55 (7)	59 (5)	17 (1)	22 (3)	98 (9)	261 (30)
XXIV	Insurance, banking, finance and business services	124 (19)	73 (6)	37 (1)	32 (1)	18 (—)	11 (—)	61 (1)	295 (27)
XXVI	Miscellaneous services	17 (6)	21 (6)	18 (4)	22 (1)	12 (—)	9 (—)	43 (1)	99 (17)
	Total	369 (81)	526 (84)	461 (70)	413 (65)	168 (17)	157 (18)	738 (100)	2,094 (335)

number of people worked in the combined public sector, including nationalized industries and national and local government and welfare services.

Trade union membership is heavily concentrated in these sectors, and so are some kinds of trade union problems. As Lord Bullock reported, unionization is stronger in the larger enterprises: Table 1.3 reveals the degree of this concentration and shows how far it was increasing during the years of full employment. Since then, it has been declining in many sectors, as we shall see in detail in Chapter 2.

Table 1.3
Unionization in larger manufacturing establishments in the United Kingdom, 1948 and 1974

	1948		1974	
	Labour force (000s)	Density (%)	Labour force (000s)	Density (%)
All manufacturing	6,709.3	52.2	7,778.9	62.2
Excluding employment in establishments with less than 100 workers	5,193.9	67.4	6,292.4	76.9
Excluding employment in establishments with less than 200 workers	4,268.4	82.1	5,422.5	89.2

Source: Price and Bain, 'Union Growth in Britain: Retrospect and Prospect', *BJIR*, XXL.

After Bullock had reported, with the fall of the Labour government and the advent of the Thatcher administration, the contraction of manufacturing industry was accompanied by further concentration in other sectors, notably that of distribution. But unions found they were working in a difficult recession.

Division of Labour and Alienation

Concentration is one side of the process of development to which trade unions must react. The other side of it has been, up to now, the evolution of an ever more minute division of labour, involving those whom it entraps in paying more and more restrictive attention to smaller and smaller details. Once again we may find this problem clearly stated at the beginning of the industrial revolution by Adam Smith. He saw this principle as the first maxim of the new science of political economy, so much so that he began *The Wealth of Nations* with a description of a visit to a pin factory, where because of their obsessive specialization on particular tasks, ten men could 'make upwards of forty-eight thousand pins in a day', whilst, had each worked separately, 'they certainly could not each of them have made twenty, perhaps not one pin in a day'.[22] The kind of centralization which has grown up in the intervening two hundred years has not only concentrated power far beyond the dreams of eighteenth-century manufacturers, it has also sharpened down the division of labour to a point where the founder of cybernetics has complained that in modern industry, people are only used to a millionth of their capacities.[23]

The two-way effect of capitalist industrialism, therefore, is to secrete vast agglomerations of unaccountable power at the top, while at the ground-level it affords individual people less and less opportunity to explore and develop their all-round abilities in the course of their work. This restriction of personal growth has profound implications for democracy, as was pointed up as long ago as 1835 by the distinguished philosopher of liberalism, Alexis de Tocqueville:

> When a workman is unceasingly and exclusively engaged in the fabrication of one thing, he ultimately does his work with singular dexterity; but at the same time he loses the general faculty of applying his mind to the direction of the work. He every day becomes more adroit and less industrious; so that it may be said of him that in proportion as the workman improves the man is degraded. What can

be expected of a man who has spent twenty years of his life in making heads for pins? and to what can that mighty human intelligence, which has so often stirred the world, be applied in him, except it be to investigate the best method of making pins' heads? When a workman has spent a considerable portion of his existence in this manner, his thoughts are for ever set upon the object of his daily toil; his body has contracted certain fixed habits, which it can never shake off: in a word, he no longer belongs to himself, but to the calling which he has chosen. It is in vain that laws and manners have been at the pains to level all barriers around such a man, and to open to him on every side a thousand different paths to fortune; a theory of manufactures more powerful than manners and laws binds him to a craft, and frequently to a spot, which he cannot leave: it assigns to him a certain place in society beyond which he cannot go: in the midst of universal movement it has rendered him stationary.

In proportion as the principle of the division of labour is more extensively applied, the workman becomes more weak, more narrowminded, and more dependent. The art advances, the artisan recedes. On the other hand, in proportion as it becomes more manifest that the productions of manufactures are by so much the cheaper and better as the manufacture is larger and the amount of capital employed more considerable, wealthy and educated men come forward to embark in manufactures which were heretofore abandoned to poor or ignorant handicraftsmen. The magnitude of the efforts required, and the importance of the results to be obtained, attract them. Thus at the very time at which the science of manufactures lowers the class of workmen, it raises the class of masters.

Whereas the workman concentrates his faculties more and more upon the study of a single detail, the master surveys a more extensive whole, and the mind of the latter is enlarged in proportion as that of the former is narrowed. In a short time the one will require nothing but physical strength without intelligence; the other stands in need of science, and almost of genius, to insure success. This man resembles more and more the administrator of a vast empire – that man, a brute. The master and the workman have then here no similarity, and their differences increase every day.[24]

H. G. Wells took this prediction literally when he wrote his novel *The Time Machine*,[25] in which time-travellers voyage out into a future in which 'masters' and 'workmen' have become two completely different species. Of course, de Tocqueville's account of what might happen to industrial civilization is a gross over-simplification, precisely inasmuch as it leaves out of account the inevitable responses of trade unions, by far the most powerful countervailing tendency. To confront the 'master', his 'brutes' must organize themselves: and in arguing with him they are liable to refine their alternative picture of what the working collective might be doing, and how it might be organized.

Yet there are constant difficulties in this process. First, in modern industrial societies, the vital information upon which decisions are taken is increasingly concentrated at the top, and selectively manipulated to facilitate obedience below. Second, workpeople always *begin* from 'the certain place in society beyond which they cannot go', which is a space in the pre-established division of labour. If they organize themselves as pin makers, this is a major achievement: but they will soon then need links with wire-drawers, and then with iron and steel workers, and at the same time with the garment workers who employ their products. Here in a sentence we have compressed the whole of that century of historical struggles which we were just discussing, from the spontaneous growth of local trade associations up to the formation of a Congress of all the Trades, the TUC. But even once this is accomplished, and a vast democratic achievement it is, the work is only beginning. As we have already seen, the division of labour in modern industry is not something fixed and unvarying. It shifts and starts like the fragments in a kaleidoscope. New inventions, and indeed, whole new technologies, constantly recast the whole social industrial organization.

questions of wages and working hours into key political issues. In some degree, the *more* a modern trade unionist places his faith in reforming devices, whether they be pay policies or 'social contracts', the *less* can he afford to treat his representatives as autonomous specialists, let alone to relate to them as he might to his greengrocer. In times or countries where bargaining is extending its influence, spilling over from areas of wage-determination into questions of industrial policy, investment decisions and product-mixes, this narrow view becomes even less tenable. Hyman quite rightly insists that trade union purposes 'must be defined in terms of the members' own aspirations'.[28] But these have always been changeable, and seldom more so than now.

Naturally, workpeople's aspirations change with changes in the overall political and economic climate. Just as people alter their immediate monetary demands, as they feel their needs altering, so too can they modify their picture of what kind of society they would most desire to live in, and what sorts of reform they see as most urgently necessary. Union rulebooks sometimes freeze these objectives for posterity: until 1977, for instance, the TUC rules still included machinery for initiating industrial action against future wars, while, in contrast, a number of affiliated bodies maintain rules committing them to support reforms which have long since been achieved. Nonetheless, there are certain broad objectives which recur from one rulebook to the next, and from one generation to the next.[29] These concern the issues of power, control, and social accountability. Thus, the TGWU rules include as a main membership commitment the need

> to endeavour by all means in their power to control the industries in which their members are engaged,

whilst the first aim of the AEU is

> the control of industry in the interests of the community.

The Foundryworkers' constitution speaks of

> developing and extending the co-operative system until a co-operative commonwealth is established which shall labour and produce for the good of all.

The NUR sees these perspectives more doctrinally as requiring

> the supercession of the capitalist system by a socialist order of society.

All these organizations, and many others, are affiliated to the Labour Party, which is pledged by rule to aim to secure 'the best obtainable system of popular control of each industry in service', in an often-forgotten section of its celebrated clause IV, the rule governing its commitment to social ownership.

We have argued elsewhere[30] that although the chosen means by which workers have pursued these goals have varied widely over the two centuries since the beginnings of the industrial revolution, it is easy to discern a strong thread of continuity, in which workpeople repeatedly reject the status of subordination and the deeply felt lack of responsible citizenship which have uninterruptedly been imposed upon them, as a basic assumption of entrepreneurial thought and managerial practice, ever since the days of Richard Arkwright and his pioneering mills. The democracy of trade unions is strongly influenced by such objectives: many activists are motivated to voluntary service by the commitment to social change which they hold out; while they are still commonly felt to imply an alternative model of what is considered desirable conduct, which is seen as very distinct from the ethics of the rat-race in which so many of today's workpeople feel themselves to be entrapped.[31] Above all, such aims put a firm question-mark over the alleged immutability of the given, inherited division of labour, and in particular over the separation of mental from manual labour, within which modern workers are caught no less remorselessly than were their grandparents before them.

This alienation has in no way diminished with the rapid postwar concentration of industrial power, both in nationalized and in private multinational companies. As such companies have become stronger, so technologies have changed more fleetingly, and so the process of workers' organization becomes more fluid and difficult. Whilst material living standards have been greatly improved, and expectations have developed accordingly, the individual worker in the 1980s is commonly employed by a more arbitrary and unaccountable power than would have been imaginable in 1945. Even governments have been known to quail at the hint of the displeasure of this power.

Mass unemployment clearly weakens the power of working people to confront it, while it increases their need for joint action and response.

NOTES

1. London, 1894: new edition, WEA, 1920. Translated into Russian by no less a person than Lenin, this book has repeatedly been quarried and requarried by authors and journalists of almost every imaginable persuasion, and criticized and recriticized by generations of sociologists of industrial relations. Nonetheless, it retains considerable value for the modern student.
2. Cf. V. L. Allen, *The Sociology of Industrial Relations*, Longman, 1971, Chapter 3.
3. The record of the founding Congress confirms this. It was republished in 1969, to commemorate the TUC centenary.
4. Cf. Ken Coates, *Work-ins, Sit-ins and Industrial Democracy*, Spokesman, 1980.
5. Cf. Ken Coates (ed.), *The New Worker Co-operatives*, Spokesman for IWC, 1976.
6. N. A. Citrine, *Trade Union Law*, Stevens, 1950, p. 296 and following for a comprehensive discussion.
7. HMSO, Cmnd 3623, pp. 205 *et seq.*
8. TUC, *Trade Unionism – Evidence to the Royal Commission*, 1966, pp. 29–31.
9. *The Wealth of Nations*, Everyman's Library edition, pp. 59 *et seq.*
10. TUC, *Trade Unionism*: cited in footnote 8 above.
11. R. M. Blackburn, *Union Character and Social Class*, Batsford, 1967, p. 18.
12. *Full Employment*, Spokesman, 1978, Ch. 5.
13. TGWU, *Minutes of Evidence to Donovan Commission*, 15.3.1966 (30) p. 1181.
14. V. L. Allen, *op. cit.*, pp. 125 *et seq.*
15. *Capital*, Volume 1, Chapter XXV 2.
16. Stuart Holland, *Strategy for Socialism*, Spokesman, 1975, p. 17.
17. *Ibid.*
18. Cited in Michael Barratt Brown, *From Labourism to Socialism*, Spokesman, 1972, p. 55.
19. M. Barratt Brown, *ibid.*, p. 56.
20. Stuart Holland, *op. cit.*, p. 29.
21. HMSO, Cmnd 6706, p. 9. See also pp. 8–19.
22. Book 1, Chapter 1. Everyman edition, pp. 4–11. Since 1776 informed commentators have nearly all reinforced Adam Smith's assumptions, until Stephen Marglin published his important essay: *What Do Bosses Do?* See Andre Gorz, *The Division of Labour*, Harvester Press, 1976.
23. Norbert Weiner, *The Human Use of Human Beings*, Boston, 1950.
24. Alexis de Tocqueville, *Democracy in America*, OUP, World's Classics, p. 427.

Not that de Tocqueville took his own argument to the consistent conclusion drawn by Wells. On the contrary, as is clear from his notebook, published in English as *Journeys to England and Ireland* (edited by J. P. Mayer, Faber), 1958, de Tocqueville clearly thought that 'the gradual development of democratic principles must follow the irresistible march of events'.

25. H. G. Wells, *The Time Machine*.
26. Richard Hyman, *Industrial Relations – A Marxist Introduction*, Macmillan, 1975, p. 85.
27. Otto Kahn-Freund, *Labour and the Law*, Stevens, 1972, pp. 52–3.
28. *Ibid*, p. 84. Hyman cites J. Child, M. Loveridge and M. Warner: 'Towards an Organizational Study of Trade Unions', *Sociology* 7, 1. They develop the distinction between 'administrative rationality' and 'representative rationality', or more baldly, between implementation on the one hand and determination of policy on the other. Too many commentators, says Hyman, quite rightly, blur this distinction, to the disadvantage of democracy.
29. For an account of union objectives in an earlier period, cf. W. Milne-Bailey, *Trade Union Documents*, Bell, 1929, Part I.
30. *Industrial Democracy in Great Britain*, vols. 1–3, Spokesman, 1975.
31. Some powerful accounts of this feeling are to be found in the two volumes of Ronald Fraser, *Work*, Penguin Books, 1968.

CHAPTER 2

Trade Union Structure

Types of Unions

In some industries, trade unions are considerably more successful than they are in others. In some sectors they are better organized and more rationally put together than in others, and in some areas they are much more representative than elsewhere. How, then, do unions recruit, and how do they organize their members? Obviously, there is no simple answer to these questions: unions come in a wide variety of sizes, shapes, and 'types': their classification is no longer the simple matter it used to seem.

The traditional discussion of trade unions divides them into three types: craft, industrial and general unions. Nowadays, the categories of 'occupational' and 'white-collar' unions are often added to this list.

Craft unionism customarily based itself on the principle of recruiting membership from some distinct skilled trade or occupation, normally entered through apprenticeship. The object was to ensure that all workers who went through such an apprenticeship, and qualified as tradesmen of a particular craft, became members of a trade union catering exclusively for it. A union which organized on this principle would enrol exponents of the skill, regardless of which industry or service might employ them.

The advantages of this form of organization were clear. By controlling the numbers of apprentices admitted into the trade, and by regulating the length and nature of apprenticeship, the union could control the supply of its type of labour and thus place itself in a strong position to name the price for that labour. Craft unionism sought also, by virtue of the same control, to ensure greater security of employment for its members. Other favourable characteristics of this model of organization included the fact that it generated fraternity amongst the members, based on their sense of a shared skill and relative equality of earnings. Because their aim was to restrict the supply of their skill, craft unions were not primarily concerned with maximum size; hence the internal problems of democratic administration and communication amongst the membership were less acute than in large organizations. Possession of a valuable skill, widely in demand, ensures a high degree of mobility amongst craftsmen, today, no less than in the past. But the value of particular skills varies and because this is so, craft unions have commonly been undermined.

In a dynamic economy, with constantly developing technology, the strongpoint of the craft is liable to be by-passed by technical change. The pace of this change has increased since the heyday of craft organization in the nineteenth century and in one industry after another the terrain has completely altered. Many examples spring to mind, from the shipwrights (craftsmen originally specializing in the skills of wooden shipbuilding) who were undermined by prefabrication, to the vehicle builders (who carried on the hand-skills of the era of coach building for horse-drawn road vehicles, and for the rolling stock of the railway age) who were overtaken by the semi-skilled processes of assembly-line technology in the mass production of motor cars. Today, printing, once a bastion of special skills, is being reduced to a new set of processes by computers and offset lithography, which challenges not only the old-established trades, but also the traditional male monopoly of them.

A craft union caught in such circumstances has two options; to seek to preserve its pure form and endure a relentless loss of numbers and bargaining strength (to the point at which it may cease to be a viable organization and be taken over by a larger union): or to alter its rules in order to admit other categories of membership; other crafts, or semi-skilled workers. In either case the structural consequence is the downfall of pure, single-craft unionism. This process, which is a continuing one, accounts in considerable degree for the prevalence of hybrid union forms in

British trade union structure. A further disadvantage of the craft union is that relatively small membership gives it little political influence: its vote at TUC and Labour Party Conferences will usually be negligible. Furthermore, its financial base will usually be insufficient to provide many of those services – research, education, legal advice – which members of a modern trade union find increasingly necessary. More: whilst the fraternity of its membership may be strong within its ranks, craft unionism may foster a sectional outlook which inhibits the growth of any wider sense of identification with the working class as a whole.

Craft unionism, then, is important not for its present position: it has been in decline for many years; but for its residual influence on trade union structures, and the contribution it has made to the inheritance of sectionalism. Of course, all trade unions have some kind of sectional base, and even within the most 'general' of organizations, there exist groupings of particular occupations having strong sectional loyalties. Trade unions could hardly ever 'take off' as permanent bodies without this immediate sense of group identity; but it is one of the virtues of trade unionism that it has shown a persistent tendency to evolve ever wider forms of association, from such sectional origins.

We may at first sight readily identify an 'industrial union' as an organization which seeks to recruit all the workers within a given industry, regardless of their occupations. On this principle, all employees of the railways, whatever their actual jobs, should belong to a single inclusive union for railway workers. The advantages claimed for this type of organization are numerous. It will be larger than a cluster of purely occupational unions, and will represent the united strength of all the industry's workers, thus overcoming some of the sectionalism of craft or occupational groupings. It eliminates the problem of multi-unionism at all those levels in the industry where collective bargaining takes place, and this greatly simplifies the processes involved: a factor which in recent years has recommended this form of organization to many employers. It brings any possible demarcation disputes within the confines of a single union, and makes it possible to resolve them through the normal processes of union decision-making. To an earlier generation of syndicalist militants, industrial unionism was the means through which class struggle could be waged until the moment of revolution, and thereafter it was the institution for the democratic administration of socialized industry. Rather oddly, perhaps, industrial unionism has also been a deliberate theory of trade union organization for those whose aim is to re-order industrial relations on more rational lines, in order the better to administer the *present* state of things.

Industrial unionism in Britain, despite the advocacy of such incompatible schools of theorists, has not been a very successful means of organization, for a number of reasons. In the first place, craft, sectional, and occupational unionism during the nineteenth century often established themselves *across* industrial boundaries, or as tightly organized segments *within* an industry, before industrial union organization was advanced. This has often meant that industrial unions have been frustrated in their ambitions to become the sole force within their chosen field.

On the railways, for instance, clerical workers have preferred to maintain their own white-collar union of railway clerks (later to embrace all salaried staff) and train drivers have evolved a form of craft unionism to organize foot-plate workers. The National Union of Railwaymen was thus faced with two stubborn forms of sectional unionism which refused to merge into an industrial organization. Complicating matters still further, the skilled men in the railway workshops have preserved their membership of appropriate craft unions, which themselves maintain membership in dozens of other industries.

The National Union of Mineworkers represented, until the defeat of the great miners' strike in 1985, the nearest approach in modern Britain to a fully inclusive industrial union in a major industry, though even here supervisory grades had a separate union (the National Association of Colliery Overmen, Deputies and Shotfirers), as did colliery managers, in the British Association of Colliery Managers.

After 1985, the NUM monopoly was further challenged by the formation of a breakaway, the Union of Democratic Mineworkers, which was reported to have recruited some 30,000 members as opposed to the NUM's claimed total of 135,000. Subsequently the UDM membership was put at much lower levels. But the decline in colliery employment will soon be reflected in sharp reductions in either or both of these estimates, even if the division has not resulted in an increase in overall non-membership. The number of miners had shrunk to below 120,000 by the end of 1986.

The National Union of Public Employees has often claimed to be an industrial union, but its membership is mainly divided between what may be considered to be two distinct industries, local government and the health service, and while in both cases it co-exists with others organizing similar grades of workers, it is weak among skilled workers, technicians, and white-collar staff. The most common union structures nowadays found within particular industries are the 'multi-craft' form (found in shipbuilding, and printing) or the combination of craft and general unionism, sometimes (as in steel) with an industrial union representing the most characteristic specific skills and processes in the industry. Thus the possibility of pure industrial unionism has usually been pre-empted by the existence of prior organization along craft or general union lines.

But there are other objections to industrial unionism, quite apart from these purely practical considerations.

In fact, the drawing of boundary lines to demarcate one industry from another is often a difficult or arbitrary process. When coal was the only source of fuel and power, the coal-mining industry defined itself fairly readily as self-sufficient for purposes of trade union organization. But in an era when gas, oil, electricity and atomic energy, to say nothing of potential future alternative sources of power, offer themselves as alternatives, it is highly questionable whether a union confined to one section of the fuel and power industry constitutes an adequate long-term form of defensive organization. Shifts in the balance between alternative power sources imply serious permanent effects upon employment patterns, and a trade union which aims to exercise influence and control over the planning of an industry's future, must be flexible enough to follow, indeed, to anticipate such changes, in the interests of its members' job security. Unions which have defined their area of recruitment in terms of particular industries at a certain stage of economic history find themselves vulnerable to large-scale shifts of resources caused by structural economic change. Thus, in the same way that membership of the NUM has shrunk, so we have seen the decline of the railway industry in the face of competition from road transport. This had already reduced the membership of the National Union of Railwaymen from 396,000 in 1952 to 130,000 in 1985. The railwaymen's difficulty is indeed very similar to that of the miners: only by embracing the whole transport industry, rather than the dwindling railway section alone, could a union develop a relevant industrial strategy. The wholesale contraction of manufacturing industry had cut deep into many other organizations by the middle 1980s.

Change is the rule, wherever trade unions operate, and even if we could draw boundaries which were appropriate for today's industrial structure, they would need to be re-drawn for every new generation. It is not simply that technology changes the division of labour within industries: the organization of large conglomerate companies increasingly disregards the industrial boundaries of the past. Nowadays the giant companies hedge their bets. Trade unions in ICI, for example, confront a common employer which spreads its manufacturing activities across a whole complex of 'industries': textiles, agricultural fertilizers, plastics, heavy industrial chemicals: whatever, indeed, the company decides to do next.

The third 'traditional' category, that of general unions, appears to suffer none of the disadvantages of craft and industrial unionism. By definition, general unions recruit across both occupational and industrial boundaries, and in theory they recognize no restrictions on their potential membership. In practice, of course, because of their historical origins in particular sectors of the economy, their membership is 'weighted' around cores in specific industries and occupations. Yet they have shown themselves flexible enough to take in new occupations, skills, and industries as these have arisen in the course of technical and economic change. Both the two largest general unions began life in the late 1880s, organizing particular groups of unskilled workers. The main parent of the Transport and General Workers' Union was the Dock, Wharf, Riverside and General Labourers' Union, and the chief forerunner of the General and Municipal Workers' Union was the National Union of Gasworkers and General Labourers of Great Britain and Ireland. We should note the significance of the phrase 'and general labourers' in the titles of both these pioneering organizations. It tells us that, *from the outset*, these unions deliberately intended that their recruitment should not be restricted to specific industries or occupations. The reason for this is not hard to find; unlike the craftsmen, dockers and gasworkers were in no position to construct a tightly exclusive barrier around their occupations. Because their jobs were casual and relatively unskilled, all 'general labourers' were potential blacklegs threatening effective trade unionism anywhere unless all could be enrolled in the union. Thus the general unions felt it necessary to construct organizations having all the flexibility which other forms of union denied to themselves. It is small wonder that they have flourished and grown to their present dominant size.

With skill levels diversifying, and a growing level of universal literacy, the most obvious advantage of the general union is no longer confined to its appeal to the unskilled. The ability to adapt organization and recruitment to the shifting patterns of occupations and industries gave general unions a strong capacity to survive and to grow, until the 1980s.

By virtue of their size, such unions can afford to provide far more extensive services for their members than can smaller organizations. Such services may well include the development of specialist groupings of members and officers catering for particular occupations and industries. Indeed, a union's willingness to do this has a strong influence on its potential for retaining its existing membership. It acts as an insurance against any tendency for minority groups to develop sectional attitudes which might lead to breakaway unionism; and it provides an incentive, attracting new groups and smaller unions to merge

Table 2.1
The TGWU and the GMBATU

(a) *Transport and General Workers' Union. Membership in trade groups.*

	1979	1985	% Change
Docks, waterways, fishing	48,126	28,895	−40
Admin., clerical, technical	158,622	109,099	−31
Passenger transport	140,373	106,622	−24
Commercial road transport	233,105	152,010	−35
Power and engineering	276,392	149,074	−46
Automotive	188,881	105,895	−44
Building	74,564	45,407	−39
Building crafts	14,195	9,109	−36
Public services and aviation	230,448	188,533	−18
Food, drink and tobacco	233,504	150,731	−35
Chemicals, oil-refining, rubber	140,984	87,153	−38
General workers	277,805	129,525	−53
Retired	37,590	32,664	−13
Free cards	31,697	41,262	+30
Textile workers	—	52,671	—
Agricultural and allied workers	—	45,355	—
TOTALS:	2,086,281	1,434,005	−31

NB. Without the mergers with Textile and Agricultural Workers' unions, the union's decline would have been of 36 per cent.

their forces into the larger collective. Data on the distribution of the membership of the TGWU and GMBATU in different industries will be found in Table 2.1.

The last and most obvious great advantage of general unions, is that their numbers enable them to play a major role in the decision-making machinery of the Labour movement as a whole; their block vote and influence at Labour and TUC Conferences is consistent and large.

Yet there are also disadvantages attached to great size. Most obviously there is a danger that bureaucratic and remote methods of policy-making may undermine internal democracy. Furthermore, in purely industrial terms, a large general union

(b) Distribution of GMBATU membership, 1984

Food, drink and tobacco	53,021
Chemicals	28,977
Engineering and shipbuilding	94,691
Bricks, glass	21,324
Gas, electricity, water	80,886
Construction	15,693
Distribution	31,727
Hotels, catering and other misc.	49,500
Health	35,596
Local government and education	201,484
Transport	6,770
Iron, steel and other metals	20,409
Motor vehicles	7,588
Metal goods	13,664
Textiles	13,723
Other manufacturing	34,784
Others	136,281
Total:	855,439

very rarely punches its full weight; within its ranks may be large groups of low paid workers for whom only a major industrial action by the whole union would suffice to raise them from their poverty. Yet unions will rarely contemplate such a deployment of their potential strength, partly because of the political implications, and partly through a fear that its members in the better paid sectors might not respond to a call for action on behalf of poorly paid members in a Wages Council industry.

In a period of falling employment and membership, the general union may be more vulnerable than some specialized unions; the TGWU's membership had fallen from 2 million in 1979 to less than 1½ million in 1986, a fall of 31 per cent, compared with the fall of 19 per cent in the TUC's remaining total affiliated strength. Things are worse still if we discount the TGWU's recent gains from mergers.[1]

But falling rolls actually increase the tempo of amalgamation, as unions seek to economize on their overheads and specialized services. The result is a concentration which, if anything, increases the significance of general unionism within the total context.

In sum: the traditional classification of unions into craft, industrial, and general unions applies, in pure form, to the merest minority of unions.

Since most existing unions do not fall neatly into any of the time-honoured categories, scholars have offered alternative and supplementary terms, such as 'occupational' union, and 'white-collar' or 'non-manual' union. 'Occupational' unions are those which organize workers in a particular occupation or related groups of occupations which are more loosely homogeneous than the apprentice-based craftsmen. Some of these occupational unions, such as the Association of Professional, Executive, Clerical and Computer Staffs, range over many industries rather like a craft society, whilst others, for example the Fire Brigades Union, confine their recruitment to one occupation within a wider industry. 'White-collar' or 'non-manual' unionism clearly describes a sector of the movement which is readily identifiable and of growing significance. But apart from unions which concentrate exclusively on non-manual occupations, the large general and semi-industrial unions usually include white-collar sections of their own. Moreover, technical change in industry, bringing the growth of new occupations like computer staffs and technicians, increasingly tends to blur the once clear distinction between non-manual and manual occupations. A worker in a computerized office may become increasingly difficult to distinguish from a worker in a computerized factory.

'Vertical' and 'Horizontal' Structures

All this has led to the formulation of other attempts to explain trade union structure. It is sometimes said that unions are organized along either 'vertical' or 'horizontal' principles. A horizontal union recruits from a grade or grades of workers spread across industrial boundaries – all clerks in the clerks' union, all supervisors in the supervisors' union, and so on. This principle corresponds closely to, and therefore includes, the craft organizations – all fitters in the fitters' union, all plumbers in the plumbers' union, and so on. The vertical union, on the other hand, aims to recruit all workers, whatever their grade or occupation, with a common industrial background, and thus corresponds to the industrial classification. These categories are useful, in that they draw attention to recognizable tendencies in union organization and recruitment strategies. They further indicate the astonishing degree of complexity of structure which emerges from the simultaneous and historical pursuit of both (opposing) principles by different trade unions in Britain.

If we represent just a very small selection from the total pattern of industrial and occupational employment, and examine the fortunes of different trade union types within it, we can establish the picture of complexity and competing forms of organization. We take a selection of industries and a few broad categories of occupation, and picture them on a chequer board of vertical and horizontal columns.

	Steel	Railways	Civil Service	Local Government	Chemicals	Engineering
Supervisors	1	2	3	4	5	6
Clerks	7	8	9	10	11	12
Engineering crafts	13	14	15	16	17	18
General and semi-skilled	19	20	21	22	23	24

It would require a major essay on its own to describe in full detail the trade union pattern which occupies all twenty-four of the segments in our diagram. A general summary must suffice. Supervisory workers are one of the major recruitment areas for the Association of Scientific, Technical, and Managerial Staffs, and they are very successfully pursued therefore on horizontal lines (390,000 people were enrolled in ASTMS in 1985). Nonetheless, in square 1, ASTMS immediately confronts the Iron and Steel Trades Confederation, a vertical or industrial union, as well as an internal management association, in British Steel. On the railways (square 2) supervisors are organized by either the vertically orientated National Union of Railwaymen, or the sectional Transport Salaried Staffs Association. In the civil service (square 3) there are purely sectional unions like the Inland Revenue Staff Federation, or the more widely based Civil and Public Service Association, catering for some supervisory grades. In local government, NALGO (National and Local Government Officers Association), square 4, occupies almost the whole territory. In chemicals, ASTMS has a clearer field (square 5), but the two major general unions also recruit here, for each of their white-collar sections. Supervisors in engineering (square 6) are one of the founding bases of the ASTMS, but even here competition is encountered from the Technical, Administrative and Supervisory Section of the Engineering Union. Clearly there is no possibility of ASTMS becoming an all-inclusive horizontal union for supervisors across all industrial boundaries. (Of course, a different selection of industries, taken to include insurance, finance or higher education, would have revealed far more hopeful fields for ASTMS recruitment.)

The Association of Professional, Executive, Clerical and Computer Staff is a horizontal union with its base in the clerical occupations, yet in squares 7, 8, 9 (steel, railways and the civil service), and 10 (local government) it encounters the same obstacles to recruitment as the ASTMS. Similarly in square 11 (chemicals), whilst doing rather better, it also encounters competition from the white-collar sections of the TGWU and the GMBATU. It has better fortune in square 12 (engineering). The engineering craft occupations, organized into the Amalgamated Engineering Union, have through prior craft organization successfully pursued horizontal unionism for these grades of its membership right across the industrial field, so that squares 13 to 18 are largely the preserve of the AEU. This effectively frustrates any hope of all-inclusive *vertical* unionism in almost any industry, as well as inhibiting it in those we have selected. The general unions, the TGWU and GMBATU, have a mixed experience of the fortunes of horizontal unionism in our selected industries. In steel (square 19) the vertical union of steel process workers, the ISTC, recruits the more skilled grades, but has left room for both general unions amongst the less skilled manual workers. In the railways (square 20), the vertical NUR effectively bars the way to any recruitment by horizontal general unions. In the civil service (square 21), there is scope for the two giants, although a sectional union for manual workers within the civil service (the Civil Service Union) enrols 47,000 members. Local government (square 22) provides ample scope for the GMBATU and the TGWU, but strong and successful competition is provided by the National Union of Public Employees. In chemicals (square 23), the two general unions have major representation of process manual grades, although they are joined here by a third general union, USDAW. In engineering (square 24), the two general unions have large membership, but compete for them with the AEU which has *vertical* union ambitions in that industry.

If we cast our eyes down the vertical columns, we find that vertical unionism is most strongly represented in our selection by the NUR on the railways, though as we have seen it is incomplete even there. In steel and engineering, there are species of partially successful vertical unionism (ISTC and AEU respectively) whilst in the civil service, chemicals, and local government, vertical unionism as such hardly exists as a distinct form.

Any exercise of this kind, then, examining trade union coverage across, or up and down, the industrial boundaries, merely reveals the extraordinary complexity of organization. Vertical and horizontal types exist as tendencies, rarely all-embracing, whilst some organizations combine both horizontal and vertical features. Others again, purely sectional-occupational unions, confine their recruitment to a single square on the board, pursuing neither horizontal nor vertical ambitions.

Our chequer board was about to be simplified early in 1987, as ASTMS and TASS prepared for a merger. This will create a very powerful union in the growth areas of technical employment in high-tech enterprises. But the EETPU is seeking recruits among the same workforce, and thus bids to conflict with the new amalgamation.

'Open' and 'Closed' Structures

We turn now to a further, and particularly helpful, method of examining structure. This, originated by Professor Turner,[2] identifies types of trade union by their different recruitment strategies, and distinguishes two basic methods, 'open' and 'closed'. A union is open when it is actively recruiting, or seeking mergers with other unions, in new occupational or industrial areas, and is closed when it concentrates on its existing territory, aiming to make that a strongpoint of organization and bargaining strength. A union, in the course of its history, may be closed at one time, open at another. Moreover it may at the same time be closed in some directions (e.g. vertically) whilst being open in others (e.g. horizontally). The extremes of the two strategies are represented by a completely closed single-craft or occupational union, and by a completely general, open union. In the course of time, a once closed union may consider that this strategy has been undermined by changes in employment demand in its territory, and revise its rules to admit new occupations. This is the process by which the once pure craft unionism of the old Amalgamated Society of Engineers has been transformed into the near general unionism of the Amalgamated Engineering Union, with its engineering, foundry, and construction sections. Within a broadly open union, there may develop strongpoints of organization around particular occupations, which the members and union then aim to close against indiscriminate new recruitment, by control of entry into the occupation. This is what has happened in the docks section of the TGWU, where the statutory dock labour scheme of employment gives the dockers a right of veto over any decision by employers to recruit new workers. In this case, the dockers' former dependence on the open strategy of general unionism gave way, after the Second World War, to a sense of self-sufficiency which led to a serious breakaway union movement in the ports. This has only been contained and reversed because the union leadership's response to the challenge was to make the docks section more democratic and responsive to members' wishes.[3]

The organizational trend has been towards a more open strategy for many unions, ever since the 1960s. It is a trend which has approached the features of a serious competitive scramble, as falling membership in the 1980s has impelled unions to seek membership anywhere, without regard to structural considerations. Unions which are equipped to compensate for lost membership here, with new sections there, will try to do so. The EETPU now enrols production workers in the glass industry, and TASS has taken over the Tobacco Workers and the Metal Mechanics, for example. Borrowing from company terminology, it now seems appropriate to speak of 'conglomerate' forms of organization in cases like this.

Demarcation and Disputes Between Unions

In one important respect, however, the trade union movement acts to control inter-union conflict and competition over recruitment and membership rights. The regulative principles, the 'Bridlington Rules' (adopted by the Trades Union Congress in that town in 1939), seek to establish a code of conduct governing recruitment practices by affiliated unions. They lay down that unions should not recruit members from another union whilst that union is engaged in a trade dispute, or whilst members are in dispute with that union, or in arrears with their contributions. Unions should not commence recruitment in an area where another union has enrolled a majority of the workforce. The TUC operates a disputes procedure to enforce these rules, and has in the past been able to make them effective through its power to suspend or, if necessary, ultimately, expel the offending union.

In the past, the interpretation of the rules has favoured the larger unions, as well as generally acting to preserve the status quo, since 'poaching' has been discouraged, in the interests of stability. Sometimes this has led to the protection of pockets of non-unionism, wherever an established union claimed that another was poaching, in plants where incumbent unions may have been complacent about the enrolment of the non-unionists. In the 1970s, the TUC Disputes Committee sought more rational solutions, but was never able to enforce a consistent policy based on agreed priorities.

Most recently, the TUC's authority has been challenged by the recruiting methods of the EETPU, which has signed single-union agreements with multinational companies giving it sole recruitment rights in plants where, under previous owners, several unions had members and spheres of recruitment.[4] We comment further on the structural implications of this trend below, and in Chapter 4.

Organizational Success

One way of testing the relative effectiveness of different forms of trade union structure is to examine the degree of organization reached (trade union membership as a proportion of employees) in different sectors of the economy, and to ask what kind of unionism prevails in each sector. When Professor Clegg did this, using data from 1964, he found that:

> The highest degree of organization is found in an industrial union, the Mineworkers, but another industrial union, the Tailors and Garment Workers, comes near the bottom. The second industrial group in terms of organization, national

government service, is covered by a bewildering variety of separate unions, whereas the distributive trades, near the bottom of the list, have only one union, the Shop, Distributive and Allied Workers. One industrial group in which craft unions figure strongly, paper and printing, comes fairly near the top of the list, whereas another, construction, comes surprisingly near the bottom. The two general unions are the most important unions in the fourth and fifth groups on the list – gas, electricity and water, and transport and communications (excluding railways) – but they are equally important in the food, drink and tobacco group near the bottom of the table.[5]

Table 2.2 confirms Clegg's conclusion for the periods beyond his findings, down to 1979. No discernible correlation exists between union density and union structure in the different industries listed here. Of course, up to 1979 there were remarkable gains in density in particular industries and sectors, notably in public employment, and in several manufacturing sectors. Subsequently, slump and mass unemployment have brought havoc not only to major industrial regions and whole manufacturing sectors of the economy, but have inflicted deep wounds on the trade unions which represented their workers. Again, trade union structural factors do not seem to be contributing to the decline(s) of the 1980s in any major way, except insofar as unions often refrain from organizing those of their former members who have lost their jobs. But union responses to the decline do have more general implications for structure. This is because of the factor already noted: that competition for members in a declining labour market threatens to break through TUC-imposed restraints, and generate a trend towards single-union agreements. These may usher in a 'reform' of structure at plant and company levels, initiated by employers and compliant unions, of a kind which was never achieved when the unit of recognition, bargaining and membership rights was the industry, rather than the establishment or company. But whilst this may tidy up structure at these levels (for whatever motives), it will perpetuate

Table 2.2

Trade union membership and density by industry, Great Britain, 1968 and 1979

INDUSTRY (in 1979 density rank order)	1968 UM (000s)	1968 PUM (000s)	1968 UD %	1979 UM (000s)	1979 PUM (000s)	1979 UD %
1. Entertainment*	97.7	113.7	85.9	128.7	114.8	112.1
2. Road transport**	432.6	521.0	83.0	451.0	449.6	100.3
3. Post and telecommunications	400.6	408.5	98.1	427.6	428.1	99.9
4. Electricity	181.5	242.3	74.9	178.3	179.9	99.1
5. Cotton and man-made fibres	146.3	180.6	81.0	112.1	114.1	98.2
6. Railways	228.9	274.5	83.4	204.2	208.9	97.8
7. Coal-mining	398.9	443.8	89.9	297.6	306.6	97.1
8. Sea transport	90.4	101.4	89.2	83.8	87.2	96.1
9. Tobacco	26.7	34.7	76.9	30.0	31.3	95.8
10. Printing and publishing	292.2	368.4	79.3	326.0	347.7	93.8
11. Water	33.5	47.5	70.5	61.4	66.2	92.7
12. National government	457.1	602.7	75.8	583.8	639.5	91.3
13. Gas	90.5	129.5	69.9	95.5	105.8	90.3
14. Air transport	41.1	62.5	65.8	78.5	92.5	84.9
15. Port and inland water transport	92.3	128.1	72.1	59.8	71.9	83.2
16. Footwear	75.6	106.4	71.1	65.2	80.3	81.2
17. Metals and engineering	2,410.4	4,249.8	56.7	3,033.9	3,809.4	79.6
18. Local gov. and education	1,366.8	2,221.2	61.5	2,232.0	2,879.9	77.5
19. Health services	369.8	976.3	37.9	971.2	1,317.9	73.7
20. Pottery	41.1	57.0	72.1	43.1	59.9	72.0

INDUSTRY (in 1979 density rank order)	1968 UM (000s)	1968 PUM (000s)	1968 UD %	1979 UM (000s)	1979 PUM (000s)	1979 UD %
21. Glass	40.2	76.7	52.4	46.6	71.4	65.3
22. Food and drink	252.0	729.3	34.6	444.3	685.4	64.8
23. Bricks and building materials	56.1	194.3	28.9	83.5	133.5	62.5
24. Chemicals	186.9	474.6	39.4	288.6	490.5	58.8
25. Paper and board	98.4	244.0	40.3	116.2	205.3	56.6
26. Insurance, banking and finance	250.3	583.0	42.9	395.3	720.9	54.8
27. Other textiles	165.6	478.1	34.6	170.5	359.9	47.4
28. Other manufacturing	95.7	331.2	28.9	143.0	330.4	43.3
29. Other mining and quarrying	21.4	54.2	39.5	22.5	52.0	43.3
30. Clothing	119.7	359.6	33.3	127.7	307.2	41.6
31. Construction	472.0	1,570.7	30.1	519.7	1,415.2	36.7
32. Leather, leather goods and furs	14.8	52.1	28.4	11.6	41.0	28.3
33. Agric., horticulture, forestry	125.4	503.7	24.9	83.5	367.1	22.7
34. Fishing	5.7	13.1	43.5	2.3	11.2	20.5
35. Distribution	294.5	2,762.9	10.7	428.3	2,872.2	14.9
36. Miscellaneous services	125.0	2,582.4	4.8	262.2	3,575.7	7.3

*Union membership and union density data for this industry are considerably overstated.
**Union membership and union density data for this industry are also considerably overstated.
UM = union membership. PUM = potential union membership. UD = union density.

Source: adapted from R. Price and G. S. Bain, 'Union Growth in Britain: Retrospect and Prospect', *British Journal of Industrial Relations*, XXL, as re-presented in G. S. Bain (ed.), *Industrial Relations in Britain*, Basil Blackwell, 1983, pp. 14–15.

in new forms the higgledy-piggledy pattern of membership across and between industries and occupations. And in any case the impact of single-union agreements will be partial and haphazard, and is still in its infancy.

Structural Reform

The lack of evidence linking structural form with organizational success may be one reason why efforts to achieve major structural reform and the elimination of multi-unionism have met with mixed fortunes when they have been attempted by the TUC. Periodic dissatisfaction with the current structure has been forcefully expressed on several important occasions in the twentieth-century history of the TUC.

In the 1920s, the 1940s, and again in 1962–3, the TUC made strenuous efforts to restructure the movement from the top. The object of these efforts was to diminish multi-unionism, and usually the means chosen was to promote industrial unionism. But craft and general unions resisted proposals for their dismemberment. In 1962, George Woodcock, TUC General Secretary, was enthusiastic for structural reform, offering Congress his famous dictum: 'Structure . . . is a function of purpose.' Empowered with a Congress resolution, he embarked on a planning operation. The obstruction which he met is exemplified by Jack Jones's reaction:

> George Woodcock told me it was a 'tidying-up operation', but it involved parts of the TGWU merging with other unions to form industrial unions, for example in the construction industry. The strength of the TGWU would be reduced without regard to the views of our members and I wasn't having any. In meeting after meeting with George Woodcock I emphasized that 'trade union members can't be treated like cattle to be bought and sold at the whim of theorists'. I stood firm and won that one.[6]

Woodcock returned to the 1963 Congress to report:

> We have come . . . firmly to the conclusion that diversity of structure – that is, unions of different size, of different shape, of different structure – is a characteristic of British trade unionism and always will be . . . We see no real alternative to a continuation for a long time, I would say as far as this Congress is concerned, for ever, of a great degree of diversity. . . .

Following the breakdown of the 1962–3 initiative, the TUC had perforce to content itself with encouraging and promoting mergers and takeovers amongst unions with common industrial or occupational interests.

A veritable spate of union mergers and takeovers broke out in the 1970s and has continued ever since, to the point where the number of TUC-affiliated unions has fallen from 160 in 1968 to 88 in 1986. The great majority of these union fusions are not the results of rational restructuring discussions convened by the TUC, but of simpler processes involving the absorption of lesser unions by greater ones; of mergers agreed for political reasons; and, as we have seen, of some fusions for the purpose quite simply of achieving a critical minimum size, in order to remain economically viable while providing necessary levels of service to members. Restructuring continues, therefore, to depend on a process deficient in overall purpose or 'theory'. It would be coincidental if the results met the criterion of George Woodcock, in which structure was related to purpose. This is particularly true of the period since 1979 when, in the face of mass unemployment and declining membership, union purpose may not extend far beyond survival. We return to consider the prospects for the future, at the end of the chapter. We should first examine the wider purposes which the unions of the 1960s and 1970s certainly proposed for themselves, and how far structural adaptation was a prerequisite for achieving them.

Since 1963, the trade union movement has constantly sought a wider role in economic planning, at all levels of the economy. This aspiration has expressed itself in its most primitive way in support for tripartite bodies such as the National Economic

Development Council, and later in involvement in the associated network of 'little Neddies' and Sector Working Parties. It has also bitten deeper, developing the concept of Planning Agreements and the demand for industrial democracy, both usually at company level. Company mergers and takeovers, and the growth of multinational ownership of capital, have led to even more comprehensive concentration of power in ever more remote boardrooms. This has stimulated both trade union and political demands for greater worker and social control over the economy, which in turn imply wider roles for the unions. Mass unemployment reinforces this need, even whilst it makes its achievement more difficult, except through a political process which, in turn, requires a changed emphasis in the trade unions' choice of methods. The growth of public sector employment in postwar Britain produced its own response in the trade union world; 60 per cent of all union members now work in the public sector.

The reversal of that trend under the privatization programme of the Thatcher government produces a further twist to the union problem, calling for a new adaptability in the public sector unions whose previous experience has been of secure memberships and full recognition and bargaining rights, in nationalized industries, in the Town Halls, and in the hospitals of the NHS. The changing composition of the labour force, away from male-dominated manual occupations in manufacturing towards part-time, mainly female work in the service sector, asks further questions of union adaptability and functional effectiveness.

Further, in an age of information revolution and high technology, unions require new kinds of resources and skills within their institutional structures. For all these reasons, they need resources and the will to provide adequate research services, an education service, mass communications to their members, technical and advisory services on safety, law, organization and method, and 'the prospect of strengthening and expanding lay participation',[7] including provision for the specific need for participation of women and ethnic groups in their ranks. None of these purposes are achievable within small, fragmented and purely sectional unions, whose even more basic function, of wage and job security bargaining, is therefore the more undermined. Hence, the drive for greater size through union mergers may be underpinned by a logic of wider import than mere survival. For without minimum size, or at least the pooling of common activities and resources, unions' functions will be subject to a progressive narrowing and frustration. How far has this conclusion, that 'bigger is better', been achieved?

Following Mr Woodcock's speech of 1962, TUC-affiliated members grew from 8,312,875 to 12,128,078 in 1979, falling back severely thereafter to 9,243,297 in 1987. The number of TUC unions fell from 182 in 1962, to 87 in 1987. Thus, the average size of TUC unions has increased from 45,675 to 106,245 in 1987 – the latter figure being almost exactly the same as in the peak membership year of 1979. It is clear therefore that falling membership has thoroughly offset the concentration-through-merger process in the last seven years, one of the less well-observed results of adversity. To show this, in Table 2.3, we take a quarter of a million as a minimum membership required for a major union to fulfil the full range of its present-day functions.

During the long period of union growth, the TGWU's success was due partly to the takeover of smaller and medium-sized unions, and partly through net additions to membership. Its growth rate of 57 per cent between 1962 and 1979 compares favourably with that of GMBATU (22 per cent) and USDAW (31 per cent), the two unions with which it is in closest contact in the general worker field.

The AEU or AUEW's growth was partly due to amalgamations with the Constructional Engineering Union and the Foundry-workers. The Technical and Supervisory Section, formerly the Draughtsmen's Union, with a 1986 membership of 220,000 now registers as a separate union, after a long period of strained relations within the AUEW amalgamation.

NALGO and the NUT, both of which maintained large memberships, were not affiliated to the TUC in 1962. Their

Table 2.3

Unions with over 250,000 members, 1962, 1979 and 1987

First seven unions are in 1962 rank order	1962	1979	1987	Rank order 1987
1. TGWU	1,318,274	2,072,818	1,337,944	1
2. AEU/AUEW	982,182	1,483,419	857,599	2
3. GMWU/GMBATU	786,138	964,836	814,084	3
4. NUM	545,329	259,966	(104,941)	12*
5. USDAW	351,371	462,178	381,984	7
6. NUR	308,050	—	(125,000)	11*
7. ETU/EETPU	252,851	420,000	336,155	8
8. NALGO	—	729,405	750,430	4
9. NUPE	—	712,000	657,633	5
10. ASTMS	—	471,000	390,000	6
11. UCATT	—	320,723	249,485	9
12. NUT	—	291,239	(184,455)	10*
Total members	4,544,195	8,187,584	5,815,314	
No. of unions	7	11	9	

*Excluded from total, as falling below threshold.

We have included UCATT as a marginal case, since it claims 515 members short of 250,000.

Source: TUC, *Annual Reports*, 1962, 1979; General Council's *Reports* to TUC, 1987.

subsequent entry was a major part of the trend towards full representativity for the TUC, including the great collectivities of white-collar and professional workers. Few significant trade unions now exist outside the TUC's orbit.

The decline of the NUM's position from fourth place in 1962 is already apparent in 1979, whilst the NUR, the other industrial union in the top league in 1962, disappears from the table in 1979.

The EETPU grew in the first period through amalgamation with the Plumbers' union and through its strategic position in the electronics industry. NUPE's growth was due to its very active recruitment drives amongst non-unionists in the lower manual and ancillary grades (including part-time workers and women), in local government and the National Health Service. Its membership in 1962 had been only 215,000. Only ASTMS's rate of growth surpassed this achievement during the sixties and seventies, through a spectacular spate of mergers in the insurance, banking, and financial spheres, and through net additions of white-collar and managerial staffs in manufacturing and service sectors under private ownership. UCATT appeared in the table in 1979 largely by virtue of amalgamations between former craft and non-craft unions in the building industry.

The 1979–86 period has seen an overall decline in TUC-affiliated membership of 2,452,349, of which 1,808,098 is accounted for by the decline in membership of 1979's top eleven unions. In turn, 638,813 of this loss is accounted for by the fall in TGWU membership. It appears that superior size is by no means a protection against membership loss in the context of mass unemployment; indeed the larger unions have been more prone than the average to decline. For the average union size, given the fall in the number of unions, actually increased slightly between 1979 and 1986, whereas the average loss amongst 1979's top eleven unions (including the NUM and the NUT, who have now fallen below the 250,000 mark) was 164,372 or 22 per cent. (Total TUC membership loss was 21 per cent.) The TGWU loss of over 31 per cent does not account for the whole of the poorer performance of the large unions. If we exclude the TGWU from the figures, the loss by the other ten top unions of 1979 is 19 per cent. Putting this trend another way, the unions with over 250,000 members accounted for 53 per cent of TUC membership in 1962, 67.5 per cent in 1979 and 63 per cent in 1986.

But it is not feasible to evaluate the changes since 1962 without consulting also the figures for overall union membership including non-TUC unions. Tables 2.5 and 2.6 give the relevant data for 1986; it should be noted that they are not strictly comparable with the TUC-only figures, since the

Table 2.4

Changes in size of TUC-affiliated unions, 1979–86

	1979			1986				
	No. of unions	No. of members	Union av. size	No. of unions	No. of members	Union av. size	Members % change 1979–86	Average size: % change 1979–86
All unions	112	12,128,978	108,286	88	9,585,729	108,929	−21	—
Unions over 250,000	11	8,187,584	744,326	9	6,036,529	670,725	−26.3	−10
Unions over 250,000 excluding TGWU	10	6,114,766	611,477	8	4,602,524	575,315	−24.7	−6
Unions under 250,000	101	3,940,494	39,014	79	3,549,200	44,927	−9.9	+15
(TGWU		2,072,818			1,434,005		−30.8	)

Certification Officer's official 1986 figures were not available at the time of publication.

The figures for 1962 and 1979 reveal the same trend of growing concentration as was found in TUC-only data, as well as the same picture of overall growth. In other words, more members in fewer unions. In the period 1979 to 1984, overall membership fell by 2,412,000, or 17.8 per cent. The loss among unions with over 250,000 members was 1,872,000, or 21.7 per cent. And the percentage of all members in unions over 250,000 was 50.8 in 1962, 63.9 in 1979, and 60.9 in 1984. It is clear that the trend towards greater concentration in the largest unions has been halted and reversed since 1979. If this reverse trend were to persist, there would be serious consequences for the effectiveness of trade unionism.

The new trend is not to be explained by a diminution of merger activity in recent years.

Table 2.5

Number of unions analysed by size of union

	1962	1979	1984
Under 100 members	129	73	67
100–499	156	124	93
500–999	63	47	38
1,000–2,499	105	58	54
2,500–4,999	61	43	32
5,000–9,999	34	24	16
10,000–14,999	24	7	3
15,000–24,999	22	19	15
25,000–49,999	18	17	19
50,000–99,999	19	15	13
100,000–249,999	10	16	11
250,000 and more	8	11	10
	649	454	371

Source: Department of Employment *Gazette*.

Table 2.6
Membership of unions analysed by size of union (thousands)

	1962	1979	1984
Under 100 members	7	4	3
100–499	39	30	23
500–999	44	34	26
1,000–2,499	173	93	85
2,500–4,999	203	154	111
5,000–9,999	299	158	105
10,000–14,999	289	84	34
15,000–24,999	410	364	294
25,000–49,999	637	633	659
50,000–99,999	1,290	933	977
100,000–249,999	1,609	2,387	2,017
250,000 and more	5,085	8,624	6,752
	10,015	13,498	11,086

Source: Department of Employment *Gazette*.

Table 2.7 records only mergers and takeovers which were brought to fruition. A great deal of inter-union negotiation occurs which may never reach that final stage. In 1983, the Certification Officer reported that seventeen proposed mergers of unions were in progress at the end of that year, and that it was known that there was a possibility of another twenty-one taking place. Most of the takeover/merger activity is concentrated on the process of ending the life of the smallest and most sectional unions, the survivors of an earlier age of unions based on craft, skilled occupations, or in particular localities. Thus, since 1979, the venerable trade of Patternmakers lost its separate identity, as did the Sheffield Sawmakers and the Huddersfield Healders and Twisters. (Much of the current merger activity centres on the textile industry, where nineteenth-century patterns of organization have survived longer than most, having the most deeply embedded local and regional loyalties.) Another casualty of recent years has

Table 2.7

Mergers and takeovers of trade unions, 1976–85

	Mergers*	Takeovers**	Total
1976	—	9	9
1977	1	10	11
1978	1	9	10
1979	—***	13	13
1980	1	12	13
1981	—	4	4
1982	4	8	12
1983	1***	8	9
1984	2	16	18
1985	1	10	11

* A merger is properly termed an amalgamation, in which a new trade union is produced, all the amalgamating bodies ceasing to exist.
** A takeover is properly termed a transfer of engagements, in which the transferring organization loses its legal identity whilst the organization to which it transfers continues in being with its legal identity unchanged.
*** Two proposed amalgamations were not proceeded with following adverse votes by the members of the unions concerned.

Source: Certification Officer's *Annual Reports*, Certification Office for Trade Unions and Employers' Associations.

been the aristocracy of the steel industry, the Roll Turners' Society.

What is patently not happening in all this is any major merger amongst the large unions themselves, which would have sustained and enhanced the earlier trend towards the domination of a few super-unions, and would, we believe, have fitted the movement better for the kind of future which it faces. As in Jack Jones's day, it seems that union leaders of large organizations are unwilling to contemplate the dismemberment or loss of independence which might follow either restructuring, or ad hoc merger. This may change, particularly if the business unionism of a few unions precipitates a crisis of rivalry between opposing union ideologies. The EETPU, for example, in the printing industry and in the glass industry, no longer considers itself limited in any way by structural considerations, readily accepting into membership production workers who have no conceivable relationship to its original industrial and occupational scope. This aggressive conglomerate recruitment could force more traditional unions into alliance and merger in self-protection.

The Problem of Multi-unionism

Despite the merger process, the problem of multi-unionism continues. At shopfloor and company levels, this requires the preservation and extension of Joint Shop Steward Committees and Combine Committees (see Chapter 5). At industry level, the TUC has sought to promote greater inter-union co-ordination through its system of industrial committees (see Chapter 4). And of course, inter-union collaboration on hundreds of Joint Industrial Councils and other joint negotiating committees is normal trade union practice.

Formal joint union bodies exist in a number of industries. The TUC listed the following confederations in 1986:

General Federation of Trade Unions
National Affiliation of Carpet Textile Unions
Northern Counties Textile Trades Federation
Council of Civil Service Unions
Confederation of Shipbuilding and Engineering Unions
Confederation of Entertainment Unions
Federation of Broadcasting Unions
Federation of Film Unions
Federation of Theatre Unions
National Federation of Furniture Trade Unions
Confederation of Insurance Trade Unions
British Telecommunications Union Committee
Post Office Union Council

Some of these bodies may well foreshadow future amalgamations; they are certainly not a complete substitute for them, particularly since they are less likely to provide for 'the prospect of strengthening and expanding lay participation'. With the final exit of those fossil organizations of the past, which have provided a veritable laboratory of democracy, and with the only partial solution through joint stewards' organization of the problem of participation in multi-union structures which seem destined for a long life yet, we must turn now to the issue of self-government, of democracy within unions, in the following chapter.

Meantime, the evidence of this chapter shows that the age of innocence and small primary (community-based) organizations has been ended, not by any greed for power within the unions themselves, but by the inexorable processes of industrial concentration. Unions, like everybody else, have no alternative but that of adapting to these cosmic pressures or becoming irrelevant.

The problem which this poses is, how to change adequately, to respond with sufficient force, without jeopardizing that 'child-like faith' of which the Webbs spoke when they were celebrating the most primary forms of union organization:

> The early trade club was a democracy of the most rudimentary type, free alike from permanently differentiated officials, executive council, or representative assembly. The general meeting strove itself to transact all the business, and grudgingly delegated any of its functions either to officers or to committees. When this delegation could no longer be avoided, the expedients of rotation and short periods of service were used 'to prevent imposition' or any undue influence by particular members. In this earliest type of Trade Union democracy we find, in fact, the most child-like faith not only that 'all men are equal' but also that 'what concerns all should be decided by all'.[8]

Equality is a vital goal, and it remains the more necessary, as power coheres in fewer and more capricious centres, that 'what concerns all should be decided by all'.

NOTES

1. However, there is a possibility that the position in some TUC unions is worse than has been reported. The decline in another major multi-sectional body, the AEU, was reported at the end of 1986 as having brought the membership down to 550,000, or not much more than half the figure claimed a year or two earlier. The TGWU has exceptionally efficient and transparent accounting procedures. Some other unions are slower to register substantial changes, if they occur.
2. H. A. Turner, *Trade Union Growth, Structure and Policy*, Allen and Unwin, 1962.
3. Even the official Devlin Report (*The Final Report of the Committee of Inquiry under the Rt. Hon. Lord Devlin into Certain Matters Concerning the Port Transport Industry*, HMSO, Cmnd 2734, August 1965) criticized the TGWU and its officials for their failure adequately to represent the interests of their docks membership.
4. See TUC, *Annual Report* 1985, p. 6, for an account of the dispute between six unions and the EETPU at the Hitachi (UK) plant in Hirwaun, in 1985. In that case, the EETPU was allowed by the TUC to retain its sole recruitment rights established by an agreement with Hitachi after its takeover of the GEC's former share in the company. Prior to this, all the complainant unions had members and bargaining rights at the plant. On any reasonable interpretation, the EETPU was in serious breach of the Bridlington Rules in this case.
5. H. A. Clegg, *The System of Industrial Relations in Great Britain*, Blackwell, 1970, pp. 59–60.
6. Jack Jones, *Union Man: an Autobiography*, Collins, 1986, pp. 156–7.
7. John Hughes, *Trade Union Structure and Government, Part 1*, Donovan Royal Commission Research Paper, no. 5, HMSO, 1967.
8. Sidney and Beatrice Webb, *Industrial Democracy*, 1913 edition, WEA, p. 8.

CHAPTER 3

Trade Union Government

Problems of Trade Union Democracy

In Chapter 1 we saw how, well over a century ago, it was already understood that the division of labour stultified people's development by compelling them to act out fixed, restrictive roles, often for years on end, without offering them any slightest opportunity to realize a fraction of the wealth of talent which lay within them. A modern study of labour markets in the Midlands shows that 87 per cent of the industrial jobs available require no more skill than is involved in driving to work. Union rulebooks reflect, all too imperfectly, the longing of millions of men and women for a society in which the individual potential of every person may become the most treasured resource of all, and in which all may reach out to the furthest frontiers of their capacities. In Chapter 2 we saw how, as well as mutilating individuals, the changing division of labour also recurrently undermined and broke up their organizations. Trade unions found their structures constantly under pressure, constantly in need of change.

There is a further problem confronting trade unions in the same principle of division of labour, however. The more complex the economy in which they operate, the more unions need their own internal division of labour, to match and pace the organizations and institutions which are ranged against them, and to respond efficiently to opportunities or threats from a whole cluster of specialized agencies. We have already discussed these pressures for increased size, which are all, in themselves, problems for any live democracy.[1]

With all the trends pushing unions to offer more and more qualified specialist assistance, more and more professionalism, it is clear that today more than ever a key element of trade union democracy consists in the struggle for membership control over leaders, and the creation of institutions imposing accountability on representatives and full-time officers.

In itself, although the difficulties it involves are undoubtedly greater nowadays than they were before, this problem is by no means new. Back in 1925, G. D. H. Cole was already writing:

> democratic control, in the large and complex modern unions, becomes a difficult matter. The rank and file feel that both executives and officials are far removed from them, and election is apt to bring to the top only the best man known over a wide area, and not necessarily the best man for the job . . .[2]

Basic Units of Organization

It was already beginning to be true in 1925, but today it is generally obvious, that the words 'rank and file' may mean more than one thing. They may be taken to mean the ordinary members as individuals; or perhaps the members at the workplace, involved in the primary levels of workshop organization; or often in a number of unions, they may refer to the members organized in branches, which are often seen as 'the basic unit in the union' as USDAW has it, or as 'the basic unit of organization', as is the case in the TGWU, GMBATU and AEU. The two views on organization, workplace versus branch, are still far from simply compatible. We consider shop steward organization separately, in Chapter 5: so here we shall confine our attention to the branch as the primary constituent of union democracy. The theory of the matter is quite simple. USDAW's home study course for union members pointed it up with a diagram, which 'illustrates the supreme significance of the branch as the basic unit on which the whole of the union's structure is building and depends'. The same handbook spells it all out verbally:

Table 3.1
The organization of USDAW[3]

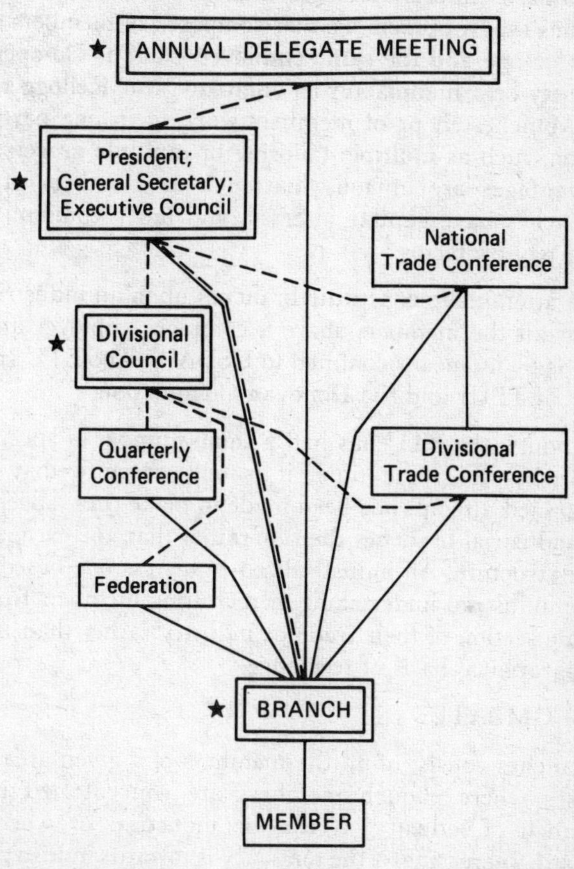

—— Illustrates the supreme significance of the branch as the basic unit on which the whole of the union's structure is built and depends.

★—The four main levels of the union's structure.

– – – –Represent the downward line of communication and representation ensuring effective consultation on and coordination of the union policies at all levels.

Every member of the Union is in one of its 1,300 or more branches. The majority of the Union's branches are organized either on a single employer or trade basis. This means that a branch is either composed of members working for one and the same employer, such as Co-operative Society or a manufacturing company, e.g. Kellogg's Ltd., in Manchester, or of members working in one particular trade, such as multiple tailoring or multiple grocery. The advantages are obvious inasmuch as members of such branches have similar interests and fairly common work and pay problems.[4]

The attempts to constitute branches upon an industrial basis, so that all the members share a common employer and workplace, is by no means confined to USDAW. The ETU (now part of the EETPU) told the Donovan Commission:

> Although the ETU has had a small number of specialized branches for some time, it is only recently that a determined attempt has been made to make these specialized or industrial branches the rule rather than the exception in our structure. An industrialized branch is one based upon one industrial undertaking or recruiting members from the same section of their trade or industry rather than upon a geographical basis of residence.[5]

In the GMBATU:

> Branches consist of all the members of a given area, or in cases where enough members are concentrated in one branch of industry, it can be industrial or work-place based. Increasingly, the tendency is towards industry, company or work-place branches. In total there are about 2,500 GMW branches.
>
> Branch administration is in the hands of either—
>
> 1. The voluntary branch secretary (who holds an ordinary job as well)
>
> *or* 2. The full-time branch secretary (who lives off commission from branch members)

or 3. The whole-time branch secretary now rapidly being replaced by Branch Administrative Officers (who get a salary based on membership, and who are in the union superannuation scheme, and do not count as lay members of the union)

or 4. District Officers.[6]

For many years the TGWU has tried to ensure that branch members are all from the same trade group, and increasing numbers of branches are based on a single workplace. Branches must normally have a minimum of fifty members, but may have as many as 5,000 or 6,000: they must meet at least monthly, but may meet more frequently if they wish. 'It is also possible to arrange to hold a branch meeting in two parts, say in a morning and evening session, to enable shift-workers to attend.'[7]

The trend to industrial branches has been resisted by the Engineers, as they explained in their evidence to Donovan:

> Unlike many other Unions, Branches of the AEU are geographically based. This is a conscious decision of the Union: one made in the light of the wider interests of the Labour Movement as a whole. Whilst it could be held to be in the interests of particular workers to base the unit of organization at factory level, it has always been felt that the AEU is not solely an organization concerned with sectional interests. It has always been one of the aims of the Union to create the framework within which the ordinary working man could become more aware of his surroundings, his true interests and his responsibility to the community. By providing the meeting place to enable him to discuss not only matters affecting himself and his place of work but also the wider issues of the day – not just within his own locality but nationally and internationally – it was held and is still held today that this makes a far greater contribution to the dignity and well-being of the working class than the more parochial attitudes most probably engendered within Branches based at factory level.[8]

It would be interesting to see the evidence for this last statement. Many very experienced trade union leaders have argued quite differently. George Woodcock, for instance, claimed that 'branches have ceased to be an important part of trade union structure', and went on to say: 'If I were an active trade unionist again you wouldn't see me anywhere near a branch; there's not enough done there to justify attendance.'[9]

The AEU thinks plenty is done, as it reported to the same Royal Commission:

> It is at the Branch, which meets fortnightly, that the ordinary member has the closest contact with his Union. It is here he is made a member; pays his contributions; collects benefits; and elects officers. It is at the Branch, too, that any member can raise matters affecting working conditions, union membership and, in fact, all matters concerning 'labour interests generally'. This means, of course, that, in practice, there is practically no subject that cannot be broached by an interested member . . . The only matters specifically barred by Rule from being discussed are 'questions of a religious nature'.[10]

Unfortunately, busy though they undoubtedly are, branches are commonly sparsely attended, and never more than when they are organized on a geographical rather than an industrial basis. A very large number of studies document the poor attendances and low participation ratios which commonly characterize branch meetings.[11] In 1974 the Sociology Department at Warwick University published a far-reaching report which had been commissioned for NUPE, as a basis for that union's thoroughgoing reform of structure. Speaking of the widespread feelings of isolation and the lack of day-to-day contact which troubled many members, the report went on:

> the initial symptoms are equally well known: poor attendance at Branch meetings; little contact with Branch officials and full time Officers alike; difficulty in finding members willing to come forward as Union Stewards and ignorance of the Union both at Branch level and beyond.

Our researches provide some evidence of all these features. For example, 67 per cent of Branches said that Branch meetings were attended by only 5 per cent or less of the Branch membership; a quarter of all Union Stewards reported difficulty in contacting some sections they represented; over three-quarters of all Branch Secretaries said it was difficult, very difficult or impossible to get members to act as Union Stewards and 37 per cent of those attending Area Conference said they did not know what happened to Area Conference resolutions once they had been passed.[12]

It is very arguable that in such cases it is the ease of accessibility to the structure that counts, rather more than the absolute numbers of people taking part in meetings on one day or another. Where is there a large organization in which attendances are *not* variable with the subject of the meeting? It seems entirely normal for people to be more interested in some issues than they are in others, and therefore quite proper to arrange trade union structure so as to accommodate this variability. But if ease of access to the union is the key to wider and more relevant participation, it is extremely difficult to justify geographically based branches in any case where industrially-founded ones are possible.

If branches were *not* 'basic units', this would not matter. But they commonly are: and what this rather obscure jargon means is precisely that they are often the main electoral foci, determining who should attend policy-forming annual conferences, involved at one or another level in electing higher committees, and sometimes making up the direct constituencies in the election of chief officers.

If branches may be structurally unrepresentative, as opposed to being simply poorly attended, this is largely because there is a limit to the percentages of members it is *possible* to involve in a dysfunctional, or irrational, structure. We might be forgiven for thinking that if a TUC General Secretary has advertised his belief that 'there's not enough done there to justify atendance', others might conceivably share his point of view.

The importance of this problem is difficult to overstress, when we take up again G. D. H. Cole's half-century-old conundrum, about how this modern rank and file is to exercise democratic control over its leaders. Cole was not the first to note that sometimes trade union leaders were not entirely in tune with their followers.

Relations Between Members and Organizers

Even earlier (in 1893), the Webbs recorded their classic description of the social stress under which full-time union officers were alleged to operate:

> Whilst the points at issue no longer affect his own earnings or conditions of employment, any disputes between his members and their employers increase his work and add to his worry. The former vivid sense of the privations and subjection of the artisan's life gradually fades from his mind; and he begins more and more to regard all complaints as perverse and unreasonable. With this intellectual change may come a more invidious transformation. Nowadays the salaried officer to a great union is courted and flattered by the middle class. He is asked to dine with them, and will admire their well-appointed houses, their fine carpets, the ease and luxury of their lives . . . He goes to live in a little villa in a lower-middle-class suburb. The move leads to dropping his workmen friends; and his wife changes her acquaintances. With the habits of his new neighbours he insensibly adopts more and more their ideas . . . His manner to his members . . . undergoes a change . . . A great strike threatens to involve the Society in desperate war. Unconsciously biased by distaste for the hard and unthankful work which a strike entails, he finds himself in small sympathy with the men's demands, and eventually arranges a compromise, on terms distasteful to a large section of his members.[13]

This is perhaps the clearest statement of the sociological process which has been presented in the theory, set out at length in 1915 by Roberto Michels, that there exists in labour movements an 'Iron Law of Oligarchy' based on the progression 'democracy is inconceivable without organization'[14] but 'organization is, in fact, the source from which the conservative currents flow over the plain of democracy, occasioning these disastrous floods and rendering the plain unrecognizable'.[15] In less high-flown language, the necessary division of labour within labour organizations is seen as generating, first an elite of labour managers, and then a definite caste of bureaucrats. In part, Michels was describing a long past labour movement based upon fairly limited levels of popular literacy. At a time when compulsory schooling to the age of twelve was an innovation, it is clear that the cadre-structure of labour organizations was likely to be set apart by the comparative rarity of its skills. Indeed, Michels made a great deal of the effect of Labour Colleges on the training of the new elite, and wrote at some length about the fostering of 'powerful orators'.[16] Today, with the mass production of a whole variety of intellectual skills, there is likely to be far stiffer competition for office in many labour organizations: oratory being one of the less significant of the requisite talents involved.

At the same time that more qualified candidates are available, the relations between labour professionals and those they serve has been transformed by the vastly increased educational attainments of the new rank and file. The 'Iron Law of Oligarchy' is perhaps a fair description of a bygone division of social labour in which the clerk was a natural aristocrat: but today's skills have certainly modified the landscape with which Michels was familiar, even if there remains a pronounced tendency for labour leaders to find themselves considering, even serving, interests somewhat distinct from some of those felt paramount by their members.[17]

Trade union full-time officers are still a rather small fraternity, in comparison with the vast armies of voluntary workers upon whom the day-to-day functions of the unions depend.

In the 1890s, there were already something between six and seven hundred permanent officials[18] at a time when the TUC counted 225 affiliates with about 1.2 million members.[19] In those days, then, the average union officer represented or serviced approximately 2,000 people. By 1952, the eighteen largest TUC unions had about 1,600 paid organizers, and this was an average ratio of one organizer to some 3,700 members. Yet this average concealed wide divergencies: the Amalgamated Union of Building Trade Workers had one full-timer for each 1,300 members, whilst the National Union of Railwaymen had one officer for each 19,000.[20]

When the Donovan Commission published its Report, in 1968, the best guess it could make was that there were about 3,000 full-time officers, or one for every 3,800 members.[21]

Taken union by union, the ratios of some major organizations were as follows:

Table 3.2

Number of members per full-time union officer in certain trade unions, 1966

Union	Members per officer
Union of Shop, Distributive and Allied Workers	1,978
Transport and General Workers' Union	2,762
General and Municipal Workers' Union	3,868
Electrical Trades Union	4,027
National and Local Government Officers' Association	4,509
Amalgamated Engineering Union	6,807

The fact that some unions were far more intensively and professionally organized than others was highlighted in a research paper prepared for the Royal Commission, which is reproduced in Table 3.3.

Yet the intensity of such servicing does not merely vary from one organization to the next: it also varies within those organizations.

A comprehensive report of developments in a particular union, since the publication of the Donovan Report, shows the trends within the TGWU.[22] During the time in question, the union had

Table 3.3
Full-time local officers: shop steward responsibilities and contacts

Name of union	Average no. of stewards for whom each officer is responsible	Average no. of stewards contacted in last 4 weeks	Proportion of shop stewards contacted in last 4 weeks
Transport and General Workers' Union	120	96	80%
Amalgamated Engineering Union	477	132	28%
General and Municipal Workers' Union	169	65	38%
Electrical Trades Union	232	94	41%
Amalgamated Union of Building Trade Workers	33	30	91%
All unions	172	89	52%

Source: Research Paper No. 10 on *Shop Stewards and Workshop Relations* cited in *Report* of the Donovan Commission, p. 189.

been pioneering in forcing forward new experiments in productivity bargaining, alongside a systematic drive to extend the influence of plant bargaining upon which the Royal Commission had recently reported. Jack Jones, then newly elected General Secretary of the union, had always been a partisan of lay participation in and control over its affairs, and had inherited a series of decisions by the union's delegate conference, which pressed in the same direction. More plant bargaining, more lay control: these pressures can only mean *less* power for full-time officers. And indeed, during the years between 1968 and 1974, that was exactly the tendency of the TGWU's evolution. Not only was the role of full-timers notably modified: the actual numbers of professionals declined very sharply at a time of rapid expansion in membership. This can be seen very

Table 3.4[23]

Ratio of members to full-time officials, Transport and General Workers' Union, 1968–86

Region	Full-time officials				Members				Ratios			
	1968	*1970*	*1974*	*1986*	*1968*	*1970*	*1974*	*1986*	*1968*	*1970*	*1974*	*1986*
1	132	123	122	123	352,623	390,285	450,608	354,813	2,671-1	3,173-1	3,694-1	2885–1
2	20	20	19	23	69,961	81,935	90,237	77,147	3,498-1	4,096-1	4,749-1	3354–1
3	35	34	33	33	112,243	129,005	137,085	100,455	3,207-1	3,794-1	4,154-1	3044–1
4*	35	28	27	24	111,618	111,438	110,666	73,192	3,189-1	3,980-1	4,098-1	3050–1
5	45	43	47	42	246,209	270,610	334,701	231,031	5,471-1	6,293-1	7,121-1	5501–1
6†	78	73	60	62	177,544	208,391	236,713	163,380	2,276-1	2,855-1	3,945-1	2635–1
7	54	48	60	52	118,011	129,369	166,559	135,199	2,185-1	2,695-1	2,776-1	2600–1
8	21	21	20	20	68,112	75,411	82,041	59,918	3,243-1	3,591-1	4,102-1	2996–1
9	27	25	25	30	71,678	89,465	87,564	85,698	2,655-1	3,299-1	3,503-1	2857–1
10	21	20	15	24	43,712	52,740	52,851	54,477	2,032-1	2,637-1	3,512-1	2270–1
11	36	35	38	37	96,220	101,709	99,738	72,061	72,2,673-1	2,906-1	2,625-1	1948–1
Head Office	26	24	19	31				5,512				
Total	530	494	485	501	1,472,505	1,638,686	1,857,308	1,412,884	2,780-1	3,317-1	3,834-1	2821–1

*Region 4 in 1968 is the previous Regions 4 and 13 added together.
†Region 6 in 1968 is the previous Regions 6 and 12 added together.
The above table shows a clear reduction in the number of full-time officials and a very marked increase in the ratio of members to officials. Region 5 is clearly outstanding as the region with consistently the highest ratio of members to full-time officials between 1968 and 1974.

plainly in Table 3.4, which gives the position for each of the union's eleven regions, together with that in its head office.

If the union had been losing members, this picture might have borne out the complaint that unions were under-professionalized. But since the union was at the time entering a period of phenomenal growth, the reduction of its paid staff could only mean that a vast burden of official work was being undertaken by voluntary workers. It will be seen that this was a most uneven process: in Region 5, covering the vast engineering plants in the Midlands, officer–member ratios had reached the level of 1:7,121 (a figure comparable with traditional levels in the NUM), whilst other regions maintained a fairly constant ratio, as most noticeably did Region 11 (from 1:2,673 to 1:2,625 between 1968 and 1974). As the TGWU membership declined in the 1980s these trends were sharply reversed. Even so, there is still a small way to go before we are back to the 1968 ratio.

This kind of unevenness is general, throughout the wider trade union movement. Not every group gets equal representation. In 1976, for instance, one estimate claimed that the thirty unions with the largest female memberships had some 2,225 paid organizers, of whom only 98 were women.[24] Ten per cent of NALGO's organizers, and 43 per cent of its members, were women. NALGO had more female organizers than any other organization and the TGWU, with 16 per cent female membership (289,000 people), had only 3 women organizers to 480 men.

The slump in trade union membership after 1979 was, at first, slow to affect the extent of professionalism. But as funds became less and less adequate, mergers accelerated. This process tends to put a slow squeeze on the numbers of full-time officers, who may not be replaced once their old organizations are fully integrated into the new amalgamations. Commonly rationalization takes time, which allows for a degree of 'natural wastage'. More recently, financial crisis has struck more brutally. A drastic decline in AEU membership which became apparent at the end of 1986 resulted in a decision to dispense with the services of some two hundred full-time officers. Such a trauma, of course, is a completely different experience from the deliberate devolution of power and responsibility to lay officers, pioneered in the TGWU a decade earlier.

Of course, there is a very great deal more to organizing a trade union than appointing a conveniently high ratio of paid officials to members, and we certainly believe that if a union can mobilize adequate voluntary participation, it may be the more democratic for having the less professional administration. Much depends on the nature of the workforce which has to be organized, and the degree to which it is concentrated or dispersed: and it would be unwise to generalize on such matters. Nonetheless, it seems fair to say that there are too few women, and too few black people, in the ranks of the trade union civil service, and it may be that some of the disputed growth areas of trade union recruitment will surrender to those organizations which are quickest to appreciate this fact.

If we are asked 'How representative are union officials?' the question can be answered in the manner already attempted in the last few pages: showing how adequately the membership is covered by union professional services, or, changing the focus of the answer, showing how far the officials as a body reflect the interests, experience and needs of the members. But most people will be seeking yet a third type of answer, which shows exactly in what ways officers are held accountable to their members, and what types of control members can exercise over their collective employees.

Elections

The first and most obvious control which suggests itself is that of election. In fact until 1984 it was always more difficult than might be expected to generalize about the election of trade union leaders in Great Britain. This situation changed with the imposition of the Trade Union Act of 1984, which regulated the election of voting members of union executives. Trade union officers are, of course, a much wider category than the limited number who are called upon to become national leaders. In most unions, but not all, the chief executive officer is the General Secretary. In some, there was traditionally a carefully defined division of responsibilities, separating the powers of a small team of leaders. Among the miners, for instance, the President has a series of duties itemized by rule, while the Secretary, again by rule, is also responsible for the union's treasury. But alongside the written rules, there has, by tradition, grown up a body of customs and practices which have still further delimited the job-descriptions of the two chief officers. For many years, the President took charge of political pronouncements, while the Secretary was the leading negotiator.

If we assume that the General Secretary is the most important functionary in most unions, then the first surprise we find is that some of these offices are not filled by elections at all. This was for a long time the case in such different bodies as the National Union of Public Employees, or BISAKTA, the old Steelmen's Union, both of whom had means of appointing their chief officers. In those where elections have always been held, the most common procedure has been to ballot either the individual membership directly, or the constituent branches of the organization. The President and General Secretary of the NUM, for example, are both elected by a pit-head ballot, which ensures a very high percentage poll. The same officers of the AEU are now elected by a postal ballot of the members. In the beginning of this arrangement, about one-third of the electorate actually voted.[25] Subsequently this turnout was to decline, while the difficulties involved in maintaining a comprehensive register of qualified electors have not been small.[26] In the shopworkers' union, USDAW, until the intervention of the 1984 Act, a branch ballot took place, in which those actually attending the branch meeting were able to cast the entire block vote of the branch's nominal roll. In this manner, a few dozen people could wield hundreds of votes. In some other unions, the Annual Conference elected the principal officers: this happened, for instance, in the TSSA (Railway clerks), the Amalgamated Weavers' Association, and the Dyers' and Bleachers' Union. Under the 1984 Act, such officials have to be elected unless they are 'civil servants', or non-voting members of their union's executive.

However, before 1984, even where such elections did take

place, they were not very often recurrent events. In the AEU all officers have to submit themselves for re-election (or otherwise) at intervals first of five, and then subsequently of seven, years. But in the other major unions, the TGWU and the GMBATU, once elected, General Secretaries will normally continue until they retire. The same rule applied in a whole series of important lesser organizations: the NUM, NUR, TSSA, among those already mentioned.

An obvious curb on the power of such life-long officers was the imposition of fixed terms of office, punctuated by regular ballots. This reform was actively canvassed for decades, with no success whatever, in the miners' union, in which not only national officials, but also all area professionals, were chosen in a once-for-all poll. Although a vigorous agitation was carried on for many years, and although many of the miners' local area officers have been chosen on the basis of manifestos committing them personally to the principle of regular five-yearly elections, the proposal only gained acceptance at the miners' Annual Conference after 1980. Then, it was applied only to newly elected officials. Overtaken by the 1984 Act, the NUM voted to amend its rules in order to clarify its procedures, so that the President would be a non-voting member of the Executive. Since this would have meant that Arthur Scargill, still a young man in his prime, would have maintained his presidency for life, the government announced proposals in 1987 for new legislation to compel recurrent elections in all such cases.

There are thus two main types of criticism of the manner in which unions appoint their officers: on the one side, from those union members who commonly want the chance to bring about greater accountability by imposing an increased frequency of elections: on the other side, from the Conservative Party, which said in 1976:

> ... we are ready to help. Public money should be made available for the conduct of postal ballots for union elections where these are requested. Firms should also be encouraged to provide time and facilities for the conduct of union meetings; this should lead to greater participation in union affairs.[27]

This proposal would have cut two ways. Branch meetings during working time, if they could be secured from managerial intervention of any kind, would obviously have a marked beneficial effect on union membership participation. But such branches could obviously not maintain a geographical as opposed to industrial catchment.

A compulsory postal ballot is by no means self-evidently the best means of increasing voting turnout in the election of officers. Since the institution of such ballots in the engineering section of the AUEW, although the proportion of votes has markedly increased, there has never been any contest without complaints about the working of the system. It is a massive task to mail out a million correctly addressed envelopes. Had the AUEW only brought its structure into line with its actual workplace organization, it would be far simpler to ballot the membership at the workplace, as do the mineworkers, who commonly poll, not one-third or less, but up to three-quarters, of those eligible to vote. In the EETPU, which also has postal votes, only one-fifth of the members normally participate.[28] When it was able to legislate, the Conservative Party did provide funds for such ballots, although the results were hardly impressive[29] beyond the fact that the new facility split the TUC, which tried initially to boycott it, on the grounds that the unions had the right to determine their own constitutions within the law. But employer provision of facilities was not improved.

The most commonly heard trade union complaint against postal voting is that it becomes the object of sustained newspaper and media coverage, much of which is a direct and obvious intervention in the union's affairs. It would be difficult to object to this if it were fair, but there is a good deal of evidence that it is not. If one or two mass-circulation newspapers intervene in such an election in favour of the same chosen nominee, it is clearly difficult for his opponents to overcome the disability under which they are consequently placed: they have no means of speaking directly to the millions of people who are reading of the merits of the person against whom they are contending or even of their own alleged demerits.

As was argued in the TUC education services' manual, *Democracy at Work*, postal votes are less than perfect reflections of union feeling:

> In a union meeting, decisions are taken in the light of discussion and debate at the meeting. In a postal ballot many members may not have full information about candidates, and, so opponents of postal ballots argue, the press and the media have been able to use this as an opportunity to interfere in the elections by selectively publicizing certain candidates.
>
> There are also administrative arguments about postal balloting – that it may be expensive to operate, and that in unions with a high turnover of membership it would be impossible to operate postal ballots fairly or effectively. One answer to these dilemmas which is sometimes put forward is to develop the role of workplace-based meetings in union elections. These could increase participation in votes while meeting many of the objections to postal ballots outlined above.
>
> Another possibility is to improve the standards of *information* available to voters in union elections.[30]

This argument has been going on for a long time in the AUEW engineering section: in 1975 the postal ballot was revoked by a National Committee decision taken on the chairman's casting vote. It was restored as a result of a court action.

Of course, newspaper influence is not confined to postal ballots, although there are many people who would question whether it would have been possible for Mr Terry Duffy to triumph over a far more experienced opponent in the AUEW presidential contest without the most intelligently co-ordinated press campaign which was waged on his behalf.[31] During the period running up to the presidential voting in the NUM, beginning in 1979, long before the incumbent, Mr Joe Gormley, need retire, a most interesting and sophisticated use was made of the newspapers. The left-wing candidates for the office were fairly evidently established: either Mr Scargill, from the union's largest area, Yorkshire; or, if the ballot were held quickly, before his age made him ineligible under rule, the Scots miners' leader, Michael McGahey, were the obvious choices. There was no very obvious right-wing contender, however. Such a candidate needed a large area for a voting-base, and the political geography of the union therefore pointed towards Nottinghamshire. Yet there existed no one of the right degree of seniority to make a remotely plausible candidate from that area. One new area official had been appointed during the previous year, and he was of a suitable age, although very much lacking in experience. To qualify him to run for national office at some time in the future it was vital to secure his early election to the National Executive Committee, and his rapid promotion within the hierarchy of his own Nottingham area. At this point, Mr Gormley announced his own premature retirement, triggering a wave of press speculation about his successor. With no evidence whatever to support the thought that this novice official had even contemplated seeking national office, a number of newspapers promptly named him as the favourite 'moderate' nominee. Whatever might be the outcome in the final contest for the NUM's national leadership, this 'news' was obviously useful to the official in question when it came to consolidating his chances of promotion in his own area. Immediately afterwards, Mr Gormley announced that he was reconsidering his early retirement, and could perhaps be persuaded to soldier on.

Obviously, this looks rather like capable management of the press: but the more that contests of this kind are influenced by newspapers, the more this will become a glaring problem for trade unions as a whole. If all possible candidates in all union elections were entitled to similar coverage, and if the press were equally open to all, no one should object to the widest possible coverage of union matters, not excluding elections. But when the press comprises a mere handful of million-plus circulation titles, all owned by diversified commercial enterprises (most of which are multinationals), all commonly hostile to many normal objectives of trade unionism, and most partisan for an explicitly Conservative political position, it is not surprising that growing numbers of trade unionists find them biased, sometimes to an extreme degree.[32]

The 1984 Trade Union Act contains provisions concerning balloting for union national executive committees. We examine these later in Chapter 10. They will lay additional duties upon officers of unions, both full-time and lay, to ensure rigorous compliance with the new legal requirements in union elections. Failure so to do is to run the risk of legal proceedings against the union by any aggrieved members. Previously unions could fix upon their own rules, as they collectively pleased, so the intervention of state regulation into their internal government departs from previous norms in the relationship between the law and the largest group of voluntary representative bodies in our society. Moreover, it is to be expected that any future Conservative administrations would seek to take this process much further. (See Appendix to Chapter 10.)

Separation of Powers

However, whatever the outcome of union elections, and whatever the impact of external influences, in practice once officers have been appointed, the real imposition of accountability and membership control over them turns upon quite other democratic mechanisms than re-election. First, as we have already hinted, many unions develop a separation of powers limiting the scope of influence of particular officers. Probably the most developed instance of this in a major union is the conscious separation of executive, juridical and legislative powers in the AEU,[33] where a policy-making National Committee legislates, and an elected final appeal court interprets the rules in all contentious disciplinary cases. A separately elected executive administers the union's affairs from day to day.

In effect, separation of powers is an attempt to develop a 'rule of law' within trade union democracy, and so it has been claimed[34] that the same principles should be embodied in union rulebooks as apply, or are thought to apply, in national government. Supporting this case, Richard Fletcher, a close observer of the union scene, argued that

> The most important of these are:
> (1) the amount of information available to the individual and the power he has to compel notice to be taken of his views.
> (2) self-restraint on the part of those who govern, not to exploit every loop-hole in the constitution to the disadvantage of the membership.
> (3) The care with which the rules are drafted and their effectiveness as a barrier against autocracy.[35]

Even where things are theoretically otherwise checks and balances of various kinds may emerge in practice, by the processes of federation between areas, or alliance between industrial or craft sectors. In many large unions the real power structure involves the balancing of central national powers against regional or sectoral autonomy: all of which means that the union 'kings' have their own problems with their 'barons'. Of course, this analogy is too facile: in contrast with King John, every modern general secretary, and all local, regional and industrial officers, have only one ultimate source of authority, which is in their membership. Even so, some memberships exert greater influence over their affairs than others.

Leadership Succession

It has often been noted that, throughout the Labour movement, there exists what has been described as 'the law of Buggins's turn'. Buggins is the man who must, in common justice, be given the opportunity to shine before his (usually long, if sometimes not over-distinguished) career of service comes to an end. Sometimes he has deputized directly for a leader, or even actually carried out a large share of the work of that leader, for a considerable time. Sometimes he has been the longest-established member of a leading committee. Sometimes he has been appointed to a special post by an outgoing leader with the express intention of ensuring continuity of policy by guaranteeing the succession.

More than thirty years ago, V. L. Allen published a detailed study of the effects of Buggins's Law. 'In most cases', he argued, 'the position of assistant general secretary is treated as a stepping stone to the chief position in a union, and is regarded as such by ordinary members.'[36] No one could deny that this happens quite often, although the evidence is not quite as overwhelming as it appeared in Professor Allen's survey: as was pointed out by Edelstein and Warner:[37]

1. An assistant top officer may be too old to qualify for nomination, under the rules, particularly in Britain, or he may not wish to compete for personal reasons, e.g. ill-health. One should, therefore, also consider top-post elections in which no assistant top officers competed.
2. There may be two or more assistant general secretaries with equal formal standing, and these may compete against each other.
3. The job title of the second-ranking full-time office is not exclusively 'assistant general secretary', even in Britain, nor is the top office exclusively the 'general secretary'.[38]
4. As Allen himself shows, assistant general secretaries are sometimes defeated for top posts. Allen cites six such instances among twenty-five elections in which such officers competed,[39] a proportion which is more than negligible.
5. There may be no full-time next-to-top officer at the national level, especially in smaller unions but even in some larger ones.

What does seem to be important, generally, is that there exist some clearly marked gradations of leadership status, which limit the effective choice in elections to candidates who have gained some real degree of confidence from wide sections of the membership. In unions which are relatively harmoniously administered, this demarcation of status may take the form of a hierarchy of assistants to chief officers, or it may take the form of regional or industrial concentrations of power. In unions which are riven by sharp internal conflicts, it may take the form of the development of clearly perceived oppositional factions, as happened when the Electrical Trades Union was split during the argument about the rigging of its ballots,[40] or when the National Union of Seamen was involved in its major reform struggle during the early 1960s. Inside the Engineers' Union, both Hugh Scanlon and his successor, Terry Duffy, were not conventional 'runners-up' or Bugginses: both having been relative newcomers to their union's small Executive Committee before they became chosen contenders for the union's presidency, each representing a different faction in the union's sharply fought and continuous political contest.

Opposition

Very often the most effective membership sanction for controlling a remote leadership arises precisely in the growth of this kind of factionalism, which sometimes reaches the point of creating a structural opposition. A classic case of this is to be found in the upheaval in the National Union of Seamen, during the years following 1960. Here a powerful oligarchy had evolved, dominating the whole union and imposing policies of blatant subordination to the employers' needs. Pyramidic appointment structures enabled the union's leaders to 'fix' most of their opponents, year after year. No marked fastidiousness was shown during this process, as was later reported after rebellion finally broke out:

> There was from the start of the conflict a feeling that coercion might be used, for it had acquired almost the quality of a tradition within the NUS and was perhaps more acceptable than might be the case in other unions. Hence the officials had closely watched the disruptive members. Lists of names had been compiled and records checked. Personal files and reports on some members

without doubt were obtained from Special Branch policemen. A smear campaign was launched. One rank and file leader had been away from the sea and had paid no union dues since 1957, a fact publicized by the officials only too readily. The Reformers were alleged to be totally self-interested communist plotters and disrupters, and this angered the men.

> There was an attack by the union on the seamen, they said we were communists, we were bandits, we were bloody rogues . . . They said I'd been highly trained in Australia, which was just bloody ridiculous . . . And this built up the anti-union feeling.

Jim Slater, the leader of the Reformers on the north-east coast, suffered attempts by local officials to force him out to sea as bosun on a trader, and others suffered equivalent harassment. Although the members expected such behaviour from the leaders, the conflict did now begin to move towards outright coercive strategies by both parties, as the bargaining assumed less-preferred forms . . .[41]

The dramatic struggle in the NUS generated some pretty tough infighting, and John Hemingway has documented some questionable practices on both sides. But the NUS was, in British terms, a quite exceptionally undemocratic organization until the final, belated, victory of the reformers. Most unions are more tolerantly conducted, and contain oppositional groupings with far better grace.

This was not always the case. Following a split in the international trade union movement, and a fierce development of the cold war in the domestic Labour movement, in 1949 the Biennial Delegate Conference of the TGWU modified its rules to bar communists or fascists from either holding office or attending Conference. The onslaught on communists was to some extent acceptable to parts of the TGWU membership in the late forties, although within a decade it had become an object of sustained criticism (it was repealed in 1968). But its effect during the early years of its imposition was greatly to reinforce the arbitrary powers of Arthur Deakin, one of the last great hierarchs of British trade unionism.

> Deakin would openly boast of his power and as openly use it. Only those he could trust to follow his line had the backing of his union when they sought election to the General Council of the TUC or the National Executive of the Labour Party. Leaders of unions who held their seats on either body with his support were frankly told that unless they could persuade their unions to support his policies he would switch his vote to some more reliable candidate.[42]

Naturally, this kind of influence was deployed not against communists, but against Deakin's opponents (notably, Aneurin Bevan) in the Labour Party. Yet it is questionable whether, if communists' factional rights had been maintained uninterruptedly, Deakin could ever have maintained such unchallenged sway: not that communists would necessarily have supported his Labour opponents (in fact, they did not), but that they would have created an imbalance which could from time to time have opened the General Secretary to effective question.[43]

The NUR still proscribes the election of communists to its highest offices, because its rules require both of those holding these posts to serve as Labour Party Conference delegates. The old Boot and Shoe Union, NUBSO (now merged into NUFLAT) had rules proscribing communist *opinions*. Aspirants to office had to complete a form saying, 'I am opposed to the principles of communism and agree that my appointment is made on that understanding.'

On the other side, communist office-holders in the ETU were tried in the courts and found guilty of an elaborate conspiracy to rig ballots in the elections of that union, thus depriving of office duly elected opponents who had fallen foul of the dominant party machine. Having learnt from this lesson, democrats of whatever political persuasion will seek to ensure the widest possible rights of assembly, communication, and access to relevant information and opinion-forming organs. Trade union rules can be designed to establish and safeguard these rights, and where necessary they should be reformed to ensure that they do.

At the same time, constitutional guarantees for democratic principles are only part of the battle to enforce genuinely democratic working practices. Rules are one thing: behaviour, often enough, is another.

Lay Government versus Professionalism

During the public employees' strikes of early 1979, towards the end of February the unions' negotiators reached what they obviously regarded as the basis for a settlement. Leaders of the GMW and the TGWU were promptly empowered to commend the employers' offer to their members. To the great surprise of the media, the national executive of the third major union involved, NUPE, then voted unanimously to recommend their balloting members to reject the proposed settlement, even though their general secretary had been actively involved in negotiating it. The lay executive felt that insufficient progress had been registered in the pursuit of their original £60 weekly minimum claim. Questioned about this, Alan Fisher had to explain his union's structure, and insist that his executive, which had appointed him, had the right to determine the policies within which he worked. When pressed by a radio interviewer who wished to know whether Mr Fisher 'had lost control of his members', the NUPE spokesman quite rightly replied that it was no part of his job to 'control' his executive, but that his executive, on the contrary, had every right to 'control' its General Secretary.

A similarly strong statement was made by Moss Evans during 1978, during the time when he was taking over the responsibility of his office. Full-time officers, said Mr Evans, should be on hand 'to service the members, rather than to tell them what to do'. As we have seen already the TGWU is perhaps classically the union in which to study lay influence. Theoretically lay members have for a time long held ultimate power, not only over the Biennial Delegate Conference (1,000 strong), and the regional and industrial sections in which they are organized, but over the central councils of the entire organization. The union's General

Executive consists entirely of working members, each of whom has been chosen for a period of two years by his relevant region or industrial group. An inner cabinet, or Finance and General Purposes Committee, is chosen by this Executive, and this ensures that working busmen or dockers can arrive at a greater degree of actual power than any professional functionary of the union other than the General Secretary himself. All the signs are that this lay power is gathering strength and self-confidence. As Roger Undy reports, in his important study on the devolution of bargaining in the union:

> Official national encouragement, and indeed promotion, of lay involvement in bargaining was a radical departure from past practice in the traditionally full-time officer dominated T & GWU. The majority of centrally or regionally appointed full-time officers were traditionally more dependent on central, rather than lay members', support for legitimization of their bargaining decisions. Thus, the use by J. Jones of the 'unique authority' vested in the position of General Secretary to reverse the past pattern of responsibilities in the bargaining field appeared to some of the Union's more long serving full-time officials to be a near revolutionary act. For this group of officials it was somewhat contradictory, to say the least, that the centralized power of the General Secretary should be used in the late 1960s and early 1970s to devolve bargaining responsibilities which were traditionally their prerogative.
>
> Finally, it can be reasonably suggested that the recent (July 1977) defeat of the now retired General Secretary J. Jones, at the T & GWU's BDC on the question of wage restraint, was not unconnected with his previous sponsorship of the procedural changes identified above. From 1945 to 1977 the platform of the Conference, helped by the 'unique authority' of the General Secretary, had only previously been defeated on two comparatively minor issues, both concerned with the formation of new trade groups. Apart from these defeats, successive general secretaries had carried the Conference. No doubt the lay

delegates in 1977, in rejecting the platform's proposals, felt disinclined to accept further nationally imposed restrictions over their relatively new-found freedom to bargain locally. Hence, paradoxically, it can be argued that defeat for the General Secretary in 1977 was the final, if ironic, tribute to the success of his previous policy of devolving bargaining responsibilities.[44]

It is because lay government reaches right up to the top in the TGWU that occasional working representatives may appear on the General Council of the TUC: Bill Jones, the London busman, or Stan Pemberton, the Liverpool steward from Dunlop Speke, or Walt Greendale, the Hull docker, or Brian Nicholson from the London docks, would not at present, without taking up full-time work as organizers, have stood any chance of joining the General Council as representatives from any other union than the TGWU. No other section of the General Council contains men and women whose diaries include slabs of time spent on the shop-floor, leading substantially the same lives as the people they represent.

The TGWU's emphasis on lay participation did not protect it from sustained press attention in 1984–5, when allegations of ballot-rigging in the election to the General Secretaryship were made and to a limited extent, upheld. But they would not have affected the overall result. Nonetheless, the General Secretary-elect, Ron Todd, overcame his executive committee's hesitation in facing the problem, and insisted upon a re-election for the post, so that there should be no doubts about the legitimacy of his succession. With both media and the law lying in wait, vigilance in the conduct of elections will become a permanent practice in all unions in future. Their funds and their administrative resources may sometimes be stretched in consequence.

The members of the policy-making National Committee of the AUEW are prevented from discharging a similar role to the lay leadership of the TGWU by the fact that they normally confer only once a year, even though their deliberations continue for a longer time than do most union annual conferences. Fifty people constitute this Committee, so that they lack the authority of a major delegate conference. But the gap between their sessions is too long to allow the Committee to hold any careful watching brief over the doings of the very small and completely professional executive, which thus constantly strays into policy-making rather than implementing policies made for it. In fact, from time to time, AEU National Committees have tried to reinforce their admitted constitutional role, by approving resolutions which have included a provision for their own recall in the event of something happening, or failing to happen.[45] The constraints which such recall might place upon the freedom of action of the executive of the union have ensured that this kind of proposal has met with small executive enthusiasm. A celebrated dispute in 1966 resulted in a decision by the union's final appeal court to censure the executive for failing to act upon such a recall motion: but union elections changed the composition of the leadership, still leaving the issue potentially liable to recur. This kind of argument has continued, and in its most recent phase it produced an opposite result, with the replacement of the members of the appeal court itself.

Sometimes lay representation is conspicuous by its absence. Executive Committees of the NUM, for instance, do not normally include many working miners, since the union's federal origins guarantee a built-in tendency by most areas to field, at executive level, their best known professional agents. Yet various problems in the history of the NUM might have been solved differently if more lay members had access to top leadership committees. Even so, NUM members have long insisted on ultimate control over the results of national bargaining, referring them to the membership.

Communications

The trade union press faces an onerous responsibility, because in general the established media are by no means over-friendly to the Labour movement. This leaves a considerable task of explanation to trade union journalists who are often amateurs, and commonly without any great resources. Quite a lot of money is spent on trade union publications, but few are distributed through any conventional channels. The NUR publication *Transport Review*, and the Teachers' weekly newspaper, are both sold through newsagents. All the other major unions produce either a regular magazine, or a tabloid newspaper, or both; and almost all of these are distributed free of charge.

In certain professional unions the journal is obviously seen as a key instrument of communication with the members and this is reflected in appropriately high circulation figures. NALGO, for instance, with 710,000 members, prints 740,000 copies of its most informative monthly journal, *Public Service*. ASTMS print one copy of their bi-monthly for each of their 450,000 members, who receive it by post. British Actors' Equity *Journal* prints 32,000 copies for 24,000 members; the *Journalist* 30,000 for 28,500 members; and most civil service unions also provide enough copies for all their members.

On the other hand, the biggest unions make no attempt to reach all their membership with their journals. The TGWU, which produces a bright tabloid newspaper, the *Record*, printed something over 400,000 copies when it had 2 million members. This compares rather well with the much stodgier *Journal* of the AEU, which only printed 145,000 for more than one million people, or the General and Municipal Workers' *Journal*, which printed 70,000 while it had a membership of 950,000. Since distribution is free in each case, there is no way of telling what proportion of these print orders is actually distributed, leave alone read.

Most unions publish their journals monthly and since many do not sell much advertising space, this can be a costly business. The SLADE *Journal*, with a circulation of 22,000, almost covers its costs through advertising receipts, but this appears to be an exceptional case. Some unions are reticent about their publishing costs, but those who were prepared to disclose an annual outlay of £20,000 or more when we surveyed this area in 1979, are listed in Table 3.5.

Table 3.5
Union journals, costs and advertising revenue

Union	Cost of journal 1978–9	Advertising revenue
APEX	£33,000	£1,000
COHSE	£70,000	£8,000
CPSA	£165,000*	
Musicians' Union	£20,000*	
NALGO	£249,000	£56,000
NATFHE	£72,000	£18,000
NUAAW	£24,000*	little
NUBE	£51,000*	£12,000
NUJ	£22,000	£1,500
SCPS	£73,000	£33,000
SOGAT	£48,000	£6,000
SPOE	£40,000*	some
TGWU	£250,000	12½%
USDAW	£100,000	

(Part of this information comes from a survey taken in summer 1978, and part from a different investigation made in March 1979. At a time of rising inflation, it is necessary to distinguish the later information with a *.)

Intelligent guesses at the printing costs of the Engineers' and GMWU *Journals* at that time would put them at £170,000 and £35,000 per annum respectively. This gives a joint expenditure, by sixteen trade unions, of £1,422,000 a year on the subsidization of union newspapers and journals.

As to whether this produces value for money, there might be room for some argument. Some journals are briskly conducted, and punchy in their style. Others have been unbelievably bad. (The *Boilermaker*, for instance, gave over numerous pages in each issue to recording the names of members who have fallen into arrears. This listing fell into a happy abeyance after the union merged with the GMWU to form GMBATU.) Sometimes a professional journalist is engaged to edit the union newspaper, but quite commonly the job is taken on by a responsible official, especially when control of the journal may contribute to some advantage in the internal political struggles of the organization. What may then be gained in direct access to a propaganda lever can sometimes be lost in readability and effective influence. Occasionally, there can be a conflict between a union journal's independent editor, and the officials of his executive, as happened in a spectacular conflict about the conduct of *Red Tape*, the newspaper of the civil servants.

A far more serious question is posed if one sets aside the union press as it is, and considers it as it might be. With modern printing technology, bright, flexible, effective publicity is cheaply available, and if it is rationally employed it can make a considerable impact. Yet the trade unions, which controlled a daily newspaper all through the twenties, thirties, forties and fifties, have been totally without any national voice in the press during two decades, through which time they have fought off more than one political offensive aimed at reducing their rights and social influence. Can the TUC remain satisfied with this unbalanced, even menacing position?

NOTES

1. Small is beautiful, and there is no doubt that Dr Schumacher discovered the power of this truth because he was so long working for the vast bureaucracy of the National Coal Board. But competition is the force which centralizes vast monopoly power, and no one has ever discovered how to run that motor backwards. Unions have to square the circle: to be big enough to exercise counter-power, and accessible enough to allow democracy to flourish in their internal affairs.
2. G. D. H. Cole, *British Trade Unionism: Problems and Policy*, LRD, 1925, p. 19.
3. USDAW, *Introducing USDAW: the Structure, Government and Administration of the Union.* Home Study Course, Part III, USDAW, 1972? p. 30.
4. *Ibid*, p. 31.
5. ETU, *Submission of Evidence to the Royal Commission on Trade Unions and Employers' Associations*, ETU, n.d., p. 4.
6. GMWU, *The General and Municipal Workers' Union – its History, Structure, Policies, Benefits and Services*, GMWU, 1975, p. 5.
7. TGWU, *Training Manual* Part 2, 1960, pp. 4–5.
8. AEU, *Trade Unions and the Contemporary Scene.* Evidence to Royal Commission on Trade Unions and Employers' Associations, 1965.

9. Cited in Jim Gardner, *Key Questions for Trade Unionists*, Lawrence and Wishart, 1960, p. 34.
10. AEU, *op. cit.*
11. Cf. J. Goldstein, *The Government of British Trade Unions*, Allen and Unwin, 1952. This offers an estimate that TGWU branch attendance never rose above 15 per cent. Controversial within the TGWU at the time of its publication, this study attempts to probe reasons for non-involvement. B. C. Roberts, *Trade Union Government and Administration in Great Britain*, claims figures as low as 4 per cent and 7 per cent, but up to 15 per cent. London School of Economics/Bell, 1956, cf. pp. 95 *et seq.*

    PEP, *British Trade Unionism*, 1948, put them between 15 per cent and 20 per cent. J. H. Goldthorpe *et al.*, *The Affluent Worker*, Cambridge University Press, 1968, 1969, found that 60 per cent of car workers never attended. This and other evidence is summarized in Robert Taylor, *The Fifth Estate – Britain's Unions in the Seventies*, Routledge and Kegan Paul, 1978, pp. 106–9.
12. Bob Fryer, Andy Fairclough and Tom Manson, *Organization and Change in the National Union of Public Employees*, University of Warwick, 1974, pp. 21–3.
13. Sidney and Beatrice Webb, *History of Trade Unionism*, WEA, 1920, pp. 466–70.
14. Roberto Michels, *Political Parties*, Constable/Dover, 1950, p. 21.
15. *Ibid*, p. 22.
16. *Ibid*, pp. 70 *et seq.*
17. There is an interesting discussion of these questions in Richard Hyman, *Marxism and the Sociology of Trade Unionism*, Pluto Press, 1971.
18. Brian Pearce, *Some Rank-and-File Movements*, Labour Review, 1959, p. 13.
19. TUC, *Annual Report*, 1978, *Details of Past Congresses.*
20. B. C. Roberts, *op. cit.*, pp. 288–9. A corrective to these figures is to be found in H. A. Clegg, A. J. Killick and R. Adams, *Trade Union Officers*, Blackwell, 1960, pp. 37 *et seq.*, especially p. 40.
21. The Donovan Report (Cmnd 5623) insisted that this ratio was on the high side: in the USA comparable figures were 'of the order of' 1:1,400, whilst in Federal Germany they were 1:1,800. 'Both Italy and France appear to have twice as many officers per member as we do.'
22. Roger Undy, 'The Devolution of Bargaining Levels and Responsibilities in the T GWU 1965–75', *Industrial Relations Journal*, 3, p. 44 *et seq.*
23. *Ibid*, p. 49. 1986 figures supplied by the TGWU.
24. The Equal Pay and Opportunity Campaign, Canonbury Park North, London N1: figures for 1976.
25. The most useful account of recent electoral struggles in both the NUM and the AEU/AUEW is to be found in J. D. Edelstein and M. Warner, *Comparative Union Democracy*, Allen and Unwin, 1975, Chapters 8 and 9.
26. See our *Trade Unions and Politics*, Blackwell, 1986, for an account of these problems and references to the literature concerning them.
27. The Conservative Party, *The Right Approach*, October 1976.
28. Cf for Robert Taylor, *op. cit.*, p. 110.
29. See the Reports of the Certification Officer, which record all disbursements for these purposes. We have analysed these reports in *Trade Unions and Politics*, *op. cit.*
30. For instance, in 1968, under the branch voting system, only 11 per cent of the AUEW's membership voted in the election for General Secretary. In 1975 38 per cent of the membership voted in postal ballots for national officials. Postal ballots

may also reduce the chances of abuse of electoral procedures, and since voting is secret, are likely to reduce the amount of 'pressure' on the voter from fellow union members. *Democracy at Work, Trade Union Studies*, BBC, p. 155.

31. The mechanics of similar previous contests are very fully described in Edelstein and Warner, *op. cit.*
32. For a summary of trade union attitudes to these questions, see *Workers' Control*, the Bulletin of the IWC, Nos. 3 and 4, 1979.
33. AEF (later to become the AUEW and then again AEU), *Structure and Function of the Union*, 1969, p. 6: 'Branches are grouped in eleven electoral divisions for the election of eleven delegates.'
34. Richard Fletcher, 'Trade Union Democracy: Structural Factors', *Trade Union Register*, 2, Spokesman, 1972, pp. 78 *et seq.*
35. Richard Fletcher, 'Trade Union Democracy: the Case of the AUEW Rule Book', *Trade Union Register*, 3, Spokesman, 1973, pp. 125–49.
36. Cf. V. L. Allen, *Power in Trade Unions*, Longman, 1954, pp. 184 *et seq.*, 271 *et seq.* This quotation is p. 206.
37. *Op. cit.*, pp. 91–2.
38. B. C. Roberts, *op. cit.*, pp. 263 *et seq.*
39. V. L. Allen, *op. cit.*, pp. 203–4.
40. Cf. C. H. Rolph, *All Those in Favour – The ETU Trial*, Andre Deutsch, 1962.
41. J. Hemingway, *Conflict and Democracy – Studies in Trade Union Government*, OUP, 1978, p. 52.
42. R. Hunter, *The Road to Brighton Pier*, cited in Gardner, *op. cit.*, p. 43.
43. The important study by Mark Jenkins, *Bevanism; Labour's High Tide*, published by Spokesman in 1979, throws much light on this question.
44. Roger Undy, *op. cit.*, p. 56.
45. Cf. Edelstein and Warner, *op. cit.*, Ch. 9.

CHAPTER 4

The TUC

The Origins and Development of the TUC

The TUC dates its inception to the year 1868, when the Manchester and Salford Trades Council convened what turned out to be the first of a continuous series of trade union conferences.[1] There had been earlier attempts to form an all-embracing forum of trade unionism, notably the Grand National Consolidated Trade Union of the 1830s, associated with the name and ideas of Robert Owen, and the National Association of United Trades for the Protection of Labour, of 1845. The early years of the TUC were dominated by the need to influence parliamentary legislation on trade union affairs.

To this end, the TUC set up its Parliamentary Committee in 1871, to lobby MPs, send deputations to ministers, and organize publicity campaigns. The work of the Parliamentary Committee, which was manned by six leading secretaries of the unions of the day, was conducted on a voluntary basis, with no full-time staff. By 1900, the TUC had progressed to the appointment of a secretary, assisted by a clerk and a part-time advisory barrister. In 1902, the salary of the secretary was fixed at £250, and in 1905 the post was made into a full-time one. The first generation of TUC leaders had been craft-oriented, cautious and even hostile to industrial action, and concerned above all to win a respected and respectable place for their version of trade unionism within a liberal capitalist society whose fundamental norms they did not seek to challenge. This search for an alliance with the Liberals led prominent members of the trade union establishment into secret dealings with the Liberal Party and with individual employers.[2]

A new wave of trade union affiliations enlarged the TUC in the 1890s, following the growth of organization amongst unskilled manual workers, and they brought with them more aggressive policies based on explicitly socialist beliefs; the younger generation of craft unionists sometimes shared these ideas.[3]

The old guard of the TUC leadership succeeded in avoiding direct involvement in socialist methods and policies, but were forced to convene the conferences out of which arose, in 1899, the General Federation of Trade Unions, and in 1900 the Labour Representation Committee, which converted itself into the Labour Party in 1906. The GFTU was intended to provide a much more co-ordinated approach to industrial action, with a common strike fund. But only a minority of trade unions joined it, and it deteriorated into a fund holder for the purely defensive mutual insurance of unions, having most significance for the smaller organizations.

Syndicalists looked forward to the time when the GFTU would supersede the TUC as the more suitable body to effect central co-ordination of trade union policies, but their hopes were never realized, and by creating a separate Labour Party, the trade unions also saw to it that the TUC was not directly involved in the alternative, Parliamentary road to emancipation. The Parliamentary Committee retained its role as a purely lobbying body, even though, between 1905 and 1919, it was formally associated with the Labour Party and the GFTU through a Joint Board.[4]

As the scope of social legislation widened in the first two decades of the twentieth century, so the role of the Parliamentary Committee increased, and in 1917 the TUC added an assistant secretary to its staff, and reinforced its clerical assistance. In 1920, under the prevailing influences of syndicalism, industrial unionism, and guild socialism, the TUC organization underwent a substantial structural reform. In place of the limited Parliamentary Committee, a General Council was created which was elected from affiliated unions divided into seventeen Trade Groups, corresponding roughly to industrial divisions. (An eighteenth element on the General Council was added in the form of special representation for women workers.) Whilst by 1919 the Parliamentary Committee had totalled sixteen members, the General Council was twice that size.

Nomination for election to represent each Group on the General Council was confined to unions within each Group, but voting for the seats was by the whole affiliated membership. The General Council was conceived as a much more dynamic, industrially active general staff of the Labour movement than the old Parliamentary Committee, and the Trade Groups were intended to foreshadow structural reform leading to industrial unionism. To initiate this trend, G. D. H. Cole, who drafted the new constitution, proposed that a start be made by establishing five industrial sub-committees within the TUC. During this period, moves to unite the TUC and the Labour Party went no further than the setting up of the National Joint Council of Labour, a consultative body comprising representatives of the Parliamentary Labour Party, the Party's National Executive Committee, and the TUC General Council.

Ambitious schemes were proposed by the radical reformers of the movement, and common departments between the Labour Party and the TUC were established for research, international affairs, and publicity. Their staff in 1925 was larger by five than the whole administrative staff of the TUC, and the TUC contributed £6,500 out of its total income of £18,500 to the joint departments. In 1926, after recording their disenchantment with the first Labour government's indifference to the TUC, the Congress withdrew from these departments, which ceased to function.[5]

The new constitution for the TUC, which was adopted when the General Council was formed, and which still forms the basis of the TUC Rules and Standing Orders, did contain overt political objectives. For example, in Rule 2, 'Objects', it is declared that Congress 'shall endeavour to establish the following measures . . . Public Ownership and control of natural resources and of services – Nationalization of land, mines and minerals, nationalization of railways, the extension of State and municipal enterprise for the provision of social necessities and services, proper provision for the adequate participation of the workers in the control and management of public services and industries.'

The advocates of the TUC as co-ordinator of industrial action achieved some success in inserting provisions in Rule 8, 'Duties of the General Council', which required the Council to 'co-ordinate industrial action' to 'promote common action . . . on general questions' and 'to assist any union which is attacked on any vital question of trade union principle'. Another interesting General Council duty which reflected the post-1918 climate of opinion was the following extract from Rule 8, later repealed:

> In order that the Trade Union Movement may do everything which lies in its power to prevent future wars, the General Council shall, in the event of there being a danger of an outbreak of war, call a Special Congress to decide on industrial action, such Congress to be called, if possible, before war is declared.

A further provision within Rule 11, 'Industrial Disputes', states that the General Council should, where its advice and assistance are being accepted by a union which is in dispute with an employer but which nevertheless finds itself in continued dispute because of the policy of the employers, 'take steps to organize on behalf of the organization or organizations concerned all such moral and material support as the circumstances of the dispute may appear to justify'.

Thus the new constitution did give the TUC powers of co-ordination, but did not fundamentally threaten the autonomy of individual unions. No central strike fund was established, and the General Council could only act with the consent of the affiliated unions. These contradictory elements in the constitution were fully exposed in the General Strike of 1926, the first and only occasion when the powers of the TUC to lead industrial action on behalf of the whole movement were tested. This is not the place for a full survey of that potent episode. It is enough to note that 'constitutionalist' opinion within the TUC became firmly established after the General Strike, resolving that such an action would 'never again' be undertaken. (See Chapter 8.) 'Never' is an injudicious word to employ in this kind of context, and it is possible to imagine circumstances, such as the threat of unjustified war, or of a fascist takeover of power in Britain, when the TUC might be under the strongest moral obligation to consider leading industrial action.[6]

Under the leadership of Walter Citrine (General Secretary) and of Ernest Bevin of the TGWU, the TUC in the interwar and war years pursued a constitutional role, and continued the historical trend towards a wider involvement in consultations with governments, and participation in the affairs of state as a very junior partner. This was particularly so during the war, and during the Labour administration from 1945–51. (Earlier, the first Labour Prime Minister Ramsay MacDonald had kept the TUC very much at arm's length, and hardly deigned to consult them at all.[7]) Moreover, in the war and postwar years, the TUC recovered and surpassed the numerical affiliated strength which had declined so drastically after 1926, and for this reason alone could claim an increasingly representative nature. For the most part, the Conservative governments of the 1950s continued the tradition of 'consulting' the TUC, but of regarding it as of limited significance for its overall policies and postures, and the TUC, under a succession of right-of-centre alliances amongst its leadership, conformed to the role assigned to it. As the economic circumstances of Britain went into relative decline, and as the hegemony of right-wing leadership in the TUC became challenged after the succession of Frank Cousins to the leadership of the TGWU, the climate changed.

The period since about 1962 has seen such large-scale and far-reaching changes in the role of the TUC that we need to look at it in greater detail.

Wages Policy and the TUC

In 1962, the Conservative government set up two organizations, the National Economic Development Council (NEDC) and the National Incomes Commission (NIC). NEDC was the first major organization to embody the concept of 'tripartite' representation in a threefold state body, being comprised of representatives of the government, the employers, and the TUC, which nominated its six most senior General Council members to represent it. George Woodcock, the TUC General Secretary, declared that 'NEDC is to us a serious undertaking indeed'. 'We go in *as a side* . . . we are linked together all the time' (italics added).[8] Consequently, NEDC has survived, although not without its trade union critics, and we shall discuss it again when we consider the general issue of tripartism.

The different TUC response to the NIC was equally unequivocal. Its purpose was seen as the enforcement of a government policy of wage restraint, and its form (it was a body entirely appointed by government, with no representative element, and with no clear accountability) made it repugnant to the TUC, which accused the government of trying to avoid the opprobrium of wage restraint. The TUC had not been invited to participate in the NIC, and indeed were only informed of its formation some hours before the announcement in the House of Commons.

Although the General Secretary was at pains to point out that he and the General Council were not averse to discussing wages within a wider context of economic planning such as might be achieved within the NEDC, the TUC advised unions to boycott all NIC investigations and hearings, and the organization did not survive the downfall of the Conservative government in 1974.

The General Council's willingness to admit wages as an item on the NEDC agenda was itself too much for the TUC as a whole at this stage. Led by the TGWU under Frank Cousins, the 1963 annual Congress rejected General Council policy, and approved a motion expressing 'complete opposition to any form of wages restraint'. In the debate, Woodcock was taken to task by Cousins and others for claiming that the TUC was now wholly concerned with Committee work in 'the corridors of power' and that 'we left Trafalgar Square a long time ago'. Yet Woodcock in one sense may have had the last word; in a remarkable anticipation of the social contract which was to emerge a decade later, he remarked, 'If you want in a democracy . . . to get restraint . . . you must seek to create, to have accepted, what Rousseau called a general will.'[9]

In subsequent years and phases of government incomes and wage restraint policies, TUC opposition rarely took the absolute form of 1963, and there are important periods when it accommodated such policies within its own strategy. This ambivalent attitude to wage restraint contrasts strongly, as we shall see, with the unambiguous and successful resistance mounted by the TUC in the 1970s against government attempts to legislate to control and limit trade union organizations and methods. It may be that the TUC has regarded incomes policies as a lesser threat to its role, because it has been regarded as a temporary measure and because in the later 'social contract' version of incomes restraint, the terms have been to some extent bargainable with government and there have been compensatory gains for the unions. Chapter 6 is devoted to the detailed questions of collective bargaining and some aspects of incomes policy.

Periodic attempts by government to control wages led in the 1960s and 1970s to a situation in which the TUC was, in effect, bargaining collectively on behalf of the whole trade union movement, and this had profound implications for its role and authority. It meant amongst other things that the TUC began to evolve negotiating targets and strategies which it then urged on the trade unions. This adaptation to incomes policies stands in contrast to the *opposition* which the TUC led when the basic organizational freedoms of trade unionism were under threat during the seventies.[10]

TUC bargaining strategy during the sixties and seventies included much attention to the question of low pay, and the setting of periodically revised targets for bargained minimum wages. More recently, and not without arousing serious divisions amongst its constituent unions, the TUC has adopted a demand for a legally enforceable minimum wage, something for which public sector unions such as NUPE have long campaigned. This represents a genuine departure from long-established principles which relegated legal minima to a fringe role in Wages Council industries.

The TUC has not confined its thinking on bargaining strategies to the minimum earnings target. Since 1968 it has published an annual *Economic Review*, a major policy statement linking economic analysis and forecasts with collective bargaining strategy, which has often enabled it to adopt an independent and critical stance in relation to government predictions and targets. The *Review*, which takes into account successful resolutions of the previous year's Congress, has consistently advocated expansionist and interventionist economic policies. Associated with the *Review*, the TUC introduced a series of conferences of union Executive Committees to debate and ratify it, thus giving a further reinforcement to General Council policies. In the 1969 *Annual Report*, the General Council affirmed that the purposes of the *Review* were to recast incomes policy along TUC policy lines, to point up the divergence between its thinking on economic policy and that of the government, to provide it with a new basis for consulting with and influencing government, and to give a policy foundation for all its participation in tripartite activities, independent of the thinking of the NEDC office.

In an overall review of TUC structure and development in 1970, the TUC devoted considerable further attention to collective bargaining strategy.[11] They argued that the TUC should be concerned not just with wages, but the total economic environment of its affiliates, including the factors which contributed to success in strike actions. The document also discussed ways and means of developing an information service for unions, through promotion of discussions with trade union research officers, through more frequent publication of TUC bulletins on economic indicators, and through a TUC initiative to pool, store, and analyse economic data and collective agreements. It was in 1970 too that the TUC renamed its Incomes Policy Committee as a Collective Bargaining Committee, with representation from each TUC Trade Group plus the General Secretary. Its objects were declared to be the discussion of bargaining targets, to review bargaining developments, and to promote common objectives amongst its affiliates. However, the Committee ceased to function after 1974, presumably because the General Council itself assumed more central authority in this field in the context of the social contract.

In 1972 the TUC produced a follow-up report on its structure and development, which continued to stress the need for co-ordination of the separate bargaining objectives of different unions. Wages Council industries particularly needed co-ordination, and the demand for equal pay should be speeded up. Non-wage benefits such as job security and redundancy agreements, shorter hours, longer holidays, sick-pay schemes and pensions schemes could be adopted as common targets. It spoke of annual holidays of three weeks as an immediate goal, and the 35-hour week, the four-week holiday, the four-day week, and more public holidays, as longer-term goals, and reported that the TUC Collective Bargaining Committee had discussed these goals with trade union negotiators in large companies. It expressed strong demands for the disclosure of information from employers, and foreshadowed later legislation to deal with employers who refused requests for disclosure of information.[12]

All this story provides strong evidence of the TUC's growing involvement in collective bargaining; the continuous battering on the door of trade union autonomy by successive government wage policies led the movement to use its central organization more and more, both as co-ordinator and policy-maker in this field. The process was incomplete – we shall refer to its further development through TUC Industry Committees later – and it encountered a persistent weakness and indecision in the key area of public sector bargaining.

The TUC and Legislative Onslaughts

The largely voluntary reforms in collective bargaining proposed by the Donovan Royal Commission in 1968 caused no profound crisis in the TUC, and in fact stimulated the early stages of TUC initiative in the collective bargaining field which we have reviewed above; six 'Post-Donovan' conferences of unions in different sectors were summoned by the TUC to consider the reform of bargaining practice and trade union organization.[13] But Donovan's voluntarism was soon overtaken by tougher government measures.

The Labour government's White Paper, *In Place of Strife*, which was published in 1969, proposed that legislation should be enacted to give governments power to order a strike ballot before a major strike, and to order 'cooling off' periods in the case particularly of unofficial and 'unconstitutional' strikes. Unofficial strikes were defined as those which were originated outside the appropriate union forum: while 'unconstitutional' strikes were those called in breach of an agreement, whether unofficial or not. The White Paper also proposed to empower a newly formed Commission on Industrial Relations to enforce its decisions in cases of inter-union disputes over recognition. These proposed measures were firmly resisted by the TUC. Other proposals were more acceptable. They included the registration of procedural agreements, the guaranteeing of workers' rights to join trade unions, and to trade unions of the right to recognition, the protection of individuals against unfair dismissal, the provision of better information for collective bargaining purposes, and extensions of the jurisdiction of Industrial Tribunals.

A major political crisis for the government developed around the TUC resistance to the 'penal clauses', and the government was forced to withdraw them. But a very important outcome was that the TUC, in undertaking to police inter-union disputes and unconstitutional stoppages more fully, assumed wider authority over its affiliated unions. In the TUC's published response to *In Place of Strife*, the *Programme for Action*, it was proposed that TUC Rules 11 and 12 should be amended to give effect to these increased central powers. On unconstitutional strikes, unions would in future be required to inform the General Council of 'unauthorized and unconstitutional stoppages of work' and to follow TUC advice as to how to deal with them. Concerning inter-union disputes, unions would be required to inform the General Council whenever an official stoppage was contemplated in an inter-union dispute, and to desist from authorizing strike action until the TUC had considered the case. If an unauthorized stoppage took place in an inter-union conflict, the union concerned was placed under the duty to strive for the resumption of work.

The opposition of the trade unions to the Conservative Government's Industrial Relations Act of 1971 provides one of the most remarkable demonstrations of the exercise of TUC authority. The details of the Act are dealt with in our chapter on Law; at this stage it is only necessary to remind ourselves that the Act carried much further the concept of legal penalties for trade unionists committing specified 'unfair practices' and introduced an elaborate system of legal regulation of trade unions, including a specification of requirements for union rulebooks.

The trade union movement was in no doubt that it should resist the legislation, and seek to render it inoperable. To achieve this end they required a united and common programme, and a sustained public campaign; these could not be achieved without a massive concentration of effort through their central organization, the TUC. Whilst the legislation was before Parliament, the TUC organized its campaign. A conference of union officers was called in November 1970, and the Education Department of the TUC produced a training kit which was used to instruct thousands of union officials and lay representatives in regional programmes. TUC regional conferences were held, 118 Trades Councils organized meetings on the Bill, and the TUC called two national demonstrations against it, the larger one summoning 140,000 trade unionists to Hyde Park and Trafalgar Square. A national petition to Parliament contained half a million signatures, and TUC press advertisements cost £51,000. TUC publications on the Bill included a film and a special gramophone record with a message from the General Secretary.

TUC policy on the Bill called for its early repeal (a necessity which did much to draw the TUC and Labour Party into closer alliance). Pending the annulment of the Act, unions were advised to insist that new clauses in collective agreements should specifically opt against their legal enforceability, to ensure that unions should continue to observe the TUC's Bridlington Rules rather than use the new legal procedures for recognition in inter-union conflicts, to boycott the statutory bodies – Commission on Industrial Relations, and National Industrial Relations Court – set up by the Act, to withdraw union nominees from service on

Industrial Tribunals, to reject the Code of Industrial Relations Practice issued under the Act and to abide instead by the independent TUC *Guide to Good Industrial Relations*. Above all, Congress mounted a vigorous campaign to ensure that no trade unions sought registered status under the Act.

This confounded much 'informed' newspaper opinion at the time, which claimed that the deregistration policy would surely fail, as one union after another would break the line and seek its own sectional salvation within the framework of the Act. No such collapse took place. It is difficult to exaggerate the effect that this episode had on the self-confidence and moral strength of the TUC in the Labour movement at that time. It must be said that the Conservative Party learned much from these events, so that its subsequent offensives were much subtler. Instead of overall confrontation and shunt, the Thatcher administration was to rely on the option of undermining legal immunities, so that unions were exposed to attacks from many sides rather than one central authority. Where direct collision was part of her plan Mrs Thatcher manoeuvred until she could isolate and divide the unions involved. She then met them with overwhelming force. But that force was at the end of a process, not the beginning. The legislation of the Heath administration certainly invited conflict: it brought state institutions into play from the beginning, at a time when they commanded no consensus, and rested upon levels of force which were, in retrospect, rather underwhelming.

The 'Social Contract'

During the period of the Heath government, the TUC was not only leading the fight against the Industrial Relations Act, but was actively preparing the political ground for its repeal and replacement, by building a more intimate alliance with the Labour Party than had been conceived at any time since the Party's foundation. The TUC–Labour Party Liaison Committee, comprising representatives of the General Council, the leadership of the Parliamentary Party and the Party's National

Executive Committee, was formed in 1972. This body gave the TUC a formidable influence on the policy-making process whilst Labour was in opposition, and its published policy documents largely comprised the election manifesto which took Labour to office in 1974. The drafts of laws to repeal the Industrial Relations Act, and to provide an Employment Protection Act, were passed through this committee during 1972–3, and the key policy document, *Economic Policy and the Cost of Living*, was jointly launched by the Leader of the Labour Party and the TUC General Secretary. The TUC followed this with its own publication, *Collective Bargaining and the Social Contract*, in June 1974, after the Labour government's election. The essence of the 'contract' was the promise by the Labour Party of legislation favourable to trade unionism, in return for voluntary pay restraint by the trade unions.

In assessing the balance sheet of this grand package deal, it is necessary to bear in mind what *Economic Policy and the Cost of Living* contained. In the field of industrial legislation, it laid down a three-stage programme. First, the Industrial Relations Act would be repealed and a new Trade Union and Labour Relations Act would take its place. Second, legislation on Employment Protection would be enacted. And third, an Industrial Democracy law would be passed. The first two items were delivered by the Labour government in the first two years of its life and the TUC was constantly consulted, and frequently prevailed in such consultations, over the details of these Acts. For good measure there was an important Health and Safety at Work Act, which contained the vital provision, which the TUC had requested, for the appointment of trade union safety representatives, and a Sex Discrimination Act, which again reflected TUC policy. But the third item, the Industrial Democracy legislation, was postponed more than once by the government, and the original TUC proposals, for 50 per cent of directors' boards in large private companies to be elected by trade union employees in those companies, had been seriously watered down. These matters concern us in a separate chapter on Industrial Democracy, but their relevance here is to demonstrate the limits of TUC influence on government policy through the social contract – limits which were clearly marked out when the CBI led a virulent opposition to the modest industrial democracy proposals in the Bullock Report.

In the passage of the Trade Union and Labour Relations Act and the Employment Protection Act, we have seen that the TUC enjoyed considerable influence. Many details of this could be cited; as an example, we may take the case of day release with pay to enable union representatives to undertake trade union training courses in working time. The original drafts of the Employment Protection Bill provided that the Advisory, Conciliation and Arbitration Service should have the power to approve courses which trade unionists could attend under this provision. The TUC successfully pressed for the exclusion of this clause, and for a new clause which established the right of the TUC, or of an individual trade union, to approve the training courses. Thus the TUC got itself written into an Act of Parliament, as a body enjoying statutory rights in this field.

In one area, the debate around the new legislation led to the TUC acquiring a new quasi-judicial function. In the original version of the Trade Union and Labour Relations Act, passed during the minority administration of Labour between the February and October elections of 1974, there was provision for legal machinery to be used by an individual who considered that he had been arbitrarily or unreasonably expelled or excluded from membership of a union. The TUC disliked this intensely, arguing that trade union internal appeals machinery was the appropriate method of ensuring that justice was done to individuals with this kind of grievance. The government, however, felt that there should be additional machinery, and suggested that an alternative to a statutory provision could be voluntary machinery established by the TUC. The TUC accepted this suggestion, and established for this purpose an Independent Review Committee, in return for which the government repealed the offending section of the law in its Trade Union and Labour Relations (Amendment) Act of 1976.

The Review Committee considers appeals from individuals

who have been dismissed from their jobs as a consequence of being expelled from, or having been refused admission to, a union in a situation where union membership is a condition of employment. The Committee has an independent chairman with legal qualifications, and two other members. All three are appointed by the TUC General Council in consultation with the Secretary of Employment and with the chairman of ACAS. The initial appointments were of Professor K. W. Wedderburn (as the chairman), George Doughty, a retired union general secretary, and Lord McCarthy, university teacher of industrial relations. The Review Committee in its proceedings must first satisfy itself that internal union appeals machinery has been exhausted, must discuss the case with the union and attempt to resolve the matter by agreement, and if this process fails, make a recommendation that the union should either accept or reinstate the individual into membership, or that the union's action was justified. There is a clear, TUC-imposed, responsibility on the part of the union to act on the Committee's recommendation. The Committee is now a functioning part of the TUC machinery. By 1985, the same Committee members had heard fifty-seven cases and adjudicated in twenty-three of them, of which fourteen led to precise recommendations. In no case where the Committee has made a recommendation have the unions involved failed to comply.[14]

This is perhaps not the place to review the whole record of the Labour government over the period 1974–8, but it is clear that TUC influence on that government was at its height in 1974–5, when the initial stages of social contract legislation were being passed. Following this, the TUC, despite regular and sustained pronouncements, was unable to dissuade the government from its chosen course of toleration for very high levels of unemployment, substantial cuts in public spending, and a generally deflationary economic policy largely dictated by the requirements of the International Monetary Fund. Nevertheless, through this later period, the TUC–Liaison Committee continued to meet regularly and frequently, and published a further general statement in 1976, *The Next Three Years and the Problem of*

Priorities (updated the following year as *The Next Three Years and Into the Eighties*), intended to serve the same strategic purpose as the 1973 statement on *Economic Policy and the Cost of Living*.

Both these documents were less specific, more muted, on the details of future Labour programmes than was the statement of 1973, and both concentrated much more on the purely economic goals of higher growth, reduced unemployment, and the control of inflation. They also recorded the failure of government to implement the commitment to planning agreements, and the consequent vacuum in economic planning which remained at the level of the large companies. Both documents, moreover, reiterated the government's pledge to legislate for 'parity representation' of trade unionists on the top boards of large companies; although it became apparent from the White Paper on Industrial Democracy finally published in 1978[15] that this objective had been indefinitely postponed by the government. Reference to incomes policy in the documents is very guarded and vague. The social contract had run out of steam, and the powerful influence of the TUC on governments over the period 1973–6 had run out with it. This fact was dramatically emphasized with the advent of the Conservative administration of 1979.

Throughout the sixties and seventies a strong tide was running in favour of what has become known as 'tripartism', the system of conducting government and quasi-governmental functions through the agency of bodies drawing representation from government, employers, and trade unions. As the central representative body for trade unions, the TUC played a major role in nominating its representatives to these bodies, and through them, was potentially in a strong position to co-ordinate trade union influence on policies by developing a system of briefing and reporting back. The list of agencies on which the TUC has representation is rather long, and when we reported on it in 1980, it included sixty-seven distinct bodies. Here we may mention some of the more significant. As we have already said, amongst the oldest of the postwar generation of tripartite bodies is the National Economic Development Council, which is supposed to deal with long-term planning objectives, and which has in membership representatives of the CBI, ministers of the government, chairmen of the nationalized industry corporations, and six senior members of the TUC General Council. It is chaired by either the Chancellor of the Exchequer, or the Prime Minister. It is backed by a servicing Office.

Whilst the TUC takes the business of tripartite planning very seriously, it is hard to detect a similar commitment on the part of governments or the CBI. When Economic Development Committees for particular industries were established, in 1963, in an attempt to take the planning process down the line from the central NEDC, the TUC sought nominations for the trade union seats on these bodies from unions with large interests in the particular industries, and the TUC was responsible for the final selection of representatives. In 1967, the TUC demonstrated its concern to make planning a serious process, by proposing on the NEDC that a National Planning College should be founded. This admirable suggestion was completely ignored. Already by 1968 the TUC was expressing concern that genuine tripartite planning on the NEDC was being replaced by the use to which government was putting the Committee – as a mere sounding board for its own policies. In 1976, the NEDC machinery was given a new look by the setting up of thirty-seven Sector Working Parties to cover various branches of the economy, and to implement what the Labour government has called its Industrial Strategy, although this strategy was, to be polite, never defined with any precision. The TUC called on the unions in these sectors to nominate lay union officials to occupy seats on them wherever possible, and it called for the discussion of Working Party recommendations to be carried down to the company and major plant levels within the sectors. This is in line with the TUC's consistent view that planning should be conceived as a total process, which operates at all levels, from the economy to the sector, the industry, the company and the plant. In fact there is no real authority in this structure at any level. In particular, the Sector Working Parties lack any means of controlling the decisions of the major multinational companies within their orbits, and at company level itself, there has been an almost total failure to implement the practice of planning agreements as envisaged in the 1975 Industry Act, despite the TUC (and TUC–Labour Party Liaison Committee) constantly calling on the government to speed up this process. When the government decided in 1975 to dilute the original concept of compulsory planning agreements between government, unions, and the largest companies, and to make such agreements voluntary, they effectively removed a key element in any overall tripartite approach to economic planning.

Since 1979, the whole concept of tripartism, and the assumption by government and employers that the TUC had a legitimate role in policy formation, or at least a right to be consulted, have been swept aside by a government and employers determined to reassert older hegemonic powers. Moreover, the combined assault on trade unionism from the law, and from economic and political forces, has not left the TUC's authority, status and cohesion unscathed.

As we have already pointed out, the Conservative administrations of 1979–83 and 1983–7 avoided the errors of the 1970–4 governments by legislating against trade unions in piecemeal fashion, not by passing a single all-embracing law such as the Industrial Relations Act of 1971. Such laws were enacted while officially recognized unemployment ran at levels rising above 3 million. Consequently, the TUC was unable, although it tried, to organize a successful campaign of resistance and defiance of the Employment Acts, 1980 and 1982, or of the Trade Union Act of 1984. At a series of Conferences and Congresses the TUC did adopt, initially, a policy of opposition and non-co-operation with the laws. However, on each occasion that resistance became necessary in practice, the General Council was unable to mobilize solidarity behind the particular unions which were caught up in the effects of the new laws. This was true of a series of disputes in the provincial newspaper industry (the Eddie Shah cases of 1982–3), in the miners' strike of 1984–5, and in the print unions' dispute with Rupert Murdoch's News International at his Wapping plant, in 1986–7.

The new laws provided no central point of vulnerability to the earlier (1971–3) tactics of the TUC. They did not construct a new legal body, such as the NIRC, but relied on the ordinary courts and on increased willingness of the employers and disaffected union members to resort to the courts. The government itself, through its appointed heads of public industries, such as steel and coal, set an example of unprecedented toughness verging on brutality. This provoked protests even from Lord Stockton, the former Prime Minister, of a different style of Conservative government. The Thatcher administration was moreover willing to finance the economic costs (not to say the considerable policing costs) of deeply damaging strikes, such as those of the printers and miners, indefinitely, up to the point of unconditional surrender from the unions. Compared with the early 1970s, unemployment had bitten deep into the willingness of other union members not directly involved to make sacrifices on behalf of beleaguered fellow trade unionists. The unions as institutions also saw not only their funds but even their very existence threatened through fines, damages, and sequestration of assets during these prolonged disputes. The TUC itself was always fearful that it would also become liable at court for any support of secondary action or secondary picketing, which could have been involved if it had sought to mobilize support, say, for the miners and printers. Even in the case of the GCHQ ban[16] on trade union membership, a simple case of government anti-unionism and of infringement of elementary civil rights, the TUC was compelled to make largely rhetorical gestures. Days of Action against unemployment, a further TUC initiative in the early 1980s, resulted in the organization of moving demonstrations and long mass marches on London, to all of which the government was impervious. At one stage, in 1984, the TUC temporarily withdrew its six representatives from the NEDC, but they returned shortly thereafter. Even so, government had no compunction about ruffling TUC feathers by using NEDC, notably in 1986, to make unilateral public pronouncement of its intended economic policies, contrary to the usually decorous tripartite customs.

After four years of this treatment, and after Labour's heavy defeat at the polls in 1983, with which defeat the TUC was strongly identified, a major debate opened around what has been called the 'new realism'. This amounted to a doctrine that the unions should distance themselves from the Labour Party, and from party politics generally, in favour of an American-style business unionism, which accepted the new laws, the new market philosophy of government, the right of management to manage, and the introduction of new technology on managerial terms. By adapting to these new forces, it was hoped to survive and prosper within the high-technology sector of the economy, whilst striving but little to alleviate the harsh effects of the new climate on less fortunate sectors of the working population. The EETPU and the AEU became two of the major exponents of the new doctrines, and the EETPU went so far as to market itself in Japan using glossy brochures carrying messages of approval from the Chairman of the Conservative Party. When the EETPU and the AEU applied, contrary to TUC policy, for the government subsidies which were available under legislation to finance postal balloting, and when the EETPU blatantly breached the Bridlington Rules in recruiting staff for the Wapping printing works, the TUC was unable to enforce customary discipline on either or both of the unions. Its decline from authority in these inter-union affairs was symptomatic of the recession of its influence.

Ranged against the EETPU and AEU within the TUC was a disparate group of unions. Some, like TASS and ASTMS, with formally left-wing politics, were in direct rivalry with the EETPU and AEU for the recruitment of highly skilled workers in electronics, and high technology generally, and were inclined to pursue their own more radical version of 'new realism'. Others, such as the public sector unions, low wage unions, and the traditional general unions, were in uneasy and uncoordinated alliance which, whilst it was against the new realism, was not all that sure of the policies of which it was actually in favour. By tradition, these unions saw their escape and rejuvenation in the election of a new Labour government. This concern led naturally to a renewed debate in the TUC–Labour Party Liaison

Committee, and also bilaterally with shadow ministers, around the legislative programme which an incoming Labour government would enact.

This in turn generated a strong debate, some of it academic and distinctly arid, around the alternatives of seeking a return to the 1906 concept of 'immunities' law, to protect unions in industrial action from the attention of the courts, and the passing of 'positive rights' law, modelled perhaps on West European practices, in which the right to strike was formally embodied. This is not the place for a lengthy discussion of this controversy.[17] But it should be noted that the positions adopted by left- and right-wing unions were not clear-cut; on the left some (for instance NUPE) favoured positive rights, whilst others (such as the TGWU) were uneasy about this policy. Similar divisions occurred amongst centre and right-wing unions.

More significantly, perhaps, the TUC showed few signs of what its response might be in the event of a third Conservative government being elected, with its advanced plans for further anti-union laws already publicized in early 1987.[18] The contrast between the TUC's firm, influential and positive role in the drafting of the social contract legislation of 1973–6, and the hesitant, divided and even pusillanimous relations between the General Council and the Labour shadow ministers in 1985–7, could not be more stark. The TUC had, by 1987, lost an old role, and failed to agree about a new one. Consequently, while hinting that they were unable to elicit a united, clear policy from their counterparts at Congress House, the Labour shadow team went ahead with their planning more or less unilaterally, with the TUC trailing, often unhappily, behind.

The Growth of Quangos

A new kind of tripartite agency was brought into existence in the first wave of social contract legislation, and the TUC nominate one-third or more seats on these bodies; the Manpower Services Commission, the Council of the Advisory, Conciliation and

Arbitration Service, the Health and Safety Commission, and the Equal Opportunities Commission. More recently in 1976–7, the TUC secured two seats on the new Commission for Racial Equality, and one-third of the seats on an Energy Commission, the existence of which was the direct outcome of a TUC proposal to the Minister.

Some of these new agencies, which were hived off from the direct control of the civil service in the Department of Employment, such as the MSC and ACAS, have acquired a policy-making role as well as a purely executive function; the MSC was initially successful in persuading government to allocate substantial funds for job creation, while ACAS was at first felt by the employers to be too much an arm of the TUC. With a change of government, and changes in personnel, both these institutions found their space, and their roles, much modified. The sharp growth of these kinds of agencies in numbers and complexity has transformed the kinds of response which the TUC has been required to make. Before the Second World War, the TUC General Council only nominated members to one dozen government-appointed committees or statutory bodies. By 1948 TUC nominees were present on 60 such bodies. In origin all of these were seen as utilitarian institutions: but in practice, some of them became sinecures, which commonly carried either a fee or a regular income, which was a valuable supplement to the retirement pension of an outgoing General Councillor.

Robert Taylor reports that Sir John Hare, the Minister of Agriculture during the 1950s, actually complained to the TUC 'about the lack of effort being put in by union nominees serving at that time on the marketing boards'. 'At this time,' he cites George Woodcock as commenting, 'there was no reporting back. We never knew what they were doing. In fact, they did damn all . . .' Taylor goes on to report that when Vincent Tewson, an earlier TUC General Secretary, served on the (now defunct) National Economic Planning Board for the TUC 'he did not even tell Woodcock what was happening'.[19]

Undoubtedly, the TUC nowadays regards its nominees on these bodies much more strictly, as trade union *representatives*; it arranges for briefings to be provided for its members of the MSC, the NEDCs, and the Health and Safety Commission, and in doing so, it works in co-operation with research officers of individual unions. In its 1977 *Annual Report*, the General Council pointed out that the TUC's own resources were too limited to effect a complete briefing service and reporting back of progress for all these agencies, and urged individual unions to come into this field much more; very few unions, it was reported, actually undertake such work. This is a serious deficiency, and things have deteriorated with financial difficulties both in the TUC itself and affiliated unions, as membership has shrunk. Tripartism as a strategy for advancing independent trade union controls in the economy and in social and welfare matters is a mask which can cover the reality of corporatism unless the unions retain their autonomy, and ensure effective briefing (or better, mandating) and reporting-back procedures. The Thatcher government initially threatened to cut a swathe through the many quangos it inherited. In the event, most survived with restricted scope. This often meant that union representatives were spending the same amount of time on activities which were less and less effective.

The TUC is heavily involved in nominating trade union representatives on the various judicial organs which now surround industrial relations. It nominates twelve trade unionists for the workers' side panel of the Employment Appeal Tribunal, it fills places on the Central Arbitration Committee, and oversees nomination to over 700 trade union places on the workers' sides of Industrial Tribunals. Royal Commissions and ad hoc Committees and Commissions on particular subjects were for a long time incomplete without their TUC nominees; recent examples include four TUC representatives on Sir Harold Wilson's Committee on Financial Institutions, and three representatives on the Bullock Committee on Industrial Democracy. Additionally, of course, the TUC rarely omits to submit carefully prepared and researched evidence to official Committees and Enquiries, on a very wide range of subjects, from broadcasting, the legal profession, the National Health Service, to metrication. When we provided a list charting the main participation by General Councillors in such organizations, it showed no fewer than 107 nominations to 67 different public bodies. Of course, this meant a number of persons had many appointments. Retired and influential trade union leaders who were not at the time members of the TUC's ruling body were not counted, although there were many of them. This was a prodigious commitment.

It is interesting to note, however, that the TUC never regarded every aspect of its work as suitable for tripartite or joint treatment. In the early 1960s, the TUC *did* draw up a joint statement with the employers' organizations recognizing that employers should be allowed a say in syllabuses, where they granted day release for trade unionists to attend educational courses. In the 1970s, however, the TUC firmly rejected this approach, and successfully insisted on its sole right to endorse courses of study which trade unionists should attend. On another issue, the TUC is insistent that trade unions which are seeking recognition from employers in a context where there is any element of inter-union rivalry, should settle such questions by reference to the TUC disputes machinery, and not by going to ACAS or the courts. In general, the TUC has tried to uphold the view that trade unions' own internal affairs should be dealt with by trade unions.

The Functioning of Congress

The TUC is primarily a policy-making, rather than an executive, body, and its main functions are to provide a federal umbrella under which the trade unions can gather to develop common policies, to administer rules governing inter-union relations, and to provide various services for its affiliated organizations. In determining policy, the TUC is not a power in itself: it depends on achieving consensus between the general secretaries of member unions. The significance of its policies depends primarily on the degree to which it represents the whole trade union movement, and also on the extent to which it can represent the working population. Table 4.1 indicates the growth of TUC-affiliated membership since its inception in 1868 up to 1987. It shows a record of sustained growth except for two periods – in the twenties and the eighties of this century. Only half a million trade unionists remain outside the TUC.

Table 4.1
TUC growth, 1868–1987

Year	No. of unions affiliated	No. of members affiliated	Year	No. of unions affiliated	No. of members affiliated
1868	—	118,367	1973	126	10,001,419
1878	114	623,957	1974	109	10,002,224
1888	138	816,944	1975	111	10,363,724
1898	188	1,093,191	1976	113	11,036,326
1908	214	1,777,000	1977	115	11,515,920
1918	262	4,532,085	1978	112	11,865,390
1928	196	3,874,842	1979	112	12,128,078
1938	216	4,460,617	1980	109	12,172,508
1948	188	7,791,470	1981	108	11,601,413
1958	185	8,337,325	1982	105	11,005,984
1968	160	8,725,604	1983	102	10,510,157
1969	155	8,875,381	1984	98	10,082,144
1970	150	9,402,170	1985	91	9,855,204
1971	142	10,002,204	1986	88	9,585,729
1972	132	9,894,881	1987	87	9,243,297

Source: TUC, *Annual Report*, 1979.

In the early 1960s there was a momentary threat to the unity of British trade unionism; in the 1962 TUC Congress, the Bank Employees' Union drew attention to the formation of a 'Conference of Public and Professional Service Organizations' and warned that this represented a dangerous initiative which could lead to the emergence of a rival white-collar, non-party political TUC. At that moment, with white-collar and public sector trade unionism poised before its major growth of the 1960s and 1970s, there was no guarantee that some of the major unions in this sector, notably NALGO and the NUT, would join the TUC. It is significant that both these unions, and after them others with a similarly middle-class professional approach to collective organization, such as the Association of University Teachers and the higher civil servants, finally chose to join the TUC. Undoubtedly one reason for this choice was the evident wish of governments not to have to consult with more than one trade union centre, and the wage and salary problems posed in the public sector during government wage restraint policies was a further compelling reason. (It is ironic that this problem has regularly proved too difficult for the TUC to tackle effectively!) It can now be said that there are no large or influential trade unions outside the TUC.

In 1985–7, the TUC avoided a split in its ranks by ducking the issue of the EETPU and AEU defiance of TUC guidelines on non-application for government subsidies for union ballots. Later, in the EETPU's case, defiance of the Bridlington Rules was overlooked on several occasions, the most glaring example being that union's recruitment of printing workers at the new Wapping plant of News International. Legal restraints helped to inhibit the General Council from following what may have been its instincts on that matter, and this provoked a bitter (and successful) rebellion on the floor of the Congress itself. But the rebels' victory was shortlived, since no action resulted from it. In earlier and more self-confident times, the TUC would certainly have suspended, and might even have expelled, the EETPU for the last offence. Had it done so in 1986, even if litigation had failed, the EETPU might have become a rallying point for all those unions, and forces within other unions, who were attracted by 'new realist' policies and methods. A rival union centre might well have emerged to challenge TUC authority and influence. But to retain unity at the cost of effective authority was no easy option to accept.[20]

The TUC is governed broadly by two elements in its constitution: the Congress, and the General Council. Congress is convened annually, when about 1,000 delegates assemble, now invariably at either Brighton or Blackpool, from Monday to Friday of the first week of September. It has three functions: to receive and consider the *Annual Report* of the General Council, to debate and vote on motions submitted by unions, and to elect the General Council for the coming year. Congress has become, particularly in the age of television, an important set-piece occasion in the political year, and its proceedings enjoy wide coverage in the media. From time to time, proposals are made to alter its timing or its procedures, and occasionally the complaint is heard that it is dominated by the will of the General Council, or that too much time at the rostrum is occupied by the general secretaries of the largest unions. But all attempts at reform have met with opposition from the General Council. In fact, Congress gets through a large amount of business during the week, and resolutions passed and motions remitted to the General Council do receive careful attention by the Council during the ensuing year. And there have been significant (if infrequent) occasions when the General Council's policy has been overturned by Congress. This happened notably in 1950, over the maintenance of wage restraint, and in 1971 on the issue of deregistration under the Industrial Relations Act. As we have just seen, it happened again in 1986 in response to the role of the EETPU in the Wapping dispute.

It is certain that proceedings are dominated by the leading full-time officials of unions, but reform here may be as much to do with the internal control of union delegations as with the TUC itself.

> . . . some General Council members who have been chairmen of delegation meetings have used their authority over procedural matters to question the competency of delegations to determine or revise policy. When everything else has failed, the opinion of delegation meetings has been flouted and union block votes have been cast to meet General Council requirements. Because the policy-making functions of delegation meetings are rarely formulated in union constitutions, their authority is frequently

determined by the need of immediate situations. Where the rules are vague, the delegation chairmen have the authority to interpret them. The Amalgamated Engineering Union has a history of procedural wrangles about the policy-making rights of delegations which has been marked by bitterness and legal action. At the 1966 TUC lay members in two unions sought legal injunctions to restrain the leaders of their union delegations from voting for General Council policies. The problem is a perennial one.[21]

The method of electing the General Council of the TUC was thoroughly amended in 1984. Prior to that date, and since the 1920s, the Council was elected by block votes of the unions at the annual Congress. For electoral purposes the unions were grouped into Trade Groups, each roughly delineating an industry or sector. Every Trade Group was allocated a quota of seats on the General Council and only unions within that Group could nominate candidates for seats within the Group. If there were more candidates than seats for the Group, a ballot vote was taken, at which all the unions were entitled to vote. This system gave rise to numerous complaints and criticisms, particularly from the smaller unions, which often failed to obtain the election of those they regarded as their own nominees, because of the contrary block votes of the very large unions. The new system, carried into the TUC's rules in 1983, has operated since that time. Under it, the General Council is constituted as follows:

Section A consists of members from unions with 100,000 members or more, with membership determined on the basis of one member for unions with 100,000 to 499,999 members, two members for unions with 500,000 to 749,999 members, three members for unions with 750,000 to 999,999 members, four members for unions with 1,000,000 to 1,499,999 members, and five members for unions with 1,500,000 and above members.

Section B consists of eleven members of those unions with a membership of less than 100,000 elected on a single list, with each union in Section B having the right to make one nomination and having up to eleven votes. Section C consists of six women members. Each affiliated union which includes women members has the right to nominate one member for election by the whole Congress to Section C.

The results of the new system in the 1983 Congress strictly reduced the old power of the large unions to determine most of the General Council's members by the use of a block vote, and the reconstituted Council proved less 'political', more cautious and 'new realist' than its predecessors, although hardly more decisive, or united.

The practice of conducting most of its business through sub-committees is in fact a longstanding one in the TUC, which behaves similarly in this respect to a local government authority. Chairmanship of the key General Council committees is keenly contested, since it gives considerable influence to the persons chosen. The Standing Committees include Finance and General Purposes, International, Education, Social Insurance and Industrial Welfare, Employment Policy and Organization, Economic, and Equal Rights. These are all manned by members of the General Council. Joint Committees, which include members of the General Council and other trade union representatives, or third parties, include the Women's Advisory Committee, the Race Relations Advisory Committee, the Trades Councils' Joint Consultative Committee, the National Economic Development Council, the Trades Union Congress and Confederation of British Industry, the Standing Advisory Committee to the TUC Centenary Institute of Occupational Health, and the TUC–Labour Party Liaison Committee. This committee structure is under fairly regular revision, as new needs arise, or as old ones disappear.

Committees which have been wound up in the past decade include the Commonwealth Advisory Committee, the Non-Manual Workers' Advisory Committee, the Wages Council Advisory Committee, the National Advisory Committee for Local Government Service, and the Nursing Advisory Committee.

The TUC's regular and extensive committee work, supported by serious 'back-room' secretariats, which in their departmentalized organization develop considerable expertise in their own fields, receives very little publicity, either in the Labour movement or in the outside world. Traditionally, all this work was directed to the business of lobbying governments, which is what George Woodcock meant when he said that 'we left Trafalgar Square a long time ago'. The TUC, he felt, did its best work in committees, and in 'the corridors of power'. However, since the advent of the Conservative governments of 1979–87, the meetings with ministers have become far less frequent, and the TUC has been intermittently involved in public campaigns as a result. But more often, it has taken on the role of directing complaints, protests and opposition towards government.

We may take as an example the work of one such committee, the Education Committee, during the year 1984–5. We find them dealing with the following issues: government cuts in education spending, participating in the campaigning of the Education Alliance (a body of trade unions and associations in the field of public education), analysing the reports of HMIs in education, opposing government cuts in school meals, commenting on a government White Paper, *Better Schools*, discussing school curricula and exams, urging education for 'economic awareness' in schools, submitting proposals to the ILEA on its school/industry project, writing to the Minister on the report of the Swann Committee on education for ethnic minorities, responding to the government's Green Paper on 16-plus examinations, welcoming proposals to widen the role of school governors, supporting moves for the phased abolition of corporal punishment in schools, pressing government for more resources for teacher training and for in-service training, regretting the end of the Advisory Committee to government on the supply and education of teachers, issuing a string of reports and comments on post-school education, on business and technical education, on the Youth Service, on the National Youth Bureau, on continuing education, on further education, and on higher education, on libraries, the arts and opera.

It also finds time to debate and oversee the TUC's own training and education programme for shop stewards and trade unionists through its Regional Education Service.

All this intense and detailed work is less and less fruitful in today's climate. Even in the last Labour government's last years, after the IMF visit of 1976, the TUC's representations on economic policy were increasingly disregarded by government. Today, we are back almost full circle to the situation of the 1920s, when Ramsay MacDonald as Prime Minister consistently ignored the existence and advice of the TUC. But now it is a Conservative government which behaves in these ways. What the TUC's method has lacked since 1983 has been any mobilizing drive to enlist the mass support of its affiliated membership behind all this staid committee work; yet the issues it takes up are all potentially popular and vital ones for trade unionists and the whole society. A daily or weekly newspaper such as the long-defunct *Daily Herald* would seem to be the necessary complement. Directing protest and opposition and dissent and cries of pain towards the government is a narrow and fruitless exercise, targeted on unsympathetic and insensitive ears. It is surely a mistake to think and act as though committee work and mass campaigning are mutually exclusive roles for the TUC. Trafalgar Square or Hyde Park and the corridors of Whitehall are, after all, very close to each other.

In 1970–1, as we have noted, the TUC, through its Education Department, did mount an educational campaign amongst its membership which had a marked effect on the successful resistance to the Industrial Relations Act. In 1979, it appeared to be prepared to enter the arena of mass campaigning again, against the effects of the Conservative government's public spending cuts. Another ideal model was the campaign (not run by the TUC but by an ad hoc inter-union committee) on the political fund ballots in 1985, which is discussed in Chapter 11. These models perhaps need generalizing, in the harsh economic and political climate which now confronts the TUC, so that its back-room studies may become the basis of an outward-facing effort of economic and political education, rather than the restricted raw material of an increasingly ingrown and frustrating lobby in the corridors of power, where the TUC's views are decreasingly welcome.

A new structure of Industry Committees was instituted in 1970, following the experience of the Steel Industry Committee set up to co-ordinate policies after the 1967 nationalization of steel. The idea of Industry Committees, on which General Council members sit with representatives of the main unions in the industry concerned, is a development which has its roots in the original concept of Trade Groups which the TUC of the 1920s saw as a precursor of industrial unionism and the co-ordination of union policies in the major sectors of the economy.

These Industry Committees do have the same potential for generating common trade union policies and overcoming the problems of multi-unionism, as the original concept. At present there are eleven of them: construction; energy; health services; hotel and catering; local government; printing; steel; textile clothing and footwear; transport; distribution; food, drink, tobacco and agriculture industries; and financial services. The Steel Committee had reached the stage of bargaining directly with British Steel in the late 1970s and served as the forum where complex problems of multi-union recognition claims in the white-collar field were dealt with. Others of the Committees have dealt with inter-union relations, with government planning of their industry (as in the case of Transport), and in general have aimed to generate common union policies in their areas. The fact that they are linked to the General Council, and are serviced by the departments and staff of the TUC, represents a considerable advance in central TUC influence over its unions. There is scope in the system for the growth of union policy-making and intervention in industrial policies. The Construction Committee, for example, devoted much time to the problem of the Lump and the decasualization of the industry, Fuel and Power was concerned with the setting up of the Energy Commission in consultation with the Minister Tony Benn, the Hotel and Catering Committee set up a joint study with the English Tourist Board on travel facilities for the disabled, the Printing Committee operates its own disputes procedure when unions are engaged in disputes with employers, and the Steel Committee was involved in setting up the Shotton Works Steel Committee, the only example of a mulit-union work-based committee involved with the TUC machinery. Jack Jones (*Tribune*, 25 April 1978) proposed that there should be systematic links between TUC, Industry Committees and Shop Stewards' Combine Committees.

All these matters and many more are fully reported in the TUC *Annual Report*, and help to shed light on and generate thinking about the normally unseen processes of policy-making and industrial negotiations, other than those directly concerned with pay. Apart from their direct functional role, the Industry Committees are seen by the TUC as an important means of meeting the criticism made by smaller unions and those without General Council representation, that the TUC does not provide a channel for them to exercise influence.

The work of the TUC's Education Department as a provider of facilities has expanded dramatically since it took over the former National Council of Labour Colleges and the Workers' Educational Trade Union Committee in 1964. The Education Department has been, until recently, the only part of the TUC structure which employs full-time staff (the Regional Education Officers) in the regions and outside Congress House.

A highly significant development in recent years has been the provision of grant-aid jointly by the Department of Education and Science and the Department of Employment, towards the cost of TUC educational services, amounting to £1.7 million in 1985–6. (This sum included an amount of £200,000 paid by government for courses which the employer had approved – a new departure in the control over the spending of the government grant, introduced by the Conservatives.) Amongst other things, this grant helps to pay the day-release course fees charged to the TUC by public educational bodies – the technical colleges, the WEA, and University Extra-mural Departments. These day-release courses (the core of the TUC's educational work) enrolled 27,500 students in 1977–8, an increase of 28.5 per cent on the previous year. The students are shop stewards and trade union safety representatives.

The regional machinery of the TUC was for a long time a threadbare and under-serviced aspect of its work. It was reorganized after 1973, and now comprises eight Regional TUC Councils, on which full-time officers from unions in the regions sit, alongside representatives of the County Association of Trades Councils, which hold 25 per cent of the seats. The Scottish unions have long held their own public Congress, and Wales was more recently accorded the status of its own Annual Conference of 300 delegates, and a Welsh General Council of forty-five, of which thirty come from union representatives in the principality, and fifteen from Welsh Trades Councils. If regionalism ever became a serious political reality in England, the TUC would still have to look seriously at its weakness in this field. The Regional Councils have potentially important functions in the field of regional economic planning, but they have until now had no full-time staff – apart from the Education Officers, who are answerable to Congress House and to a Regional Education Advisory Committee.

The purely local link in the chain, the country's 441 Trades Councils, have suffered a drastic eclipse of influence since their heyday in the nineteenth century. As the officially recognized representatives of the TUC in the localities, they are regarded rather paternalistically by the central body, and have periodically been a source of TUC–Establishment anxieties over the presence in their ranks of left-wing influence. Their relationship with head office has therefore sometimes inhibited them, and although they have worthy functions such as nominating trade union representatives on a variety of local committees and institutions (e.g. the governing bodies of local educational establishments), they are so frequently disregarded by local trade unionists that only 25 per cent of the country's trade union branches actually affiliate to them. A separate chapter deals with the international trade union activity of the British trade union movement; we record here merely the remarkable fact that for a long time it consumed a larger share of TUC revenues than any other aspect of its affairs. Recently financial stringencies have curtailed this involvement.

The second largest item in the TUC accounts is the cost of running Congress House, at £900,000, largely devoted to salaries. The TUC education service costs it £687,000. The TUC's total income is a modest £5 million. In 1987 a serious crisis in TUC finances was reported in the *Observer*: while demands for central services were increasing, falling membership was reducing revenues in a dangerous way.

> Mr Norman Willis, the general secretary, has initiated a review of 'all aspects of TUC work' in a bid to avoid exhaustion of the organization's reserves by the end of the year.
>
> He has also asked all 100 members to submit 'urgently' their 1986 membership figures so that an increase in affiliation fees can be agreed quickly.
>
> Describing the situation as 'very sombre', Mr Willis last week told the General Council in a document marked 'private and confidential' that the TUC deficit this year would be £496,500. It comes on top of a deficit of £134,095 for 1986.

Such losses meant the effective exhaustion of the Congress's reserves, and necessitated stringent spending cuts. Even the Tolpuddle rally, deeply engrained in tradition, was now put in question, reported the *Observer*. Long before the emergence of this crisis, it was clear that the trade unions prefer to maintain their central organization on modest, non-bureaucratic lines. The TUC itself argues that, as a policy-making rather than an executive body, this is the best arrangement, and accordingly has always urged individual unions to compensate for the low level of TUC resources by stepping up their own expenditure on services. Yet not every union can afford expensive modern aids to effective trade unionism, such as research and education staff. Small unions, which it might be thought could have benefited from a wider TUC servicing role, lack the muscle to insist on its provision: while some, indeed, undoubtedly lack any ambition to see education and research developed effectively. Rationalization and centralization of trade union services would seem sensible on economic grounds, but in the past few years, the TUC has rejected proposals to provide a centralized Legal Department, a Research Bureau, and a central computer service for the unions.

NOTES

1. B. C. Roberts, *The Trades Union Congress, 1868–1921*, is a standard source on the early history of the TUC, although it has been seriously criticized by V. L. Allen in *The Sociology of Industrial Relations* (Longmans, 1971), which itself contains a series of valuable essays on key moments in TUC history. The relative dearth of literature on the TUC as an institution is possibly due to the peripheral role it has played, until the last two decades, in industrial relations. H. A. Clegg argued that most of the work of the TUC (and of the CBI) 'belongs to a study of political pressure groups rather than to a book on industrial relations' (*The System of Industrial Relations in Great Britain*, Blackwell, 1970).
2. See V. L. Allen, 'The Establishment of the TUC, 1868–1875', *op. cit.*
3. V. L. Allen, 'The TUC Before Socialism, 1875–1886', *op. cit.*
4. V. L. Allen, 'The Re-organization of the TUC, 1918–1927, *op. cit.*
5. V. L. Allen, *op. cit.*
6. For an account of the General Strike, see Ken Coates and Tony Topham, *Trade Unions and Politics*, Blackwell, 1986, Chapter 7.
7. Fred Bramley, the TUC General Secretary from 1923 to 1925, said that he did not have more than five minutes' conversation with Ramsay MacDonald during his first premiership in 1924.
8. TUC, *Annual Report*, 1962.
9. TUC, *Annual Report*, 1962.
10. But note that the TUC, in entering into its so-called 'Concordat' with the Labour government in February 1979, offered its support to the notion that 'reforms' were needed (albeit voluntary) in picketing, strike decisions, and the closed shop. These were to become the subject of legislative intervention by the Thatcher administration.
11. TUC, *Annual Report*, 1970.
12. TUC, *Annual Report*, 1972.
13. The proceedings of these conferences were published in six booklets by the TUC in 1969.
14. TUC, *Annual Report*, 1985.
15. *Industrial Democracy*, HMSO, Cmnd 7231, May 1978.
16. Government Communications HQ: see TUC *Report*, 1984, pp. 46–53.
17. These issues are comprehensively reviewed in Ken Coates (ed.), *Freedom and Fairness*, Spokesman, 1986.
18. See Chapter 10, Appendix.
19. Robert Taylor, *The Fifth Estate – Britain's Unions in the 'Seventies*, Routledge, 1978.
20. Throughout 1987 the EETPU continued to arouse opposition from other unions, notably the TGWU, by the negotiation of single-union deals. A heated exchange ensued during the 1987 TUC.
21. V. L. Allen, 'The Centenary of the TUC, 1868–1968', *op. cit.*, 1971.

CHAPTER 5

Shop Stewards and Workplace Trade Unionism

The Development of Workplace Representation

For all the national prominence given to full-time general secretaries of trade unions, and the role of the TUC, the trade union movement remains heavily dependent on the work of voluntary, part-time trade union representatives. In an earlier time, the base of trade unionism was the local branch, and the key officers were the branch secretary and chairman. After the Second World War the focus of organization and activity became the workplace, and the key figure was thus the workplace representative of the membership, usually termed the shop steward, whose function has been to represent the interests of trade union members at plant level.

Not all industries and unions apply the term shop steward to their workplace representatives; in printing they speak of the 'Father of the Chapel', among draughtsmen of the 'corresponding member', and in white-collar occupations of 'staff representatives'. In some few industries (for example, agriculture) the shop steward system has not appeared, while in large areas of non-manual employment (for example among local government officers) the system grew to maturity only in the last fifteen years. Across employment as a whole, however, the appointment of working employees to represent trade union members in the workplace is almost universal, covering for example 95 per cent of employees in metal manufacture, 88 per cent of office workers, and 78 per cent of distributive workers.[1] An estimate in 1971 put the total number of stewards in Britain at between 250,000 and 300,000.[2] In 1973, it was found that shop stewards existed in four-fifths of unionized establishments.[3] By 1980, the number of stewards overall was reliably estimated at

317,000, and the most recent calculation, for 1984, puts the figure at 335,000 of whom 172,000 are manual workers, an actual decline of 10,000 since 1980. The number of full-time convenors or senior stewards is, on the reckoning of the researchers who arrived at these totals, some 4,200.[4]

It was not always so. While we may suppose that from an early period in the industrial revolution work groups often threw up informal and unrecognized spokesmen, there is no evidence that shop stewards achieved any widespread significance much before the First World War. Workplace representation certainly did exist in some nineteenth-century industries. Legislation in 1860 provided for workers' representatives (checkweighmen) to be appointed in coal mines, and representatives were recognized in the North-East coast steel industry conciliation machinery from 1869. Engineering shop stewards had achieved a presence for some years before the turn of the century, collecting stewards with a bargaining role appeared in the gas industry in 1889, and the collectors of the old Workers' Union were acting as spokesmen before 1914.[5] Undoubtedly, however, the first major manifestation of steward organization came with the First World War, when both their numbers and their powers expanded considerably, particularly in engineering and munitions.

After the war, in the interwar period of mass unemployment, the steward system went into decline, although not before it had been partially recognized in the formal procedures of industrial relations in some industries, such as engineering. In the later 1930s stewards re-emerged, significantly in industries such as aircraft manufacture which first felt the resurgence of demand associated with re-armament. In the Second World War, they again became prominent in the major manufacturing industries, often associated with the spread of Joint Production Committees in the plants, to promote war production.[6] After the war, the continuation of full-employment conditions meant that there was no collapse of shopfloor trade unionism, which went from strength to strength, at any rate up to the onset of mass unemployment in the late 1970s.

The growth of informal plant-level bargaining activity by shop stewards in the 1950s and early 1960s gave rise to much concern and hostility from employers, trade union leaders and the mass media, who commonly identified them with the twin 'problems' of 'wage drift' (the tendency for total earnings to rise above the rate of growth of officially determined wage rates negotiated by national industry-wide bargaining) and the rising incidence of plant-level unofficial strikes. These concerns were largely responsible for the setting up of Lord Donovan's Royal Commission on Trade Unions and Employers' Associations in 1964. From some of the research work carried out for this Commission[7] and from an earlier survey of 1960[8] statistical evidence began to accumulate about the nature, functions and activities of shop stewards. The moderating influence of this work (which showed that stewards were normally 'lubricants, not irritants' in workplace industrial relations, and that plant managers usually preferred to deal with shop stewards rather than full-time trade union officials) was ignored by the more extreme advocates of penal sanctions to deal with the shop steward 'problem'. The Commission in its Report nevertheless expressed a central anxiety about the gulf which had developed between the formal and informal systems of industrial relations, and recommended that employers and trade unions should close this by evolving more formal systems of procedural agreements at plant and company level, and by incorporating stewards more fully into trade union machinery. Although there has been an expansion of formal written procedures in industry since then, and although trade unions have given greatly more attention to the shop steward's role, later research continued to emphasize the element of informality and custom and practice in workplace industrial relations. An authoritative survey of the period from 1966 to 1972 found that 'of the Donovan Commission's enthusiasm for the formalization of factory-wide agreements there was remarkably little evidence'.[9]

In the meantime, the wave of productivity bargaining which accompanied the Labour government's incomes policies in the late 1960s, whilst being part of the managerial strategy for incorporating shop stewards in more formal procedures, served in part to stimulate further growth in steward numbers and to diversify their functions.[10] The method of penal sanctions to curb plant-level initiative and to reduce the shop steward to a subordinate and dependent role was successively frustrated (with the 1969 withdrawal of Labour's legislative proposals in the White Paper *In Place of Strife*) and then tried and repealed (in the case of the Conservative government's Industrial Relations Act of 1971–4). The legislation of the 1974–9 Labour government included measures which provided some legal protection for shop stewards and which promoted a widening of their representative role,[11] whilst at the same time the pay restraint policies of these same governments restricted the influence of plant bargaining by shop stewards on their members' earnings. New fields of concern for stewards simultaneously opened out, as unemployment and company mergers made issues such as job security and company investment policy much more important. Thus as the economic, political and legal environments underwent a series of changes in recent decades, the shop steward system successfully adapted to them, showing remarkable resilience and capacity for growth. Stewards also continued to retain the confidence of the members whom they represented: three-quarters of them are still normally elected to office without opposition.[12] In a Sheffield enquiry of 1977, it was found that only 16 per cent of AUEW stewards were opposed in their first election to office, and only 10 per cent in subsequent elections.[13]

Shop Steward Facilities and Functions in the 1980s

The facilities which shop stewards enjoy to further their work and effectiveness grew substantially through the 1970s. In 1975, the Employment Protection Act gave all union lay representatives the legal right to paid time off work for attendance at training courses organized by unions and by the TUC, which uses public adult education institutions to provide the teaching. Time off without pay is also provided, in the same statute, for attendance at trade union meetings and to discharge public duties. Facilities provided by the majority of employers can include all or any of the following: rooms for stewards' and trade union meetings, a telephone, a noticeboard, free access to new employees to explain about union membership, names of new employees, an office on the premises for use of the stewards, a desk, storage space, typewriter, photocopier or duplicator, facilities to meet union full-time officials on the premises, use of printing facilities, supply of stationery, dictating machines, even use of the company telex. In the survey conducted by the Labour Research Department in 1986, from which this list was compiled, only one company afforded access to the company telex. This was EMI Records, which allows the joint shop stewards' committee to use it to communicate with trade union representatives at EMI Pathe Marconi in France. The dominance of multinational companies surely makes this a most significant facility for the future.[14] Except for time off for training and public duties, most of these facilities are not covered by legal requirement, but many are recommended in an ACAS Code of Practice. Of course, such amenities depend partly, even mainly, upon bargaining by the unions and stewards to obtain, retain and extend them.[15]

Hard bargaining is often necessary, and according to one witness, 'The facilities we have are the result of prolonged struggle with the employer, who at the first opportunity would destroy them.'[16] The Labour Research survey was conducted amongst highly organized sectors of the economy, such as engineering, and it cannot be expected that, in weaker sectors, even these facilities are available to the majority of stewards and to their joint shop stewards' committees. Yet it may well be that in the single-union deals which are being introduced in high-technology and multinational company agreements, especially but not exclusively in Japanese-based enterprises, the company emphasis on intimate relationship with the chosen union might bestow quite lavish facilities on the stewards, if only for management's own purposes. Many such single-union arrangements simply shrink shop-steward facilities, though. The dividing line between a facility which advances the autonomous role of the stewards, and one which undermines it, is a fine one, and it may move with changes in the economic situation of the company.

The question as to what extent shop stewards' roles and effective powers have suffered from the climate of high unemployment, hostile laws and a hardened and often aggressive management style, all characteristic of the 1980s, is one which is difficult to answer without qualifications. The evidence which is available seems to indicate that, whilst steward numbers have actually risen in some sectors during the 1980s, there have nonetheless been significant changes for the worse in their total situation.

Shop stewards engaged in plant- and company-level bargaining in the 1950s to the 1970s were able to generate wage improvements above base rates throughout private manufacturing industry. This fact gave rise to much talk about wages drift, a large part of which was ill-founded. In today's climate, the upwards adjustment of wages in line with company prosperity as well as with the cost of living is more problematic, many companies being able to prevail on their workforce to forgo wage increases altogether for a period. The Trade Union Research Unit reports that company profits in the UK rose by 45 per cent between 1981 and 1984, while real pay rose by only 2 per cent in the same period. In terms, therefore, of a very basic function, unions generally, and this must include their shopfloor representatives, were failing to maintain the relative share of wages in the distribution of company income, to a considerable extent.[17] But cost of living, rather than company efficiency, remains the most common basis for settling wage increases at plant level.

In the 1980s the numbers of shop stewards in manufacturing industry have shared the decline of their sector of the economy, as workplaces where employment fell substantially had relatively high union and steward density (60 per cent), while workplaces in which employment had grown (by a smaller amount) had very low densities (20 per cent) of members and of stewards. (It is a truism that steward density and union density correlate closely.[18])

The shop stewards' most hospitable homes have been in the traditional male-dominated, heavy manual manufacturing and extractive industries, together with transport. In this connection, it is significant that 'the decline of union membership, union recognition, and the closed shop in the private sector is clearly associated with the falling numbers of large workplaces employing predominantly male, manual, full-time employees . . .'[19] The staff representative has thus become more typical than the manual shop steward. There is also firm evidence of a decline in trade unionism in workplaces dominated by ethnic minorities. The number of workers in closed shops has recorded a decline of about 1.2 million in the period 1980–4, to a figure of 3.5 million. Again, the more the company had reduced its labour, the more likely it was to have a closed shop than the growing, smaller companies which were taking on labour. The whole scope for bargaining had reduced and the emphasis of bargaining had switched from wages to employment.[20]

However, the number of shop stewards in private manufacturing had declined by less than the number of workers in this sector, so that density of shop stewards had actually increased. Also, there was no change in the proportion of industrial relations procedures negotiated by management and unions, in the private sector. Furthermore, the survey showed no overall increase in the use of short-term fixed contracts in the period reviewed, but in the public sector, notably in education, there had been a marked increase. Elsewhere, the use of freelance workers had declined. But a tendency is creeping in, which has up to now been ignored in the surveys. This is the difficult-to-quantify practice of employers who single out individuals on the pay-roll with whom they make a confidential individual contract of employment, ignoring the collective terms negotiated by the unions and by the stewards. In these circumstances, which prevail for example in British Steel in Port Talbot, the workforce has no means of knowing which of their fellow workers are on a private contract, and which remain dependent upon the stewards' bargaining skills.

Foreign-owned companies are now making significant changes

in customary shop-level industrial relations, especially in private manufacturing, and in financial services. Professionally qualified personnel staff have higher status among them than in their UK-based counterpart companies, and it is to this skilled staff that the shop steward must relate. Frequently, these specialists practise high levels of communications direct to the workforce, and may thus undermine many of the stewards' former autonomous roles. Perception of the need for joint shop stewards' committees is also reduced in these environments, whenever single-union deals are made, as is increasingly common among foreign firms.

Single-union, no-strike agreements, with pendulum or other built-in arbitration, are a new and growing feature of British industrial relations. They are dealt with also in Chapter 6; here we are concerned with their impact on shopfloor organization and on the role and status of shop stewards. These 'new realism' agreements sprang into prominence in 1985, with the initiatives of Toshiba in Plymouth, of Nissan and Hitachi in the North-East and South Wales, and also of course with the efforts by Eddie Shah and Rupert Murdoch, in the printing industry, to obtain single-union, legally binding deals. At the Hitachi plant, five unions lost recognition rights.

An important case study was published by Region 10 of the TGWU in January 1986[21] which reviewed that union's experience at the Norsk-Hydro plant at Immingham on South Humberside. N-H, a Norwegian-based multinational company, is the largest producer of fertilizers in the world. It has plants in Sweden, Holland, the UK, West Germany, France, the USA and Qatar. It bought out the British company Fisons in 1982, and in this transaction it acquired a site where there was a long tradition of multiple unionism. This had always involved recognition of four unions, the TGWU, EETPU, AEU and ASTMS, together with an agreement according full rights to five full-time convenors and a joint shop stewards' committee. In 1985, N-H withdrew recognition from the national combine committee of stewards linking the fifteen former Fisons UK plants, and also withheld all rights for the local JSSC. It also pulled out of the industry's JIC in 1985. It then presented the workforce directly, through the post, with a 'New Personnel Package' stating that a crucial £80 million investment plan for the site, to be decided on by the parent company in Norway, depended entirely upon acceptance of this deal.

The package provided for sole bargaining rights to belong to the TGWU. It also imposed an 'Advisory Council' made up of management and directly elected employee representatives, and a series of big changes. These included complete flexibility and mobility of labour, emphasizing the 'team concept'; simplified pay structures; a three-year pay deal, ending the annual round of negotiations; continuous shift patterns of working; bell-to-bell working; and a new disciplinary procedure. On the advisory council sit the senior steward (the company having unilaterally abolished the five full-time convenor posts), and thirteen other employees, regardless of union membership or shop steward status. These employees are joined by six members of management, plus the managing director. All collective issues are handled by this council. Procedure for handling collective issues provides for escalation from senior steward level to the council, from whence it rises by steps to the national trade union officer. The final stage is not (as in many US and Japanese agreements) 'pendulum' arbitration, but a secret ballot of the employees, with management having the right to determine with the union the wording on the ballot form.

When the unions first opposed this package, they were met with threats by the company not to proceed with the planned investment, which was vital to a region of higher than average unemployment. There followed direct approaches, over their heads, to the workers through the post. In these communications, the company acknowledged that the new agreement 'reduces significantly the position the trade unions have previously held on site'. In the event, a company-run ballot on the proposals resulted in a majority decision in favour of the package. Thereafter the unions' campaign of opposition folded up. Following this, the new investment programme was approved by the company. It constituted the largest investment on the Humber banks for nearly twenty years.

It is not only in green-field sites, therefore, that these new shopfloor practices are being forced through by tougher managements. Shell, Esso, Mobil, Kellogg, Caterpillar and Babcock have all established similar routines in recent years. British Leyland and the GCHQ have afforded examples in British ownership and direction. There is no doubt that they involve a direct attack on the role and structures of shopfloor unionism, by introducing the Advisory Council concept, by derecognition of all but a single union, and by the withdrawal of convenor status and other basic facilities from the stewards. (At Immingham the senior steward was deprived of a proper office, filing system, and all privacy for his work, following the new agreement.)

> On the face of it the unions at N-H Immingham were well organized with a long history of recognition, a joint shop stewards' committee, five full-time convenors, and well established procedures. Yet the N-H site union organization was comprehensively outflanked by the company, suggesting that the formal, institutional appearance cannot be trusted to give a true indication of the strength of workplace organization.[22]

And further:

> . . . the TGWU organization at the site now faces the practical problem of dealing with the new advisory council and changed bargaining procedures, and the very real threat that the site union could become peripheral to the resolution of collective issues.[23]

Yet, at the same time, the alternative to the acceptance of such deals by unions is the spread of non-unionism in face of intransigent firms who hold all the bargaining cards at a time of hostile legislation and mass unemployment. At Nissan in the North-East, only one of the six worker representatives recently elected to the 'company council' is a union member, and it is widely reported that workers there see little benefit from joining the union, suggesting that non-unionism may well follow even the last-ditch concessions of new deals by the unions. Unions must study all these cases with great care if they are to identify a counter-strategy capable of holding off these dire prognoses. It is noteworthy that personnel managers in the Humber region meet regularly, across company boundaries, to study the N-H agreement and its workings.

In the public sector, the changes in recent years are different from both the private manufacturing and the private service sectors. In the public sector union density is higher, and remains high despite unemployment. This is true for both manual and non-manual workers. But bargaining remains highly centralized in this sector, and shop stewards have never had a significant wage-bargaining role. Nevertheless, the number of lay representatives has actually increased in the public sector, and they are involved in significant area bargaining over non-wage issues. They are also active above plant or office or school levels in co-ordinating the industrial actions which now characterize this sector more than manufacturing, notably in education.[24]

While the survey on which we have drawn concludes that there is much continuity of experience on the shopfloor from the 1960s to the 1980s, in practice the mere counting of stewards and recording of their formal activities may well miss the point.

> Social institutions can remain unchanged from the outside, while their actual function and significance changes completely: form may survive, content evaporate. Shop stewards might survive, but only on management sufferance, tolerated because of their insignificance.[25]

Wage drift above the rate of inflation still happens. But often it may well be due, in part, to the ability of managers in prosperous high-technology sectors to buy the acceptance of new technology, and the redundancies which often follow its introduction: or to induce changes in working practices in the direction of greater flexibility, paying for increases in real earnings out of faster escalating profits.

The office of shop steward was incorporated into trade union rulebooks often after they had spontaneously emerged, and exercised varying degrees of influence for some time, and consequently the rules are often vague as to their functions and mode of appointment. An exception to this is the EETPU whose rules stipulate that shop stewards are under the control of the area full-time official and of the Executive Committee. The GMWU rules specify that the shop steward has no authority to call strikes (in fact this is universally true, but most rulebooks do not include such a specific restriction)[26] and in unions with craft traditions, such as the AEU, stewards are subject to the formal control of the union's District Committee. Most rulebooks simply provide that shop stewards 'shall be appointed', without indicating the method. In practice a shopfloor show of hands is the most common method, and shopfloor appointments are five times as common as appointments at branch meetings. In fact whilst regular re-appointment of stewards is general, its method is controlled largely by local custom and practice. Most union rulebooks are similarly vague about the stewards' functions, usually referring only to their role in recruiting and retaining members. Nor do they lay down how many shop stewards there should be. In fact, most of the surveys from the late 1950s onwards reveal a remarkable consistency in the average size of shop stewards' constituencies, of between fifty and sixty members.[27] The relationship between workplace democracy and the formal organs of trade union authority from the branch upwards are seldom defined in rules; the widespread practice of shopfloor members' meetings (convened by stewards outside the formality of the branch meeting) is ignored.[28] It is true that some unions (such as the EETPU and NUPE) have instituted official national meetings of stewards in particular industries or sectors, but these have only consultative status; they are not part of the union's policy-making machinery.

In some unions, the branch secretary or chairman undertakes the representative and negotiating functions normally discharged by shop stewards. This happens in the civil service, bus transport, the railways and former nationalized sections of the port industry, in each of which these officers *are* much more fully integrated into the formal structures of the unions.

It is quite commonly found that shop stewards are 'pushed'

into taking up office by members' pressure; only a minority actively seek the job. One study distinguished several reasons for the occupancy of the role. Among those who were 'pushed', some arrive because of a crisis in the plant, some because of their popularity, and some simply by accident. Among those who actively seek the job some are motivated by the need to solve workshop problems, some by ideological considerations, and some by personal ambition.[29]

Most generalizations about shop stewards have been based on studies of the engineering industry where, as we have seen, the system developed early. In engineering, and also in printing, shop stewards developed naturally because the industry was characterized by a multitude of separate firms, exercising strong local management control, and where scope for workplace bargaining was correspondingly wide. Following these precedents, the system spread to the other manufacturing industries, and to the bulk of the private sector manual workforce, in the 1940s and 1950s. An exception is building, where stewards were only recognized by employers in 1964. In important sectors of public employment, the system is of much more recent origin. NUPE only introduced shop stewards in the 1960s, winning recognition for them in local government in 1969, and in the National Health Service in 1971. NALGO, the white-collar union in local government, pioneered a shop steward system as recently as 1973; a study of a 6,000-strong NALGO city branch found that the system had begun to stimulate a more active trade union membership than hitherto.[30] One of the problems of plant-level organization in such sectors as local government is the geographical dispersion of the workforce in small groups, which tends to inhibit the growth of the more sophisticated internal steward organizations common in manufacturing.[31] Elsewhere in the public sector, institutions such as the Post Office and British Rail have long traditions of centralized management which have also acted to limit shop steward functions in those industries.

Shop stewards obviously function more effectively if they have access to certain facilities. Trade unions and the TUC in the 1970s mounted a campaign to induce employers to grant extended facilities, and the Employment Protection Act (1975), and the Health and Safety at Work Act (1974), have given statutory backing to this drive in some respects.

Surveys in 1972[32] and 1979[33] found that most shop stewards claimed that they had the right to hold workplace meetings with members, many of them in working hours. In 1972, one-third of stewards remained dissatisfied with their facilities.[34] Improvement as a result of legislation and the active promotional work of ACAS may not be sustained: we have already noted that shop stewards' facilities are under threat of diminution or even, in some cases, worse, from the new kinds of single-union, no-strike deals which have been introduced in recent years by multinational companies in the UK.

One of the earliest functions of the stewards historically was the recruitment of members and the collection of union subscriptions. The spread of the closed shop (more recently the 'union membership agreement' under the Trade Union and Labour Relations Act, 1974 and 1976) and of the check-off system reduced the burden on stewards in both these areas. The check-off, whereby union contributions are deducted from pay by the employer and paid over to the union, has been well-nigh universal in the public sector, and one regional organization of the TGWU, with most of its members in the private sector, collects three-quarters of its members' subscriptions in this way.[35] If the withdrawal of the check-off facility follows the ending of the closed shop, which is threatened by the new kind of single-union deal which we have noted, then a very basic function of dues-collection and elementary union organization – often in a hostile environment – will devolve back to the shop steward, whose role may begin again to resemble what it was in the 1890s in engineering.

The Functions of Shop Stewards

The wider modern functions of shop stewards can be classified into (1) bargaining and representative functions on behalf of the membership and (2) communicative functions on behalf of the union. A more complex classification is offered in a report in the *Industrial Relations Journal*, where it is suggested that shop stewards evolve the following pattern of activities: (1) spokesman for the work group, (2) disseminator of information between the organization and the group, (3) minor bargaining over grievances, (4) monitoring of information, (5) liaison, with other groups and with managers, (6) exercising leadership, to strengthen the cohesion and therefore the bargaining power of the group, (7) decision-making, (8) formal negotiation with senior management.[36]

Shop stewards do not all see their job in the same light. One writer distinguishes four different functions amongst stewards; those of a mediator, of a welfare officer, of a problem-solver, and of a representative of trade union principles. The welfare concept was most common, and the embodiment of principles the least common.[37] The day-to-day initiatives of shop stewards give us examples of these roles. A welfare function may arise whenever members have domestic problems, particularly those which infringe upon life at work. For example, a tacit agreement between unions and management stipulates that the week's holiday due during the winter period shall not be taken in Christmas week, since everyone would want to be off work at that time. A member has a sick wife, and he desperately needs to ensure that at least some Christmas shopping is done for his family. The shop steward takes this case to management and persuades them to treat this as a special and deserving case. They thus waive the agreement.

A mediating role is common where shop stewards represent more than one work group whose interests over such things as overtime working or grading may conflict and require reconciliation. Some stewards also believe that their role includes that of liaising with management over the maintenance of production. Problem-solvers amongst stewards seek out and tackle a whole range of plant-level issues and 'attempt to establish general precedents from individual cases'. And trade union principles are upheld when a steward calls for solidarity action, such as refraining from undertaking any work normally done by other workers who are in dispute with management, or blacking the products of another company where a strike is in progress. The latter type of action is now of course illegal, and its frequency in an era of mass unemployment is in any case greatly reduced. Stewards in the docks industry were particularly noted for this kind of action, yet they are also – and this is far less well-known – among the most advanced practitioners of an extended 'welfare' function, reaching well beyond their own members. The Hull docks shop stewards' committee regularly purchased and presented TV sets for hospital wards and Old People's Homes, and in 1979 they won their members' agreement to hand over all the back-pay to which they were entitled with the award of a new wage increase, to a fund for purchasing an expensive item of equipment for brain surgery for a local hospital.

A minority of shop stewards are consciously and actively political. But among the Sheffield engineering stewards a trade union and Labour-socialist family background appeared to be important for many, although the commonly shared work experience of the whole sample tended to produce similar attitudes regardless of family background. The shop stewards' trade union role was often supplemented by wider leadership roles in the local community.[38]

Different types of stewards have been observed in a number of studies. Some, usually the least experienced, confine themselves to a 'spokesman' role, merely expressing the grievances of their members as they are defined by the group; others are more active, shaping a conscious strategy and taking much more initiative. The longer the tenure of a steward in office, the more likely he is to evolve towards a leadership role of this last kind. One analysis[39] classifies stewards as 'leaders', 'nascent leaders', 'populists', and 'cowboys'. The 'leaders', usually though not always the convenors and senior stewards, are those with the most extensive networks and shopfloor organizations, who build 'strong bargaining relations' with managers, and who occupy the top of the shop steward hierarchy. They tend to take a long-term view of the interests of the members and the union, are cautious but tough negotiators, and are the most successful stewards. The 'populists' are those who are content simply to reflect members' immediate wishes, whilst the 'cowboys' are erratic and unpredictable personalities, who come and go quickly. Naturally these types are not altogether exclusive.

The 'leaders' are most successful when achievement is measured by their members' earnings, and most conscious and effective in protecting the 'frontier of control' against management encroachments. They tend to have a lower level of recourse both to strike action and to the use of the formal rules of procedure. But at the same time 'leaders' may become so involved with management that they become divorced from their members. The result may be member revolt and the demise of 'leadership'.[40] The fact that 'member revolt' in these circumstances remains a possibility represents an important safeguard against the entrenchment of a permanent and invulnerable bureaucracy amongst senior stewards.

The effectiveness of shop stewards depends not only on their personalities and the degree of leadership they exercise, but also on the work environment in which they operate. Important factors here include the mobility which his job allows to a steward – e.g. an inspector can move about more freely than a machine operator, the presence or absence of piece-work pressure, the relative isolation of the shop or bay in which the shop steward works, the degree of craftsmanship in the job, the sex and colour of the workforce, the facilities provided by management, the level of labour turnover, and even the availability of public transport to and from the plant, which affects the possibility of holding mass meetings of members and stewards' committee meetings.[41]

Continuity of office is important for the effectiveness of shop steward representation, and the relatively high rate of turnover amongst stewards has been a source of concern to trade unions. The Donovan Commission's research found an average turnover rate amongst stewards of 15 per cent per annum. Recent attention has focused on the factors affecting turnover. It has been shown that this is lower where stewards exist in groups in the larger plants, providing each other with mutual reinforcement. This effect is strengthened where stewards share a common ideology. Amongst other factors, longer tenure is associated with large plants, larger numbers of shop stewards per plant, higher skills, co-operative management and good shop steward facilities, good relations between the stewards and the outside unions, a leadership rather than a populist role, and commitment of the steward to the wider political goals of the Labour movement.[42] Stability in office was measured in a survey covering 453 workplaces employing 330,000 manual workers across a wide range of industries. It was found that the proportion of stewards with more than four years' experience ranged from 40 per cent in engineering to only 29 per cent in local authorities. Plants with under 500 employees and under 10 shop stewards showed much the greatest instability.[43] As with hierarchy and leadership amongst shop stewards, it may perhaps be feared that *too* great a stability amongst stewards would reinforce bureaucratic tendencies. But Batstone and his colleagues found that there was no inevitable tendency for a particular pattern of shop steward power to become permanently stabilized; 'random shocks' could lead to changes amongst stewards, and while 'leader' stewards were more stable than 'populists', their continuity in office was still conditional on member satisfaction and success. 'Shocks', of course, might not be altogether 'random', in that they might follow major policy changes, or crises in the plant. Such 'shocks' are increasingly likely. 'New realism' deals, and new management initiatives generally, may bring about an altogether more fragile style of shopfloor representation.

Joint Consultation

Joint consultation was a favourite device of management in prewar days, during the war, and for some time thereafter. It has returned to favour in management's eyes as part of the 'new realism' and of single-union agreements which are spreading today. Whereas it was originally practised as a method of providing a semblance of workers' participation separate from trade unionism and hostile to the growth of shop steward influence at plant level, it first declined and then was transformed in postwar years into a further method of advancing shop stewards' roles in the sixties and seventies. Writing in 1966, for the Donovan Royal Commission, W. E. J. McCarthy (Lord McCarthy) said that 'shop stewards . . . do not [agree with] . . . separate institutional arrangement for . . . dealing with so-called "conflicting" and "common interest" questions, and any committee on which they serve which cannot reach decisions . . . they regard as . . . an inferior . . . substitute for . . . negotiating machinery.'[44]

In that era, therefore, joint consultative committees which survived became changed into a vehicle for extending stewards' bargaining role. In the 1980s, however, management has often regained the initiative and developed new institutions, the so-called Company Advisory Boards or Councils, on which elected employee representatives sit regardless of trade union membership. These may sit with a token shop steward presence alongside them, but most of the initiative and all the decision-making authority will rest in management's hands.

Steward Organization in the Plant

The power bases which shop stewards build up vary from plant to plant. Except in very small plants with fewer than three stewards, some form of shop steward organization and hierarchy develops, with full-time stewards, steward committees, and the election of steward executive committees by the stewards themselves. Half the stewards surveyed in 1973 had regular meetings amongst themselves.[45] Hierarchical organization tends to appear where there are ten or more stewards in a plant, and 50 per cent of workplaces with over 500 employees had full-time stewards, although the presence of full-time stewards is more marked in private manufacturing than in the public service.[46] 'Leader' stewards built up resources and sanctions largely through their network of relations with other stewards, and a major resource in this respect is the existence of shop steward committees.[47]

Although some slight decline has been noted in plant-level multi-unionism since 1966[48] it remains a very common phenomenon. In 1973, it was found that 50 per cent of manual workers' establishments had more than one union, and 30 per cent of non-manual establishments.[49] In the earlier postwar years unions were critical of inter-union joint shop steward committees for developing 'private' unions, and for becoming self-governing organizations despite the formal allegiance of stewards to individual unions. At plant level, unions have become much more tolerant of joint committees of stewards on multi-union lines – we refer to the wider phenomenon of company-level combine committees later. At plant level, multi-union steward organization is frequently of a more developed and hierarchical character than in the single-plant union; union heterogeneity seems to encourage stronger steward organization, which in turn makes inter-union co-operation more manageable.[50] Conversely, poor inter-union relations are to be found in plants with low levels of steward organization. Single-union deals of course are in the process of transcending, for better or more usually worse, the problem of multi-unionism at plant and company levels.

The most obvious base of shop steward authority is the membership – the workforce as organized into trade unions. Ever since the 'human relations' school of industrial psychology in America in the 1920s 'discovered' the informal work group, it has been recognized that the workforce in modern industry is not an undifferentiated mass of physical atoms, but a complex social organization. The original American research studied the work group in isolation from trade unionism; in Britain more attention has been given to the relationship between work groups and shop stewards, and it is clear that there is no single, universal type of group. Task groups, human relations groups, friendship cliques and interest groups co-exist and overlap on the shopfloor.[51] Work groups have been classified as (a) apathetic – a condition found amongst low paid, unskilled workers with individual jobs, such as cleaners and lavatory attendants, (b) erratic – amongst low status groups with identical, physically demanding jobs, such as assembly-line work, (c) strategic – skilled, relatively well-paid, individual jobs such as metal finishers and process workers in iron and steel, and (d) conservative – the most skilled elite of maintenance craftsmen.[52]

This type of analysis emphasizes the influence of technology and occupation on the relative powers of work groups and stewards, but technology by no means explains the observable differences in shopfloor power; groups need to be aware of their power and prepared to use it and these aspects of consciousness derive from the nature of their trade unionism. Growing experience of collective action in response to grievances and claims builds up something which is stronger than a loose coalition, and develops a group commitment to continued reliance on collective methods.[53] Moreover, there is no simple one-to-one relationship between stewards and work groups. In a case study of nineteen stewards in six factories, it was found that the average number of distinct groups represented by each shop steward was five.[54]

Work groups are thus autonomous with respect to shopfloor trade union organization; they are not necessarily coterminous with shop steward constituencies. This implies that stewards must consciously strive to retain the confidence and support of the groups they represent. They are not always successful in this; an important study of industrial relations in the car industry identified the phenomenon of the 'unofficial-unofficial' strike, in which workers strike in defiance not only of the outside union, but of their own shop stewards.[55] Clearly, the recent tendencies for numbers of stewards to increase, and for improved facilities to hold meetings with their members, enhance the possibility for stewards accurately to represent their groups' feelings, and the existence of autonomous group pressure constitutes a permanent check on the growth of shop steward bureaucracy. However prominent the role of the 'leader' stewards, decision-making must ultimately be shared with the work group; only a small minority of shop stewards can 'always' get their own way with the members.[56]

Relations with the Unions

The relationship between shop stewards and their trade union organization, though not easy to define, is of fundamental importance. Union support for and endorsement of the stewards' office, and protection against victimization, is essential. Unions also offer practical advice and guidance for stewards, provide training courses on an increasing scale, and facilities for forming policy. Trade union principles provide powerful reinforcement at the ideological level, for shop stewards. In turn, without stewards, trade union administration and cohesion, as we know it, would collapse. Yet the links between the shop stewards and union branches and higher committees is (with some exceptions such as the AEU and NUPE) based more on the personal commitment of stewards than on constitutions. It is usually the hard core of active stewards who keep branch life going, and who serve on the unions' higher committees. The trend towards plant-based branches (as distinct from branches which cover a geographical area) is helping towards a closer relationship between stewards and union structures. At present, the branch serves as a much more important forum and meeting place for stewards in the public service than in manufacturing, as it does generally for smaller and dispersed workforces.[57] District Committees vary in influence over the plant; in the AEU they are very important but elsewhere the full-time official is more significant. Industry or trade conferences of stewards at regional and national level are held by the GMBATU, USDAW, and the EETPU, but their impact is limited and they have no authority in the unions' constitutions.

All the published studies tend to show that for stewards their relations with full-time union officials are more important than are those with the branch or higher union committees.

The principal influence on the relationship between stewards and full-time officials is that of plant size. The large plant develops its own resources, convenors, steward committees, and facilities. In this context, the convenor may easily come to rival the full-time official in skill and experience. Size of plant outweighs other variables, but within this limitation, full-time officials can influence the growth of steward organization, by encouraging or hindering styles of bargaining which foster the independence of the plant stewards.[58] Beyond the attitudes taken up towards steward initiatives by individual unions, there is the policy of the TUC as a whole, which from the 1950s onwards has reflected a shift from authoritarian to permissive responses, and then, in the 1970s, towards democratic attitudes to steward organization. The TUC's official training manuals even encourage stewards to strengthen links with their fellows in other plants, by forming combine committees: something which would have been unthinkable to the draftsmen of the famous 1960 statement on 'disputes and workshop representation', which condemned such initiatives.

Combine Organization

So far, we have considered shop stewards as operating purely at plant level. A further dimension of their activity, which has been important at key moments in shop steward history, and receiving renewed attention today, is the association of workplace representatives in multi-plant companies. Given the trend towards takeovers and mergers leading to the current concentration of ownership which we discussed in Chapter 1 (in which a hundred companies account for half the UK's manufacturing output and employment, most of which is in multi-plant, multi-union enterprises), the growth of Combine Committees of stewards in these companies was inevitable (the fiftieth largest company had six plants in 1958; in 1968 it had twenty, and the number must be even larger today).[59] Today, stewards from half of all manufacturing companies hold at least some meetings with stewards from other workplaces of the same employer.

In the multi-plant firm, bargaining at plant level alone leaves most of the key decisions in the hands of top management. They may therefore positively seek to confine their stewards to operation at the plant level. However, leap-frogging claims between plants may in some cases (as happened in British Leyland) force management to consider company-level bargaining as an alternative. Some companies have indeed favoured company bargaining from the outset, hoping thereby to negotiate only with national full-time union officials. This was the strategy of Fords, in particular. But the internal union reforms of the last two decades led in that case to the eventual involvement of shop stewards in the national company-level negotiations. The whole logic of such company bargaining tends to call forth company-level shop steward organization. Combine Committees have in fact been quite common throughout the postwar years in engineering and in the motor industry; prominent contemporary examples of such Combines include those at British Leyland, Fords, Dunlop-Pirelli, Lucas Aerospace, and Vickers.[60]

The Lucas organization is a particularly interesting example. Set up in the 1960s in response to fears of rationalization and redundancies the Combine Committee took over four years to develop its mature functions and structure. It has set up a number of advisory services for stewards and workers in the company, including one on company pensions, and another on science and technology. It publishes a four-page bi-monthly newspaper of which it distributes 10,000 copies to workers. Its principal achievement, which has made it widely known far beyond the boundaries of company industrial relations, is the researching and publication of an 'Alternative Corporate Plan' which advocates the adoption of a whole range of new company products, selected after canvassing the workforce and after detailed technical and commercial studies, and based on considerations of social usefulness (e.g. kidney machines, and new forms of energy generation). For this work the Committee has been proposed for a Nobel Peace Prize. The Combine set up, jointly with the North-East London Polytechnic, a Centre for Alternative Industrial and Technological Systems. Other Combine Committees which have developed alternative product plans to combat rationalization and redundancy include those at Vickers, Parsons, and Chryslers.[61]

Unfortunately, Combine Committees are constantly threatened by plant sectionalism; often arising in response to a job crisis in the company, they may find it hard to consolidate their organization and to ensure its continuity. Failing recognition by the company, the Combine's role may become limited to one of exchanging information between plants, though it should be said that this in itself can be a very useful function. This poses the question of whether Combine Committees should seek company recognition and a formal collective bargaining role. For some committees this has been a dilemma, since they have been wary of undermining the strength and independence of their constituent plant steward organizations. Yet recognition and a bargaining function may well overcome the organizational difficulties which beset them. Two students of Combine Committees have gone so far as to claim that 'the future effectiveness of collective bargaining rests on whether Combine Committees can cope'. They conclude that 'we can expect to see officially recognized Combine Committees becoming more common and consequently increasingly effective as bargaining agents'.[62]

For those whose persistent efforts have failed to secure from their employers any modicum of recognition, these words may seem slightly optimistic. Today, Combines are increasingly under threat. There is a strong management drive to isolate and fragment the labour forces by restricting the shopfloor trade union role to plant level only.

Combine Committees, of course, carry with them their own problems, as well as opportunities for the extension of the trade union role. Obviously, by concentrating attention upon company affairs, they risk neglecting the wider, industry and class loyalties and unities which lie beyond that level. In this sense, they may substitute new sectionalisms for older (e.g. craft) loyalties. Yet considering the still predominantly plant-level nature of shop steward organization, and the overwhelming corporate power which is embodied at company level, in the large, conglomerate corporations, an increase in these 'problems' would mark a substantial advance from lower to higher and more effective levels of shop steward organization. The aim to meet, bargain with, and control the corporate decision-makers of Fords, with its twenty-three plants in the United Kingdom alone, represents something more than narrow sectionalism. A high level of strategic thinking can be provoked in the striving for wider and wider forms of shop steward association in a major company, including the need for international and multi-company links. This is illustrated by the experience of leading convenors in Ford's UK factories.[63] Multi-company participation in the evolution of shop stewards' alternative planning about the whole motor industry is exemplified in the Motors' Group of the Institute for Workers' Control, whose published deliberations involved representatives from Chrysler, Vauxhall, Ford, British Leyland and Wilmott Breedon.[64] In another industry, the Coventry Machine-Tool Workers' Committee, with shop steward and convenor representation from five major companies in the industry, commissioned their own report on the economics of their industry.[65] The possibilities for organizing joint trade union initiatives of this kind, across a group of companies, or of embracing a whole industry or sector, are enormously strengthened by the prior existence of company-level Combine Committees. Yet the tendencies towards co-ordination of shop steward activity – in the plant, with the growth of full-time convenors, and in the company, with the growth of Combine Committees – has led some writers to reflect on the dangers of the 'bureaucratization of the rank and file',[66] and to resurrect a modified version of Michels's 'iron law of oligarchy'. Whilst Hyman, for example, acknowledges the desirability and inevitability of some degree of 'centralization' of workplace organization, he also advocates that 'the types of strategy long associated with "unofficial" struggles must now be reinterpreted and reapplied within shop steward organization'.

The aspirations of workers and their stewards' organizations, embarked as they are on the early stages of a sustained and difficult evolution to create working trade union structures which can face up to the powers of multinational companies, may well bring them into conflict with such proposals. To pose the possibility, or desirability, of constructing unofficial rank-and-file organization in opposition to convenors and Combine Committees is to conjure up an infinite regression of reactive organizations. There could be little reasonable doubt that if such a movement developed, it too would in its turn become 'bureaucratized' in the eyes of such critics, and so on, as it says in the poem: big fleas have little fleas, upon their backs to bite 'em; and little fleas have lesser fleas, and so ad infinitum. This is not to say that the time-honoured trade union controls of election, report-back, and recall, should not be applied to shop stewards, convenors, and Combine Committees, and indeed to all other representatives. It is, however, to argue that recent developments in the field of Combine and multi-company stewards' initiatives require a positive response from trade unions and perhaps even from commentators upon trade unionism.

Just as trade unions and the TUC must define and practise a new role in the 1980s and 1990s, shop stewards and their organizations must gear up for the new tasks thrown upon them by the adverse circumstances of mass unemployment, hostile laws and more subtle as well as more aggressive managements.

NOTES

1. S. R. Parker, *Workplace Industrial Relations, 1972*, HMSO, 1974.
2. Commission on Industrial Relations, Study no. 2, *Industrial Relations at Establishment Level: a Statistical Survey*, HMSO, 1973.
3. S. R. Parker, *Workplace Industrial Relations, 1973*, HMSO, 1975.
4. Neil Millward and Mark Stevens, *British Workplace Industrial Relations, 1980–84*, Gower, 1984, pp. 84–5.
5. H. A. Clegg, *The System of Industrial Relations in Great Britain*, Blackwell, 1970, and H. A. Clegg, A. Fox and E. F. Thompson, *A History of British Trade Unions since 1889*, vol 1: *1889–1910*, Clarendon, 1964.
6. See Jack Jones, *Union Man, an Autobiography*, Collins, 1986, Chapters 10 and 11.
7. W. E. J. McCarthy, *The Role of Shop Stewards in British Industrial Relations*, Research Paper 1, Donovan Royal Commission, HMSO, 1966, and W. E. J. McCarthy and S. R. Parker, *Shop Stewards and Workshop Relations*, Research Paper 10, Donovan Royal Commission, HMSO, 1968.
8. H. A. Clegg, A. J. Killick and Rex Adams, *Trade Union Officers*, Blackwell, 1960.
9. M. G. Wilders and S. R. Parker, 'Changes in Workplace Industrial Relations, 1966–72', *British Journal of Industrial Relations*, vol. 13, 1975.
10. In an unpublished Sheffield University research report (by R. Jones, J. Halstead, and M. Barratt Brown, 1977) it was recorded that among plants surveyed in the local engineering industry, the number of shop stewards doubled in 1968–9 with the emergence of productivity bargaining.
11. In the Employment Protection Act, 1975, and in the Health and Safety at Work Act, 1974.

12. M. G. Wilders and S. R. Parker, *op. cit.*
13. R. Jones, J. Halstead, and M. Barratt Brown, *op cit.*
14. Labour Research Department, Bargaining Report, *Facilities for Shop Stewards*, 1986.
15. *Ibid.*
16. *Ibid.*
17. Trade Union Research Unit, Ruskin College, *Nowt for Nowt*, Economic Appraisal No. 41, December 1985.
18. Millward and Stevens, *op. cit.*, the DE/ESRC/PSI/ACAS Surveys, Gower, 1984.
19. *Ibid.*
20. *Ibid.*
21. Ian Linn, *Single Union Deals, A Case Study of the Norsk-Hydro Plant at Immingham, Humberside*, TGWU Region 10, 1986.
22. *Ibid.*
23. *Ibid.*
24. A sea-change may be pending in public service industrial relations, in consequence of the government's privatization programme for many local government and NHS services. Government spokesmen in 1986 and 1987 expressed their wish to see the break-up of centralized Whitley-type wage-fixing machinery, although the employers' sides, as well as the unions', are reluctant to pursue this. The government has, however, abolished collective bargaining for schoolteachers, and its imposition of compulsory competitive tendering for NHS and local government services opens the way for such multinational private firms as Hawleys – an international cleaning and security business with a turnover of £1 billion – to invade further the hitherto stable shopfloor relations in these sectors. In 1986, Hawleys and its subsidiaries already controlled one third of all cleaning contracts in the NHS, central and local government. Its security business includes the export of equipment to South Africa. See *Labour Research*, June 1986. See also TUC, *Bargaining in Privatised Companies*, February 1986.
25. Roderick Martin, 'The Quiet Triumph of the "New Realism"' in *Times Higher Education Supplement*, 30 January 1987.
26. Robert Taylor, *The Fifth Estate*, Routledge and Kegan Paul, 1978.
27. In R. Jones, J. Halstead and M. Barratt Brown (*op. cit.*) the average was 60; in H. A. Clegg, A. J. Killick and Rex Adams (*op. cit.*) the average was 51; in W. E. J. McCarthy and S. R. Parker (*op. cit.*) the average was 60; and in W. Brown, R. Ebsworth and M. Terry, 'Factors Shaping Shop Steward Organization in Britain', *British Journal of Industrial Relations*, vol. XVI, no. 2, July 1978, the average was 51.
28. W. E. J. McCarthy, *op. cit.*
29. N. Nicholson, 'The Role of the Shop Steward: an Empirical Case Study', *Industrial Relations Journal*, vol. 7, no. 1, 1976.
30. N. Nicholson and G. Ursell, 'The NALGO Activists', *New Society*, 15 December 1977.
31. W. Brown, R. Ebsworth and M. Terry, *op. cit.*
32. M. G. Wilders and S. R. Parker, *op. cit.*
33. Labour Research Department, Bargaining Report 5, November/December 1979.
34. S. R. Parker, *Workplace Industrial Relations, 1973, op. cit.*
35. Data supplied by the Transport and General Workers' Union Region 10, for the second quarter of 1978.

36. B. Partridge, 'The Activities of Shop Stewards', *Industrial Relations Journal*, vol. 8, no. 4, 1977–8.
37. N. Nicholson, *op. cit.*
38. R. Jones, J. Halstead and M. Barratt Brown, *op. cit.*
39. E. Batstone I. Boraston and S. Frenkel, *Shop Stewards in Action*, Blackwell, 1977.
40. *Ibid.*
41. R. Jones, J. Halstead and M. Barratt Brown, *op. cit.*
42. *Ibid.* See also Graham Winch, 'Shop Steward Turnover and Workplace Relations', *Industrial Relations Journal*, 1980.
43. W. Brown, R. Ebsworth and M. Terry, *op. cit.*
44. W. E. J. McCarthy, *op. cit.*
45. S. R. Parker, *Workplace Industrial Relations, 1973*, *op. cit.*
46. W. Brown, R. Ebsworth and M. Terry, *op. cit.*
47. E. Batstone, I. Boraston and S. Frenkel, *op. cit.*
48. M. G. Wilders and S. R. Parker, *op. cit.*
49. Commission on Industrial Relations, *op. cit.* In W. Brown, R. Ebsworth and M. Terry (*op. cit.*) it is reported that two-thirds of stewards were in multi-union workplaces.
50. W. Brown, R. Ebsworth and M. Terry, *op. cit.*
51. B. Partridge, *Towards an Action Theory of Workplace Industrial Relations*, University of Aston Management Centre, Working Paper no. 50, 1976.
52. L. R. Sayles, *Behaviour of Industrial Work Groups: Prediction and Control*, Chapman and Hall, 1958.
53. B. Partridge, *op. cit.*, 1976.
54. J. F. B. Goodman and T. G. Whittingham, *Shop Stewards in British Industry*, McGraw-Hill, 1969.
55. H. A. Turner, G. Clack and G. Roberts, *Labour Relations in the Motor Industry*, Allen and Unwin, 1967.
56. S. R. Parker, *Workplace Industrial Relations, 1973*, *op. cit.*
57. W. Brown, R. Ebsworth and M. Terry, *op. cit.*
58. I. Boraston, H. A. Clegg and M. Rimmer, *Workplace and Union*, Heinemann, 1975.
59. W. Brown and M. Terry, 'The Future of Collective Bargaining', *New Society*, 23 March 1978.
60. Case studies of these and other committees are provided in H. Friedman, *Multi-plant Working and Trade Union Organization*, WEA, 1976.
61. For an account of the Lucas Combine Committee see K. Coates (ed.), *The Right to Useful Work*, Spokesman, 1978.
62. W. Brown and M. Terry, *op. cit.*
63. See Bernie Passingham and Danny Connor (TGWU convenors at Ford Dagenham), *Ford Shop Stewards on Industrial Democracy*, IWC Pamphlet no. 54, 1977.
64. See IWC Motors' Group, *A Workers' Enquiry into the Motor Industry*, IWC, 1978.
65. See *Crisis in Engineering: Machine Tool Workers Fight for Jobs*, Coventry Workshop and the IWC, June, 1979.
66. Richard Hyman, 'The Politics of Workplace Trade Unionism: Recent Tendencies and some Problems for Theory', in *Capital and Class*, vol. 8, Summer 1979.

CHAPTER 6

Collective Bargaining

The Range of Trade Union Methods

In their study of trade unionism, Sidney and Beatrice Webb had already distinguished three approaches by which trade unions sought to achieve their aims: the method of Mutual Insurance, the method of Legal Enactment, and the method of Collective Bargaining.[1]

Even while the Webbs were describing it, it was clear that the first of these was withering considerably: it belongs classically to the period of craft unionism, and a time when collective bargaining was far from widespread. The method of mutual insurance (apart from its formal insurance aspect in the provision of cash benefits for sickness, industrial injury, retirement and death) involved the use of trade union funds to provide 'out-of-work' benefit, and travelling allowances, to individual workers to enable them to refuse jobs offered at below the rate agreed amongst the union members; the Webbs christened this technique the 'strike in detail'. That it was a time-honoured method of trade unionism, designed to maintain labour's prices against the employers' market power, is attested by Fred Knee, an old militant who, also writing in the early years of this century, complained bitterly about its supersession by collective bargaining, which he regarded as a distinct compromise, and a compromise for the worse.

> It surprises me when I hear 'collective bargaining' spoken of . . . as the first principle of trade unionism. You may search the 'objects' of the older unions for this precious 'first principle' but you will not find it. The object of trade unionism used to be to uphold the price of labour *against* the encroachment of the employers, not in agreement with

> them. 'Collective bargaining' is an afterthought forced on Capital and Labour alike because of this straining after 'industrial peace' . . .[2]

Obviously the method of mutual insurance, which required no formal recognition of trade unions by employers, and indeed no necessity for a bargaining process, was a response to a time when industrial relations were rudimentary and undeveloped, when employers insisted successfully on their prerogatives, and when trade unions were small and confined to defined crafts and particular occupational skills. Yet such unions were not necessarily impotent. Another method, not separately categorized by the Webbs, which is suited to such circumstances, revived strongly in the postwar world of mass unionism and full employment; that of unilateral workers' regulation. When groups of workers place unwritten and informal, but effective, limits on their earnings, under systems of payment-by-result, when they administer the fair distribution of overtime among themselves, or when road haulage drivers place limits on the scheduling of their vehicles, or when a thousand and one informal 'norms' established by custom and practice are observed in industry, then no bargaining, and no recognition of unions, is required. Ironically, this most primitive form of regulation may prove to be the most tenacious and effective method of workers' control left alive on the shopfloor in the new age of industrial relations now developing under the influence of Japanese companies.

But, whatever Fred Knee thought about it, it is hardly possible to conceive of a *mass* trade union movement, enrolling people of diverse skills and people of no specific skill, exerting its postwar level of influence on labour's terms and conditions of employment without the widespread use of the method of collective bargaining. Moreover the supplementary function of mutual insurance, the provision of welfare cash benefits, was also most appropriately associated with a system of craft unions with relatively high subscriptions, in a pre-welfare state society, and has consequently declined with the historical evolution (which is itself largely attributable to the trade union method of legal enactment) of state provision for unemployment, sickness, accidents, and retirement. It is hardly conceivable that mutual insurance could be revived as an important trade union method, despite the present shrinkage of state welfare (for example in health provision). The shrinkage of trade union finances is even greater and modern members are unwilling to pay nineteenth-century craft rates of contributions.

We are left inevitably with collective bargaining as the classic function of a trade unionism which, inheriting some of the liberal suspicions of legislative 'interference', and strong on the doctrine of self-reliance, turned to legal enactment only in respect of specific areas of weakness and dependence, such as the protection of women and child labour. More recently, of course, the balance of emphasis in trade union methods between collective bargaining and legal enactment has shifted somewhat in favour of the law, but even today the British trade union movement as a whole (unlike some European unions) has only recently and, in the case of some unions, reluctantly, accepted the notion of legally enforceable minimum wages and is still indifferent to the legal enforcement of standard working hours. There are some unions (notably NUPE) which have strenuously argued for a legal minimum wage, but they are in a minority.

Wages and hours have in fact provided the staple diet for orthodox collective bargaining; for long periods, these have been the only subjects (along with 'conditions of work' rather narrowly defined) on which bargaining rights have been ceded by employers, or demanded by trade unions. One of the most dynamic and significant changes in trade unionism during the 1960s and 1970s was the areas of managerial control which are subject to the joint regulation of collective bargaining. At the same time, the traditional claim to legitimacy for wage bargaining has itself been increasingly challenged by the state in its pursuit of incomes policy, which in the sixties and seventies, and to a lesser extent even in the fifties, signalled an end to the prevailing assumption of the past two hundred years, that the state should leave wage regulation to the market, or to the bilateral regulation of employers and unions. The governments of the 1979–87 period, of course, have reverted, at least in their ideology and their public pronouncements, to the laissez-faire mode.

At a much earlier period of history, government regulation of wages both centrally and through its local Justices of the Peace, goes back to the sixteenth century and earlier. The grounds for a challenge to this state paternalism were prepared earlier in this country than elsewhere, with the rise of capitalist employment relations in agriculture from the sixteenth century onwards; the rising industrial capitalist class of the eighteenth century took up the struggle against the regulatory and paternalist state, and won the argument to the point where state control of wages was allowed first to deteriorate through neglect, and then was formally abolished.[3] During the transitional period, workers were to be found in the late eighteenth century petitioning governments for the enforcement of the old laws on minimum wages and other working conditions. When they found these approaches treated first with indifference and then with official hostility, they were thrown back on their own resources in their struggle to control the dominant new force of the labour market. By a painful and prolonged process of struggle, workers evolved over the next hundred years the means (trade union organization), they compelled the concession from employers (trade union recognition), and they elaborated the method (collective bargaining), by which to bring the labour market closer towards their own interests.

The Development of Collective Bargaining

Over the two hundred years history of trade unionism, collective bargaining has evolved from (a) 'primitive' workplace bargaining, reinforced by the method of mutual insurance, to (b) district or local agreements in particular industries (the majority situation before 1914), to (c) national-level, industry-wide agreements (the traditional aim of trade unionism, laying down a 'common rule' on wages and hours, and resting 'on the capacity of the two parties to make an agreement which will apply to the whole industry'),[4] to (d) the post-1945 situation, in which national agreements, particularly in the private sector of the economy, have been supplemented by widespread plant bargaining by local managers and shop stewards. Into this last pattern has been sketched, at certain postwar periods, a further level of proto-bargaining by (e) TUC negotiations with the state over the content of government incomes policies. While this was developing there was also growth of separate negotiations at company level.

Trade unions during much of the nineteenth century were too weak to enforce their rights to negotiate. Before the First World War the majority of workers were still either unorganized, or were conducting their negotiations with individual employers or groups of employers at local level only, which led to great variety of rates throughout the country in each industry. In 1910 only one-quarter of all industrial workers were covered by negotiated agreements of any kind, and the period from 1910–14 was characterized by many national-level strikes and disputes revolving round the issue of national-level recognition and national wage bargaining. The First World War greatly accelerated the trend towards national-level industry-wide bargaining. There was increasing intervention by government in industrial relations: industries such as mining and the railways were administered by the state at a national level. Growing unofficial labour unrest, spearheaded by the shop stewards' movement, led government to set up a wide-ranging enquiry under the chairmanship of Mr J. H. Whitley, MP, deputy speaker of the House of Commons, 'on the relations between employers and employed'.

The Whitley Reports (1916–17) have, ever since, been identified as the founding charter for the subsequent evolution of the British system of industrial relations, which later generations have continued to use and to amend, but not to overthrow. Its outlines remain in place today, although both its spirit and its substance have been watered down recently. The Whitley Reports recommended: (i) the establishment of Joint Industrial

Councils, representative of employers and trade unions, to make formal national, industry-wide agreements in particular industries, (ii) subordinate District Committees below the JICs, (iii) works committees for consultative purposes in particular companies and plants, (iv) the extension of the Trades Boards system of statutory wage regulation in industries where collective organization was inadequate to sustain collective bargaining, (v) a permanent arbitration board available for voluntary settlement of disputes, and (vi) recourse to government-appointed Courts of Inquiry to aid the understanding and settlement of major, intractable disputes. The principle on which the Whitley enquiry based its recommendations was 'the advisability of a continuance, as far as possible, of the present system whereby industries make their own agreements and settle their differences themselves'.

The advance towards a uniform system of national negotiations industry by industry was not uniform during the interwar years. Yet, the creation by mergers of the two large general unions in the 1920s added weight to the pressure on employers to concede the principle of national machinery; the TGWU and GMWU became the most active propagandists for Joint Industrial Council machinery in the trade union world. The changing character of industrial organization assisted the growth of national agreements – the appearance of large combines in such industries as chemicals, flour milling, and cement was one sign of a general shift away from small family business towards large-scale enterprise, managed along professional lines. Trade union professionalism, concentrated at national level, became the counterpart, the two sides converging on national agreements. In the aftermath of the failed General Strike of 1926, employers and union officials found common ground in their search for 'constitutional' forms of joint regulation.

The Second World War gave a further impetus to the setting up of national negotiating machinery, fifty-six new Joint Industrial Councils being created during 1939–45. At the end of the war, the Acts which established the nationalized industries all contained clauses compelling the newly created authorities to set up negotiating machinery with the appropriate trade unions. By 1946 already, some 15½ million workers in industrial and service occupations were covered by collective machinery, or by statutory Wages Councils. Since the war, some 70 per cent of the working population have had their wages and working conditions regulated by these means.

The forms taken by collective bargaining vary widely as we shall see, but at the national level they all require an adequate degree of organization and representation on the part of unions and employers. Since multi-unionism is the norm in British industry, then at national, company, and even at plant level, it is usually necessary for unions to 'recognize' each other's claims to represent a part of the workforce, and to form joint teams of negotiators to engage in bargaining. (In recent years, the increased pace of trade union mergers, and the onset of the new fashion for single-union agreements at company level, are eating into the common, multi-union situation.) Sometimes these joint arrangements are formalized into Federations, such as the Confederation of Shipbuilding and Engineering Unions, the National Federation of Furniture Trade Unions, and the Federation of Broadcasting Unions. TUC co-ordination of unions for bargaining purposes is embryonic although the TUC Steel Committee has some bargaining functions with British Steel. In other cases, unions simply negotiate amongst themselves about their relative share of seats on Joint Industrial Councils or Whitley Councils. Inter-union rivalries are sometimes manifest in this process, for example between NUPE and the general unions on Local Government and Health Service Committees, but there is a surprising degree of co-operation and mutual tolerance within many of these arrangements. Differences of policy between unions on the same negotiating body can emerge, as was the case between the TGWU and AUEW and the GMWU and EETPU, over whether support should be given to shop steward opposition to settlement of Ford wage claims in 1969. Only rarely do such disputes reach the stage of threatening the disruption of the bargaining machinery itself, and by the spread of their membership across many industries, the large general unions in particular acquire vast experience and expertise in operating joint union representation in literally hundreds of negotiating bodies.

Joint employers' organization is necessary where the bargaining structure embraces more than a single firm, as is the case with the major national bargains in the private sector. Like trade unions, employers' associations have undergone a process of rationalization and mergers: in 1936 there were 270 national federations of employers, whereas today the number is 172. In the past and particularly before the First World War, employers' associations were major innovators in the field of industrial relations, particularly in developing conciliation machinery and district agreements. Since the Reports of the Whitley Committee, government and unions have been more likely to initiate changes in bargaining practice, at least until the Report of the Donovan Royal Commission in 1968, since when individual companies, rather than associations of employers, have assumed a greater role in reforming structures and procedures, and the introduction of such things as 'fringe benefits' has been developed at company, rather than association, level. Of course, some associations retain overall control in major national bargains, such as the Engineering Employers' Federation, whose negotiations with the CSEU cover 2 million workers. But the Donovan Report concluded that the most useful functions retained by employers' organizations were their provision of access to an industry-wide disputes procedure, and their symbolic representation of their members' commitment to the formalities of collective bargaining.[5] Today only 20 per cent of private sector workers are covered by multi-employer agreements such as Joint Industrial Councils, which used to be standard. Thus the collective bargaining functions of employers' associations have continued to diminish. More and more companies prefer to withdraw from the old structures and to bargain directly with the unions through industrial relations departments or specialist directors.

Collective Bargaining Institutions

Collective bargaining takes place through a wide variety of institutions, and at several different levels. It is usual to distinguish between national, industry-wide bargains conducted either through a Joint Industrial Council or through more ad hoc meetings of the two parties, through public sector machinery arranged according to JIC (or Whitley) principles, through centralized bargaining in each nationalized industry, through independent ('non-federated') private sector company bargains, and through Wages Councils. These constitute what the Donovan Commission called the 'formal' institutions of the industrial relations system. In addition, though varying in significance between sectors and industries, there is widespread supplementary bargaining activity between shop stewards and local managers, at the level of the individual plant or workplace, – what Donovan called the 'informal' aspects of the system.

As we have already pointed out, Joint Industrial Councils were originally set up in response to the Whitley Committee's recommendations, with formal constitutions and a representative composition of employers, their associations, and the appropriate unions. Between 1918 and 1921, seventy-three Councils were formed; between the wars the numbers declined to a total of forty-five in 1938. The Second World War saw a revival of the form, and in postwar Britain there have been around 200 Councils.[6] Some large private sector industries rely on purely ad hoc meetings for bargaining, and avoid the setting up of elaborate constitutional machinery. This is the case in engineering, where either the CSEU or the EEF can request a meeting of the two sides whenever necessary.

The civil service and the National Health Service have elaborate structures of national bargaining committees going under the generic name of Whitley Councils divided into separate Councils for particular branches and grades of employees. Local government has a similar structure of national bargaining committees, and each of the nationalized industries conducts its own separate national bargains with the recognized unions. A feature of many of these formal structures is that separate machinery, and separate bargains, are maintained for craftworkers, semi- and unskilled workers, and for non-manual employees.

Wages Councils are statutory bodies established to provide a means of settlement of wages and certain basic conditions in industries where voluntary collective bargaining has not evolved; they too are composed of employer and union representatives, but in their case with a third element of independent members appointed by government. Unlike the voluntary system, minimum wages determined by Wages Councils have the force of law, though enforcement in practice is often a difficult matter in back-street industries policed by an inadequate number of government wages inspectors. The jurisdiction of Wages Councils over the wages of young workers has been ended, while the number of government wages inspectors has been further reduced, in the 1980s.

Broadly speaking, the distribution of the various forms of collective bargaining among the working population is as follows:

(1) Multi-employer agreements at industry level cover 20 per cent of private sector workers.
(2) Wages Council rates cover 5 per cent of private sector workers.
(3) Single-employer agreements at company, divisional or workplace level cover 50 per cent of private sector workers.
(4) 25 per cent of workers in the private sector are not covered by any form of collective agreement or statutory regulation.
(5) In the public sector, some form of negotiated collective agreement has been well-nigh universal, although in 1987 the government proposed to end the negotiation of teachers' salaries and conditions of employment in favour of a consultative process which left the government itself as the unilateral decision-maker in these matters.

In general, the public sector's 7 million workers have traditionally been governed by highly centralized agreements, particularly in health, local government, education, central government administration and the police service. In some of these sectors there is scope for the supplementing of national pay standards by local bargains over bonuses, piece-rates, etc. In 1987, government sentiment was strongly in favour of ending the standardization of national rates in the public sector, in favour of regional differentials. The privatization of a wide range of services in local government and health is tending in the same direction. In the public corporations covering energy, transport, communications and some manufacturing, privatization, governmental and commercial policies combine to introduce decentralization of bargaining in industries which formerly bargained centrally to fix national terms and conditions.

An alternative breakdown of the different forms of agreements is given in Table 6.1. The table indicates a significant shift away from collective bargaining in the seven years covered, which is part of a trend reaching back at least to the earlier 1970s.[7] The decline in coverage for manual grades, both male and female, is greater than for non-manual workers. The figures also illustrate and confirm a change in the structure of bargaining. The decline in coverage is almost wholly in the category of 'national and supplementary agreements'; all males, and manual females, register an *increase* in coverage in the case of company and local agreements.

To explain the decline and the structural changes we need to examine the multiple causes at work. Dominant amongst them is the rise of unemployment. This makes institutions of collective bargaining very vulnerable. In the great slump of the interwar years, there was a similar and even greater collapse of collective bargaining. National-level, Joint Industrial Council bargaining took particularly hard knocks. Trade unions try to resist this, but in unhelpful conditions. Employers, on the other hand, often happily withdraw from JICs and similar bodies, as two large affiliates did from the Engineering Employers' Federation in 1979, whose membership has declined from 6000 to 5000 firms since 1981.

More: changes in the employment structure have reduced and are reducing the classic areas of densest unionization and stable formalized bargaining in manufacturing. The relative expansion of the service sector, important parts of which are much less organized, does not compensate in union recruitment for losses

Table 6.1

Coverage of collective agreements (full-time workers only), 1985 compared with 1978

	Percentage affected by					
	National and supplementary company etc. agreement	National agreements only	Company, district or local agreement only	No collective agreement	Total on collective agreements	Percentage difference, 1978–85
All males	14.5 (22.4)	37.7 (37.2)	12.0 (11.1)	35.8 (29.1)	64.2 (70.7)	−6.5
Manual males	19.3 (29.3)	37.6 (36.4)	13.7 (12.6)	29.4 (21.7)	70.6 (78.3)	−7.7
Non-manual males	8.4 (11.7)	37.9 (38.5)	9.8 (9.4)	43.9 (40.5)	56.1 (59.6)	−3.5
All females	10.4 (15.6)	45.8 (43.7)	7.8 (8.7)	36.0 (32.0)	64.0 (68.0)	−4.0
Manual females	17.0 (25.6)	32.2 (32.9)	12.8 (12.4)	38.1 (29.1)	62.0 (70.9)	−8.9
Non-manual females	8.3 (11.2)	50.3 (48.4)	6.2 (7.1)	35.3 (33.3)	64.8 (66.7)	−1.9

Source: *New Earnings Survey*, Part F, 1985. Figures in brackets = 1978 (from *NES*, Part F, 1978).

Note: There are approximately 4.98 million full-time females in Great Britain and 11.5 million male workers. Applying the percentages to these gives a *broad* indication of numbers of workers affected. (However we should remember that collective agreements will also cover some *part-time* females.*) Thus around *7.38* million full-time men and *3.18* full-time females are covered by some kind of collective agreement.

*approximate number of part-time females = 4.16 million

elsewhere. Trends away from manual work to white-collar work, from male to female employment, from the North of Britain to the South, and from full-time to part-time work, to self-employment and the black economy, all warren the ground beneath collective bargaining. Supporting all these objective influences is a government ideology which, since 1979, has been avowedly disrespectful and discouraging towards the pluralist traditions of collective bargaining. The same philosophy is seen to be taken up by managements, not least amongst newly privatized and foreign-owned companies. The government has systematically withdrawn long-established state supports for collective bargaining, such as the Fair Wages Resolutions, or Schedule 11 of the 1975 Employment Protection Act. It has weakened the coverage of Wages Councils. In its own sector, where it is the source of funds for pay, it has shown, as in the teachers' case, a lack of sympathy not only for collective bargaining, but for voluntary arbitration, the last supportive stage in that process.

Plant-level Bargaining

If national-level bargaining was dominant in the 1940s, the postwar years saw an impressive growth in significance of plant-level bargaining between shop stewards and local management, particularly in the private large-scale manufacturing sector. This method grew during the fifties and sixties to the point where it became the main source of anxiety about 'disorder' in British industrial relations. The restoration of 'order' was the principal motive behind the setting up of the Donovan Royal Commission on Trade Unions and Employers' Associations, which reported in 1968. The Commission found widespread evidence that ad hoc plant bargaining over a range of issues had created an 'informal' system of industrial relations alongside the 'formal', JIC, method of determining pay and conditions. Amongst other matters, shop stewards regularly determined or negotiated on the distribution of overtime, piece-rates, bonuses, and manning, together with other issues subject to local variations. The Commission's principal recommendation was that all this activity should be formalized, in plant- or company-level agreements covering procedures and standards for these bargains, to bring the informal arrangements into line with formal arrangements at higher levels.

This and other recommendations were given a strong impetus in succeeding years from the impact of incomes policies. Under successive governments in the sixties and seventies, these allowed and encouraged departures from restrictive pay norms where companies or plants negotiated productivity agreements. Of necessity, these were more formal than much previous practice, and they became widespread in both private and public sector pay bargaining. Management invested increased resources in the industrial relations aspects of their total planning, and evolved new methods of wage payment, using job evaluation and measured day work, in their efforts to control hitherto free-wheeling and ad hoc plant-level negotiations.

But the hoped-for constraint on the total national pay bill did not evidently materialize. Neither was the formalization of structures envisaged by Donovan very widely applied. Where it was applied, it did not seem to have been effective in curbing shop stewards' autonomy and powers. Nor did strike levels, a concomitant anxiety of Donovan, decline under the influence of new managerial methods.

With the end of the postwar world industrial and trade expansion and stability in the early seventies, and with the accompanying crises of increased price inflation and of the balance of payments, attention shifted from the shopfloor to the major national pay bargains. As these came into conflict with tight government pay norms, particularly in the public sector, they produced a rapid growth in strike activity, under the governments of both Edward Heath (in 1972–3) and James Callaghan (in 1978–9). These conflicts were severe enough to produce a press campaign against trade unionism which aroused serious popular resentment of the unions. They were particularly criticized for large set-piece collisions over public sector pay, because the resultant strikes invariably hit, not the employers' profit, but the provision of public or social services. (Government, indeed, actually saved money during such strikes, because they cut the wage bill.) This set the scene for the Conservative governments of the 1980s to demote collective bargaining from its former sacrosanct position as the normal, consensual way of determining people's pay and conditions.

How has this combination of factors affected the bargaining relationships at plant level? Much depends upon the style of management; Brown and Sisson have usefully distinguished four types currently on view in Britain.[8] The first, 'sophisticated paternalism', aims to avoid collective bargaining and even to refuse recognition to trade unions. American firms in Britain are noted for this approach. IBM(UK) is a classic example, refusing recognition to British unions, deploying a battery of human relations techniques to ward them off, and proudly proclaiming a strike-free record reaching back to its foundation in 1951. It has 18,000 employees in the UK, engaged in about forty sites, so it is no negligible example. Moreover, it encourages neighbouring companies in Scotland and in other electronics corporations to pursue a comparable anti-union policy. In a survey of its workers which was conducted by ACAS, only 4.36 per cent could be found to support the introduction of collective bargaining, and only 4.9 per cent wanted to join a union. '. . . IBM refuses to recognize trade unions, not because of their potential nuisance value, but because their collectivism runs wholly counter to the company's fundamentally individualist philosophy.'[9] In the early months of 1987, there were reports of moves towards the actual abolition of collective bargaining in companies with UK bases and with hitherto traditional industrial relations policies. Scottish Agricultural Industries, a wholly owned subsidiary of ICI, withdrew recognition of bargaining rights from three manual worker unions, the TGWU, the GMBATU and the AEU. Annual wage bargaining is now superseded by a pay review carried out by a purely consultative committee, in which employee representatives will advance their views, followed by a management-determined pay award. The company has claimed that the workers concerned had shown no signs of resisting the change, which was part of a package of reforms aimed at introducing greater flexibility and single-status terms and conditions of employment. On South Humberside, a subsidiary of BP took similar steps in March 1987, and the workforce supported them despite trade union opposition.

One of the consequences of these developments in the petrochemical industry may well be a decline in safety standards, as trade union safety representatives' bargaining role is diminished, and as process workers with minimal training are called on to carry out maintenance work on pipes and valves. Fatal and serious accidents in the chemical industry have increased by 35 per cent since 1981, according to a report by the GMBATU, which draws its evidence from the industry's own trade association.

A second type of management style, 'constitutionalist', sees collective bargaining as fundamental, and its refinement and formalization as a central managerial task. Procedure and written agreements are the chosen means of regulation; communication with the workforce is through these mechanisms and the shop stewards. This approach harmonizes with the Donovan pluralist philosophy, and at least preserves the trade union role in the plants.

The third, and currently rising, style is called 'consultative' by Brown and Sisson. It accepts collective bargaining, and even 'conducts it with great professionalism', but at the same time seeks to confine it to the narrowest compass feasible, replacing it wherever possible with 'problem-solving' through elaborate formal consultative methods. This approach is widely associated with the Japanese companies and their single-union, 'no-strike' deals which have been recently introduced into Britain, often assisted, or indeed even promoted, by the EETPU. But they are not confined to Japanese companies, and many other unions apart from the electricians have concluded such deals. Sometimes unions have been impelled into such agreements by their own membership, recognizing the power of big transnational companies to insist on these deals or go elsewhere in a buyers' market for labour. The management style of such companies often extends to the constitution of Company Advisory Boards or Councils, on which employee representatives are elected without regard to union membership or to shop steward tenure, even if the senior steward is usually a co-opted member. Collective issues are then handled in this machinery, and not with union officials, whether lay or full-time. Such arrangements impose flexibility of work, sometimes even establishing a single grade of worker untrammelled by written job-descriptions, and accompanied by a much simplified and more egalitarian pay structure. Employees all enjoy the same status in respect of canteens, car parks, and even a company uniform worn by management and workers alike. Finally, unresolved issues are referred to 'pendulum arbitration' and strikes are often specifically foresworn by the union signing the deal. (In practice, this has not prevented outbreaks of strikes at some of the companies which have adopted this method; for example, Bowmann Webber, a mirror and glass manufacturer, experienced a two-week stoppage eighteen months after signing its no-strike agreement with the EETPU in 1985.[10]) Nothing in these agreements can in fact exclude the possibility of unofficial strike action. The EETPU signed some seventeen or eighteen no-strike single-union deals, mainly in electronics, between 1981 and 1986. The car industry has also featured elements of these deals; significantly the industry is dominated by multinational ownership (Fords, GM) and the new managerial initiatives are practised worldwide in such companies. We are witnessing an international convergence in this field.[11] Bassett distinguishes this style from that of IBM:

> Japanese companies, including those in the UK, forge a corporate whole through collectivism, made most obviously manifest in the rigorous similarity of the uniforms which employees are required to wear. There are no uniforms at IBM: even the coffee served by machines in the . . . restaurant is individually ground.[12]

Pendulum arbitration, a recent innovation in Britain, is a

strong feature of the new consultative style of management. In orthodox arbitration, the arbitrator is required to find a solution acceptable to both parties, which normally involves an element of compromise between the two disputants' final positions. Thus, it is criticized by the advocates of pendulum bargaining for its lack of principle, and for its tendency to 'split the difference'. In pendulum, or 'last-offer' arbitration, the arbitrator must award his verdict to one or the other of the two sides' final positions. In its favour, it is argued that this prospect forces the two sides into more realistic negotiation, and draws them towards an agreed solution, since they must fear that extravagant demands or mean offers will, if they reach the stage of arbitration, be rejected as unreasonable. Thus bargaining is enhanced and reference to arbitration will in practice be less frequent. It is in this context that strikes become unnecessary. Sir John Woods, chairman of the Central Arbitration Committee, objects to the new process, however, arguing that often the issues are too complex to resolve by a simple choice between two positions, and that in the compromise of traditional arbitration, there is a helpful element of face-saving involved, while in pendulum arbitration one side must go away utterly defeated.[13]

Despite this novelty, the new agreements described here have much in common with the managerial methods of advanced companies such as ICI in the slump interwar years, especially the creation of company-controlled non-union joint consultative councils. Although the full method is practised only by a minority of companies today, elements appear very frequently in recent company strategies, and could become more common, especially in the high-technology private sector, in future.

The last style identified by Brown and Sisson is 'pragmatic' or 'ad hoc'. This, they believe, rules in the majority of companies in the private sector. In this category, bargaining is traditional and relatively unsophisticated, and personnel management is a 'fire-fighting' role, acting to solve crises as and when they arrive. In this style, the shop stewards function relatively undisturbed, but market pressures on industry tend to make it a less than satisfactory method for management.

The institutions of collective bargaining in the public sector have for a long time seemed relatively stable compared with the volatile shifts of structures in the private sector. Public authorities have operated highly centralized bargaining, depriving the shopfloor and local levels of many bargaining duties. In recent years this has been changing. The government has sought to decentralize bargaining, insisting that national pay rates should be replaced by regional differentials reflecting different labour markets in different regions. So far, this policy has made little impact, but it undoubtedly remains a long-term commitment of any future Conservative administration. It is significant that a National Local Authority Co-ordinating Committee was established in 1983. Local government is a service with little previous evidence of national-level shop steward initiatives. But this initiative creates what is effectively a shop stewards' Combine Committee, affiliating the Joint Shop Stewards' Committees of some thirty major local authorities. Some of these groups participate with the encouragement of their employing authorities. This move undoubtedly represents a response to novel pressures for decentralization and regionalization of industrial relations in local government.

The other important initiative of government has been its privatization programme, which has affected both the commercial and manufacturing part of the public sector (such as gas, aerospace, shipbuilding, or road passenger transport) and also the services in local government and the NHS. In the commercial sector, more competitive industrial relations practice has been introduced: the use of bargaining over working practices, or even the unilateral introduction by management of flexibility, and consultative methods. Privatization has been widely followed by the abrogation of collective agreements by the new managements, by the individualizing of employment contracts, by demanning, subcontracting, and decentralization of bargaining and procedures.[14]

In health and local government, the process of tendering for the private operation of services such as refuse collection and hospital catering, cleaning and laundering, has disrupted industrial relations in many locations and is impelling the employers towards modern flexibility deals. It poses a major dilemma for the unions, which know that privatization is often accompanied by non- or anti-unionism in the contractor companies. To protect itself and its membership numbers, the union often finds it necessary to support an in-house contract which concedes new and tighter working practices and greater managerial control over the work process, as well as lower pay, the loss of overtime and bonus earnings, and the loss of legal protection for workers who become part-time instead of full-time. One union official gave as his opinion that his union would lose 10 per cent of its members (disgruntled at the union's support for the deal), 10 per cent on pay, and 10 per cent on working conditions. These losses he saw as the costs of retaining most of his members by adopting in-house contracts competitive enough to succeed against the cost-cutting private tenderers. Such deals have been widely imposed in the health service.[15] The same problem faces all local authority unions in the near future, given the government's plans and timetables for compulsory tendering in that sector. Since we are dealing with labour-intensive employment there is ample scope for such changes. The shopfloor level of bargaining under private contracting itself is primitive or non-existent. The limited role of plant-level bargainers under centralized pay determination in public services gave the process a degree of stability which is now radically disturbed by all these developments. Against this argument, a recent academic survey has suggested that the evidence for major changes in plant-level bargaining and in the powers of trade unions and shop stewards should be treated with some caution, and that there is in fact some considerable continuity over the recent slump and difficult years. But this investigation was confined to manual workers in large-scale private manufacturing and relied upon answers to a questionnaire addressed only to personnel managers.[16]

We must also note the spread of the device of subcontracting. Such things as component manufacture may, on the model of Japanese industry, give rise to a core of relative employment security inside the company while this is surrounded outside by firms supplying parts to the main assembly centre. Such modes of work are beginning to spread in Britain, and it is certain that plant trade unionism is difficult to sustain in the subcontractors' employment areas. Nor are these methods confined to manufacturing. Courage Breweries in 1987 announced the turning-over of 900 managed public houses to tenancies, thus transforming the landlords (who are unionized) from wage-earning employees into self-employed entrepreneurs, carrying the risks and insecurities of a small business. Tenants may also be sold equities in their pubs by Courage's Australian parent company. Similarly, Northern Dairies intend to dismiss all their milk-roundsmen (unionized in USDAW), offering them in return first refusal of self-employed contracts to continue delivery in defined neighbourhoods. Within some industries, employers are offering confidential and financially favourable subcontractual status to individual workers who continue to work alongside traditionally employed, collectively covered colleagues. This is happening, for example, in British Steel. The disruptive effects of this scheme upon plant-level trade unionism are not hard to envisage.

The Subjects and Results of Bargaining

Traditionally, collective bargaining has encompassed wages, hours of work, holidays, and conditions of work (narrowly defined). In the postwar boom, unions and their members developed much wider ambitions, and sought to push the frontiers of bargaining ever wider to include, amongst other things, shop stewards' facilities, manpower planning, job and income security, guaranteed weeks, health and safety measures, pensions, sick pay, discipline and dismissals, and disclosure of information. Some of these endeavours bore fruit, especially when reinforced by some of the social contract legislation of 1975 and 1976 (see Chapter 10 on the law). Employers resisted these trends, sometimes refusing outright to bargain on the wider issues, or sometimes offering consultation rather than negotiating rights, in these areas. The unions might at one stage have become involved in negotiations over the whole of companies' corporate plans had the Planning Agreements sections of the 1975 Industry Act not been diluted in its final version so that they became optional for companies and not compulsory. In the event, only one such agreement was ever made, by Chryslers; shortly afterwards that company made its exit from the plants in question, and from the agreement with them.

This proved to be the beginning of a prolonged retreat. From the frontiers reached by union bargainers in the years of full employment, we now see, in a harsher economic and political climate, new conditions. Employers have been enabled to withdraw from bargaining, or to impose more restrictive terms upon it. On pay, we have already given evidence to show that the numbers covered by collective agreements are shrinking, and the evidence from the spread of single-union, no-strike agreements suggests strongly that true bargaining processes are being supplanted by what is not much more than consultation. There is conflicting evidence on the question of whether or not more employers are succeeding in their drive to attach productivity and flexibility strings to their pay bargaining. A recent survey reports that 'Neither the establishment's recent financial performance, nor the trend in its output, nor the sensitivity of its product prices to the level of demand appeared to have any overall impact on the considerations that influenced pay settlements . . .'[17] On the other hand, the CBI in early 1987 reported that pay was effectively being linked to flexible working and productivity. Grass-roots evidence confirms this: more and more workers are accepting multi-skilling and flexibility merely in return for local wage gains of 4 or 5 per cent, in the engineering industry.[18] Government encouragement of performance-related pay is evident in the introduction, in 1987, of income-tax relief on elements in the pay packet which are geared to the profits of the company.

The forty-hour week was established by bargaining in the early 1960s, but progress towards further reductions has been slowing, despite an official TUC policy goal of a thirty-two-hour week and six weeks' annual holiday entitlement. Insofar as there is one, the standard working week for manual workers is now thirty-nine hours, and for many white-collar sections, thirty-seven and a half hours. Currently, prolonged and difficult negotiations are taking place between the Engineering Employers' Federation and the seventeen unions in the Confederation of Engineering and Shipbuilding Unions over the introduction of a phased reduction of the working week to thirty-seven hours. The EEF has seized the initiative, and has tabled a series of demands on which they require agreement in return for the reduction. These include full utilization of working hours, the employers' right to arrange those hours annually, half-yearly, or monthly, and drastic changes in the disputes procedure. They also insist that hours worked should not include washing-up or tea breaks, and on the variation of the working week – twenty-five hours one week, forty-five the next, according to employers' decisions. All these imposts are to be linked to single-union agreements under which other unions lose bargaining rights, and 'an end to all demarcation'.[19] While these conditions would drive a coach and horses through the bargaining norms of the past, engineering workers reflect that, at plant and company level, they are often already in process of conceding these terms, without the benefit of the shorter working week which is on offer nationally. Bargaining in the hitherto staid, administrative public service tradition in local government and health is now also imbued with new managerialist goals and methods, using job evaluation and flexibility clauses to obtain concessions in return for pay increases.[20]

Public sector pay bargaining of course never escapes overt or covert incomes policies: a question to which we will return.

The impact of new technology on labour has preoccupied unions (and the TUC) for some years. Indeed, back in 1979, the TUC urged its members to embark on a programme of New Technology Agreements.[21] Under such a programme unions would only accept the introduction of new technology in return for safeguards in the fields of health and safety, pay, job security, and information disclosure. Few unions have since been successful in securing agreements, and a major survey of more than 2,000 workplaces in 1987 found that 'So great has been the support of workers and trade union representatives for technical change that managements have not had to use consultation, participation, or negotiations to win their consent to change. Even major changes have been introduced with surprisingly little consultation.'[22]

Another TUC priority during the present decade has been that of low pay. In 1977, male earnings in the lowest decile were 43 per cent of those in the highest decile. This proportion had fallen to 36 per cent in 1986. Amongst women the comparable figures were 44 per cent in 1979 (their highest point), falling to 40 per cent in 1986. In 1987, some 3 million full-time workers (or 30 per cent of the full-time labour force) earned less than £100 per week, the majority (some 2 million people) being women. There may be as many part-time workers earning less than the hourly equivalent (about £2.60 per hour). In a major consultative document the TUC affirms that 'The bedrock of TUC policy for combating low pay . . . will remain collective bargaining', although, in response to pressures from unions such as NUPE, and a Congress resolution in 1986, '. . . the question of general statutory support for collective bargaining . . . is being considered . . .'[23] Some definitions of low pay are given in Table 6.2.

However, bargaining over minimum pay is no easier in current conditions than is bargaining on any other subject, and is virtually certain to be accompanied by employers' demands for productivity concessions. In a strategy paper, even a sympathetic local authority, seeking to tackle the problem with its trade unions, calls for 'flexibility in work arrangements . . . performance of certain identified additional duties, . . . co-operation in efficiency studies . . . preparedness to work overtime if necessary'.[24] Collective bargaining in the mid-1980s is clearly unable to protect the real take-home pay of many groups of workers. A recent regional study by Michael Somerton shows that for the lowest decile earners amongst single men, pay

Table 6.2
Some definitions of low pay, 1985

Royal Commission on Income Distribution and Wealth (lowest decile male manual gross weekly earnings)	£100.40
Trades Union Congress (two-thirds of male manual gross weekly average earnings)	£109.07
Low Pay Unit (two-thirds of all male gross weekly median earnings)	£115.20
Council of Europe (68 per cent of male and female average gross weekly earnings)	£116.28
Family Income Supplement Eligibility Level (two children under 11)	£109.00
Supplementary Benefit Earnings Equivalent (two-adult, two-child family, aged 11–15 and under 11)	£116.90

has fallen by 4 per cent from 1978 to 1985, and by 3.2 per cent in the same period for married men. (For lowest decile single women it has risen by 4.5 per cent.) That this is part of a general widening of the gap between rich and poor is shown in the same survey's figures of real take-home pay for the top decile, which has risen by 12.4 per cent (single men), 20 per cent (single women) and 11.6 per cent (married men).[25]

Further disparities in bargained rates, and widening inequalities, are to be apprehended from government's sustained pressure for the termination of national bargaining across the whole field of the public sector and for the widening of regional differentials in pay. This pressure, deriving from a quixotic hope that market forces applied to labour may provide a cure for unemployment in the worst-affected regions, has been maintained despite the evidence of the 1987 Family Expenditure Survey, that average household income in the South-East is already 45 per cent higher than in the North. Trade unions have not been able to hold the line for the national 'rate for the job'.

The collective bargaining process overall has been unable to

Table 6.3

Shares of profits and wages in national income

	Average 1960–74	1975	1977	1979	1980	1981	1982	1983	1984
As % of net domestic product (FC)†*									
Net* trading profits and rent of industrial and commercial companies	11.8	5.3	10.0	10.0	9.1	9.4	10.5	12.3	14.9
Income from self-employment	9.9	9.3	9.2	9.1	8.6	8.9	9.1	9.3	10.0
Wages and salaries	68.6	72.8	66.3	67.8	69.5	68.9	66.9	65.6	64.6
As % of gross domestic product (FC)									
After providing for stock appreciation	14.2	9.1	13.5	13.7	13.1	13.5	14.2	15.7	17.9
GR, TR, Profit of industrial/ commercial companies									
Self-employment	9.6	9.1	9.0	8.9	8.4	8.6	8.7	8.9	9.5
Income from self-employment	67.5	72.5	67.3	67.6	68.9	68.3	66.5	65.5	64.4

*Net = after providing for capital consumption and stock appreciation
† = at factor cost

Sources: *1985 UK National Accounts*, Table 3.5 and Table 3.3, as presented in *Nowt for Nowt? or Who Got What, When?* Economic Appraisal no. 41, Trade Union Research Unit, December 1985.

maintain the relative share of wages and salaries in the national income, as Table 6.3 demonstrates.

In the face of deteriorating conditions for collective bargaining among the diminishing core of full-time workers, particularly among manual workers, the two large general unions have embarked on campaigns to recruit and represent the growing numbers of temporary and part-time workers, women, young people and ethnic minorities, who loom larger in the labour force and who have rarely or never hitherto been covered by collective agreements.

Ron Todd, General Secretary of the TGWU, told the rally which launched his union's campaign in 1987, that it 'marked the first serious attempt by any union to face up to the new reality of the British economy and the growth of five million part-time and 1.5 million temporary workers'.[26] A pilot scheme drive was launched from this rally aimed at the non-unionized hotel and catering industry. John Edmonds, General Secretary of the GMBATU, has spoken of the same fundamental problem. For him, while 'Throughout large areas of industry trade union membership has survived remarkably well and has pretty consistently delivered benefits to the workers', elsewhere 'millions of workers live in an entirely different world. For them, the real concern is getting off first base: winning the right to trade union membership, raising poverty wages, avoiding discrimination or victimization, dealing with arbitrary and aggressive management . . . Their attachment to unionism is weak . . . and . . . we do need to acknowledge the remarkably low esteem into which unions have fallen.'[27]

Procedures

Collective bargaining, the joint regulation of industrial relations, includes procedural rules as well as the substantive matters with which we have so far been concerned in this chapter.

In outline, the pattern looks like this:[28]

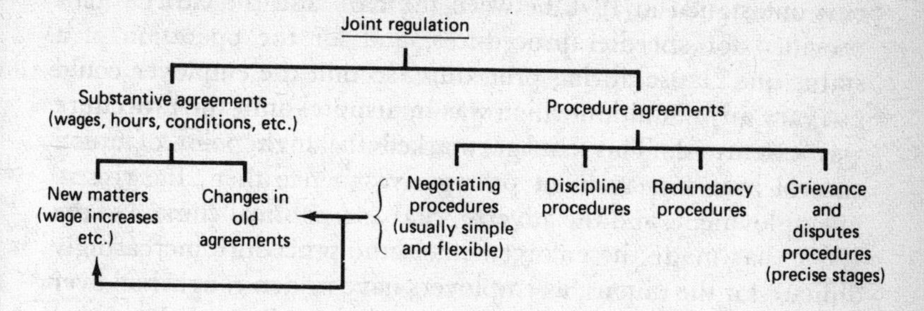

This carefully constructed network of procedures in industrial relations was the outcome of much conflict and much effort at its resolution, over the modern era of trade unionism; its structured solution reflects the dominant pluralist and voluntary philosophy of the postwar consensus.

The realities of power within the structure have varied over time with the fortunes of trade unions and with the employment level. The procedure agreement covering the 2 million workers in engineering is quite typical. In the period from about 1910 to 1922, the unions gained much ground, both in terms of national recognition and bargaining procedures on substantive matters at national level, and at plant level in the growth of shop stewards' influence. In 1922, the employers won a prolonged lockout and in its aftermath reasserted managerial prerogatives by insisting on grievance and disputes procedures which gave them unilateral rights to vary conditions before entering into retrospective bargaining. The agreement was enshrined in the well-known York Memorandum and under its sway, grievances and disputes originating at the shopfloor level had to be processed through elaborate, time-consuming stages to a national conference during all of which time the employer's decision which had sparked the dispute remained in operation. When the unions regained their strength during and after the Second World War, these arrangements were frequently by-passed by the strengthened shop stewards' movement and much unofficial and unconstitutional action directly resulted in the 1950s and 1960s. The 1922 agreement was finally abandoned in 1971, and a new one signed in 1976 between the EEF and the CSEU. This provided for speedier procedures, and for the operation of a status quo clause during procedure, so that the employer could not vary any condition which was in dispute, until the procedure was exhausted. This change marked the high point of union control over management prerogatives. Since then, the rise in unemployment, and the adverse legal and political climate of the 1980s, has made the enforcement of the procedure increasingly difficult for the unions, as employers have ridden roughshod over agreed procedures in the areas of discipline, redundancy notification and bargaining, and individual and group grievances. This is not to say that all power has transferred to unilateral employer decision-making, but even where the more even-handed procedures survive (and what has been said of engineering applies very widely wherever collective bargaining has been practised in both private and public sectors), they are not always honoured by the employers' side, and the enforcement of their terms is an up-hill task for the unions. Much of what has been said in earlier sections of this chapter, about the spread of new managerial initiatives and practices, reinforces this generalization.

Professor B. C. Roberts has provided a useful summary of the likely future trends in British bargaining relations.

> The fundamental thrust of industrial relations in Great Britain is likely to continue to be centred on the establishment and the enterprise. Collective bargaining will inevitably reflect this trend, but with weakened union organization and more positive and open management it is possible that it will become more narrowly focused on pay, with other aspects of working conditions and work procedures being determined through a greater involvement of employees in the decision-making process.[29]

Arbitration and Conciliation

Some industries, notably in the public sector (such as railways and the civil service), have their own specific arbitration tribunals to which disputes are finally referred. Others – the vast majority – use the government-financed but independent services of the Advisory, Conciliation and Arbitration Service (ACAS) and the Central Arbitration Committee (CAC). The origins of these services date back to the late nineteenth century. Then the government, impressed by what it observed of private arrangements for conciliation operating in a number of industries such as steel, and the boot and shoe industry, assumed powers under the Conciliation Act 1896 to provide arbitration and conciliation services. These were henceforth to be available freely, whenever they were requested voluntarily by both parties to a dispute. Thus the principle was established that government would offer a service, but would not impose any obligation to use it. Following this precedent, a permanent arbitration court, adhering to the same principles, was set up in 1919 (the Industrial Court Act). An element of compulsory, unilateral arbitration was introduced during both world wars, when strikes were illegal. This became a permanent feature after the second war, enabling first the Industrial Disputes Tribunal, and later the Industrial Court to make legally binding awards to apply where employers were judged not to be observing minimum standards of pay established by collective bargaining. The former Industrial Court has undergone several changes in title, and has now been succeeded by the CAC established under the Employment Protection Act 1975. The CAC provides traditional voluntary, mutually acceptable arbitration in single industrial disputes, and also compulsory unilateral judgements on minimum wage questions (under Schedule 11 of the Employment Protection Act), union recognition, and disclosure of information. The conciliation services formerly provided successively by the Board of Trade, the Ministry of Labour, and the Department of Employment, have now been hived off to the independent, tripartitely administered ACAS. The creation of such a service, independent of government and the civil service, was felt to be necessary to restore confidence in the whole method, following long periods in the postwar years when unions felt that government was influencing arbitration awards and its conciliation officers in the interests of state wage restraint policies. ACAS is governed by a Council which is appointed by the Secretary of State for Employment. Its Chairman works full-time, and the nine other members are part-time. The Secretary of State consults with the CBI and the TUC about the appointment of two groups, each of three members, who will remain broadly in tune with one or the other of these constituencies, while the remaining one-third are 'independents'. The ACAS Council has declared that it will not be an 'interpreter, monitor, or enforcement agent of an incomes policy'.[30]

Conciliation is a process in which a third party assists the two sides to resume talks after a breakdown or deadlock in negotiations. It is a voluntary procedure, and conciliators make neither awards nor pronouncements concerning the issues at stake. Their diplomatic skills are deployed to bring about renewed discussion, and once talks reopen, the conciliators' role is at an end.

During the 1960s, ministry conciliators were handling some 200–300 disputes a year, 40–50 per cent of which were about pay, 30 per cent about trade union recognition, and 10 per cent about redundancy and dismissals.[31]

As their successor, ACAS had, by 1985, a staff of 648 (most of them based in seven regional offices) who conciliated in 1,337 disputes during that year; 1,104 of these cases were successfully brought to settlement. The usual subjects of dispute were again wages, union recognition, dismissal and discipline, and redundancy. Trade unions asked for conciliation services in 40 per cent of cases, employers in 11 per cent, 46 per cent were joint requests, and in 2 per cent, ACAS took the initiative itself. Up to the end of the 1970s business had been brisker, involving about twice as many conciliations, and employing almost 200 more staff. But the recognition of the service had become more stable, as is reflected in the increase of joint requests for intervention, which more than doubled as a percentage of all requests, during the same time.

Table 6.4

Completed conciliation cases analysed by cause of dispute[32]

	1977		1979		1981		1983		1985	
	No. of cases	%	No. of cases	%	No. of cases	%	No. of cases	%	No. of cases	%
Pay and terms and conditions	1,601	(55.4)	1,336	(58.5)	969	(56.4)	966	(59.6)	769	(57.5)
Recognition	635	(22.0)	392	(17.1)	247	(14.4)	216	(13.3)	211	(15.8)
Demarcation	32	(1.1)	20	(0.9)	17	(1.0)	13	(0.8)	8	(0.6)
Other trade union matters	143	(4.9)	125	(5.5)	82	(4.8)	57	(3.5)	49	(3.7)
Redundancy	134	(4.6)	90	(3.9)	153	(8.9)	103	(6.4)	80	(6.0)
Dismissal and discipline	239	(8.3)	219	(9.6)	204	(11.9)	178	(11.0)	162	(12.1)
Others	107	(3.7)	102	(4.5)	44	(2.6)	88	(5.4)	58	(4.3)
Total	2,891	(100)	2,284	(100)	1,716	(100)	1,621	(100)	1,337	(100)

Source: ACAS, *Annual Reports*, 1977, 1979, 1981, 1983 and 1985.

In addition to collective conciliation cases, ACAS has a duty to conciliate in cases where individuals complain of loss of rights to an Industrial Tribunal. The service handled 42,887 such cases in 1985, of which 38,255 were cases of unfair dismissal; 48 per cent of these cases were settled by conciliation, and 25 per cent were withdrawn. This left 27 per cent which went forward to hearings of Industrial Tribunals. As may be expected at a time of mass unemployment, individual cases occur at very nearly the same frequency as they did in the earliest years of the service, reflecting none of the drastic decline which has been registered in the numbers of collective cases.

ACAS also provides an arbitration, investigation, and mediation service. In the case of arbitration (which differs from conciliation in that the arbitration body makes a definite decision, or award, to settle the dispute) ACAS may appoint a single arbitrator, or an ad hoc arbitration board, or may refer the case to the Central Arbitration Committee. Mediation may be defined as a more formal type of conciliation, and is a variant on the services offered by ACAS. In 1985 ACAS appointed 135 single arbitrators in disputes, set up 13 ad hoc boards, referred 2 cases to the CAC, and appointed outside mediators in 12 cases. A measure of the range of the ACAS conciliation service can be obtained from Table 6.4.

The CAC is made up of a chairman, a panel of deputy chairmen, and panels of members with experience as representatives of employers and of workers. For any one case, the Committee will comprise a chairman and one representative each from the employers' and unions' panel. Its function as arbitrator in voluntary cases arising from orthodox industrial disputes became a small part of its total workload as ACAS got into its stride; out of a total of 836 awards made in 1978, only 3 were voluntary arbitration cases;[32] 519 cases were brought in that year under Schedule 11 (Terms and Conditions of Employment) of the Employment Protection Act, 7 cases involved trade union recognition, and 10 were disputes about disclosure of information. Awards made under Fair Wages Resolutions totalled 271, and the rest of the cases concerned CAC powers to arbitrate under specific pieces of legislation applying to particular industries (like the Road Traffic Act 1960, or the Road Haulage Wages Act 1938), or to particular groups (like the Equal Pay Act 1970). Subsequent amendments to the Employment Protection Act and changes in government policy towards public sector employees have reduced recourse to the CAC to the merest trickle of cases.

In outline, then, we have the British collective bargaining system: based on trade union rights to organize and negotiate, on employers' recognition of these rights, covering wages and conditions for the vast majority of the labour force, but expanding into new areas of decision-making, embracing both substantive agreements and voluntary procedural rules, and supported by officially sponsored, statutory, but independent conciliation and arbitration services. Up to this point, we have chosen to ignore a major anomaly, which in most years since the Second World War has challenged the assumptions of voluntarism and independence on which this system has rested. We have passed over government wages and incomes policies. We must now put this right.

Incomes Policy

Our chief concern in looking at incomes policy is to appraise its implications for the traditional, and indeed for any alternative, role for trade unions. Before attempting this, however, a brief summary of incomes policy experience is necessary. The traditional role of the state in wage-fixing, since the repeal of the Combination Laws in 1824–5, up until the Second World War, has usually been assumed to have been one of 'non-intervention'. In fact this has only been true insofar as market forces in the labour market, and trade union weakness and immaturity, were in such a condition that wage movements did not threaten the stability of the capitalist market system. In both world wars, when there was a great shortage of labour, the government did not hesitate to impose compulsory arbitration. This was clearly intended to prevent trade union bargaining power from 'pushing up wages too far'. And in 1925–6, at the climax of half a decade of conflict generated by employers' attempted wage cuts, the Prime Minister, Mr Baldwin, explicitly embraced a 'wages policy' when, following the return to the gold standard at the pre-1914 parity, he told the TUC leaders that 'we must all accept wage cuts to put the country on its feet'.

But it is of course with the post-1945 experience of much more overtly interventionist government policy on wages that trade unions must now be most concerned. That experience has moved through a number of phases. The 'Stafford Cripps policy' of 1948–50 consisted of official government pronouncements and appeals calling for wage restraint, rising to a call for a wages freeze in 1949. Although the government took no direct powers to enforce wage limits, it applied its policy in the public sector, and won the support of the TUC for its general policy for a period of eighteen months. Rising inflation provoked by the devaluation of the pound, and the Korean war, led to increasing opposition from the trade unions, and to the defeat of the TUC General Council's commitment to the continuation of the policy, at the 1950 TUC Congress.

During the 1950s, Conservative governments tried to obtain agreement for a policy of voluntary wage restraint. These met with little trade union sympathy. Government influence on statutory wage-fixing bodies was resented by the unions, who rejected the policies advocated by a government-established Council on Prices, Productivity and Incomes (the Cohen Council).

In 1961, the government went further towards direct wage restraint by imposing a 'Pay Pause'; again no statutory powers were invoked, but the government used its influence in the public sector and amongst arbitrators, to ensure a measure of adherence to the policy. The Pause was followed in 1962 by an attempt to establish a long-term incomes policy, and a 'norm' of 2–2½ per cent wage increases was proposed. A National Incomes Commission was established to police the policy, which the TUC opposed and boycotted.

The returning Labour government in 1964 abolished the Conservative's NIC, and initially operated a voluntary policy on incomes, prices and productivity, based on a Joint Statement of Intent signed by government, the TUC, and the employers. A new body, the National Board for Prices and Incomes, was set up to examine particular cases of wage claims. A White Paper in 1965 laid down the criteria on which the Board would judge both proposed price and wage increases, and a norm of 3–3½ per cent for wage increases was announced. Increases above that amount were only to be justified by acceptance of 'improved working practices' leading to higher productivity.

The TUC, still anxious to make the policy work voluntarily, set up its own 'early warning' system for vetting pay claims by their affiliated unions; the government created a statutory early warning system of its own, requiring companies and unions to notify it of proposed wage and price increases. In 1966, the government decreed a statutory freeze on wages and prices which lasted six months. Orders preventing increases had the force of law, and striking against them was illegal. A 'nil norm' followed during 1967, only exceptional cases for increases based on stringent productivity criteria being allowed. The government retained its statutory authority to enforce this degree of restraint. In 1968 a 3½ per cent norm of wage increases was introduced, and the government continued to foster productivity deals. During these years these became a widespread method of obtaining the wage increases demanded by union members, since the cost of living was specifically ruled out as a criterion on which extra pay increases might be conceded. Such policies persisted through 1969; in 1970 a new norm of 2½–4½ per cent was decreed, and the policy was relaxed to accept claims based not only on productivity, but on the general ground of low pay, public sector pay, and equal pay for women. By the end of the Labour government's period in office, the policy was visibly breaking down. It went out in the tumult of an unprecedented wave of major strikes.

The Conservative government of 1970–4 began by abolishing the NBPI and the government's wage restraint powers. Following substantial pay settlements in the public sector in

1970–1, a government policy of reducing each subsequent settlement by 1 per cent was enforced in that sector. This provoked several major official strikes. Following the failure of Downing Street talks in 1972 between the Prime Minister and TUC and employer representatives, which were aimed at achieving a voluntary code of co-operation on restraint, the government imposed a ninety-day statutory pay and prices freeze – Phase 1 of its Counter-Inflationary Policy.[33] This was succeeded by Phase 2,[34] which set up a Pay Board and propounded a norm of £1 a week increase plus 4 per cent on the average pay bill per head up to a ceiling of a £250 annual increase for any individual. The statutory Phase 3[35] extended the role of the Pay Board and created a norm for increases of £2.25 or 7 per cent (whichever was greater) in the average pay bill per head, plus 1 per cent flexibility margin, plus threshold payments geared to the rise in the cost of living, up to a maximum of £4.80. There was also a maximum of £350 per annum for individual increases.

The assault on these policies was led by the miners, in 1972 and 1973–4, and the subsequent General Election in February 1974, called at the height of a miners' strike, led to the defeat of the government.

The Labour government of 1974–9 commenced its period in office with a voluntary policy, agreed with the TUC, and based on TUC guidelines calling for wage increases simply to keep pace with increases in the cost of living.[36] In July 1975, the government, after difficult bargaining with the TUC, again obtained endorsement for a limit on wage increases, of a flat rate supplement of up to £6. The TUC's guidelines were actually reproduced in the appropriate government White Paper.[37] A person earning more than £8,500 was denied any wage increase. On the insistence of the TUC, and especially of Jack Jones, this phase was the first which had created a flat rate, as opposed to a percentage, norm. In 1976–7 (the government and the TUC having by now succeeded in adopting an agreed annual wage round running from July to July) the TUC again bargained with government to establish guidelines subsequently endorsed in a

White Paper.[38] On this occasion, a further supplement on earning was agreed: it was fixed at up to £2.50 per week for those earning under £50 a week, up to 5 per cent for those earning between £50 and £80 a week. A £4 flat rate was applied to those earning more than £80 a week. By 1977, the strains of these successive policies within the trade union movement were beginning to make themselves felt; differentials had been seriously distorted and the call for a return to free collective bargaining was strongly pressed at TUC meetings. Between 1977 and 1978, the government's unilateral creation of a 10 per cent norm[39] fared badly in some major private sector settlements and provoked strikes in the public sector – notable amongst which was an official strike of firemen. In 1978–9, government was again faced with determined trade union requirements for an end to norms, and a return to unfettered collective bargaining. It persisted however in seeking to impose a 5 per cent norm[40] (substantially below the rise in the cost of living) and had to face a winter of severe strike action, involving lorry drivers, and many groups in the public service. The government's powers to penalize private firms which settled above the norm (by denying them contracts or financial supports) were removed by the House of Commons, and the 5 per cent policy was commonly held to have been an important factor in the defeat of the Labour administration in the election of May 1979.

The restoration of a Conservative government, under the radical new leadership of Mrs Thatcher, maintained continuity in one respect alone: all these policies were once again reversed. Officially, the Thatcher administration denied any interest in incomes policy, and indeed repudiated the very idea of intervention in wage determination.

Reliance on monetary policies and increased unemployment combined to squeeze out a substantial proportion of the ailing manufacturing sector of British industry. Subsequently there was a covert abandonment of raw monetarism, although non-intervention remained the watchword in general industrial policy. But although there was no overt intervention in private sector pay bargaining, we should not accept governmental protestations at their face value. In fact, Mrs Thatcher intervened very strongly to restrict unions, and at the same time she maintained very stern incomes policies for a most significant group of people. Seven million people work in the public sector, and for two decades that sector grew steadily until its expansion stalled in the early 1980s. Health, education and local government account for 1½ million employees apiece. In the early 1980s, before the onset of major privatization schemes, 2 million worked in the public corporations. The armed forces and the police accounted for a further half a million. Government policy towards pay settlements in these sectors is clearly an influential fact in the wider economic balance.

In fact, four distinct incomes policies have been evolved, affecting the different parts of this variegated workforce in different, even contradictory ways. Brown and Sisson have identified these four mini-policies.[41]

First, there is the policy of indexation to national average earnings, which applies in the police, the fire service and the armed forces. Second, there is the more advantageous policy of *comparability* with the private sector. This applies to doctors and dentists, politicians, judges and, for a long time, to the civil service. In general this system is associated with the establishment of permanent review bodies. Thirdly, in public industries trading in the general market place, there exists a modified system of collective bargaining, although this will be subjected to strict limits where Exchequer subsidies are necessary to the operation of the industry, or where government control over price rises is in force. Fourthly, there is a straightforward policy of cash limits, which applies in the main public services, including health, education and local government.

Like all incomes policies, these four mini-policies are subject to infinite variations. Limits can be relaxed when it is convenient so to do. It may well be convenient in the run-up to General Elections. Limits can also be tightened, and we might expect that this would be convenient, other things being equal, in the period immediately after elections. Public sector trade unions could thus be excused for reviving the old Chartist demand for annual parliaments. 'Comparability' may fluctuate with electoral timetables, as may the degree of restraint on public subsidies or changing prices. In previous incomes policies, comparability was always seen as a threat to the imposition of fixed norms. But these mini-policies have provoked deep resentments. Public sector wages have not kept up with the private sector, and public sector unions have not usually been able to do much about it. Of course, there have been attempts to try, most noticeably, recently, in the education service. Brown and Sisson conclude that a comprehensive public pay policy could only emerge 'from further expensive disputes. Governments will always be tempted to use pay restraint for public employees as an early and apparently easy means of restraining inflation.'[42] Nonetheless, we are bound to agree that there is a price to be paid for the use of this convenient mechanism. Our public services rely on people who are often labouring under a profound sense of injustice and neglect, and who, in consequence, may work with something below peak levels of enthusiasm.

This account has necessarily been brief, and has not spelt out the detailed effects of incomes policies on governments and trade unions at any stage. In fact it can be said that wage restraint has been a rock on which successive governments have foundered in the postwar years, and it has been a factor introducing great uncertainty in the minds of trade unionists. It is now necessary to appraise this experience, and to ask what it implies for the future of trade unionism.

NOTES

1. Sidney and Beatrice Webb, *Industrial Democracy*, first published 1897, Longman Green edition 1926.
2. Fred Knee, 'The Revolt of Labour', in *Social Democrat,* 1910, reprinted in K. Coates and T. Topham (eds.), *Industrial Democracy in Great Britain*, 3rd edition, vol. 1, Spokesman Books, 1975.
3. Alan Fox, 'The Social Origins of Present Forms and Methods in Britain and Germany', in *Industrial Democracy; International Views*, SSRC, 1978.
4. TUC, *Trade Unionism*, 1966.
5. Royal Commission on Trade Unions and Employers' Associations, 1965–68, *Report*, Cmnd 3623, HMSO, 1968, paras 81–2.

6. Ministry of Labour, *Industrial Relations Handbook*, 1964. This useful compendium, long out-of-date, was succeeded by a new volume prepared by ACAS.
7. In 1973, 83.2 per cent of manual male workers, 60.4 per cent of non-manual males, 71.7 per cent of manual females, and 64.8 per cent of non-manual females were covered by the various types of collective agreement (full-time workers only). E. J. Thomson, C. Mulvey and M. Farbman, 'Bargaining Structure and Relative Earnings in Great Britain', *British Journal of Industrial Relations*, July 1977.
8. Willy Brown and Keith Sisson, 'Industrial Relations – the Next Decade', in *Industrial Relations Journal*, vol. 14, no. 1, Spring 1983, pp. 9–21.
9. Philip Bassett, *Strike Free: New Industrial Relations in Britain*, Macmillan, 1986, p. 164. See also M. George and H. Levie, *Japanese Competition and the British Workplace*, CAITS, 1984.
10. See *Industrial Relations Review and Report*, no. 370, June 1986, pp. 14–16.
11. See *The Auto Industry*, International Labour Reports: Educational Packs for Trade Unionists, 1986.
12. Philip Bassett, *op. cit.*, p. 164.
13. Sir John Woods, 'Last Offer Arbitration', *British Journal of Industrial Relations*, vol. XXIII, no. 3, November 1985, pp. 415–24.
14. TUC, *Bargaining in Privatized Companies*, 1986.
15. Evidence in an unpublished study by Daniel Vulliamy, University of Hull Industrial Studies Unit.
16. See Eric Batstone, *Working Order: Workplace Industrial Relations over Two Decades*, Basil Blackwell, 1984.
17. Neil Millward and Mark Stevens, *British Workplace Industrial Relations, 1980–84*, the DE/ESRC/PSI/ACAS Surveys, Gower, 1986.
18. Interviews with AEU district officials.
19. 'This Deal Undermines Trade Union Principles', *Tribune*, 28 November 1986. In April 1987, almost all the 24 motions on the subject scheduled for debate at the AEU's policy-making National Committee's annual conference called for the union to withdraw from talks on the deal, and criticized the secrecy of those talks. In November 1987, these 'flexibility' negotiations finally collapsed after four years of talks. The Confederation of Engineering and Shipbuilding Unions (CSEU) was divided. Opponents of the deal included TASS and the General Unions. Supporters were the AEU and EETPU. For their part, the Engineering Employers' Federation (EEF) had been pressurized by governments to pursue a flexible agreement of the kind that has foundered. Thus the future of both federations is in some doubt. Certainly their roles and influence will change.
20. Maurice Smart, 'Performance Management Reaches County Hall', *Manpower Policy and Practice*, vol. 1, no. 1, Autumn 1985, Institute of Manpower Studies, Gower Press.
21. See TUC, *Strategy of Technology Agreements*, 1979, and also Peter Carter, 'New Technology: the Challenge which the Unions Must Face', in *Tribune*, 31 October 1986. Between 1980 and 1984, eighteen trade unions published guides to New Technology Agreements.
22. W. W. Daniel, *Workplace Industrial Relations and Technical Change*, Frances Pinter with PSI, 1987.
23. *Fair Wages Strategy: National Minimum Wage*, a TUC consultative document, April 1986.
24. *A Low Pay Strategy*, Humberside County Council consultative document, 1987.
25. Mike Somerton, *Fair Pay of Foul Play; Low Pay in Humberside* Low Pay Unit Pamphlet no. 44, May 1987.

26. *Guardian*, 27 February 1987, and 'Link-Up!', in *The Record*, TGWU monthly paper. See also the TGWU's organizers' pack, *T & G Link-Up Campaign*, 1987.
27. John Edmonds, 'Uniting the Fragments', in Ken Coates (ed.), *Freedom and Fairness*, Spokesman for the Institute for Workers' Control, 1986.
28. Diagram taken from Tony Topham, *The Organized Worker*, Arrow, 1975.
29. B. C. Roberts, 'United Kingdom', in J. P. Windmuller *et al.*, *Collective Bargaining in Industrialized Market Economies: A Reappraisal*, International Labour Office, 1987, p. 299. This whole volume represents the most authoritative and up-to-date comparative account of its subject, confirming many of the trends which we have noted in this chapter.
30. ACAS, *Annual Report, 1978,* 1979.
31. Ministry of Labour, *Industrial Relations Handbook*, HMSO, 1964.
32. See CAC, *Annual Report 1978*, 1979.
33. Cmnd 5125 (November 1972), HMSO, 1972.
34. Cmnd 5205, 5206 (January 1973), and 5267 (March 1973), HMSO, 1973.
35. Cmnd 5444 and 5446 (October 1973), HMSO, 1973.
36. TUC, *Collective Bargaining and the Social Contract*, 1974.
37. Cmnd 6151 (July 1975), HMSO, 1975.
38. Cmnd 6507 (July 1976), HMSO, 1976.
39. Cmnd 6882 (July 1977), HMSO, 1977.
40. Cmnd 7293 (July 1978), HMSO, 1978.
41. W. Brown and K. Sisson, 'Industrial Relations in the Next Decade', *Industrial Relations Journal*, Spring 1983, vol. 14, no. 1.
42. *Ibid*, p. 16.

CHAPTER 7

The Experience of State Intervention

Upon what principle should wages be allocated? The question, which is involved in any attempt at incomes policy, poses greater difficulties than are commonly admitted in newspapers, although some informed people have always been willing to confess that it has perplexed them. Speaking a hundred years ago, for instance, Judge Ellison, who had been invited to umpire a mining dispute in Yorkshire, allowed himself to be recorded as saying:

> It is [he said] for [the employers' advocate] to put the men's wages as high as he can. It is for [the men's advocate] to put them as low as he can. And when you have done that it is for me to deal with the questions as well as I can; but on what principle I have to deal with it I have not the slightest idea. There is no principle of law involved in it. There is no principle of political economy in it. Both masters and men are arguing and standing upon what is completely within their rights. The master is not bound to employ labour except at a price which he thinks will pay him. The man is not bound to work for wages that won't assist (subsist) him and his family sufficiently, and so forth. So that you are both within your rights; and that's the difficulty I see in dealing with the question.'[1]

Almost certainly the judge was at that time unaware that an identical point had been made by Karl Marx, in *Capital*, which had been published in German twelve years earlier. 'There is here', he had written, 'an antinomy, right against right, both equally bearing the seal of the law of exchanges. Between equal rights, force decides.'[2] In this tradition, there grew up a long-term socialist opposition to what became known as 'the bondage of wagery', in which the whole relationship of employees to employers, or, as it was described, the system of wage-labour was exposed to powerful criticism.

In modern England this may seem strange, since 'free collective bargaining' is nowadays commonly perceived to be a war-cry of militant trade unionists, and left-wing *opposition* to such bargaining may not be easily understood. Yet such opposition was at one time widely argued.

Judge Ellison was, of course, speaking when there was a comparatively free market in operation, as compared with today's multinationally cartelized economy. If labour markets have always been less 'free' than many economists have believed, today we stand on the brink of major technological changes which could radically worsen the bargaining position of labour. At the same time, the concentration of ownership and the growth of industrial scale have produced recurrent and persistent pressures for incomes policies in order to 'plan' the distribution of pay, and thus limit the force of labour market pressures on companies.

Here it is important to distinguish between the relatively profitable meso-sector of giant transnational companies, which can commonly afford high wages and remain viable, and a growing slum sector of the economy in which dire market pressures might squeeze out employment altogether if what many would regard as minimal conditions of work and reward were established. Both these sectors are privately controlled. Under public control there is a similar mix, with a greater concentration of ailing industries, and the perennial problem of welfare services which are never adequately funded to meet the need they have uncovered.

This dual economy poses problems for any government which wishes to tax industrial concerns, since it positively needs an elastic measure if it is not to choke life out of the uncompetitive sector at one extreme, or to feather-bed the great quasi-monopolistic concerns at the other. The same issue already applies to trade unions, and is likely immeasurably to complicate the discussion on any future incomes policies unless the manufacturing basis of the British economy can be miraculously resuscitated.

Table 7.1

Income shares as a percentage of gross national product at factor cost: United Kingdom, 1860–1978[4]

Years	Employee compensation	Income from self-employment Farmers	Others	Corporate profits	Rent	Total domestic profits	Net property income from abroad	Gross national product
1860–9	45.2	6.4		30.6	14.8		3.0	100
1870–9	45.2	4.5		32.1	13.7		4.5	100
1880–9	46.2	2.7		31.4	13.9		5.8	100
1890–9	48.0	2.4		30.8	12.5		6.2	100
1900–9	47.7	2.3		31.3	12.1		6.6	100
1910–14	47.3	2.5	13.7	17.1	11.0	28.1	8.4	100
1921–4	58.5	2.1	15.1	13.0	6.8	19.8	4.5	100
1925–9	58.1	1.3	14.8	12.5	7.5	20.0	5.8	100
1930–4	59.3	1.6	13.4	12.5	9.0	21.5	4.2	100
1935–8	58.9	1.6	11.6	15.0	8.8	23.8	4.1	100
1946–9	65.3	2.9	9.4	16.8	4.0	20.8	1.7	100
1950–4	65.3	2.8	7.8	18.0	3.9	21.9	2.1	100
1955–9	67.0	2.3	6.9	18.0	4.5	22.5	1.3	100
1960–3	67.4	2.1	6.3	17.9	5.1	23.0	1.2	100
1964–8	67.6	8.0		16.8	6.4	23.2	1.2	100
1969–73	68.9	9.0		13.2	7.6	20.8	1.3	100

Income shares as a percentage of gross national product at factor cost: United Kingdom, 1860–1978[4]

Years	Employee compensation	Income from self-employment Farmers Others	Corporate profits	Rent	Total domestic profits	Net property income from abroad	Gross national product
1974	70.6	9.3	10.0	7.5	17.5	1.7	100
1975	73.5	8.8	9.3	7.4	16.7	1.0	100
1976	71.5	8.5	10.6	7.3	17.9	1.1	100
1977	69.7	9.4	13.0	7.5	20.5	0.4	100
1978	69.5	9.2	13.2	7.6	20.8	0.5	100

Economic laws will increasingly allow that rewards in the two sectors remain different, whilst their members will continue to shop in the same supermarkets. Free collective bargaining, if it is not prevented, may well expose the limits of these differences, but it will provide no machinery for passing over them. Legislative enactment (for shorter hours or longer holidays, or for minimum wages) could have some limited impact, but in the mid-term this would only be effective if it were backed by entrepreneurial intervention (possibly by the state or workers' co-operatives as well as or instead of the current directorship) to overcome the capital and planning starvation of the weak enterprises.

The traditional argument for incomes policies was summed up by Harold Wilson, speaking at the 1964 TUC:

> We have the right to ask for an incomes policy because we are prepared to contribute the three necessary conditions. First, an assurance of rising production and rising incomes, so that the sacrifice, the restraint, for which we ask is matched by an assurance that it will result in increased production and increased rewards. Second, an assurance of equity and social justice, in that our policies will be directed to the benefit of the nation as a whole and not to the advantage of a sectional interest. Third, an assurance that what we ask for in wages and salaries will apply equally to profits and dividends – and rents.[3]

It is, to say the very least, difficult to apply these assurances during a prolonged slump with stagnant production and falling real incomes, in which it is clear that superhuman efforts will be required to enable any prospect of recovery to be maintained.

In fact, even in times of relatively rapid growth, the mechanisms of incomes policy did not secure the kind of redistribution of the social product which was commonly advanced as their purpose. In fact, the sector of wages and salary incomes improved by 0.2 per cent of the Gross National Product during the four years of this policy. In the next four years, after the collapse of the policy it further improved, in the course of a veritable tidal wave of strikes and industrial unrest, by 1.3 per cent. During the cataclysm in which the Heath administration was carried off, it improved in one single year by 1.7 per cent. In the first and only deliberately redistributive year of the social contract, 1975, it improved by 2.9 per cent. Thereafter it declined, and in 1978 it was once again below the 1974 level.

Profits, by 1978, were restored to the same level (20.8 per cent) at which they had been in 1969–73. Incomes policy during the majority of these years had registered rather limited direct gains for the whole sector of wages and salaries, when compared to the effects of its indirect impact, through the strikes and unrest which it invariably provoked. Only in 1975 was there a conspicuous exception to this pattern.

But although the sector of wages, taken in relation to other broad sectors, went through a cycle during the second half of the seventies, in which at the end it arrived back close to its starting point, there was nonetheless a certain tendency inside that sector for differentials to be reduced.

This appears quite markedly when we examine the gross weekly earnings of full-time workers. A certain egalitarian movement has taken place among manual workers, between non-manual and manual workers, within the limits we have already discussed between men and women, and last, but very important, between private and public sectors. This can be clearly seen in Table 7.2.

However, this modest degree of levelling had not at all taken place in the context described by Mr Wilson, but rather at a time of severely restricted growth or actual decline, during unrelenting inflation, with rising unemployment and heightened social tension. Hardly surprisingly, it has not therefore been seen as an unmitigated or universal benefit. Indeed, as insecurity has become widespread, there has been a considerable increase of resentment at the erosion of these time-honoured differentials, and many people would ascribe to this fact the main reason for Mrs Thatcher's remarkable success in winning votes from trade unionists during the 1979 election. If economic growth certainly gives no guarantee of redistribution of income, lack of such growth most assuredly does not make it any easier. We arrive

Table 7.2

Gross weekly earnings of full-time workers: differentials, 1970–7

Workers	1970	1974	1975	1976	1977
Male manual workers					
Top decile % of median	149.6	145.3	145.8	145.9	145.6
Top decile % of bottom	230	219	216	214	212
Male non-manual workers					
Top decile % of median	178.8	173.9	168.2	169.7	166
Top decile % of bottom	309	293	282	282	274
Non-manual median % of manual median	123	115	116	118	119
Women median % of men median					
Manual	51	55.5	59.5	62.5	64
Non-manual	52	55	59	61.5	62
Public % of private					
Men manual	93	97	105	102	100
Non-manual	103	102	106	110	106
Women manual	100	106	112	108	105
Non-manual	140	132	140	137	130

Source: Social Trends, 1979, and NIESR, *Economic Review*, February 1979.

once again at a truism, that questions of income are intimately connected with degrees of effective social power, and that without a significant shift in the balance of power, no serious change in distribution of income is possible.

Even if it is temporarily eclipsed during the upsurge of monetarist policy which accompanied the political rise of Mrs Thatcher, the argument on incomes policy will probably continue as long as the capitalist form of industrial enterprise survives. What it shows no signs of doing is finding any more solid basis for answering Judge Ellison's question than he himself could discover a hundred years ago.

NOTES

1. Quoted by the Webbs in *Industrial Democracy*, WEA, London, 1913, p. 229.
2. *Capital*, vol. 1.
3. TUC, *Annual Report*, 1964, pp. 384–5.
4. Cf. Michael Barratt Brown, 'The Growth and Distribution of the National Income', in Ken Coates, *What Went Wrong?* Spokesman, 1979, pp. 60–1. Source of figures in this table: 1860–9 to 1960–3: C. H. Feinstein, *The Distribution of National Income*, Macmillan, 1968, Table 1, pp. 116–17, as adapted by J. King and T. Regan, *Relative Income Shares*, Macmillan, 1978, Table 1, p. 19. 1964–8 and 1969–73: King and Regan, *op. cit.*, Table 1, p 19. 1974–78: Michael Barratt Brown, from National Income and Expenditure Data.

CHAPTER 8

Strikes

The Occurrence of Strikes

The author of the classic book on strikes offers us the following definition: a strike is, he tells us: 'a temporary stoppage of work by a group of employees in order to express a grievance or enforce a demand'.[1] This formula draws attention to the central features of a strike – its temporary nature (the strikers intend to return to work eventually), the fact that it is an action by employed persons (not self-employed or employers), and the fact that it is purposeful, that there exists an objective to be achieved. It is noticeable that there is no reference to trade unions. Strikes by unorganized groups of workpeople can and do take place without the presence or engagement of a union. At the same time, strikes have a most intimate relationship with trade unionism, and it is one of the purposes of this chapter to explore this.

Strikes are simply the most visible and measurable manifestation of conflict between the owners and/or managers of industry, and their employees. There are many other forms which this conflict may take, including lockouts, autocratic forms of supervision, speed-up of work, disciplinary sackings, output restriction, labour turnover, sickness and accident rates, absenteeism, overtime bans, working-to-rule, sit-ins, work-ins, and sabotage. Some of these forms are deliberate and organized, some spontaneous and unplanned, some are initiated by workers, some by managers.[2]

If strikes are only one expression of industrial conflict, they are themselves a complex phenomenon; they cannot be regarded as 'a simple category of social action' since the social conditions which stimulate some kinds of strike, can lead to the diminution of other kinds.[3] For some thinkers, the continued presence of discontent among workers, as expressed in the postwar records of strikes, must be a puzzling affair, difficult to explain rationally. For instance, Talcott Parsons believes that:

> Through industrial development under democratic auspices, the most importantly legitimately-to-be-expected aspirations of the 'working class' have, in fact, been realized.[4]

This kind of thinking leads in the direction of a 'unitary' theory of industrial relations, which claims that within the employment relationship employers and employees share common goals and mutual interests, which should normally produce a state of industrial harmony. If working people are indeed satisfied in their aspirations and employed in socially harmonious conditions, then only two possible explanations of strikes appear credible: either workers are ignorant of their true situation, and therefore act irrationally when they strike, or they are deliberately misled by 'trouble-makers' and political extremists. The remedies for strikes which follow from these theories then vary between attempts at the improvement of 'communications' between management and workers on the one side: and the disciplining and dismissal of strike leaders, or political or legal constraints on strikers and trade unions, on the other. These remedies have been tried from time to time, with none but a temporary effect; indeed they have sometimes led to an increase in strike action. A considerable body of academic literature on strikes has shown that the conspiracy theory is to say the least implausible:[5] while there is no evidence that an improved flow of information from management to workers will dissipate workers' grievances. On the contrary, there are times when it may well augment them. Since 1979, government (invariably) and employers (less consistently) have acted in disputes according to the unitary view of strikes. During this period, the incidence of strikes has fallen substantially. However, the relationship of cause and effect between the two factors is not simple; strikes become more infrequent for other reasons: above all, because of prolonged large-scale unemployment, but also because of associated fragmentation in the labour markets. Trade union weaknesses have played their part in this story, to say nothing of the hostile legal climate in which contemporary strikes take place.

Strikes are best understood by combining a study of the social and economic circumstances in which they occur, with studies of the beliefs and attitudes of strikers; including, of course, their interpretation and understanding of their place in industry and society, which in turn are influenced by specific experiences of industrial relations in particular countries, industries, companies, and plants, and by the forms of collective organization (trade unionism) which have developed there. In the Western world at least, the alienation of the worker which generates conflict is certainly attributable to capitalism's treatment of labour as a commodity – a thing to be bought and sold in the pursuit of profit. Whether this conflict expresses itself in strikes will depend on a complex of factors: Talcott Parsons notwithstanding, one of the main achievements of industrial capitalism is that it has created 'legitimately-to-be-expected' aspirations even larger in volume and richer in cost, while not always meeting them. Most recently, strikes have been less about the expression of aspiration, and more about the defence of existing status, either on wages or job security. It is entirely reasonable to claim that:

> Strike action shows every sign of being endemic to capitalism. It is an historical phenomenon which has persisted through radical changes in living standards. It is a spreading phenomenon which is overcoming all manner of social barriers . . . It has defied all prescribed solutions, both prophylactic and punitive.[6]

Industrial conflict and strikes occur also in the socialized economies of Eastern Europe and Soviet Russia,[7] sometimes, as in Poland, accompanied by considerable violence. Whilst strikes may be 'endemic' to capitalism, they are not unique to it; alienation may also be produced by bureaucratic, undemocratic administration of large-scale industrialized societies under public ownership. Even in the worker self-management system of Yugoslavia strikes are fairly common, and have been intelligently ackowledged by the authorities in that country as symptoms and indicators of the malfunctioning of that system.[8] The incidence of small, short, 'unofficial' strikes, principally about wages in an economy of 100 per cent annual inflation, and invariably successful, rose sharply in Yugoslavia during 1986. This phenomenon has some curious parallels with the sociology of the UK strike pattern of the 1950s and 1960s. The Yugoslav workers appear to be following the British into more difficult, prolonged strikes in 1987, a year in which government policies are generating a large increase in job losses in Yugoslav manufacturing industry, and a wage freeze.

Measuring Strikes

An important aspect of the study of strikes is the analysis of strike statistics.

The official source of this information in Britain is the Department of Employment's monthly *Gazette* which together with its predecessors from the Board of Trade and the Ministry of Labour, has been collecting and publishing information on strikes since the last decade of the nineteenth-century. Most Western industrial countries have a similar central source of information, and international strike statistics are collected and published by the International Labour Organization in its *Year Book of Labour Statistics*. British statistics are limited as follows:

> The official series of statistics of stoppage of work due to industrial disputes in the UK relates to disputes connected with terms and conditions of employment. Stoppages involving fewer than ten workers or lasting less than one day are excluded except where the aggregate of working days lost exceeded 100. Workers involved are those directly involved and indirectly involved (thrown out of work although not parties to the dispute) *at the establishment where the dispute occurred*. The number of working days lost is the aggregate of days lost by workers both directly and indirectly involved (as defined). It follows that the statistics

do *not* reflect repercussions elsewhere, that is, *at establishments other than those at which the disputes occurred.*[9]

Notice that these limitations mean that political strikes are excluded, and whilst these have normally been of the most negligible significance, they have, since 1970, become more important, as we shall see. Very small and short-lived strikes are also excluded, and Professor Turner has estimated that 30 per cent of mining strikes, and 80 per cent of strikes in the car industry, have been excluded from the official statistics for this reason.[10]

Whilst this represents a deficiency in the official statistics, it is important that it should not be exaggerated, as the *Sunday Times* has attempted to do.[11] For instance, the privately collected car manufacturers' statistics which are the basis of Turner's comparisons with those of the Department of Employment, included such minor 'stoppages' as 'shop stewards coming back late from lunch-hour committee meetings' and another of a strike costing a mere seventeen man-hours.[12]

The Department of Employment relies for the collection of its figures upon information supplied by managers, supplemented by the monitoring of the press both local and national. The role of management in this process gives rise to some concern, since 'management often have the power to define a situation as a strike or not' and there is some evidence that where management feel themselves to have been in the wrong, they may not always notify the authorities fully about what has happened.[13]

This may lead to the under-representation of strikes on issues such as safety and working conditions, and a consequent exaggeration of strikes about wages, in the official statistics. A further omission from the information is the level at which strike action occurs – work group, section, plant, company, industry – a dimension which has major sociological interest.[14]

These reservations do not invalidate the use of official statistics; the omission of the smallest and shortest strikes does not amount to the neglect of anything of serious economic consequence – these brief affairs are best considered as part of the unquantifiable but sociologically significant underworld of endemic industrial unrest – and the official series are consistent in their criteria, thus enabling us properly to use them to identify *trends* in strikes. The same things may be said about comparative international strike statistics; although different countries have different criteria for their statistical series, so that there is legitimate controversy about their absolute position in the international league table,[15] the internal consistency of the multiple series makes possible, as we shall see, a valid comparison of relative trends between countries.

Three key measures are available in the British figures: the number of strikes, the number of workers involved, and the number of 'working days lost'. The latter official terminology has been rightly criticized as emotive and questionable; a more neutral description which we shall use is 'number of striker days'. From these statistics can be derived also the average duration of stoppages, and the average number of workers per strike. The Department of Employment also publishes tables indicating the causes of strikes as reported to it, on the number of strikes of varying duration, disaggregated figures for the major industries and regions, and figures of strikes 'known to be official' as compared with what are assumed to be unofficial strikes.

Beyond these bare figures of strike incidence lies the question as to how much economic disruption is caused by strikes. What do strikes cost and who bears the cost? We shall deal later with the cost of strikes to strikers themselves and to their unions. At this stage we are concerned with the cost to the employer and the economy. In fact there is little or no statistical evidence about this aspect of strikes, but what there is suggests that the economic effects of strikes are frequently exaggerated and that they are in general of a minimal nature. For example, one of the few case studies available, of an official strike in printing in 1959, showed that the 2½ per cent pay rise which was conceded by the employers to settle the issue would, if not passed on, have reduced employers' profits by 1¼ per cent of total turnover.[16] There have been some spectacular cases of employers making a profit from a strike. This happened in the major national dispute in the Post Office in 1971, when the loss-making postal service closed down, whilst the profit-making telephone side of the organization's services expanded. In other instances, notably in the car industry, strikes are sometimes provoked and 'used' by employers as a substitute for lay-offs during periods of slack demand, or during re-tooling for a new model.[17]

Of course, it is true that some strikes, which take on the aspect of a major trial of strength in strategically key areas of the economy, may inflict economic damage. In the first half of the 1920s, in the early 1970s, in 1978–9, and again in 1984–5, such contests assumed high significance; industries in this category include coal, rail, steel, the ports, the merchant service, gas, water and electricity, and finally education. But even here, the economic effect is likely to be temporary.

An important controversy arose around the conclusion of the Donovan Royal Commission in 1968 that the short, small, unofficial and unconstitutional strikes (which dominated the strike statistics at the time) were peculiarly damaging because they were unpredictable, and inhibiting of management initiative. Apart from the consideration that it is unlikely that this type of strike was a particularly British phenomenon, the comment of Dr W. E. J. McCarthy is apposite:

> . . . I have always thought that the Donovan Report grossly oversold the psychological deterrent effect of strikes; it has always seemed to me a managerial excuse, the first refuge of the lazy and the last ditch of the cowardly.[18]

In most successful strikes, there is an increase in the solidarity of the workforce, which often carries over after the dispute, in increased collective willingness to work overtime, or to raise output under incentive payment schemes. The workers may be additionally motivated to do this by their need to recoup lost wages. All this minimizes the economic loss of the strike. This effect was powerfully demonstrated, not just for short plant-level stoppages, but on a national scale, in the three-day week (which was tantamount to a partial national lockout) during the coal dispute of 1973–4; because managers and workers had a common interest in maintaining production, much co-operative ingenuity was applied to the problem, and the result was a remarkably sustained level of total output. Evans and Creigh concluded their essay on the economic costs of strikes by saying that 'many of the charges levelled against strikes on economic grounds seem to rest on rather dubious evidence'.[19] Of course, strikes which result in defeat may well create demoralization, and therefore lower productivity, in the aftermath.

This conclusion, it may be argued, may apply to allegations about the 'loss of production' but is surely invalid if we consider the effect of strikes upon wage-price inflation?

The same authors maintain the same scepticism in this matter also, citing in support the evidence of other specialist research, which concluded that 'the role of strikes [in money-wage inflation] was a minor one',[20] and that 'the direct effect of strikes in pushing up wages or arresting their fall does not seem to have been very great'.[21] By itself, the single year of 1974, which saw a large strike incidence and a wage explosion of unprecedented proportions, cannot offer evidence to refute the much longer-term studies of the earlier years. That year merits careful analysis, not because it was typical, but because it shows us a window on to the limits of our present system of industrial relations.

It is worthwhile also to point to the figures of other causes of lost production in weighing these controversies; in 1970 for example, whilst 10 million days were 'lost' through strikes, industrial accidents accounted for 20 million days, unemployment (at 1 million workers) for 200 million days, and certified sickness for 300 million days.[22] Another calculation, in 1973, showed that 'the average union member goes on strike once (and sometimes more) every twelve years, for a period of about two and a half days at a time'.[23]

Of course, average figures may conceal major variations in the experience of different industries (we return to this subject later) and between different establishments within an industry. The peculiarly strike-prone *plant* is a well-known phenomenon and in these cases economic loss may be real enough. In engineering, an apparently strike-prone industry, it has been shown that, in the period from 1960 to 1966, only 9 per cent of the 1,000 federated firms investigated experienced any unconstitutional stoppages (a category of strike which accounted for 96 per cent of all stoppages by manual workers).[24] In another study, it was shown that of 432 engineering establishments surveyed, 38 per cent had been free of strikes (even including brief stoppages down to a half-hour duration), that under 1 per cent (just three establishments) had over 40 per cent of the strikes; and 5 per cent had 65 per cent of them. Almost 80 per cent of the managements 'would think of themselves as strike free'.[25]

Table 8.1

Number of strikes, number of workers involved, and striker days in the UK, 1889–1987

	Number of strikes	Number of workers involved (000s)	Striker days (000,000s)
1889–91*	1,050	340	7.1
1892–6	760	360	13.3
1897–1901	720	210	7.1
1902–6	410	160	2.6
1907–11	570	440	7.2
1912–16	890	660	13.2
1917–21	1,120	1,660	31.8
1922–6	570	950	41.8
1927–31	380	310	4.4
1932–6	520	250	2.5
1937–41	1,020	370	1.6
1942–6	1,960	580	2.4
1947–51	1,590	430	1.9
1952–6	2,100	680	2.5
1957–61	2,630	830	4.6
1962	2,449	4,420	5.8
1963	2,068	590	1.8
1964	2,524	872	2.3
1965	2,354	868	2.9
1966	1,937	530	2.4
1967	2,116	731	2.8

	Number of strikes	Number of workers involved (000s)	Striker days (000,000s)
1968	2,378	2,255	4.7
1969	3,116	1,654	6.8
1970	3,906	1,793	11.0
1971	2,228	1,171	13.6
1972	2,497	1,722	24.0
1973	2,873	1,513	7.2
1974	2,922	1,622	14.8
1975	2,282	789	6.0
1976	2,016	666	3.3
1977	2,703	1,155	10.1
1978	2,471	1,001	9.4
1979	2,080	4,583	29.5
1980	1,330	830	12.0
1981	1,338	1,499	4.3
1982	1,528	2,101	5.3
1983	1,352	573	3.8
1984	1,206	1,436	27.1
1985	887	643	6.4
1986	1,053	538	1.9
1987**	574	705	3.1

* Figures for the years 1889–1961 have been given as five-yearly annual averages, except for 1889–91, which is a three-year annual average.

** First seven months of the year.

Source: Department of Employment.

Table 8.1 presents the historical record of British strikes in the twentieth century, derived from the official statistics. With its aid we can trace the main trends and delineate the different phases into which this history falls. Column 1 of the table measures the number of separate occasions per annum on which some group of workers took action. Column 2 indicates the number of workers involved in actions during the year, and column 3 the number of striker days. Thus columns 2 and 3 provide different measures of the scale and severity of the strikes recorded in column 1.

Historical Patterns

The 1890s were marked by some severe contests as trade unions came under attack from anti-union employers who were determined to reverse the gains made by the 'new unions' in the 1880s. The older craft unions were also subject to a prolonged rearguard action in 1897 in the engineering industry. After a lull in the first decade of the twentieth century, the first wave of modern, large-scale, industry-level strikes occurred during the syndicalist period of 1910–14, involving notably the mining, inland road transport, docks and railway industries, in which a new generation of militants fought with considerable success for recognition, negotiating rights, and wage increases.

During the First World War, strikes were made illegal, and the official national strike almost disappeared, to be replaced by an escalating number of short, localized, unofficial disputes associated with the rise of the shop stewards' movement. After the war, the militants resumed their large aggressive actions but were soon, after the short postwar boom of 1919–20, driven on to the defensive, from which position they sustained what was historically the highest ever level of strike action (particularly as measured by the scale of the strikes, rather than their number) against wage cuts and a mounting offensive by employers against union encroachment on their prerogatives. This phase culminated in the General Strike of 1926, in which year it should be noted that of the 162 million striker days, only 15 million were caused by the General Strike itself; the rest were the result of the prolonged lockout of the miners which lasted from May to November.[26]

The General Strike and the miners' lock-out represent the most severe defeat ever suffered by the British trade union movement, and the ensuing demoralization, decline in union membership, and the onset of the world slump in 1929 which persisted through most of the thirties combined with a new mood of subservience and respectability amongst trade union leaders to produce through the 1930s the lowest records of twentieth-century strike action. However, during the Second World War, when strikes were again made illegal, the number of strikes rose sharply, yet because these strikes were of a different character from the 1920s, being short, small, and unofficial, the number of striker days remained at the low levels of the 1930s.

The wartime experience is instructive; the legal ban on strikes and the institution of compulsory arbitration in disputes were totally effective in dissuading unions from supporting strikes, but were clearly ineffective in preventing unofficial stoppages. One, then youthful, strike leader has testified to the casual and disrespectful attitude which he and his fellows harboured towards the law.

> Six of us, apprentices at Metro-Vickers and other factories in Manchester, were dragged into court in 1941, probably one of the prosecutions under the new regulations which Ernie Bevin had introduced at the Ministry of Labour during the war. You were supposed to give twenty-one days notice of disputes, but we were only kids, between 16 and 20, and we didn't know about niceties like that . . . Eventually they found us guilty and bound us over not to do it again. Platts Mills in court tried to hold things up by trying to get them to make Ernie Bevin come up from London and give evidence that he hadn't been notified of the strike. And there were hilarious scenes in court when they tried to prove that we were out on strike.[27]

By October 1941 there had been over 1,000 illegal strikes, but only six such prosecutions. Another of these was the famous affair of the strike by 1,000 miners at the Betteshanger colliery in Kent, whose mass summons was made the occasion for a carnival procession by the local mining community, complete with brass bands, the result of which was to ridicule the Regulation.[28] Despite this, in 1944, Bevin's Department forged a new weapon in the Defence Regulation 1AA, which made even incitement to strike an offence; the Regulation was never used and was hastily revoked the following year.[29]

It is useful to compare the strike record of the war years for another reason. This concerns the common assumptions made in newspapers (and elsewhere) about the relation between agitators, particularly communists, and the incidence of strikes. Between 1939 and 1945 the figures were as shown in Table 8.2.

Table 8.2

Number of strikes, number of workers involved and number of striker days, 1939–45, Great Britain

Year	Number of strikes	Number of work-people directly and indirectly involved (000s)	Striker days (000s)
1939	940	337	1,356
1940	922	299	940
1941	1,251	360	1,079
1942	1,303	456	1,527
1943	1,785	557	1,808
1944	2,194	821	3,714
1945	2,293	531	2,835

At the beginning of the Second World War, the Communist Party policy was to support strikes. The result was that in 1940 there were eighteen *less* strikes, involving 416,000 less workdays than had been the case in 1939. When Russia was attacked in mid-1941, the Communist Party adopted a policy of strong opposition to strikes, and worked hard to make a success of joint production committees. Its wartime conferences of shop stewards were thenceforward widely and sympathetically reported in the press. The result? Strikes increased to 1,251 in 1941, and then, each year, to 1,303; 1,785; 2,194 and 2,293, while striker days rose to a peak of over 3,700,000 by 1944.

(This number of strikes was the highest hitherto recorded, yet the number of striker days is not high by either the standards of the twenties or the seventies.) All this evidence casts doubt on the assumptions of those who think they can reduce industrial discord by hunting for witches. A postwar triumvirate of Will

Lawther (NUM), Arthur Deakin (TGWU), and Tom Williamson (GMWU), controlled TUC policy and held together a firm anti-strike policy, in keeping with their uncritical loyalty to the Labour government. This included a continuing tolerance of the wartime Order 1305 banning strikes, into peacetime circumstances. Between 1945 and 1950, there were nevertheless 10,000 strikes – all of them illegal.[30] There were no postwar prosecutions, and in 1951 the Order was repealed. Between 1933 and 1953 there had not been one single official national strike.

After resuming their legality, the characteristic strike of the 1950s and 1960s continued to be the short, small, unofficial dispute, although official strikes began to make their reappearance on the railways, the docks, and in printing in 1955, in shipbuilding and engineering in 1957,[31] and on the London buses in 1958. In the last two cases at least, a new factor was to emerge as central to an understanding of postwar trends: namely government wage restraint policies.

In the London bus strike the TGWU, led by Frank Cousins, the more militant successor to Arthur Deakin, gave official support to its members, whose pay claim was resisted by the government (the ultimate sources of finance for the London Passenger Transport Board) in the name of its declared policy of wage restraint.

As the strike became more and more prolonged, and was clearly being undermined by private car transport and the London underground, Cousins approached the TUC for support, citing Rule 11 of the TUC's constitution. The initial response of the TUC was to declare its support for the strike, and its conviction that its cause was to be laid at the government's door.

> Government policy has brought London's buses to a standstill. Having mismanaged the economy the Government has chosen the pay claim of London's busmen to put pressure on a public employer to conform to its policy of holding down wages and to bolster the resistance of private employers . . . This strike has been made unavoidable by the Government's determination to hold down wages in publicly-owned industries and services, which, in times of rising prices, can only be done by cutting the living standards of the workers concerned.

The TUC General Council participated in negotiations with the government, including meetings with the Prime Minister, during which the TGWU accepted the initiatives of the TUC and collaborated with them. These negotiations collapsed, and Frank Cousins was faced with the question, which he posed to the TUC General Council, as to 'how soon was this strike going to be developed into something that somebody was going to take notice of?' He proposed an extension of the action, to call out TGWU members who drove petrol bowsers into London, and who worked in London's power stations. The government responded by cancelling weekend leave for troops in the London area, and affirmed that it would ensure supplies of petrol and electricity to the capital. Cousins then asked the General Council whether they would follow 'normal trade union practice' by treating energy and fuel supplied by troops as 'black'. A positive response to this request would have seemed almost mandatory for the General Council, bearing in mind the wording of Rule 11(d) of its constitution, under which its participation in the dispute was taking place. The clause reads:

> Where the Council intervenes [in a dispute] as herein provided, and the organization or organizations concerned accept the assistance and advice of the Council, and where despite the efforts of the Council, the policy of the employers enforces a stoppage of work by strike or lock-out, the Council shall forthwith take all steps to organize on behalf of the organization or organizations concerned all such moral and material support as the circumstances of the dispute may appear to justify.

This clause (which still exists today) appears almost tailor-made for the 1958 London bus strike. Yet the General Council members beat a hasty retreat from their previous stand of verbal and financial solidarity with the strike, and in an angry debate with Cousins, in which there were many references to the dangers of a 1926 type of conflict with government, told him that they would not support the proposed extension of the strike, and even threatened that any such extension would result in the withdrawal of the TUC's earlier appeal for financial support from other unions for the strikers. The Council bluntly advised Cousins to resume negotiations; the busmen were thus effectively isolated and compelled to accept a compromise settlement. The implications of this episode, which highlights the self-imposed limitations on solidarity action by the TUC, are of permanent significance during the whole subsequent period to the present day; public service strikes have constantly posed the same questions for the TUC as Frank Cousins did in 1958, and the TUC has constantly avoided the issue.[32]

During the 1950s and 1960s, a significant trend was at work which was concealed within the aggregate figures of numbers of strikes. The mining industry in the 1950s dominated the strike field. This predominance came to a peak in 1957, when mining accounted for 2,224 strikes out of a total of 2,859. These miners' strikes were overwhelmingly local affairs, caused either by disputes over rate-fixing in the decentralized system of incentive payments then in operation, or by disagreements on the interpretation of such contracts. Yet by 1968 a remarkable reversal of the situation was completed; in that year there were a mere 219 strikes, following a steady fall over the previous ten years. The decline was the result of the reduced bargaining power of the miners in a multi-fuel market in which oil and gas competed more and more lethally, and a consequent large-scale reduction in the mining labour force. This was complemented in 1966 by the conclusion of a new National Power Loading Agreement between the NCB and the NUM, which effectively centralized wage bargaining and ended local tonnage rates.[33]

Remarkably, outside the mining industry, there was a fivefold increase in numbers of strikes during the very years of the decline in mining strikes. The credit for uncovering this trend belongs to Professor H. A. Turner[34] but the phenomenon was soon the focus of less dispassionate attention, and the examination of the rise of non-mining strikes, most evident in engineering and the car industry, but spreading to other manufacturing, came to dominate the literature and the political debate about Britain's 'strike problem' in the 1960s. It received much attention from the

Donovan Royal Commission and provided some of the rationale behind the proposals of the Labour government's White Paper *In Place of Strife*, of 1969, and of the Conservative Party's policy document *Fair Deal at Work*, of 1968, each of which set out to create legal penalties for certain types of strike. But both sets of party proposals ignored the more sophisticated pluralist views of the Donovan Commission, and leaned heavily on a simplistic unitary view of industrial relations, the Tories comprehensively, and Labour at least in respect of shopfloor conflict.[35]

But hardly was the ink dry on these proposed remedies, than the nature and scale of strike incidence began to change. Whilst during the furore over the unofficial strikes of the early and middle sixties the number of striker days increased hardly at all compared with the whole previous period back to the 1920s, it did grow with remorseless regularity thereafter. In 1966 there were 2.4 million days involved: this had risen to 24 million days in 1972, a figure which had not been remotely approached since the 1920s. Clearly this provides yet another distinct phase in the recent history. This new period was characterized by the re-establishment of a pattern of long, official national strikes. Only a few of these are required in any year to send the number of striker days rocketing: for example, the forty-five-day strike by the UPW in 1971 accounted for 6.3 million days out of the year's total of 13.6 million. Whilst, during the early sixties, only five really large strikes per year had been occurring there were twenty of this type in the years 1969–70.[36] During the years following 1969, strikes spread to previously strike-free groups, especially amongst public employees such as dustmen, teachers, hospital workers, and postmen. Trade union membership was growing rapidly at this time (after its long postwar plateau at around 8 million) and an increasing number of strikes involved groups seeking recognition and negotiating rights. Long-quiescent groups and long-unionized industries in clothing, steel and glass[37] took up the strike weapon, and there were revivals of strikes amongst car workers and above all by the miners.[38]

This last case is instructive. We have shown that the NCB and NUM had previously, in 1966, brought wage bargaining in the industry under central direction. Undoubtedly at the time this reflected a managerial strategy to regain control of wages, to check wage drift and reduce pit-level strikes. But the effect on the miners and their union was to re-create the much earlier tradition of concern for the *industry* wage level, to make them aware of their declining position in the national wages league[39] and to eliminate their bargaining power at any level lower than that of the *whole* union. The oil price explosion was a late contributor to the rediscovery of the miners' power, and together these causes issued into the two great national mining strikes of 1972 and 1974.

The increasingly political character of the large strikes of the 1970s is clearly evident, and the role of government wage restraint policies was central, so that the collapse of the Conservative government after the second miners' strike was predictable. Yet Mr Heath was defeated in a General Election, not an insurrection: and he lost votes whilst his opponents failed to win them. Not only incomes policy, but the whole trend of legislative intervention from the Industrial Relations Act in 1971, to the social contract legislation of 1974–6, was bound to involve the state more actively in the strike scene. And the changing nature of trade union leadership (as evidenced by the initiative of two new leaders, Jack Jones and Hugh Scanlon, who early in their tenure of office took decisive steps to recognize and support the unconstitutional strike at Fords in 1969) combined with the increasing militancy and frustration of the membership under successive incomes policies ensured that official strikes became much more common. 1972 was a peak year, and only 1979 and 1984 record levels of strikes comparable with it; the most notable feature of the 1970s and 1980s is the volatility of the figures. In certain years, particularly 1973 and 1975–6, workers and unions appear to accept the wage norms imposed by incomes policy. At other times the dam bursts and strike action rises again. This happened most recently between 1977 and 1979. Of course there was undoubtedly a political element in the explanation of the lull of 1975–6, when Labour in office was delivering some of the most important parts of the promised social contract legislation, for the unions. If the strike wave broke during the 1980s, its collapse was interrupted by a succession of large, spectacular strikes in mining, printing, steel and education. This new pattern has been caused by a number of factors. These include: the changing composition of the workforce, leading to a divided and fragmented labour force; mass unemployment; the new laws which aim to discourage and penalize strikers and their unions; the decline in the social and economic status and power of trade unions consequent upon the first three causes; more active, even sometimes fierce police action against pickets and demonstrators; employer intransigence arising from enhanced bargaining power; and the withdrawal by government of social security payments for strikers' families. In some cases, also, there has been a misreading of the workers' total situation by trade union leaderships. Further, of course, some pressures which had caused high strike levels were actually taken off by reduced rates of inflation.

The decline of strikes during the 1980s is somewhat disguised to the casual observer, because a very few large-scale stoppages have held up the overall statistics of incidence, as witnessed by the following;

> in *1979* a strike by *engineering workers* accounted for 16.0 million (54 per cent) of the total of 29.5 million working days lost in that year; a strike by *public service and hospital ancillary workers* contributed 3.2 million days (11 per cent); and a stoppage by *drivers and other grades* in the transport and communication industry was responsible for another million lost days (3 per cent);
>
> in *1980*, the *national steel strike* accounted for 8.8 million (74 per cent) of the total of 12.0 million working days lost;
>
> in *1981*, one dispute by *civil servants* contributed 0.9 million days (20 per cent) of the total of 4.3 million working days lost;

in *1982*, three strikes, two of which were in connection with a dispute involving *National Health Service* staff and the other involving *railway workers*, accounted in total for 2.3 million (43 per cent) of the 5.3 million days lost in that year;

in *1983*, a dispute by workers in the *electricity, gas and water* industry accounted for 0.8 million (20 per cent) of the total of 3.8 million days lost;

in *1984*, the *miners' strike* in protest over pit closures accounted for 22.3 million (82 per cent) of the total of 27.1 million working days lost;

in *1985* the continuation of the *miners' strike* accounted for 4.0 million (63 per cent) of the 6.3 million days lost, whilst national strikes by *teachers* over pay contributed a further 0.8 (13 per cent) million days lost;

The above illustrations show that it is not uncommon for figures for a particular year to be affected by the incidence of one or more large stoppages. As a result, comparisons among individual years need to be made in the light of the incidence of large stoppages.[40]

The total of 6.4 million striker days in 1985 compares with 27.1 million in 1984 and a twenty-year average for 1965–84 of 10 million. There were eleven occasions in the twenty-year period when more striker days were recorded than the total for 1985. If the United Kingdom has now entered a phase of 'industrial peace', it has done so at enormous cost to morale, equity, efficiency and sheer human kindness. What the country has certainly not entered into is a state of unitary bliss; the conflicts of interest remain, even whilst their expression is suppressed – more or less effectively – by repressive laws, oppressive government/employer responses, and a mass of unemployment, itself a conscious by-product of government policies. The government would claim lower inflation as a positive gain from their repression of the strike; but wage increases still in 1986–7 outstrip the rate of inflation, so cause and effect are by no means demonstrated in this matter.

Table 8.3

Striker days per 1,000 workers in mining, manufacturing, construction and transport, 1970–84*

Countries: in rank order for 1970	1970	1972	1974	1976	1978	1980	1982	1984	Rank order of averages for 10 years 1970–9	5 years 1980–4
United States	2,210	860	1,480	1,190	1,070	540	300	160	6th	10th
Canada	2,190	800	2,550	2,550	1,930	1,510	1,410	930	1st	2nd
Italy	1,730	1,670	1,800	2,310	890	1,630	1,930	730	2nd	1st
India	1,440	1,300	2,480	830	1,650	—	—	—	3rd	—
Australia	1,040	880	2,670	1,430	960	1,360	900	510	4th	4th
Belgium	830	190	340	560	650	140	—	—	12th	14th
United Kingdom	740	2,160	1,270	300	840	1,150	460	3,120	9th	3rd
Irish Republic	490	600	1,240	840	1,610	650	630	650	8th	7th
New Zealand	470	300	360	950	790	750	710	960	11th	6th
Finland	270	520	470	1,310	160	1,250	220	690	7th	8th
Spain	240	120	310	2,540	1,820	—	—	—	5th	—
Japan	200	270	450	150	60	50	20	20	14th	18th
France	180	300	250	420	200	170	260	170	13th	13th

Striker days per 1,000 workers in mining, manufacturing, construction and transport, 1970–84*

Countries: in rank order for 1970	1970	1972	1974	1976	1978	1980	1982	1984	Rank order of averages for 10 years 1970–9	Rank order of averages for 5 years 1980–4
Denmark	170	40	330	220	90	210	100	150	10th	12th
Netherlands	140	300	—	10	—	30	60	—	17th	17th
Norway	70	—	490	70	90	140	390	60	16th	15th
Sweden	40	10	30	20	10	2,240	—	20	18th	9th
Germany (FR)	10	10	60	40	370	10	—	510	15th	16th
Average for the year:	692	608	975	874	771	739	567	620		
Index of yearly average:	100	88	141	126	111	107	82	90		

— = not available.

Source: International Labour Office

*The figures are restricted mainly to these four relatively strike-prone industry groups by the ILO to reduce the effects of different industrial structures and so improve the basis of comparison of strike rates between the countries.

International Comparisons

Reference to Table 8.3 shows that Britain's position in the international league table of strike-proneness varies considerably from year to year. There is nothing here to indicate a unique degree of industrial unrest for this country. It could be said, however, that Britain appears to belong in the top half of the table, amongst countries which have volatile records. In the bottom half of the table there is more consistency; Denmark, Netherlands, Norway, Sweden and West Germany have a consistently low record of strikes. (Even here, however, we must record the 1983 German engineering strike, which was certainly big, and Denmark's mini general strike of 1983.)

Britain's reputation for strikes seems to depend on the record of a slightly earlier period than that covered by the table. Between 1951 and 1974, Britain shared top place with Australia in the growth of the number of striker days, but only thirteenth and twelfth place respectively in growth of numbers of strikes and numbers of workers involved. Britain shared in the rising incidence of strikes from the 1950s to the 1970s, and its record reflects the fact that strikes in this country changed character through the postwar period, from predominance of small disputes to large ones.

From 1970, as we can see from the index numbers in our table, the strike-wave of the 1950s and 1960s peaked in 1974, and thereafter the tide turned. The decline which set in was only arrested in 1984. But in that year, the up-turn was entirely due to Britain's figure of 3,120 striker days per 1,000 workers in the selected strike-prone industries of the table. In other words, the much-vaunted claim of the British government to have solved the strike problem with its new laws and 'new realism' only holds up to scrutiny if it is allowed that the very largest strikes, such as the miners' dispute of 1984–5, don't count!

General Explanations of Strikes

Our review of recent trends adds interest to the literature on strikes which seeks general explanations of the causes of strikes. One of the earliest modern enquiries is that of K. G. J. C. Knowles.[41] His work inevitably suffers from being outdated, but remains a valuable general discussion of the subject. In particular, he suggested a threefold classification of strikes according to different causes, as follows: (a) Basic issues, including wage increases and decreases, other wage questions, and hours of labour, (b) Frictional issues, including the employment of certain classes of persons, other working arrangements, rules and discipline, (c) Solidarity issues, including trade union principles and sympathetic action. The sub-categories are derived from the original official statistics of the Ministry of Labour, and the use of 'single-cause' classification is subject to the reservation that most strikes are 'multi-causal'. The results of the analysis, based on the years 1927–36, show for example that the mining industry was high on solidarity strikes, but low on basic strikes, which serves to illustrate the limitations of an investigation confined to a few years, since in the years both before and after these, miners' strikes were overwhelmingly about basic issues. But Knowles's work does draw attention to the important category of 'frictional' issues, to which we shall return.

Ross and Hartman conducted a famous enquiry on an international basis.[42] They explained strikes as the products of industrial relations 'systems' in which key influences included the age of the Labour movement and the stability of trade union membership, factionalism and the presence of a Communist Party influence in the trade unions, the degree of employer recognition of trade unions, and a consolidated bargaining structure, the role of Labour parties and Labour governments, and the role of the state in industrial relations. They found in the British case a low level of trade union member involvement in strikes, which were mainly of short duration. The proportion of British trade union members engaging in strikes had fallen from 16.1 per cent in 1900–29, to 5.9 per cent in 1948–56, and the average duration of strikes from 23 days to 4.3 days. They found this to be part of a general 'withering away of the strike' internationally, which they explained by reference to the ending of the historical struggle for trade union recognition, the evolution of a mature trade union–management relationship, and an organized labour market which 'institutionalized' industrial conflict, together with the turning of labour's attention to the political sphere and the election of Labour governments. This analysis may offer a partial explanation of the period studied, but has clearly proved, in the light of subsequent experience, to be hopelessly lacking in predictive value. Above all it ignores the fact that the balance of class power established in the slump years of the 1930s and carried over for a time into the early postwar period, was disadvantageous to labour, which would seek to redress the balance, given the opportunity.

Kerr and Siegel were responsible for another well-known attempt at a global analysis of strike records.[43] They studied the comparative strike levels of different industries in eleven countries, and concluded that the high strike-proneness of mining, the merchant service, the docks, lumber and textiles was due to their characteristics as single-industry communities, with little occupational differentiation, the geographical or social isolation of their communities, and strong group cohesion. Low strike-proneness in agriculture, trade, railways, clothing, gas, electricity and water, and in services like hotels and restaurants, they attributed to the opposite characteristics; these industries are located in multi-industry communities, with considerable occupational differentiation, integrated into the general society, or experiencing individual isolation, as on farms. In this interpretation, group cohesion is treated as crucial, and it clearly contributes to an explanation in the case of *some* groups such as, perhaps, dockers and miners. Even there it should be used with caution: some of the most close-knit mining communities have been among the least strike-prone, for instance. But it certainly does not apply consistently across all countries to other industries, and is a contributory factor anyway in so much of mass-employment manufacturing industry that it loses its edge as a specific causal influence in particular industries. The spread of strikes to wider and wider sectors of employment, such a notable feature ever since the 1960s, and occurring after the Kerr and Siegel work, is hard to explain in these terms.

Certainly, strike-proneness is a feature of some industries in Britain. Apart from mining, which as we have seen has been through a peculiar and unique evolution in postwar years, the top British industries for strikes are docks, motors, shipbuilding, iron and steel, aircraft and general engineering. Lowest strike figures are usually recorded for agriculture, distribution, finance and administration, gas, water, electricity and clothing. Several studies have however drawn attention to the increased spread of strikes in recent years, to industries previously immune.[44] Whilst the *level* of strikes remains uneven between industries (from 5 minutes per worker per year in distribution, to 6½ days per worker per year in docks, in 1973) the *trend* towards increased strikes has been *even*, across industries.[45] Hyman, following Goodman, notes that the top five industries accounted for 69 per cent of strikes in 1952, 52 per cent in 1965, and 47 per cent in 1970. (The trend has been slightly reversed since then; the figure for 1977 is 52 per cent.) In the light of this kind of evidence, theories which concentrate on explaining the situation in especially strike-prone industries will ignore much that is significant in the recent scene.

G. K. Ingham has subjected the Ross-Hartman thesis to searching criticism in the course of his comparative study of British and Scandinavian patterns of industrial conflict.[46] He finds that, far from belonging to a common 'North European' pattern of industrial relations, Britain and Scandinavia diverge in many respects, and the differences help to explain the higher strike figures in Britain. His thesis is that industrial concentration and a simple, specialized industrial structure in the small Scandinavian economies have led to centralization of industrial relations there, and a high level of 'institutionalization' of industrial conflict, and that the reverse is true of Britain. He contrasts, for example, the British TUC, 'which has displayed chronic constitutional and *de facto* weakness throughout its entire history' with its counterpart in the authoritative Swedish LO. The British economy he finds to be characterized by 'complexity, product differentiation, and relatively low industrial concentration', the results of being the first country to industrialize, so that craft workshop, mass production and automation technologies all co-exist and overlap. The employers' associations in the contrasted economies reflect the same features – there were 1,350 such associations in Britain in 1968, but only 44 in Sweden in 1961. British employers only succeeded in forming a unified central body (the Confederation of British Industry) in 1965, almost a hundred years after the foundation of the TUC. The structural complexity of British trade unionism contrasts with the simple industrial union structure of the Scandinavians. Hence the abiding character of British industrial relations, with its fragmented and decentralized collective bargaining and the strength of custom which survives at plant level, which contribute potently as sources of conflict and strikes. Britain's 'failure' to achieve the transition from customary to formal industrial relations lies at the heart of Britain's strike 'problem'. As a contribution to the debate, Ingham's thesis is certainly fruitful, but probably remains content with too great a dependence on the study of institutional superstructures. Surely the deeper reasons for the relative strike-proneness of Britain as compared with Scandinavia lie buried in the fundamental class divisions, historically and continually sharper and more antagonistic in Britain than in Northern Europe.

There is something in common between Ingham's thesis and that of the Donovan Royal Commission, which found Britain's industrial relations problem to consist in a lack of formality in collective bargaining. A study of a sample of 45 plants chosen from amongst both strike-prone and strike-free establishments in six different industries, throws some interesting light on this influential theory.[47] The strike records of the plants were examined for 1966–70 and correlated with various characteristics of management, and it was found that:

> . . . so far from declining with the establishment and development of formal collective agreements, conciliation procedures and consultative arrangements, or with increasing provision for regular trade union activities and representation within the enterprise, the incidence of labour unrest appears, if anything, to increase.[48]

Was the formalization of industrial relations a cause or an effect of labour unrest? The authors incline to the view that it was a cause. 'At the least, the proposition that formal arrangements for bargaining and union activity at the enterprise level necessarily encourage industrial peace must be highly suspect.'[49]

High and rising levels of trade union membership and high levels of strikes have often been correlated in British history, from the time of the Owenite movement in the 1830s, through the syndicalist period of 1910–14 and its succeeding phase up to 1926, and in the recent period of the late 1960s to 1977. The causal relationship between the two quantities is complex; it can as well be argued on the evidence that strikes stimulate trade union recruitment as that trade unions cause strikes. Certainly some of the most central features of British trade union structure and organization, such as the general unions, were born and expanded in the context of strike actions. But equally, the minimal commitment to collective action implied in *joining* a trade union is commonly required before workers will contemplate going on strike. Non-union strikers, where this precondition does not apply, invariably have as one of their purposes, the formation of a union organization and the obtaining of employer recognition for this: although of course this demand may be elaborated in the course of the dispute itself.

The relationship between strikes and the level of employment also deserves attention. The one durable period of full employment in our history, from 1940 to 1967, was characterized by relatively large numbers of small, short, unofficial strikes. These had no economic significance, though they were heavy with social and political meaning. The most severe and prolonged period of unemployment, from 1929 to 1937, was the nearest to 'industrial peace' which has been experienced in the twentieth century, and it has usually been assumed that experience of unemployment is a deterrent to strike action. Yet the period from 1967 to 1979 was one of rising unemployment associated with a rising incidence of strike activity. This coincides most closely with the period from 1919 to 1926, and we might conclude that severe, large, prolonged strikes are associated with periods of economic dislocation and nascent slump, a time when workers' organizations are still strong, undefeated in major conflicts, and when workers are most conscious of what they have to lose, in terms of living standards and job security. Insecurity caused by slump conditions and technological change is undoubtedly one of the factors driving more workers to join trade unions, and we have argued that rising trade union membership at least coincides historically with rising strike action.

Moreover, the 1970s had a further disturbing element absent from the 1919–26 phase, that of inflation. Dislocation and disturbance of established norms, expectations and income differentials are some of the consequences of inflation which, like job insecurity, can be expected to turn workers towards trade unionism and the collective defence of living standards. The severe inflation of the 1970s has 'weakened the hold of traditional frames of reference for judging pay'.[50] This is a profoundly disruptive trend, since it implies the destabilization of that delicate balance of expectations which has, in the past, related one reference group to another. And this has been associated, in the British case at least, with the increasing tendency for the state to impose wage restraint policies, which bite with particular effectiveness in the public sector, and it is clear that the pincers of inflation and wage control go far to explain the recent outbreaks of strikes in this sector. Indeed, in the light of the evidence for a worldwide strike wave in the 1970s, it is feasible to discover a common, global causation in the universality of inflation, technical change, and dislocation caused by rising unemployment. In the 1980s, the depressive effect on strike levels resulting primarily from mass unemployment brought us to a new phase of low incidence. Extrapolation of this trend is hazardous, and we do not attempt it.

Causes of Unrest in Britain

We may turn now from general theories of strike causation to examine the evidence on causes as provided in official British statistics. These figures must be treated with some care, since (a) the stated cause of a strike may not be its 'real' cause; discontent on a whole range of grievances may finally surface in a strike which is ostensibly about wage arrangements; (b) the source of information for the stated cause is usually management, rather than the strikers themselves, and (c) strikes are usually (one source believes 'invariably)'[51] multi-causal. The official classification on strikes by cause was altered in the Department of Employment in 1973, but a reworking of the old series was provided in the Department's *Gazette* back to 1966. Table 8.4 gives percentage figures of numbers of strike by cause for selected years between 1938 and 1966, using the old classification; Table 8.5 provides similar percentages for the period 1966–85. Comparing the number of strikes due to wages, across the two tables, we can see that this tended to rise over the whole postwar period, and to have been particularly high in the years of greatest

Table 8.4

Number of strikes, by cause, in selected years, 1938–66, as percentage of all strikes (old classification)

Cause	1938	1942	1946	1950	1954	1958	1962	1966
Wages	39	62	43	44	47	46	46	45
Hours of work	5	4	3	3	2	2	—	1
Demarcation, disputes on employment and discharge (inc. redundancy and other personnel questions)	29	13	13	15	12	13	19	21
Other working arrangements, rules and discipline	15	19	36	34	37	36	29	29
Trade union status	11	1	4	2	2	2	4	3
Sympathetic	1	1	1	2	—	1	2	1
Strikes in year (number)	875	1,303	2,205	1,339	1,989	2,629	2,449	1,937

Source: Ministry of Labour *Gazette*, Employment and Productivity *Gazette*.

Table 8.5

Number of strikes, by cause, 1966–87, as percentages of all strikes (new classification)

Cause	1966	1967	1968	1969	1970	1971	1972	1973	1974	1975
Wage rates and earnings levels	43.0	44.8	51.8	56.6	62.0	51.0	57.0	47.1	61.5	55.3
Extra-wage and fringe benefits	2.8	2.0	2.0	2.8	2.0	1.8	2.4	3.2	4.3	2.5
ALL PAY	45.8	46.8	53.8	59.4	64.0	52.8	59.4	50.3	65.8	57.8
Duration and pattern of hours worked	2.1	3.2	2.1	2.0	1.4	1.9	2.2	2.5	1.8	1.1
Redundancy questions	3.6	3.5	3.3	2.7	3.1	6.9	12.6	3.0	2.9	5.1
Trade union matters	7.7	8.5	9.5	8.5	8.1	7.9	6.6	8.2	6.3	6.2
Working conditions	7.8	8.4	5.5	5.0	5.7	5.7	5.2	8.2	5.3	6.8
Manning and work allocation	18.7	15.0	12.0	11.0	7.4	10.3	10.5	13.4	9.0	12.1
Dismissals and other disciplinary measures	13.1	13.8	13.2	10.5	7.4	14.2	10.4	13.4	8.9	10.9
Miscellaneous	0.4	0.7	0.4	0.7	0.6	0.3	0.4	0.4	—	—
Strikes in year (number)	1,937	2,116	2,378	3,116	3,906	2,228	2,497	2,873	2,922	2,282

Cause	1976	1977	1978	1979	1980	1981	1982	1983	1984	1985	1986–7*
Wage rates and earnings levels	39.2	52.4	58.2	56.9	45.0	45.2	40.9	39.0	36.1	38.0	34.1
Extra-wage and fringe benefits	4.2	5.2	3.4	2.3	2.7	1.7	1.9	1.6	0.9	2.4	2.8
ALL PAY	43.4	57.6	61.6	59.0	47.7	46.9	42.8	40.5	37.0	40.0	36.9
Duration and pattern of hours worked	3.3	1.7	2.0	1.3	2.7	3.2	6.1	3.6	1.5	5.6	4.1
Redundancy questions	4.3	2.8	2.5	2.9	6.0	10.9	8.0	10.0	26.2	11.6	7.4
Trade union matters	8.2	7.0	4.5	6.5	5.7	5.0	6.0	5.2	24.8	4.3	2.6
Working conditions	10.7	9.3	7.7	7.6	8.4	8.2	10.0	10.0	1.9	10.0	15.6
Manning and work allocation	19.8	13.1	12.5	13.0	17.4	16.1	17.7	21.3	5.5	11.6	23.0
Dismissals and other disciplinary measures	10.4	8.5	9.2	9.6	12.2	9.6	9.4	9.4	3.2	10.9	10.5
Miscellaneous	—	—	—	—	—	—	—	—	—	—	—
Strikes in year (number)	2,016	2,703	2,349	2,080	1,330	1,338	1,528	1,352	1,272	903	1,046

* Twelve months from July 1986.
Source: Department of Employment *Gazette*.

strike incidence in the late 1960s and 1970s. The heavier the strike incidence, the more likely it is to be about wages.

The old series category of 'other working arrangements, rules and discipline' corresponds roughly with the new classifications of 'working conditions', 'manning and work allocations' and 'dismissals and other disciplinary matters'. It can be seen in Table 8.4 that this category rose from its 1938 level of 15 per cent of all strikes, to an average of over one-third in the postwar years. Examining this trend in 1963, Professor Turner argued that:

> One could say that these disputes all involve attempts to submit managerial discretion and authority to agreed – or failing that customary – rules: alternatively that they reflect an implicit pressure for more democracy and individual rights in industry . . . it seems clear that here one is dealing with a strong contemporary current of feeling, which has not so far been satisfied by the limited development of joint consultation.[52]

In the subsequent years, the three relevant categories in the new series have maintained this 'current of feeling' right through the period of steadily rising strike incidence, at an average of 30 per cent of all strikes, from 1966 to 1977, although as a proportion of striker days they account only for an annual average of 14 per cent, showing that strikes on these issues are smaller and shorter, than those on wages and other matters.

The remarkable evidence of the figures for the 1980s is that strikes about wages have now fallen to the level of prewar 1939, whilst strikes about working hours and redundancies have reached unprecedented proportions. So, Professor Turner's comment on non-wage strikes remains true in today's quite different circumstances. The difference is, of course, that whereas in the 1960s such strikes tended to be local, short, often unofficial, and successful, the same causes in the 1980s produced national, prolonged, official and usually catastrophically unsuccessful strikes.

Of the other categories of strike, it is noteworthy that hours of work, trade union 'status' or trade union 'matters' (which include recognition and closed shop disputes) and 'extra-wage and fringe benefits' are all quite minor causes, and contrary to popular opinion, more detailed enquiries have revealed that demarcation alone accounted for only 2–3 per cent of strikes during the 1960s,[53] and that multi-unionism is a factor in not more than 5 per cent of strikes.[54]

It is interesting, after this examination of causes according to official statistics, to look at what workers have had to say about their reasons for striking. In an extensive case study of a large engineering plant, Batstone *et al.* found that 'the most dominant vocabularies attribute blame to management' and that amongst management behaviour which provoked strikes were the breaking of agreements, 'conning', 'adopting a hard line', ignoring men's efforts, goodwill, or intentions, and adopting an aggressive approach. Security of earnings and loss of money appear twice as often amongst reasons for striking, as a desire to increase earnings, and 'an average of five types of reason existed for each strike or near-strike which we observed'.[55]

A very specific and potent cause of the 1970s increases in strike figures in Britain has, we have argued, been the juxtaposition of high inflation rates with statutory or near-statutory incomes policies. These circumstances have borne particularly heavily on public sector workers, especially since incomes policies have been tightened up to exclude the traditional public service unions' claims for 'fair comparisons' with outside industries. Along with the imposition of cash limits on public expenditure, monetarist economists, whose self-destructive influence has spread deep into the Treasury and into the front benches of both major political parties, have called for the deliberate abandonment of the concept of a 'going rate' of wages, so that the claim for parity by public service workers can be removed from the collective bargaining scene. Since the wide public debate of incomes policies has the effect of making everyone more conscious of their relative pay, it is small wonder that the public sector has been driven more and more frequently into intransigent collective action. The persistent failure of the public service unions and the TUC to co-ordinate this action has meant that it has frequently been less effective than it might have been. We wrote at some length about this in 1972, and everything we said then is still relevant.[56] The fact that the governments since 1979 have foresworn the language and conceptual framework of incomes policy does not alter the analysis for this later period, since it is evident in every year that, despite the monetarist terminology, governments have sought to restrain wage increases in the public sector, and have often ended up, despite their free labour market philosophy, in paying roughly similar increases (6 to 8 per cent in 1986–7, for example) across the board.

Strikes with an overtly political motive have usually been a very small proportion of total stoppages, and are indeed excluded from the official statistics. During the period from 1910 to 1926, and particularly in the prewar years of 1910–14, syndicalist philosophy, which regards strikes as a training ground for social revolution, and the General Strike as the ultimate political weapon, had some influence in British trade unionism[57] but it is impossible to ascribe political motives to the mass of strikers, and the General Strike when it came in 1926 seems to have been regarded by most trade unionists largely as a defensive action of solidarity with the miners.[58] The aspirations of those who saw the strike as a political offensive against the state were rudely overridden by the behaviour of the TUC leaders, who backed away rapidly when the political implications of their actions became evident to them. A few years earlier, the militants of the Triple Alliance had called unsuccessfully for a general strike to force an end to the government's physical intervention against Soviet Russia, but in 1920 the Council of Action set up by the TUC, the Parliamentary Labour Party, and the Labour Party, did in fact contemplate such action, and may well have influenced the government in its withdrawal of support for the anti-Soviet Poles.

More recently, industrial action on a considerable scale was directed against the Industrial Relations Bill in 1971. There were four one-day unofficial strikes against the Bill, accounting for 350,000, 180,000, 1,250,000 and 1,250,000 striker days. Between 1970 and 1974, official estimates record that there were 3,300,000 striker days against the Bill and the Act, 1,000,000 striker days against decisions of the National Industrial Relations Court, 1,600,000 striker days against incomes policies, 100,000 striker days of postmen against the sacking of their chairman, 200,000 striker days against the government's decision to let Upper Clyde Shipbuilders go bankrupt, and 85,000 days in protest against unemployment, a total of political or near-political striker days of 6,285,000.[59] Ingham's study, already cited, includes this apposite statement:

> . . . if this 'politicization' of industrial conflict continues, governments in Britain are likely to change the pattern of industrial conflict from that which we witnessed in the last decade. The existence of a clearly identifiable and coercive source of grievance in the form of the state will almost inevitably increase the size and scope of industrial disputes.[60]

We have no researched catalogue of political strikes in the period since 1979, but it would not seem far-fetched so to classify a considerable proportion of the strikes of this period. Although few of them started out for political reasons, many were transformed in their progress into political issues as government and police combated the strikers' goals and picketing respectively, to the point where the combatants included not only workpeople and employers, but also government, police and courts. Thus we might include in any such list the public sector strikes of 1978–9 (the 'Winter of Discontent'), the 1980 national steel strike, the 1981 civil servants' strike, the 1982 strikes in the National Health Service and on the railways, the 1983 strikes in electricity, gas and water, the 1984–5 miners' strike, the series of strikes in printing, culminating in the Wapping dispute of 1986–7, and the teachers' running industrial action through 1985 and 1986.

Implicit in our discussion so far have been certain distinctions between different types of strike – long, large stoppages and short, small strikes, official and unofficial strikes. To these classes we should add also so-called 'constitutional' and 'unconstitutional' strikes. The long, large strike, intended by both sides as a serious trial of strength, is a quite different kind of social action from the small, short strike intended by workers mainly as a demonstration of feeling.[61] The major trials of strength occur, as we have seen, mainly around national industry-level wage claims and redundancies, whilst the short, local demonstration strike may have a hundred and one different causes in local grievances.

Unofficial Stoppages

Most of the latter strikes are unofficial, which is to say that they lack the authority of the strikers' union behind them. This may mean that the union disapproves in an active sense, or it may mean that it maintains a largely benevolent neutrality. Whilst the right to strike appertains to individuals, to persons, there is no legal ground for such distinctions as 'official' or 'unofficial', since all strikes equally involve people, whilst only some involve organizations.

The censure of unofficial strikers in the press is almost entirely unhelpful and inappropriate. Trade union leaders can rarely act in advance of their members[62] and hence official support is often a matter of policy, late in being declared, by which time many strikes will have already finished. In other cases, union funds may be too low to allow the union to risk recognizing the strike. Even where the trade union definitely opposes the strike, the degree of discipline which it can exert is strictly limited by the very nature of trade unions, and by most union rulebooks. (Only three union rulebooks of a large sample investigated give specific authority to discipline unofficial strikers, and only one gives the authority for the executive to expel members in these circumstances.[63]) It is in any case a dubious proposition to suggest that any union ought to have this kind of power over its members; the only legitimate control which unions should enjoy over members is that which comes from the expression of members' grievances and aspirations, *not* from suppressing them.

In practice, then, unofficial strikes present a complex

phenomenon. One writer has distinguished as many as five different categories:[64] (a) those in which the union executive supports the strike but does not wish to finance it, (b) those in which the union gives tacit support, to shift the employers' position, (c) those to which the union would have given recognition had the strike not been too short, (d) those which have the support of the district union organization, but not of the national centre, (e) those which the union fully opposed, which probably means that they were at least partially directed *against* the union. That these latter two categories are a small proportion of the whole is indicated by the evidence of the TUC which found (in 1959–60) that 'in about half the cases reported to the General Council where strikes began without official sanction, the union paid dispute benefit'.[65] Even were their numbers greater, it would be at some risk to liberty that they were ever prevented. If a union is out of favour with its members, they may have arguments on their side.

During the 1970s, the official records of the Department of Employment showed that over 90 per cent of strikes, year in and year out, were classified as unofficial. However, the proportion of striker days in official disputes, which was 31.3 per cent in the 1960s, rose to an annual average of 46.6 per cent in the strike wave of 1969–74. (In 1971 and 1972 it rose to 74 and 76 per cent.) In the social contract years of 1975–6 it fell to 19 and 14 per cent. And all of the very sizeable strikes of the 1980s listed above were official. It seems that, in prosperous times, strikes are usually short, local, unofficial and successful.

The distinction between 'constitutional' and 'unconstitutional' strikes is between those which are called only after the appropriate disputes procedure is fully exhausted, and those which are called 'in breach of procedure'. We have very little statistical evidence about their relative significance, but we should expect that some unofficial strikes were also unconstitutional. The annual reports of the Engineering Employers' Federation claim that for 1961–71, three-quarters of all staff strikes in their industry, and 96 per cent of manual workers' strikes, were unconstitutional.[66] But this evidence may be atypical, since the procedure agreement in engineering at that time was outrageously cumbersome, slow, flagrantly biased in favour of the employers, and outdated. Perhaps we might *expect* unconstitutional stoppages to be common in the absence of effective, fair and speedy disputes procedures. These particular rituals had been imposed in the 1922 lockout, and remained unchanged until the mid-1970s, only because it had been possible to ignore them for such a long time. The remedy is clearly not to bewail the lack of constitutionality, but to create honest and practicable procedures.

Recognition Strikes

There is a further type of strike which deserves a special category to itself and which looms large at least in the consciousness of the active trade unionists; what we may call the 'intransigent recognition strike'. These occur at company level (usually a small company which yet has powerful backers or a strong parent company which remains in the background) when an anti-union employer digs in his heels and refuses recognition to his employees' trade union. These have often proved to be the most testing type of strike for the whole trade union movement, being frequently prolonged for months or years, involving major hardship for the strikers, and sometimes exposing the inability of the trade union movement to act with effective solidarity. Amongst these famous affairs we may list the Roberts-Arundel strike,[67] the Fine Tubes strike,[68] the Jersey Mills strike,[69] the Grunwick strike,[70] and the Sanderson fork-lift factory strike of 1977–8.

The struggle for union 'recognition', for its normal status, was an element in many of the big strikes of the 1980s. For example, in the miners' strike of 1984–5 the very existence of the union was threatened in court proceedings, and a breakaway union (the UDM) emerged during the course of the strike in the Nottingham coalfield. In the print workers' dispute with News International at Wapping, the conflict involved not only job loss but also the continued status of two unions, the NGA and SOGAT 1982. In earlier strikes against the provincial press of Mr Eddie Shah, the issues included the status and continued recognition of the print union, the NGA.

Conclusions

Finally, we should note that research on the question of who finances strikes, makes clear that union strike benefit provides only minor financial relief for strikers and none for their families, whilst social security payment to strikers' families, which has always been uncertain, is now subject to severe limitations as a result of government legislation and orders in the 1980s. The majority of strikes are financed mostly from the strikers' own savings, from the grey economy, and from the acquiring of debt by the strikers and their families.[71]

Finally, we may ask the question, 'how far do strikes succeed in achieving their aims?' To this there is no glib statistical answer, although investigations that have been undertaken in mining[72] and in a multi-industry study[73] have found a positive correlation between militancy and relative wage rates. Over the historical period of the twentieth century, we can identify the 1910–14 period as one of successful strikes, the 1919–26 period as one of major defeats, the 1950s and 1960s as a period when the small, short, unofficial strikes were usually successful; and the period since 1969 as one of major official strikes, requiring more detailed scrutiny.

Even on a most cursory view, however, these have included some spectacular victories (the miners particularly, in 1972 and 1974) together with some tough 'draws' (perhaps the firemen in 1977–8) and some unambiguously lost strikes (for example the Post Office in 1971).

Of the large strikes of the 1980s, those which concerned wages were still proving successful at least to some degree, whilst those concerned with resistance to job loss, privatization and other government or employer initiatives tended to end as defeats for the strikers and even to imperil the viability of their unions. Whilst we should not be understood as enthusing over strike action, since in any given situation there may be very cogent reasons for avoiding it,[74] in the broad sweep of social history there is little doubt that strikes have contributed positively to the nurturing and sustainment of trade union organization, to advance wages, and to wrest more democratic controls over working conditions and managerial decision-making, throughout industry.

No consideration has been given here of the impact of labour and trade union law on strikes. Readers are referred to Chapter 10.

NOTES

1. K. G. J. C. Knowles, *Strikes: a Study in Industrial Conflict*, Blackwell, 1952.
2. See M. P. Jackson, *Industrial Relations*, Croom Helm, 1977. Also Geoff Brown, *Sabotage*, Spokesman, 1977.
3. J. E. T. Eldridge, *Industrial Disputes*, Routledge and Kegan Paul, 1968.
4. Talcott Parsons, 'Communism and the West', in *Social Change* (eds. A. and E. Ezioni), Glencoe Ill., 1964, quoted in G. K. Ingham, *Strikes and Industrial Conflict*, Macmillan, 1974.
5. J. Hemingway, *Conflict and Democracy: Studies in Trade Union Government*, Clarendon, 1978, describes Harold Wilson's allegations that the 1966 seamen's strike was led by 'a tightly knit group of politically motivated men' as 'quite implausible'.
6. V. L. Allen, *Trade Union Militancy*, Merlin Press, 1966.
7. See for example Mary McAuley, *Labour Disputes in Soviet Russia, 1957–65*, Clarendon, 1969.
8. Milojko Drulovic, *Self-management on Trial*, Spokesman, 1978.
9. Department of Employment *Gazette*. Italics in original.
10. H. A. Turner, *Is Britain Really Strike-Prone?* Cambridge, 1969.
11. 'The Truth about Britain's Strikes', *Sunday Times*, 29 October 1978, and 'The Awful Truth about Strife in our Factories', *Sunday Times*, 12 November 1978.
12. H. A. Turner, *op. cit.*
13. E. Batstone, I. Boraston and S. Frenkel, *The Social Organization of Strikes*, Blackwell, 1978.
14. *Ibid.*
15. See W. E. J. McCarthy, 'The Nature of Britain's Strike Problem', in *British Journal of Industrial Relations*, vol. VIII, 1970, wherein the author challenges the interpretation of international strike statistics to be found in H. A. Turner, *op. cit.*
16. Ministry of Labour *Gazette*, vol. LXVIII, 1960, cited in E. W. Evans and S. Creigh, 'Introduction' in their *Industrial Conflict in Britain*, Frank Cass, 1977.

17. H. A. Turner, G. Clack and G. Roberts, *Labour Relations in the Motor Industry*, Allen and Unwin, 1967.
18. W. E. J. McCarthy, *op. cit.*
19. E. W. Evans and S. Creigh, *op. cit.*
20. K. G. Knight, 'Strikes and Wage Inflation in British Manufacturing Industry, 1950–68', *Bulletin of the Oxford Institute of Economics and Statistics*, vol. 34, 1972.
21. K. G. J. C. Knowles, *op. cit.*
22. R. Hyman, *Strikes*, Fontana, 2nd edition 1977.
23. M. Silver, 'Recent British Strike Trends: A Factual Analysis', *British Journal of Industrial Relations*, vol. XI, no. 1, 1973.
24. A. I. Marsh and W. E. J. McCarthy, *Disputes Procedures in British Industry*, Research Paper no. 2, Part 2, Donovan Royal Commission on Trade Unions and Employers' Associations, HMSO, 1966.
25. A. I. Marsh, E. O. Evans and P. Garcia, *Workplace Industrial Relations in Engineering*, Federation Research Paper 4, Engineering Employers' Federation, 1971.
26. See Coates and Topham, *Trade Unions and Politics*, Blackwell, 1986, Chapter 7, 'Class Politics and the General Strike which Did Not Come'.
27. Dick Nettleton, former apprentices' leader, in R. A. Leeson (ed.), *Strike: a Live History, 1887–1971*, Allen and Unwin, 1973.
28. A full account of the Betteshanger prosecution, factual yet ironic, is given by the wartime Ministry of Labour's Chief Industrial Commissioner, Sir Harold Emmerson, in Appendix 6 of the Report of the Donovan Royal Commission, Cmnd 3623, HMSO, 1968.
29. E.Wigham, *Strikes and the Government, 1893–1974*, Macmillan, 1976.
30. *Ibid.*
31. See H. A. Clegg and R. Adams, *The Employers' Challenge*, Blackwell, 1957.
32. TUC, *Annual Report*, 1958, which contains a detailed 10-page report on the whole history of the strike and the TUC's involvement.
33. See R. H. Heath, 'The National Power-Loading Agreement in the Coal Industry and some Aspects of Workers' Control', in Michael Barratt Brown, K. Coates and T. Topham (eds.), *Trade Union Register 1969*, Merlin Press, 1969.
34. H. A. Turner, *The Trend of Strikes*, Leeds University Press, 1963.
35. We are indebted for this point to Bruce Spencer.
36. R. Hyman, *op. cit.*
37. See T. Lane, and K. Roberts, *Strike at Pilkingtons*, Fontana, 1971.
38. R. Hyman, *op. cit.*
39. See J. Hughes and R. Moore, *A Special Case?* Penguin, 1972.
40. Department of Employment *Gazette*, August 1986, p. 325.
41. K. G. J. C. Knowles, 'Strike Proneness and its Determinants', in W. Galenson and S. M. Wiley (eds.), *Labor and Trade Unionism*, Wiley, 1960.
42. A. M. Ross and P. T. Hartman, *Changing Patterns of Industrial Conflict*, Wiley, 1960.
43. Clark Kerr and A. Siegel, 'The Inter-Industry Propensity to Strike – an International Comparison', in A. Kornhauser, R. Dubin and A. Ross (eds.), *Industrial Conflict*, McGraw-Hill, 1954.
44. J. F. B. Goodman, 'Strikes in the U.K.', *International Labour Review*, vol. 95, 1967, and H. A. Clegg, *The System of Industrial Relations in Great Britain*, Blackwell, 1970, for the 1960s; and R. Hyman, *op. cit.*, for the period up to 1975.
45. M. Silver, *op. cit.*

46. G. K. Ingham, *op. cit.*
47. H. A. Turner, G. Roberts and D. Roberts, *Management Characteristics and Labour Conflict*, Cambridge, 1977.
48. *Ibid.*
49. *Ibid.*
50. R. Hyman, *op. cit.*
51. E. Batstone, I. Boraston and S. Frenkel, *op. cit.*
52. H. A. Turner, *The Trend of Strikes, op. cit.*
53. J. F. B. Goodman, *op. cit.*
54. H. A. Clegg, *op. cit.*
55. E. Batstone, I. Boraston and S. Frenkel, *op. cit.*
56. *The New Unionism*, Penguin Books, 1972.
57. Bob Holton, *British Syndicalism*, Pluto Press, 1977.
58. See Coates and Topham, *Trade Unions and Politics, op. cit.*
59. E. Wigham, *op. cit.*
60. G. K. Ingham, *op. cit.*
61. R. Hyman, *op. cit.*
62. *Ibid.*
63. J. Gennard, *Financing Strikers*, Macmillan, 1977.
64. M. P. Jackson, *op. cit.*
65. TUC, *Annual Report*, 1961.
66. M. Silver, *op. cit.*
67. See J. Arnison, *The Million Pound Strike*, Lawrence and Wishart, 1970.
68. See Tony Beck, *The Fine Tubes Strike*, Stage 1, 1974.
69. See Mike Taylor, 'The Machine-Minder', in Roland Fraser (ed.), *Work 2*, Penguin, 1969.
70. See Tom Durkin, *Grunwick: Bravery and Betrayal*, Brent Trades Council, 1978.
71. J. Gennard, *op. cit.* See also J. W. Durcan and W. E. J. McCarthy, 'The State Subsidy Theory of Strikes: an Examination of the Statistical Data for the Period 1956–70', *British Journal of Industrial Relations*, vol. XII, no. 1, March 1974; L. C. Hunter, 'The State Subsidy Theory of Strikes: a Reconsideration', *British Journal of Industrial Relations*, vol. XII, no. 3, November 1974; and J. Gennard and R. J. Lasko, 'The Individual and the Strike', *British Journal of Industrial Relations*, vol. XIII, no. 3, November 1975.
72. John Hughes, 'The Rise of the Militants', *Trade Union Affairs*, no. 1, 1960–1.
73. H. A. Turner, G. Roberts and D. Roberts, *op. cit.*
74. A fascinating account of *workers'* reasons for *not* striking is contained in E. Batstone, I. Boraston and E. Frenkel, *op. cit.*

CHAPTER 9

Industrial Democracy

'The very discovery of improved industrial methods, by leading to specialization, makes manual labourer and brain-worker alike dependent on the rest of the community for the means of subsistence, and subordinates them, even in their own crafts, to the action of others. In the world of civilization and progress, no man can be his own master. But the very fact that, in modern society, the individual thus necessarily loses control over his own life, makes him desire to regain collectively what has become individually impossible. Hence the irresistible tendency to popular government, in spite of all its difficulties and dangers.'[1]

It was in 1897 that the Webbs drafted this conclusion to their work on *Industrial Democracy*. Undoubtedly their recognition that 'no man can be his own master' was tempered by the earlier defiant insistence, by their contemporary, William Morris, that 'no man is good enough to be another man's master'.

However, the 'desire to regain collectively what has become individually impossible' has moved through many troubled phases during the civil tumults of the twentieth century. There have been times when it has been a bold and captivating demand, loudly upheld by vast numbers of people. There have been other times when it has survived as a whispered memory, while mass unemployment has intimidated millions of trade unionists into silent conformity. While people have lived through these phases, they have commonly come to share the illusion that they were permanent. We can see this illusion showing its face in the once-standard text on trade unions by Flanders. Writing in the mid-1950s, he captured the dominant mood of the immediate postwar years, when he took up the theme first stated by the Webbs.

> Unfortunately it seems also to be true that modern society tends to destroy the individual's confidence in his capacity to control his own life and thus to weaken any feeling of personal responsibility for his social environment.[2]

This opinion adequately reflects the official climate of the years after 1945, which, in retrospect, now appear to have been the end of an interlude in British labour politics. Since then there have been heady years in which industrial democracy has been high up in the imaginations of working people. These have more lately been followed by a darker time in which it has been way down. A look at our history, however, will persuade us that the idea will rise again.

Periods of Concern: a Historical Background

The story of this century seems to have been characterized by a vast discontent which has recurrently created widespread interest in the ideas of industrial democracy and workers' control.[3] The first third of the century, culminating in the General Strike of 1926, was characterized by the rise of the Labour Party, the prewar 'great unrest', and a proliferation of syndicalist, guild socialist and industrial unionist agitations. After the 1926 defeat, trade unionism was put on the defensive, shop steward organization was disrupted and smashed in large parts of industry, and the unions only began to recover some of their former powers with the onset of rearmament and the war itself. Up to 1940 unemployment remained over the million mark, and it took trade unionists some years to recover their old self-assurance with the conquest of full employment.

When the Labour Party came to power in 1945, the call for industrial democracy was commonly equated with and reduced to the nationalization programme, even though many far-sighted trade unionists complained at the time that this was a mistaken policy. Writing while this disappointment was already becoming articulate, Allan Flanders recognized the historical commitment of the trade union movement:

> The growth of trade unionism . . . had undoubtedly contributed to the awakening among employees of a fuller awareness of their own dignity and importance, and this has found expression in demands for more than a larger pay packet and greater leisure. There is a long tradition among British trade unions in favour of the workers having some share in the management and control of the industries in which they are employed, as well as in the determination of their wages and working conditions.[4]

In the years after the fall of the 1951 Labour government, there was a constant strengthening of trade union shopfloor responsibility and power, and from the late 1950s onwards, a marked renewal of interest in a wide range of prescriptions for democracy in industry. This was checked, but not annulled, with the restoration of mass unemployment from the late 1970s onwards.

The Historical Perspective

At its strongest, the call for industrial democracy has always been revolutionary in its implications. From near the beginning of the century, James Connolly expressed it very clearly in his work *Socialism Made Easy*,[5] a classic which has frequently been reprinted by the Irish Transport and General Workers' Union. Connolly took the dictum, 'Political institutions are not adapted to the administration of industry', and turned it against those who used it as a conservative defence of the power of property. He developed the argument for an industrial franchise, replacing the territorial division of power upon which rests the foundation of modern states:

> The delegation of the function of government into the hands of representatives elected from certain districts, States, or territories, represents no real natural division suited to the requirements of modern society, but is a survival from a time when territorial influences were more

potent in the world than industrial influences, and for that reason is totally unsuited to the needs of the new social order, which must be based upon industry . . . What the Socialist does realize is that under a social democratic form of society the administration of affairs will be in the hands of representatives of the various industries of the nation; that the workers in the shops and factories will organize themselves into unions, each union comprising all the workers at a given industry; that said union will democratically control the workshop life of its own industry, electing all foremen, etc., and regulating the routine of labour in that industry in subordination to the needs of society in general, to the needs of its allied trades, and to the departments of industry to which it belongs; that representatives elected from these various departments of industry will meet and form the industrial administration or national government of the country.

This, said Connolly, would constitute a true social democracy 'from the bottom upward', in place of capitalist political society 'organized from above downward'. Connolly's trade union based socialism would reduce states, territories, and provinces to 'geographical expressions', having 'no existence as sources of governmental power, though they may be seats of administrative bodies'.

Connolly's ideas met and merged with a vast pre-1914 war wave of strike actions which shook the whole British Establishment. The upturn of the trade cycle was accompanied by sharply rising living costs and a remarkable growth of trade union membership. At the same time, the Labour Party's arrival in Parliament in 1906 had already generated some considerable disillusionment with what some critics were to call the 'decorous and hypothetical socialism of Labour MPs'.

In 1908 there had been a wholesale lock-out of woodworkers and a national cotton strike. Next year and the year after there were major disputes in mining. Also in 1910 the boilermakers were locked out: so that, in one industry after another it became increasingly clear that the gain of direct Parliamentary representation would be simply ignored if the work of self-defence were not also carried on by an active rank-and-file movement. As this awareness extended itself, so the rolling strike wave became more and more aggressive, integrated and solid. In 1911 victory after victory was gained, through strikes by seamen, dockers, railwaymen and others. It was no accident that industrial unionists and syndicalists took leading parts in these turbulent events.

While they demanded the democratization of industry and society, the trade union agitators also tried to rationalize the inherited trade union structure. In 1909, there were 1,168 separate union organizations, and it is not surprising that the call for amalgamation and consolidation aroused very wide echoes.

These were particularly clearly heard on the railways, where the formation of the National Union of Railwaymen, in 1913, embodied for a whole generation of militant workpeople the principles of industrial unionism. Such ideals were summed up in a tract published a little after the birth of the NUR, as 'the permeation of labour with a class spirit' and equipment of the workers 'with an organization capable of supplanting capitalism'. This was the view of G. D. H. Cole and William Mellor, as expressed in an elegantly printed pamphlet called *The Meaning of Industrial Freedom*, which continued:

> The industrial structure brings into a single union all those who are engaged in a factory, a mine, or a service. It follows the line not of occupation, but of industry: it has regard not to what a man is doing, but to the branch of production in which he is employed. This gives the workers far greater power in fighting the employers, and enables them to negotiate with far greater success . . . but it does far more than that. For the first time, it puts them in a position to end the wage-system.[6]

It was in pursuit of this goal that the engineers were incited to emulate the railwaymen, amalgamating all their various craft associations into one body, and embracing also the semi-skilled and unskilled labourers.

The outbreak of war predictably defused the industry-wide strike movement, but it paradoxically heightened the demand for workers' control in the day-to-day argument on the shopfloor, particularly in an engineering industry which was working flat out, to meet an insatiable demand for munitions, under the handicap of great labour shortages. The official union leaderships concluded agreements with the government to promote 'dilution' (the waiving of traditional training and apprenticeship practices), the outlawing of strikes, direction of labour, and the suspension of many trade union protective practices. This created innumerable grievances, and a veritable upheaval in the working conditions of precisely the most skilled and indispensable part of the workforce. There was a remarkable growth in the shop steward movement, which proved under such pressures to be easily open to the doctrines of industrial unionism, syndicalism, and their fashionable variant, guild socialism.

All these currents of thought vied with one another for influence, but they also reinforced each other in criticism and passionate debate. Elsewhere we have documented parts of this argument, which can be very clearly traced in the different appeals made by its partisans within the coal-mining industry, some of whom coupled the call for state ownership with a series of elaborate and detailed proposals for popular self-management, while others counterposed to 'reformist' nationalization proposals the demand for overall revolutionary change. Before the First World War came to an end, the Russian Revolution of 1917 raised yet further hopes and promoted the idea of Soviets or workers' councils, which bore a remarkable similarity to some of the proposals first advocated in these islands by James Connolly. He himself, however, had meantime been shot, in reprisal for his part in the Easter rising in Dublin in 1916. A remarkable convention in Leeds in 1917 brought together all wings of British socialism, and numerous key trade union leaders, to acclaim the first Russian Revolution, and to call for the establishment of workers' and soldiers' councils in this country too.[7] In its earlier years the young Soviet Union appeared to be following a path rather similar to that prescribed by Connolly, and this attracted many industrial unionists, guildsmen and syndicalists to the new communist party which grew up in the early twenties.[8]

It was in the heat of such passions that the Labour Party ratified its new (1918) constitution, which included a commitment to the 'best obtainable system of popular control' of publicly owned industries.

Revolution was in the air, even though King George V was reassured by Will Thorne after the Leeds Convention that no ill would come of it. 'This seemed to relieve his mind', wrote the labour leader, 'and he spoke to me in a most homely and pleasant way. I was very pleased.' Thorne, however, also told the King that 'there will have to be many political and industrial changes during the next few years'.[9] It was in this context that the government-appointed Whitley Committee recommended widespread experiments with joint consultation (in 1917) and that (two years later) the Sankey Commission reported in favour of nationalization of the mines. Instead of reform and industrial peace, though, the trade unions were to suffer prolonged mass unemployment, lockouts, and victimization. The 1922 engineering lockout established that the 'prerogative' of management was absolute. Shop stewards were sacked in droves. The dole queues provided the overwhelming majority of employers with all the 'consultation' they wanted. And then, in 1926, the defeat of the General Strike registered the beginning of a long moratorium on trade union pressures for greater control over the place of work.

This is not to say that the desire for industrial democracy was extirpated: on the contrary. Throughout the 1930s the issue of workers' control continued to be debated at Labour Party Conferences, and even after the formal victory of the Morrisonian model of nationalization (based upon the experience of Herbert Morrison in the creation of a bureaucratically administered Passenger Transport Board for London, and argued with strenuous appeals to the managerial example of Stalin's Russia,[10] which had long since dispensed with all forms of democracy, including industrial democracy) there remained a continuous and determined opposition which kept alive the ideas of syndicalism, guild socialism, and similar schools of industrial democracy, sometimes in fullblooded forms, and sometimes considerably diluted in a variety of compromise proposals. By the time that a Labour government could be elected, in 1945, this opposition was in a distinct minority, however.

Nationalization of coal, gas, electricity, railways, road haulage, airlines and steel brought something like a fifth of British industry into public control, under vast centralized corporations. Two concessions were made to the idea of industrial democracy: token trade unionists were usually appointed to the national boards of these industries, and an obligation to establish a framework of joint consultative committees was written into the main nationalization Acts. The first of these made little difference. In the absence of any direct electoral link with the trade union constituency, or even the most limited forms of accountability, the union-orientated directors soon came to look exactly like all the others. As George Orwell put it in a different case but a similar situation:

> The animals looked from pig to man, and from man to pig, and from pig to man again; but already it was impossible to say which was which.

The second expedient was at first more promising: in the earliest days there is some evidence that managers were sensitive to the part which was intended by legislators to be played by joint consultative institutions, and many JCCs began their work with earnest enthusiasm. In at least one case a colliery manager actually handed over powers of decision to such a committee, until a court action (which arose inadvertently) established that his legal responsibility could not be divested, whatever the claims of democracy.

The Limitations of Joint Consultation

In this climate, whatever the hopes in which it began, joint consultation soon came to be seen as at best an inadequate expedient, at worst a positive menace, preventing unions from defending their members as resolutely as they might. Seldom were the committees able to exercise real influence on policy: but they were commonly given responsibility for certain types of personnel questions, such as difficult disciplinary cases, or absenteeism: thus incorporating what might otherwise have been the trade union defence into the management prosecution team.

A very clear example of this was given by Arthur Scargill, in his contribution to a discussion on industrial democracy which was organized by the National Union of Mineworkers.

He described how union branch officers, serving on a colliery consultative committee, accepted responsibility for judging cases of absenteeism. At last they agreed to the dismissal of a man who still retained strong support from his workmates. He appealed over the heads of the branch committee to his full branch meeting. Under the threat of strike action the Coal Board then agreed to reinstate the man.[11]

In practice, the institutions of consultation took on somewhat different significance in different areas: where unions were determined to play an adversary role, they could do so: but where they agreed to go along with the pressure to discharge minor policing functions, there were frequently quite similar complaints that the union's identity was being compromised. On the other side of the coin, one beneficial result of the process was that it frequently permitted workpeople to inform (or threaten to inform) higher management of some of the derelictions of middle management so that it could sometimes conduce to a more humane working environment: but this improvement commonly came about as a result of paternalist concern, and could hardly be presented as a form of democratic self-regulation.

Vesting day (when nationalization took effect) in the coal industry was at the beginning of 1947: by 1948 consultation was already rather obviously less than 'the best obtainable system of popular administration and control', promised in the Labour Party's objectives: so that considerable unease was being expressed both in the Labour Party Conference and at the TUC. These protests were muted upon appeal from Conference organizers, however, and it was agreed that joint discussions would be initiated between the Party's National Executive Committee and the Congress.

By this time, the international alignments which have dominated the world since 1945 had crystallized: cold war was already raging, and a by-product of it was the circumscription of communist activities in a number of trade unions, some of which determined upon an actual ban on office-holding by Communist Party members. In 1949, such a proscription was agreed by 426 to 208 votes at the biennial conference of the TGWU. Interestingly, at the same time, by 433 to 170, the conference agreed

> that trade union representatives should be placed on the boards and executives . . . with the right of the members to recall such trade union representatives as and when considered necessary.[12]

These two simultaneous decisions show how far the industrial visions of James Connolly had become separated from the communist doctrine, in the minds of many ordinary union members: they also show how far these workers still desired effective self-government, whatever harm the undemocratic evolution of the USSR might do to the reputation of socialism. Paradoxically, many of those who suffered proscription were themselves ardent supporters of workers' control, who had become communists precisely inasmuch as they believed that Soviet institutions embodied a strong commitment to industrial democracy. An enormous confusion, based upon a vast flow of misinformation, characterized this whole period, and made the whole issue very difficult to discuss.

When, also during 1949, the TUC reported on the questions which it had been set about reform of nationalization, it confined itself to proposals for improving formal representation by unions on National Boards, and increasing consultation. Two years later, the Labour government fell, and then, for thirteen years, fundamental democratic restructuring of the nationalized industries was no longer an immediate practical option.

In the meantime, the same cold war which had begun to divide British unions had brought Yugoslavia into conflict with the

USSR, and thus created the preconditions for that small country's remarkable experiments in industrial democracy.[13] These were to exert wide influence in later years.

The Content of the Modern Movement

Throughout this time, the movement for industrial democracy in Britain took three connected forms: first, full employment aided a growth in shopfloor negotiating power and control over specific conditions of employment; second, a lobby for more democratic forms of public ownership; and third, as a result of the intensified difficulties of the British economy, and the consequent demand for governmental incomes policy, a tendency to create more and more elaborate mechanisms to involve union leaders in some form of overall planning mechanism. Other democratic options, such as the growth of the co-operative idea, were not to mature until a good deal later on. Later, in the late 1970s and afterwards came a significant shift to the development of democratic forms of local enterprise, usually as a result of decisions by Labour councils in an effort to meet the new problems of unemployment and the collapse of local industries.

This modern movement for industrial democracy has had to pilot its way through an extremely complex mish-mash of terminology. 'Workers' control' is an ambivalent term because the word 'control' in the English language is capable of bearing a variety of different meanings. On the one hand, we speak of 'controllers of British industry', meaning the most powerful corporate owners and directors. On the other hand, control can signify a shifting relationship of supervision, surveillance and monitoring. European languages are commonly exempt from this difficulty: control usually means the second type of activities, and a different phrase is used to describe the first. When a Frenchman wishes to speak of the workers taking charge of the running of industry, he calls this process 'self-management'.[14] Many English trade unionists, however, speak of workers' control when they are seeking to argue for self-management, and this sometimes creates a certain amount of misunderstanding. An increasing consensus limits the use of the words 'workers' control' to cover the extension (encroachment) of direct powers of working people over the immediate environment in which they work. It is in this sense that the growth of shopfloor powers is most easily understood. The whole process has been graphically described by Philip Higgs, a convenor in the aircraft industry in Coventry:

> Earnings are one of the principal controls, but by no means the only one. Over the past four or five years, pretty much since I became convenor, a fair part of my time along with other stewards has been spent encouraging and helping workers in a department or section to form a gang. This is a powerful weapon in the struggle for control, because the employer can no longer pick on the individual worker but is forced to negotiate with a collective. Some sections of our plant, such as final assembly of engines, have always worked in gangs because this was the best for the company. So we took the decision that what was best for the company under certain circumstances was good for us all the time. At that time there was real inequality of earnings in some sections and a lack of strength in negotiations with rate-fixers, as well as a failure to be able to control labour-loading. We presented our arguments to the lads: the gang was a collective in which weaker members could be safe-guarded; everyone would get the same wage; there would be more control of conditions; and it could improve earnings when one man – the democratically elected ganger – could be almost full time on rate-fixing problems and the organizing of work. Since foremen are usually busy at production meetings, filling in forms or doing progress work, the ganger ends up by having some control over the allocation of work. Of course, this organization of the work process by the workers themselves in fact helps the company; but when it reaches the stage where the company feels it is losing control over the organization and earnings of the shop floor, it reacts.[15]

This initiative resulted in short, considered partial disputes which were quickly effective at a time when the company was anxious to avoid disruption in other production.

> In a well-organized factory where the strategy is to go for limited advances, long mass strikes shouldn't be necessary. Of course, there are bloody-minded company managements who don't care at all if they are wrong, who prefer a total shutdown to a compromise . . . With each such advance we secure a little more control, a little more of managerial function is taken from management.[16]

In this sense of the word 'control', dock workers have controlled hiring and firing in their industry so that no one may be engaged or turned out without the permission of the dockers' representatives. Yet shop workers quite commonly enjoy no such security. It thus seems reasonable to speak of the dockers exercising greater controls in this domain than the shop workers. Of course, neither dockers nor shop workers have attained anything like self-management.

Encroachment of Powers

Even so, during the long postwar boom, shop stewards reached far beyond the point described by Philip Higgs, to wield considerable influence over large areas of decision-making which, a decade or so before, had been entirely the property of management. Control of hiring and firing by workpeople, however, became a qualitatively new issue when full employment began to give place to continued high levels of unemployment. Beginning with an unsuccessful attempt to prevent factory closures and redundancies in the Merseyside plants of GEC, the movement of factory occupations, work-ins and sit-ins became a major phenomenon after the pioneering struggles of the workers at Upper Clyde Shipbuilders, in 1971.[17] Under the slogan of 'the right to work' this exemplary battle soon had imitators all over the country, and within three years more than two hundred such initiatives had been recorded. Sometimes these raised the question of co-operative self-management, to which we shall return. More commonly, they were concerned with workers' control in the narrow sense employed in this chapter: they were attempts to limit arbitrary managerial powers by the exercise of joint trade union action.

Naturally, resistance to plant closures or mass redundancies implies a challenge to the decisions which bring these policies into practice: accordingly there have been a whole series of attempts to bargain about such heartland 'management' matters as investment priorities, product-mixes, and alternative corporate planning.[18] The Transport and General Workers' Union began to introduce elements of environmental protection into its claims, during the early seventies.[19] Before long, as the demand 'open the books' was taken up both in bargaining around the table, in political action and then in legislative responses, so it became more and more frequent to find investment policies subjected to scrutiny, and sometimes opposition.

This process culminated in two types of action: firstly, the political call for formal planning agreements, intended to be made obligatory in the major multinationals which were dominant in British manufacturing industry, and thus to involve tripartite negotiations between unions, management and government in determining a range of strategic issues; and secondly, the alternative corporate plan which emerged as a trade union response to a threat of serious contraction in employment at Lucas Aerospace.

Planning Agreements

The first of these approaches was canvassed in the 1973 programme of the Labour Party:

> The key to our planning effort is the domination of the economy by a few leading firms. For by concentrating our efforts on to these firms – and especially the 100 or so major firms in manufacturing – we can ensure that our planning is

> kept both manageable and straightforward. We will harness directly the energies of these giants – leaving the numerous smaller firms to our more general planning policies.[20]

It was insisted that trade unions 'must have the right to take part' both in drawing up the plans which were to be presented to the government, and in the consultations about the final agreements. Later plans were announced to involve the 30 most important companies in such agreements by December 1976, and to comprehend the top 100 by the end of 1978. Twelve items for discussion were listed in the White Paper *The Regeneration of British Industry*: these covered economic prospects, company strategy and objectives, sales in the United Kingdom and overseas, investment, employment and training, and productivity. They also extended to questions of finance, pricing policy, industrial relations procedures, consumer and community interests, and product and process development. The last five of these items being more complex than the first seven, it was suggested that they might be tabled for consideration in a subsequent stage.

In fact, nothing happened, because the Prime Minister, Mr Wilson, personally intervened to ensure (after his governmental reshuffle following the 1975 referendum on membership of the European Economic Community) that planning agreements were made 'voluntary' instead of compulsory.[21] Only one such agreement was ever concluded, and this was with Chrysler Motors at the moment between their collapse and subsequent governmental resuscitation. This agreement was unilaterally abrogated when the company was later taken over by French interests, and no further argument was heard about it.[22] But the idea of such agreements dies hard, and it may well recur if ever a reforming government comes into office with the will to do anything to widen the scope of economic planning and popular participation.

Alternative Corporate Plans

The Lucas initiative was altogether more elaborate and far-reaching than this fiasco. Shop stewards from the aerospace combine approached Mr Tony Benn while he was Secretary for Industry, with the complaint that contractions in armament budgets would imply serious unemployment unless counter-projects were launched. He invited them to propose alternatives, and after an elaborate programme of discussion and enquiry, the shop stewards' combine committee put forward more than 1,000 pages of reasoned argument about how alternatives might indeed be developed.[23] This involved consultations with 180 leading authorities, universities and institutions outside the firm, and a vast effort inside it. As a result no less than 150 ideas for relevant new or developed products were set forward. These were refined and grouped into six major product ranges, some of which were extensions of existing commitments (pace-makers and kidney-machines, for instance) while others represented the application of high technology to areas of unmet social need:

> Before we even started the corporate plan our members at the Wolverhampton plant visited a centre for children with Spina Bifida and were horrified to see that the only way they could propel themselves about was literally by crawling on the floor. So they designed a vehicle which subsequently became known as Hobcart – it was highly successful and the Spina Bifida Association of Australia wanted to order 2,000 of these. Lucas would not agree to manufacture these because they said it was incompatible with their product range.[24]

As Mike Cooley, one of the leading stewards involved, reports:

> the design and development of this product were significant in another sense: Mike Parry Evans, its designer, said that it was one of the most enriching experiences of his life when he actually took the Hobcart down and saw the pleasure on the child's face – it meant more to him, he said, than all the

> design activity he had been involved in up to then. For the first time in his career *he actually saw the person who was going to use the product that he had designed.* It was enriching also in another sense because he was intimately in contact with a social human problem. He literally had to make a clay mould of the child's back so that the seat would support it properly. It was also fulfilling in that for the first time he was working in the multi-disciplinary team together with a medical type doctor, a physiotherapist and a health visitor. I mention this because it illustrates very graphically that it is untrue to suggest that aerospace technologists are only interested in complex esoteric technical problems. It can be far more enriching for them if they are allowed to relate their technology to really human and social problems.[25]

Other prototypes were tested, and some of these aroused worldwide interest. They included a rail-road car which could drive on and off a railway, thus avoiding the need to incur vast expense in laying down railway lines through inclines or tunnels; a hybrid power pack which could both conserve energy and reduce pollution and noise; and a whole area of work on heat pumps.

While the company refused point-blank to negotiate on this alternative corporate plan, although the government was unwilling to press the company to take up the matter, the argument reached a point at which it became impossible for ministers to ignore the plan, and in 1978 the Labour Party warmly endorsed the whole scheme.

In February 1979 the Lucas shop stewards published a further 400-page document: *Turning Industrial Decline into Expansion.*[26] After some considerable initial difficulties with some of the national officials of their various trade unions, the stewards secured the recognition and endorsement of the Confederation of Shipbuilding and Engineering Unions for their corporate plan. In the words of Ernie Poland, a TGWU steward:

> It took a lot of persistence, much campaigning and much resolution but eventually, on 25 April 1978, an historic

meeting was held in a Brummie pub under the auspices of the Confederation of Shipbuilding and Engineering Unions (CSEU) – we had become legitimate.

This meeting brought the shop stewards' demands right into the orbit of trade unionisms most powerful organization within the engineering industry. Their cause was taken up, endorsed and acted upon.

They won the backing of 2,500,000 workers, whom the CSEU represent.[27]

The stewards had discovered that between 1971 and 1977 Lucas had 'made an overall profit of £250 million, paid tax on £10.6 million and yet received grants from the government of £10.1 million. Since 1973 deferred tax has amounted to £179 million and in 1978 deferred taxes of about £75 million exceeded the company's profits . . .' reported the Transport and General Workers' *Record*.

This juxtaposition of trends provides an example in a nutshell of how trade unions recognized the necessity to seek to bargain about investment decisions, at any rate in their relation to manpower commitments. The Lucas campaign succeeded in preventing the imposition of many redundancies; secured a stay of execution of others; increased the manpower budget at a new plant in Huyton from 500 to 800; and, after stormy and long argument, secured at last some agreement by the company to discuss the stewards' proposals. Meantime, similar projects were evolved at Vickers, and not unrelated ones at Parsons, the generator manufacturers. At Parsons, constructive and successful negotiations did take place, and the management accepted many of their workers' proposals.[28]

If these were the responses of shop stewards, what was the approach of the central councils of the trade union movement?

Worker-Directors and the Bullock Report

From the early seventies onwards, the TUC was drawn deeper and deeper into the argument about appointing worker-directors on to company boards, which it had already entered, tentatively, in 1966. Beginning with reaction to the celebrated Draft Fifth Directive of the European Economic Community, published in 1972, and the EEC's paper on a draft for European Company statutes, the General Council found itself compelled to develop more and more detailed responses on this issue. The EEC proposed to generalize throughout Europe what were essentially variations on current German Company Law, providing for the appointment of works councils representing all employees, whether unionized or not, and for two-tier company boards, separating out 'supervisory' or overall policy functions from 'management' ones. Workers would elect a minority of the directors on the supervisory boards. In reply to governmental requests for comments on these suggestions, the General Council published a statement on Industrial Democracy in 1974,[29] which argued the case for equality of representation for both workpeople and shareholders upon the supervisory boards of companies employing 2,000 or more workers, provided that worker representatives were elected 'through the trade union machinery'.

Although the Labour Party contested the two 1974 elections on manifestos which included direct commitments to industrial democracy, 'in both the private and public sectors', and specific promises to 'introduce new legislation', no such legislation was ever brought forward. Instead, at the very end of 1975, the government established the Bullock Committee, comprising a mixture of TUC representatives, industrialists and independents, to look into the effects of proposals to place representative workpeople on boards of directors. This committee reported in 1977,[30] in favour of legislation to require the election of worker-directors on to the single-tier boards of large companies. 'Parity' would require equality of numbers between worker and shareholder representatives, but an intermediary group of directors would be appointed by mutual consent of the two sides, or by an Industrial Democracy Commission in the event of their failure to agree. This was designated the '2x + y' formula, where 'x' was the equal number of directors elected by shareholders and workpeople respectively, and 'y' the smaller quota of independents, who might hold the balance in the event of deadlock between the two 'x' contingents.

Subsequently, although promises of legislation were repeated several times before they were written into the Queen's Speech opening the 1978–9 session of Parliament, no legislation was in fact tabled. But during this prolonged delay, the proposals of Lord Bullock's team were continuously diluted, until from the point of view of the strength of proposed worker representation, they finally reached a specific gravity somewhat lower than that of the original EEC directive, with the publication of a White Paper (Cmnd 7231) in May 1978.

During all this time, the Bullock proposals aroused considerable debate between national union spokesmen. Whilst Jack Jones, General Secretary of the TGWU, who had served as a member of the Bullock Committee, called for legislation on its proposals to be tabled the same year, Hugh Scanlon of the AUEW opposed the Report, posing against it a call for 'an extension of collective bargaining, to which we know no limit'.[31]

The lines of argument cut across conventional left–right alignments, uniting both factions of the (normally bitterly divided) AUEW with the (right-wing) EETPU and the (left-wing) Draughtsmen, against any kind of worker representation on the boards of capitalist concerns; and leaving a similarly wide spectrum of forces lined up with the TGWU in favour of implementing the Report. The defeat of the Callaghan administration in 1979, however, put an end to this argument for at any rate the time being, since the Conservatives had no interest in enacting any legislation even remotely similar to that proposed either by the TUC, or by the Bullock Committee, or even by the Labour government's hyper-cautious Cabinet sub-committee on Industrial Democracy.[32]

If the fate of proposals for worker-directors in privately owned industry has not been very encouraging for the advocates of this reform, it does throw light on another issue. Various people have in the past argued that there has been a complete divorce between ownership and control of industry, so that the concept of property has ceased to have any fundamental importance in industrial affairs. Of course, the concentration of economic scale has meant that many small and medium shareholders have been effectively disfranchised in the process of industrial government: but this process has merely served to augment the real powers exercised by oligarchic minority owner-controllers.[33] How important these powers remain may be diagnosed from the remarkable resistance which was offered to the Bullock proposals (moderate though they must have seemed to all who thought ownership an irrelevant issue) from the very first moment of their publication.[34]

In the field of the nationalized industries, this problem was thought no longer relevant. Since these industries are nominally social property already, many trade unionists claimed that there was no solid reason why they should not be democratically administered, unless it can be proved that democratic forms of administration are inherently incompetent. The same TUC Report in which parity representation was mooted for company boards also addressed the issue of public sector management, and recommended 50 per cent trade union membership of all relevant policy-making boards. The other half of board members 'should be appointed by the Minister, but there is scope for further discussion about the composition of this 50 per cent' the Report went on. Although the October 1974 election manifesto of the Labour Party spoke of 'socializing' the nationalized industries, the terms of reference of the Bullock Committee specifically excluded them. Instead, a separate internal governmental enquiry was established under the co-ordination of Mr Alan Lord, Second Secretary at the Treasury. This was a 'private' attempt to monitor the exact position of participatory involvement in different nationalized industries, and it resulted in a memo which tabulated the different stages of participation already reached and offered the opinion that it would be difficult to enforce any single specific policy.[35]

At the level of national trade union initiative, complex discussions took place within the National Union of Mineworkers and between the NUM and the Coal Board;[36] while an experimental scheme involving national union representation in the management of the Post Office was agreed and began to operate. The real interest in change, however, has made itself more keenly felt lower down. The call for direct forms of self-management has been increasingly frequently heard from workers in the nationalized and about-to-be-nationalized industries.

Perhaps the first modern call for a democratic mode of public ownership came from steelworkers, when they were contemplating the renationalization of their industry during the mid-1960s. After several informal seminars, a programme was drafted,[37] which became the basis in 1967 for a full-fledged programme drafted by the National Craftsmen's Co-ordinating Committee of the Iron and Steel Industry.

This called for the constitution of a public board, consisting of a chairman and twelve members, responsible to Parliament through the Minister in a manner roughly analogous to previous nationalization measures. But the directors would be forbidden to hold any other interlocking directorships and would retire in rota after serving a five-year term. The vice-chairman of the board and four of its members would be appointed by the Minister from a panel of names submitted by the various trade unions in industry. The craftsmen also defined extensive powers for the proposed corporation, including the power to develop joint operations with state and private companies operating overseas. They spelt out their plans for rationalization of the industry and for the constitution of workers' councils that varied at combine or group level. At plant level there would be boards which consisted of elected representatives of the different parts of the workforce. At shop level the appointment of shop managers and a wide variety of other powers would be the responsibility of elected shop committees. None of these recommendations, however, came into force.[38]

The nationalization measure which was actually brought in was a repeat of those of the late 1940s, except that a token force of 'worker-directors', without specific powers or accountability, was built in at the last moment. These were appointed by management, as one of them subsequently described:

> One morning, our general manager sent for me and said, 'Oh, the managing director wants to see you.' 'What the hell for?' I said, 'I haven't done any bloody thing!' [39]

Twelve such persons, chosen from a list submitted by the TUC without the intervention of any of their workmates, and sworn to preserve the confidentiality of whatever boardroom secrets they might inadvertently uncover, soon came to the opinion 'We're accountable to BSC . . . we're not representatives of the unions at all.'

Setbacks in steel did not prevent others from pressing for greater powers, however. After the work-in at Upper Clyde Shipbuilders, when the demand for nationalization of the shipbuilding industry was accepted by the Labour Party, a group of workers in the industry at Barrow met with their Member of Parliament, Albert Booth, to discuss plans for a management structure for public ownership. They, too, reached agreement on parity representation on the predominant policy-making board.

But in the aircraft industry, also scheduled for nationalization by the 1974 Labour administrations, workers raised their sights. Half a year before the return of Mr Wilson to Downing Street, the Bristol workers of the British Aircraft Corporation published a thorough and detailed plan for the administration of their industry by a controlling council of worker representatives, elected by trade unionists, which would hire and fire management. 'We reject worker-directors', they wrote: 'the essence of our system is that management is hired by the workers to run the industry.'[40]

> The TUC's latest proposals, though somewhat unclear, can be seen as a movement towards meeting our objectives although in one basic and fundamental regard they are unacceptable. We discuss this below. Here we reproduce the summary of the proposals for the Public Sector as set out in paragraph 96 of the TUC's latest report:
>
> 'If the proposals put forward above for a form of worker representation on the boards of private industry were adopted, then it would obviously be desirable if similar

> forms of representation could be established within the nationalized sector. The 1973 Congress affirmed the importance of this principle. However, the present boards of the nationalized industries already include outside appointments representing wider interests, including trade union appointments from outside the industry. In this sense the existing nationalized boards already perform a function not dissimilar to a supervisory board; indeed, in certain nationalized industries there is also an executive or operating board subordinate to the main board. It is proposed that this system – which is in effect a two-tier system – is retained, but that 50 per cent trade union representation should be provided for on the first-tier board (i.e. that concerned with overall policy-making). This top-tier board would not be the operative body so far as wage negotiations were concerned. The representation should be direct, without involving the Minister, but based on the trade union machinery in the nationalized industry so as to represent the workers employed in the industry. The TUC's role in this would only relate to determining respective unions' interests where necessary. The other 50 per cent of the board should be appointed by the Minister, but there is scope for further discussion about the composition of this 50 per cent. There must therefore be a commitment to a new set of statutes for the nationalized industries.'

If this means that the 50 per cent trade union representation shall be directly elected via the trade union machinery in the nationalized industry so as to represent the workers employed in the industry then to that extent it is a movement towards the objectives we have raised earlier. We now come however to our fundamental and basic objection:

> What we would ask is the significance of the 50 per cent representation? The question surely is, does this or does it not give control?

If not, it does not matter much whether the representation is 5 per cent, 10 per cent or 50 per cent. On the other hand if it is supposed that the proposed representation could mean the exercise of effective control over decision-making (albeit in certain areas) what are the arguments against a complete break with considerations about what different numerical representations might mean and give overall control to elected worker representatives? The Report would seem to suggest that the trade unionists on a public board can represent workers, help to arrive at decisions and presumably as individuals make an equal contribution as any one of the other 50 per cent nominees, but that they could not be 'trusted' to make the 'right' decisions on their own. This is a strange reflection when considered in terms of local authorities up and down the country where elected councillors are responsible for the expenditure of considerable public funds and important policy decisions.

We cannot therefore understand why both the TUC documents fail even to discuss the proposition that the overall policy-making body of a publicly owned industry could be composed entirely of directly elected trade unionists who work in the industry concerned and that they should be clearly answerable and responsible to those who elected them.

Similar attitudes were expressed by the dockworkers of Hull and London, when they prepared their plan for the nationalization of the ports. With quite unambiguous directness, they spelt out their view of industrial democracy: 'Industrial democracy', they insisted, 'does not mean union leaders sitting on directors' boards without any responsibility to the industry's workers.' Neither, they thought, did it mean privileged treatment for elected worker-directors, or the delegation of subordinate responsibility for redundancies, speed-up and managerial experiments. Workers should accept that their councils would report back to them on all their proceedings, that the same democratic constituencies which elected representatives should have the power to recall them, and that duly elected people should have access to all commercial secrets. 'Open the books' was a strong demand of the dockers, but of course this was shared by many others.

The New Worker Co-operatives

If the newly nationalized industries came nowhere near to meeting these expectations, they were partially met in the various experiments in co-operation which took place after 1974. Starting in very inauspicious conditions, usually involving bankruptcy, various factory occupations, work-ins, or sit-ins, gave place to worker-organized co-operatives. The three largest of these were formed after governmental intervention, at the *Scottish Daily News*, Kirkby Manufacturing and Engineering, and Triumph Motorcycles at Meriden.[41] By early 1979 the first two had failed from capital starvation, and the third was precariously balanced upon the brink of failure. Yet all three had aroused widespread sympathy, concern and discussion. Smaller co-operatives were considerably more successful, especially in traditional, labour-intensive manufactories.[42]

Problems of Technological Innovation

The most recent stimulus to trade union strategic thinking on job control and industrial democracy has come from the introduction of 'new technology' in the shape of the micro-processor. There are two aspects of this development which carry serious implications for trade unionists – the threat of massive job loss, with few prospects of compensating growth in employment in non-automated industries and services, and the threat of more arbitrary managerial control over work.

> The new technology offers increased opportunities for management supervision. This is because micro-processors can be programmed to monitor work rates automatically. The exact speed at which people are working can be noted

> immediately, or stored for later use. This may well make it possible for management to set worker against worker. It certainly means that management will be given the tools to squeeze a greater pace of work from the workers.[43]

These problems produced a spate of trade union literature[44] in which the common themes had much to do with the great debates of the 1960s and 1970s on workers' control. The union publications tended to recommend a common strategy, which can be represented by a summary of the TUC's proposals.[45]

The TUC recommends that unions should negotiate New Technology Agreements with companies, and provides a checklist of objectives, which insist that all change must be by agreement and that the status quo should apply in the case of any dispute until negotiations have resulted in agreement for change.

The TUC also insists upon the need for full disclosure of information on management plans for new technology, and for the negotiation of agreed plans for 'maintaining and improving employment'. Not only should there be no redundancies, but 'negotiators should look critically at proposals for using natural wastage to change the size of a workforce . . .' Moreover, 'negotiators can press for exploration by joint management/union teams of new markets for existing products, alternative product ranges, the scope for import substitution . . .' (The influence of the Lucas shop stewards' pioneering initiative is to be noticed here.) The TUC also believes that the health and safety aspects of new technology need careful controls by unions, and that 'no information acquired by computer-based systems shall be used for individual or collective work-performance measurement'.

A number of unions produced model agreements to develop the TUC recommendations. That of APEX insisted, 'There shall be no job loss as a result of the introduction of new systems.' Slump has ensured that this sensible injunction has been more and more difficult to enforce.

The defeat of the Labour government in 1979 put a moratorium on any thought of reform in the nationalized industries, other than the 'reform' of privatization. Increasingly, public sector unions became preoccupied with defensive concerns, since heavy rationalizations were frequently imposed in order to create conditions in which nationalized corporations were easier to sell off.

The roster of privatization was formidable.[46] Beginning in 1979, 5 per cent of British Petroleum was put up for sale. The following year, more than half of British Aerospace came on the market, together with £195 million worth of North Sea Oil licences. There followed the British Sugar Corporation, Cable and Wireless, Amersham International, Britoil, British Rail Hotels and a host of lesser entities. The value of such sales rose continuously from £377 million in 1979 to £2,444 million in 1984/5. The later sales, such as that of British Telecom, sought to extend share ownership over a wider area. Subsequently, the sale of British Airways reverted to earlier practices, aiming at a narrower business constituency. But whether shares were sold widely or not, concentration of holdings was usually rapid. Shareholders in British Aerospace, for instance, shortly fell from 158,000 to 27,000. The huge revenues from these sales became an increasingly important part of the government budgetary strategy, as the advantage of selling off the seed corn began to make itself felt in Treasury circles. There were very widespread criticisms about the flotations which commonly disposed of public assets at prices considerably below their true value.

Coupled with an onslaught against public service workers, as cleaning and ancillary services were put out to tender in the health service and local government, this sales drive certainly created major problems for the trade unions, and undermined powers which had long been taken for granted. Workers found themselves virtually tendering for their own jobs, so that all the processes of collective bargaining were put into reverse. Whilst Mrs Thatcher's government made continuous propaganda play of proposals to 'democratize' the unions, democratization of industry itself was no part of the new dispensation. Instead, as was frequently heard during the miners' strike, the issue was once again reduced to the crude question of 'management's right to manage'. This had been the war cry of the engineering employers far back in 1922, but trade unions thought it had died with the onset of full employment.

In retrospect, we can see that the defeat of the Bullock Report occurred at the highest moment of postwar trade union strength, and was a reverse for the whole idea of collective bargaining. The TUC's proposals for industrial democracy had in fact represented an extension of the principles of collective bargaining into the boardroom. These proposals had been clearly rational and relevant, since they corresponded to the experience and needs of active rank-and-file trade unionists. In choking this impetus, the Wilson administration was guilty of an immense apostasy. If there had been better methods of trade union advance, the TUC had not articulated them, so that to frustrate those specific proposals which the trade unions had actually advanced was to close down the whole prospect of constructive development. That the same Labour government which foreclosed on industrial democracy also began Britain's flirtation with monetarist policies, and established a degree of respectability for mass unemployment, meant that the trade unions were suffering a desperate mauling at the hands of the very government they had worked to install.

The Development of Industrial Strategies by Local Government

Disillusionment with central government policy was an inevitable result of these processes. In the unions, it produced a polarization to the left and to the right. Many rank-and-file workers defected to vote for other parties. The most skilled workers and the poorest workers were involved in two quite distinct rebellions, in favour of differentials (the toolroom workers in the engineering industry), and against privation in the public sector (in the 'Winter of Discontent', which brought low paid public sector workers into mutiny against a 5 per cent pay policy at a time of raging inflation). But while many workers changed their political allegiance at least temporarily, others moved sharply into more intransigent socialist positions, to express their deep displeasure at the evolution of the Labour government. A significant part of this radicalism was to unfold in the development of local government. While such initiatives as those of the workers of Lucas Aerospace had received an equivocal or even hostile response from Labour and trade union leaders, local activists were enthralled by their potential. Workers' corporate plans sought to find means to relate unused resources to unmet needs, and thus struck a deep chord among a new generation of local Labour councillors. Just as independent trade union action was beginning to be circumscribed by mass unemployment and adverse legislation, so these heady ideas found new and powerful advocates in the Town Halls and Labour local authorities. Symbolically, Mike Cooley, one of the main inspirers of the Lucas project, was victimized by his company with the tacit support of his union leaders. Equally symbolically, he quickly found himself re-employed at the very centre of activity in the local authorities' resistance to mass unemployment. As key members of the Greater London Enterprise Board, established to co-ordinate both rescue operations for ailing concerns and the inauguration of new models of co-operative and social production, Mike Cooley and his colleagues found themselves able to carry some of the Lucas proposals from the drawing-board into production, with the support of the Greater London Council.[47] Enterprise Boards were quickly developed in other areas, notably the West Midlands.[48] District and Borough Councils entered the same field, sometimes with the establishment of Co-operative Development Agencies, and sometimes with wider-ranging initiatives. Different authorities organized their intervention in radically different ways, but the results moved very much in similar directions. The mobilization of resources to prop up ailing firms was accompanied by a policy of close support to trade unions, whose economic knowledge was increasingly necessary to local administrators seeking to orient themselves in unfamiliar worlds of industry. We discuss some of the more spectacular local authority supports for trade union groupings below, in Chapter 12. No doubt these far-reaching commitments of the local councils contributed to the decision of

Mrs Thatcher's administration to seek to curtail the autonomy of local government, as well as that of trade unions. The middle 1980s became the occasion for a systematic onslaught on pluralistic institutions, whether unions, local authorities or any other foci of autonomous thought and action. These were not good years for the development of practical examples in the field of industrial democracy. But they certainly provided abundant instances of what the Chinese call 'negative example'. No doubt trade unions will do their best to scrutinize and learn from this.

The consistent prejudice of the Conservative administrations of the 1980s is reflected in their policies towards industrial democracy. The right to extend collective bargaining was discouraged, as we have seen in Chapter 6. Any industrial action beyond the immediate boundaries of the workers' own employment unit is now unlawful, under the 1982 Employment Act, even when it affects plants in the same group of companies. The same is true of any other industrial pressure to extend either recognition or the scope of consultation with unions. In recent years, obligatory disclosure of information by companies to the unions has been narrowed down by successive decisions of the Central Arbitration Committee.

Joint consultation is still imposed by law on the (diminishing) nationalized industry sector, but in the fields of health and safety, of proposed redundancies, and of impending company transfer or takeover, previous advances in trade union rights have been pared back.

A 1985 White Paper proposed relaxing some of the regulations of the 1975 Health and Safety at Work Act. The requirements in the Employment Protection Act of 1975 to give notice of and consult on proposed redundancies have suffered similar dilution at the hands of the courts. On the obligation to give notice of transfer of company ownership, EEC Directives and Regulations have been characterized as 'a very substantial burden on an employer', by UK government spokesmen, and their enforcement by unions has consequently not been supported or encouraged. The EEC Vredeling Directive, if enforced, would create new duties on multinational companies to inform and consult with unions, but although the requirements are not onerous, the British government has firmly denied the need for any such law.

Going against this tide, the 1985 Social Security Act is accompanied by regulations which may impose a duty on the employer to disclose to members of an occupational pension scheme *and* to independent recognized trade unions, information about rights, administration and finances of the scheme. More consistently, the government's withdrawal from enforceable rights is replaced by an addition to the Companies Act which requires the directors to 'report' on their voluntary efforts to establish and operate schemes of consultation and employee involvement. The state's promotion of 'wider share ownership' belongs within the same stream of policy, which is directed towards promoting individualistic, company-oriented attitudes to work, and away from collective responses to the employment relationship.

NOTES

1. Sidney and Beatrice Webb, *Industrial Democracy*, WEA edition, London, 1913, pp. 849–50.
2. Allan Flanders, *Trade Unions*, Hutchinson University Library, 1957, p. 118.
3. We have presented a good deal of evidence on this matter in our *Industrial Democracy in Great Britain*, MacGibbon and Kee, 1967. This covers the development of the argument during the twentieth century.
4. Flanders, *op. cit.*, p. 118.
5. Excerpts from this work are reprinted in volume I of our *Industrial Democracy in Great Britain*, pp. 30–4.
6. Allen and Unwin, n.d., p. 18. This pamphlet was printed by the Pelican Press of Francis Meynell, and its typography is a considerable achievement in craftsmanship.
7. 'What Happened at Leeds?' in Ken Coates (ed.), *British Labour and the Russian Revolution*, Spokesman, 1972.
8. Cf. Raymond Postgate's contemporary work, *The Bolshevik Theory* (Grant Richards, 1920) for a good example of this.
9. S. R. Graubard, *British Labour and the Russian Revolution*, OUP, p. 41.
10. Herbert Morrison, *Socialization and Transport*, Constable, 1933, pp. 208–10.
11. Arthur Scargill, 'The Case Against Workers' Control' in *Workers' Control*, Bulletin of the Institute for Workers' Control, no. 37, pp. 13–14.
12. Flanders, *op. cit.*, pp. 121–2.

13. The best available account of these is Milojko Drulovic, *Self-Management on Trial*, Spokesman, 1978.
14. We have discussed this terminology in greater detail in *The New Unionism*, Penguin, 1972, Chapter 4.
15. R. Fraser, *Work*, volume 2, Penguin, 1969, pp. 116–17.
16. *Ibid*, p. 119.
17. For a brief account, see K. Coates, *Work-ins, Sit-ins and Industrial Democracy*, Spokesman, 1980.
18. For a number of examples, see K. Coates (ed.), *The Right to Useful Work*, Spokesman, 1978. See also Vickers' National Combine Committee of Shop Stewards, *Building a Chieftain Tank and the Alternative*, Newcastle-upon-Tyne, 1978; *Alternative Employment for Naval Shipbuilding Workers*, Barrow, 1978; *Economic Audit on Vickers Scotswood*, Newcastle-upon-Tyne, 1979; *C. A. Parsons' Unions Explain*, Bulletin of the IWC, no. 36, p. 20; *An Alternative Strategy for Power Engineering*: C. A. Parsons' shop stewards; *Workers' Control*, Bulletin of the IWC, New Series, no. 1., p. 9.
19. See, for example, the ICI claims of 1971 and 1974. The first was published by the T & GWU under the title *A Positive Employment Programme for ICI*: it proposes joint safety committees with a remit to consider environmental matters.
20. Labour's Programme, 1973.
21. Cf. Tom Forester, 'The Neutralization of the Industrial Strategy', in Ken Coates (ed.), *What Went Wrong?* Spokesman, 1979.
22. Cf. Chrysler, *The Workers' Answer, Workers' Control*, Bulletin no. 32, May–June 1976, pp. 12 *et seq*. There were at least two versions of the Chrysler Agreement, and even the abridged one was marked 'confidential'.
23. Lucas Aerospace Combine Shop Stewards' Committee, *The Lucas Plan*, IWC Pamphlet, no. 55.
24. Mike Cooley, 'Design, Technology and Production for Social Needs', in *The Right to Useful Work*, Spokesman, 1978, p. 201.
25. *Ibid*, p. 202.
26. Lucas Aerospace Confederation Trade Union Committee, Interim Report, February 1979 (Hayes, Middlesex).
27. Transport and General Workers' Union, *Record*, July 1979.
28. *Workers' Control*, Bulletin of the IWC, New Series, no. 1, pp. 9 *et seq*.
29. TUC, *Industrial Democracy*, first edition, 1974; second edition, 1977; third, revised and expanded edition, 1979.
30. Cmnd 6706, January 1977. See also K. Coates and T. Topham, *A Shop Stewards' Guide to the Bullock Report*, Spokesman, 1977.
31. *Morning Star*, 27 January 1977.
32. Of which the TUC spoke with less than fierce enthusiasm in the 1979 reprint of *Industrial Democracy*. 'The General Council considered that the Government were proposing a very protracted timetable for the attainment of . . . modest objectives' (p. 58).
33. This phrase comes from P. Sargant Florence, *The Logic of British and American Industry*, Routledge, 1953 and reprints. See especially Chapter V.
34. The influence of the CBI in co-ordinating resistance to the Bullock proposals deserves closer scrutiny than it has received. See, in particular, Michael Useem, *The Inner Circle: Large Corporations and the Rise of Business Political Activity in the US*

and UK, Oxford University Press, pp. 157–60. See also Hilary Wainwright and Dave Elliott, *The Lucas Plan: a New Trade Unionism in the Making*, Allison and Busby, 1982.
35. John Elliott, *Conflict or Co-operation*, Kogan Page, 1978, Chapter 17.
36. These talks culminated in a forum at Harrogate in December 1977, reported in *Workers' Control*, no. 37, pp. 11 *et seq.*
37. Cf. K. Coates and T. Topham, *Workers' Control*, Panther, 1970, p. 385.
38. Coates (ed.), *Can the Workers Run Industry?* Spokesman, 1968, pp. 154–6.
39. P. Brannen, E. Batstone, D. Fatchett and P. White, *The Worker Directors*, Hutchinson, 1976, p. 120.
40. Bristol Aircraft Workers, *A New Approach to Public Ownership*, IWC Pamphlet, no. 43, 1974, pp. 10–11.
41. Cf. Coates (ed.), *The New Worker Co-operatives*, Spokesman, 1976.
42. As at Grantham, where former Courtaulds' employees established a dressmaking co-operative after the closure of their shirt-factory. See Harold Frayman in *Workers' Control*, New Series, 1978, no. 2, pp. 13 *et seq.*
43. TGWU, *Micro-Electronics: New Technology, Old Problems, New Opportunities*, 1979.
44. In addition to the TGWU booklet referred to above, see also: APEX, *Office Technology: the Trade Union Response*, 1979; ASTMS, *Discussion Document – Technological Change and Collective Bargaining*, 1979; NUJ, *Journalists and New Technology*, 1978; POEU, *The Modernization of Telecommunications*, 1979; AUEW/TASS, *Computer Technology and Employment*, 1978; TUC, *Employment and Technology*, 1979. See also Clive Jenkins and Barrie Sherman, *The Collapse of Work*, Eyre-Methuen, 1979; Counter-Information Services, *Report: the New Technology* (Anti-Report no. 23), 1979; and Chris Harman, *Is a Machine After Your Job? New Technology and the Struggle for Socialism*, Socialist Workers' Party, 1979. For a theoretical discussion see Steve Bodington, *Computers and Socialism*, Spokesman Books, 1973.
45. TUC, *op. cit.*
46. Cf. Kate Ascher, *The Politics of Privatization*, Macmillan, 1987. Also, OECD, *United Kingdom 1984/5*, pp. 24–5, and *Westminster Bank Review*, November 1965, with Labour Research Department, *Privatization: Paying the Price*, 1987.
47. Tony Topham, *Planning the Planners*, IWC/Spokesman, 1983; M. Barratt Brown, *Study Packs*, 1–6, GLC Industry and Employment Branch, 1983–5 (especially no. 3); GLC, *London Industrial Strategy*, 1985; GLEB, *Corporate Plan*, 1984–5; M. Mackintosh and H. Wainwright, *A Taste of Power*, Verso, 1987.
48. WMEB, West Midlands County Council, *Action in the Local Economy*, 1984.

CHAPTER 10

Trade Unions and the Law

Judicial Fictions

'Law is a technique for the regulation of social powers.'[1] In the field of labour relations, the law as an institution does not recognize this rather self-evident truth. Common law, which is based on the decisions of judges, is concerned almost exclusively with the rights of individuals, and therefore relates uneasily, and commonly throughout history in a hostile manner, to the collective behaviour of workers and their trade union organizations. This tendency has been greatly enhanced in the period since 1979, as we shall see, although it was already gathering momentum during the previous fourteen years. At the same time, the law persists in treating modern companies, and indeed any employer, including multinational corporations and publicly owned bodies, as if they were individuals. Despite their vast collective power, it further grants to companies the unique privilege of limited liability. The fiction of 'personality' attaching to the corporation or company becomes ever more unreal with the widespread growth of the device of the subsidiary company. A whole chain of firms may, in reality, be under a single holding company's direction, often concealed behind a 'corporate veil'. Just one of these companies may claim independent personality at law, with sometimes devastating consequences for their workers and the unions involved.[2]

The fiction of corporate 'personality' derives from another fiction, which is crucially influential in judicial intervention in labour law. This is the assumption that the contract of employment made between employers and workers is the outcome of an individual agreement between two free and equal parties. In fact, of course, the bargaining power of an *individual* worker is usually minimal, whilst that of his *corporate* employer may well be vast. This is the moral and social rationale behind the formation of collectivities of workers, normally taking the form of trade unions. Yet the common law views such organizations with deep suspicion. So it is not surprising that the courts find crimes and torts (civil wrongs) arising from workers' actions largely in consequence of these basic legal distortions.

Judges and the Law

For trade unions and workers' collective action to have any legal status at all against this common law background, it has been necessary that Parliament should repeatedly, at critical moments in history, legislate to protect these organizations and initiatives, to give them 'immunity' from laws which penalize actions 'in restraint of trade'. Only such intervention has ensured that trade union functions were not constantly restricted by case law which found them illegal and therefore punishable or liable, either in criminal or civil suits. Legislation designed to provide such immunities, that is to promote trade unionism, was passed on many occasions in the hundred years from 1871. On each occasion, sooner or later, judges in the ordinary courts found ways to reimpose liability on trade unions for their collective actions; hence the history of labour law between those years, and to some extent also between 1974 and 1979, is a record of the conflict between judges and Parliament. Since 1979, this has changed: judges and Parliament seem to have joined in consensus. Before 1979, throughout this conflict, trade unions exerted their own political pressures to support the principle of non-intervention of law in their affairs, and in industrial relations generally. Their experience led them to endorse what has been called 'collective laissez-faire', and a wide political agreement was eventually built around this approach.

The judges were never reconciled to this restriction of their powers; so frequently have they re-entered the field that one is bound to question how far their behaviour has been motivated in part by their own class and social background. Most judges come from public schools and the ancient universities, although the position is changing. One confessed, with uncharacteristic honesty, in 1923, that

> the habits . . . the people with whom you mix, lead to your having a certain class of ideas of such a nature that . . . you do not give as sound and accurate judgements as you would wish. This is one of the great difficulties at present with Labour. . . . It is very difficult sometimes to be sure that you have put yourself into a thoroughly impartial position between two disputants, one of your own class and one not of your class.[3]

More direct in impact than unconscious social bias is the positive dislike of many judges for the immunities of trade unions, which they prefer to interpret as 'privileges'. In company law, however, the principle of limited liability, which exempts individuals from the consequences of their actions, is not at all normally seen as a privilege, however much loss it may inflict on innocent parties.

Freed from almost all legislative restraint in the 1980s, the judiciary has so indulged its own law-making powers that, in the eyes of one serious journalist writing on the case of the printing unions in their legal collision with the newspaper proprietor Rupert Murdoch, the employer 'does not just have the best cards, he's got the entire pack'.[4] The Law Lords, Britain's final court of appeal, have now registered their deepest antagonism to the tradition of non-intervention, stating that union 'immunities stuck in their judicial gorges'.[5]

The Outlook of Trade Unionists

Along with their distrust of the law on collective organization and action, the unions have also held traditionally to a cautious and restricted view of the benefits to be derived for working people from legal enforcement of individual workers' rights, and of minimum standards of pay and conditions. In this field, of 'regulatory' legislation (as distinct from the 'auxiliary' law governing collective relations), unions have sometimes endorsed special cases as suitable for Parliamentary intervention. Notable examples include the establishment of Wages Councils to enforce minimum wages in low paid industries, health and safety statutes, and more recently the laws against sex and race discrimination in employment. But, as with auxiliary law, these former props to the self-regulation of industrial relations have been substantially reduced since 1979. Parliamentary enactment had given trade unions considerable space in which to pursue their chosen method of collective bargaining; it had supplemented that method with piecemeal regulation in specific industries and in certain defined fields. State employment practice – particularly after the Whitley Reports of 1917 (see Chapter 6) – had encouraged the collective bargaining method, and had endorsed its results in such matters as fair wages in public contracts by enforcing collectively bargained wage rates through arbitration and by keeping the judges at bay. The state had also refrained from any but minimal interference in trade unions' internal affairs.

In one area, that of trade union political funds, statute law, although acceptable to most trade unionists, became and remained intrusive after 1913. We consider this question in our next chapter. But all this, and more, was swept away by the new statutes of 1980, 1982 and 1984, and common law was invited by those measures 'to resume its dominion over industrial conflict, union security and the power relations inherent in employment'.[6] In this new and inhospitable legal climate, trade unions are rethinking traditional policies and values. Before discussing the new laws, however, we must first survey the paths which have been trodden to reach them.

The Development of Labour Law

The medieval state had forbidden workers' combinations as early as 1351, having empowered local magistrates to fix wages in

1349. Statutory regulation continued for four centuries but broke down before the advance of commercial and industrial interests in the eighteenth century, to be followed by the classical era of laissez-faire and freedom of contract. The prohibition of workers' combinations was reaffirmed in 1799, but withdrawn in statutes of 1824–5. However, strikes and other collective actions were punished by criminal laws relating to 'threatening', 'intimidation' and 'molestation'. Master and Servant Acts regulated the contract of employment, under which workers were liable at criminal law for any breach, whilst employers were merely held subject to (highly unlikely) civil proceedings. The common law crimes of conspiracy and 'action in restraint of trade' were applied to trade union organization and action.

In the 1860s and 1870s, more effective trade unions emerged, though limited to craftsmen and certain skilled industrial sections. Having formed the TUC in 1868, they began campaigning for an amelioration of the laws. Their lobbying, encouraged by the extension of the franchise first to some, and then to the majority of working-class males, resulted in two important statutes. One, in 1871, nullified the 'restraint of trade' doctrine, thus giving unions a more secure legal status and protection at law for their funds. But it set the pattern for subsequent legislation, by conferring not a *right* to organize, but an immunity from the common law consequences of so doing. We have recorded this formula in Chapter 1.

Moreover, in the same year, Parliament passed the Criminal Law Amendment Act which provided for the continuing operation of criminal conspiracy charges against strikers. A renewed and effective trade union lobby yielded the Conspiracy and Protection of Property Act of 1875, which gave immunity (again) to strikers from the crime of simple conspiracy in the context of a trade dispute, and which further afforded some legal protection for peaceful picketing. But penalties still attached to specific offences such as intimidation; these were always liable to hostile application by the judges. Despite this, the Acts of 1871 and 1875 marked a significant milestone in the trade union struggle to obtain, through Parliament, protection from judge-made law for trade union organization and for strike action.

Thwarted in their use of criminal conspiracy, the judges turned to civil conspiracy, a doctrine which they deployed against a revived and militant trade unionism in the 1880s and 1890s, finding strike action to be a civil wrong, or tort, for which the injured party (the employer) could claim damages. The case of the Taff Vale railway company against the Amalgamated Society of Railway Servants in 1901 was the most influential moment; the union was found liable in tort for the effects of its strike on the company, and had to pay £42,000 in costs and damages. The case completely undermined the right to strike, or rather removed from strikes the immunities which had been thought to exist by virtue of the statutes of 1871–5.

So the trade unions returned to Parliamentary pressure, this time through their enhanced affiliations to the newly formed Labour Representation Committee which, in 1906, won twenty-nine seats in the Commons, and transformed itself into the Labour Party. In that year, strengthened by this historic development, the unions persuaded the Liberal government to pass the Trades Disputes Act which forbade legal action against strikers in tort, and provided union action with the most widely based immunities up to that time.

This law prevailed until the 1960s (albeit with an aberration between 1927 and 1946), and set the scene for the growth and eventual dominion of collective bargaining relatively free from legal intervention. Yet this Act belonged also to the category of immunity law, and *individual* strikers remained in principle liable for breach of their contracts of employment during strikes. It should be added that this offence was now confined to civil law, having lost its old criminal status as a result of the Employers and Workmen Act of 1875.

Within three years of the passing of the 1906 Act, the Law Lords, in the Osborne Judgement, found another loop-hole through which to attack trade unions. They deemed it to be illegal for trade unions to spend any of their funds on political functions, thus depriving the infant Labour Party of its main source of income. Yet again, the unions required statutory redress, which they obtained with the Trade Union Act of 1913. It provided that unions may spend funds on politics, but only out of a separate account, not to be supported from their general funds. A separate levy on the members had to be made for this purpose, and any member could 'contract-out' of paying it. Furthermore, the unions had to hold a special ballot of their members to determine their right to operate this system. Without a majority in favour, political objectives remained *ultra vires*. In fact, most unions immediately held successful ballots, and abandoned their initial hostility to the Act, which they had at first regarded as an unhappy compromise. (From 1910 to 1913 they had argued that it represented a discriminatory circumscription of trade union rights to determine their own affairs by internal democratic processes.) The trade union minorities recorded in the ballots can still quite legally evade the majority decision and withhold their support for the political fund by contracting-out. But company directors can, in flagrant contrast, 'contract-in' their shareholders, customers and workers, to political subscriptions without consulting any of them. 'The unions operate in a goldfish bowl, the employers behind a two-way mirror.'[7] We shall return to this subject when we encounter the 1984 Trade Union Act.

The state had taken its first step to endorse the settlement of wages by collective agreement in 1891, when Parliament passed the first of its Fair Wages Resolutions, which stipulated that government contractors should observe the terms and conditions of employment generally operating in their industry. In 1896, the Conciliation Act established the principle that government had an obligation to provide a professional conciliation service in industrial disputes, setting a precedent which has been observed, though governed by numerous subsequent statutes, down to the present day, when the Advisory, Conciliation and Arbitration Service (ACAS) fulfils this function. This is briefly described in Chapter 6.

Another step in harmony with the prevailing view of the state as an auxiliary to collective bargaining was taken in 1909, with the passing of the Trades Boards Act, which created machinery for statutory determination of minimum wages in certain 'sweated' trades, such as tailoring, paper-box making, lace and net making, and chain making. The criterion for the establishment of a Trades Board was simply low pay; in 1918 this was broadened to include low levels of union organization, and much later, after the Second World War, enlarged in Wages Council legislation. This sequence of measures is a classic exception which proves the rule; for in effect the state was endorsing the general practice of voluntary collective bargaining precisely by identifying those industries where it was not present, or was ineffective, and only there breaking the convention by legislating for enforceable minima.

The conclusions and recommendations of the Whitley Reports of 1917, which were commissioned by government in the wake of what it regarded as serious industrial unrest during the First World War, adhered faithfully to the prevailing philosophy. Whitley's principal recommendation was that voluntary collective bargaining between trade unions and employers or their associations should be the norm of industrial relations, and that state intervention should support, but not override it. Thus, voluntary arbitration machinery should become a permanent state service (having been compulsory during the war years), and the Trades Board system should be extended. We have already seen that this proposal resulted in legislation. The Industrial Court Act 1919 did the same in respect of voluntary arbitration. The government itself instituted the 'best practice' recommendation in establishing, with the unions, central negotiating machinery in the civil and public services.

In opposition to this trend towards harmony, the government passed its Emergency Powers Act in 1920, to give itself powers, including the requisitioning of troops, to 'secure the essentials of life' for 'the community' in cases of serious strikes in essential industries such as transport and power supply. This Act is still on the statute book, and can be used, not to ban a strike, but to break it by, for example, sending in troops to provide the absent labour. Another repressive measure was the Trades Disputes Act 1927, visited by government on the trade unions as a punishment for their temerity in calling the 1926 General Strike. Quite irrelevantly to that event, the Act forbade the closed shop in public sector employment, and decreed that civil servants must join only unions confined within the service, which must also be barred from any political affiliation. Strikes to 'coerce the government' were declared illegal, picketing rights were restricted, and in a vindictive irrelevance, 'contracting-in' was substituted for 'contracting-out' of the unions' political levy. The whole of this 1927 law was repealed by the Labour government in 1946.

An important practice which should be subsumed under the category of auxiliary support for collective bargaining, was First adopted during the Second World War, when strikes were outlawed and compulsory arbitration reimposed as in the first World War. Tribunal awards under this regime became legally binding on trade union and employer alike, and after the war this power was extended to impose upon a single non-conformist employer the obligation to pay the 'going rate' in his industry or service. This was a most powerful endorsement by the state of the terms and conditions arrived at by collective bargaining. It was perpetuated in different forms by Labour and Conservative administrations between 1951 and 1975. It was abolished, as we shall see, by Mrs Thatcher's government in the 1980s.

In the immediate postwar years the Fair Wages Resolutions of the House of Commons, whose origin we have already noted, were extended and mirrored in similar measures adopted by local authorities and public corporations. The Resolutions also required that 'the contractor shall recognize the freedom of his workpeople to be members of trade unions'. Otto Kahn-Freund believed that these measures did more than any other act of state to spread collective bargaining rates throughout industry.[8] They certainly amount to formidable evidence that the promotion of collective bargaining and therefore of trade unionism was a matter of established state policy. This policy enjoys a contradictory relationship with government-imposed wage restraint (incomes policy), which sometimes had the force of law behind it, during several periods in the 1960s and 1970s. An arbitrary but necessary division of our subject has led us to discuss incomes policy in the chapter on collective bargaining; it could belong equally well here, since clearly stated involvement in the determination of personal income may require strong legal intervention for its enforcement, the more so since the law lacks any equitable principle on which to determine incomes.

The 1960s ushered in a new phase in the history of labour law in other respects as well as that of incomes policy. The state became increasingly interventionist, for example in its endeavour to promote labour efficiency with the Industrial Training Act 1964, and labour mobility in the Redundancy Payments Act of 1965. But the most startling developments in labour law of this and subsequent decades were set in motion by the ancient means of another adverse judicial finding in an industrial dispute. In 1964, the Law Lords discovered, in the *Rookes v Barnard* case, an obscure tort of intimidation. Its proof in the court depended upon the interpretation of a shooting incident in a private trade war between two British merchant vessels off the coast of the Cameroons in the eighteenth century. Such are the Gilbertian absurdities from which stem the injustices of English common law as applied to trade unionism. For this ancient (and, strangely, *civil*) wrong, trade unionists in the twentieth century were once again found liable for the effects of normal industrial action, or rather the threat of it. The decision, said the union's counsel, 'drove a coach and four' through the 1906 Trades Disputes Act.

In 1965 the Labour government legislated to provide temporary restoration of the 1906 immunities but at the same time, bending before a widespread agitation by the media, employers and political opposition about the more extensive activities of shop stewards in the postwar climate of full employment, it set up a Royal Commission on trade unions and employers' associations, thus signalling its willingness to hear evidence bearing upon possible change in established labour law. Calls for fines on unconstitutional strikers and for 'other acts of indiscipline' and for the legal enforceability of collective agreements came thick and fast from employers' associations, the CBI and the newspapers. The Commission, true to the tradition of such bodies, commissioned, heard and read an encyclopedic volume of research evidence. (Within its limitations, this is not a bad tradition; it is certainly to be preferred to the current government's arrogant rejection of research and empirical evidence in favour of reliance on prejudice and ideology in industrial relations.)

Donovan and After

The Donovan Commission (whose Report appeared in 1968) avoided endorsement of extreme demands for legal intervention in strikes and union affairs, and has appeared to many commentators to reaffirm the abstentionist tradition. But, whilst the weight of its authority was thrown behind the voluntary reform and formalization of collective bargaining, it also proposed that the immunity in strikes conferred on all by the 1906 and 1965 Trade Disputes Acts should in future be withdrawn from unofficial actions and, further, that after a period during which collective bargaining procedures should be reformed, legal sanctions would be justified. Therefore Donovan actually represented the thin edge of a wedge against the abstentionist tradition. The TUC, and trade unions individually, were content in evidence to the Commission to restate the values of non-intervention and the voluntary tradition. The TUC's tone, in particular, was defensive, or assertive only of the status quo; absent from its concerns was any evaluation of the need for a new set of legal rights or 'workers' charter'. This critical comment seems indeed restrained, given the hindsight that we now possess in the 1980s.

The Labour government started the push for restrictive legislation with the publication of its White Paper *In Place of Strife*, in 1969. Going beyond Donovan's recommendations, it would have given governments powers to order a twenty-eight-day compulsory return to work for 'conciliation' in an unconstitutional strike, and to order the conducting of a strike ballot. There would have been fines for non-compliance. A compulsory recognition procedure was also envisaged. These commitments caused a deep political crisis between trade unions and government, which was resolved only by the government's withdrawal of its proposals. The TUC in return gave a 'solemn and binding' promise to be more active in seeking to prevent unconstitutional and unofficial strikes.

The turn of the High Tory lawyers had now come; their proposals, prefigured in a Party document of 1968 – *Fair Deal at Work* – were legislated for by the Conservative administration elected in 1970, in the Industrial Relations Act 1971. This was a comprehensive, restrictive legal code, abolishing the foundations of labour law as embodied in statutes from 1871 to 1906, and overtly aimed at curbing trade unions and strikers by legal penalties, and at regulating trade union internal affairs by means of state registration of unions which conformed to legal requirements in their rulebooks.

New civil wrongs, called 'unfair industrial practices', were created, which rendered much official, but particularly unofficial action, and all action by unregistered unions, liable to damages. Disregard of these laws led to contempt of court proceedings, fines, and eventually imprisonment for the offenders. Unions could avoid these impositions only by disciplining and expelling offending officers, including shop stewards. The intention was to turn unions into an industrial police force.

Collective agreements were made legally enforceable, except where employer and union agreed to insert an escape clause. The closed shop was outlawed except in very special circumstances (as in the merchant navy), and an elaborate legalistic procedure for 'agency shops' was substituted for it. The right to belong, or not to belong, to a (registered) union was guaranteed. The state was empowered to order compulsory strike ballots and a sixty-day cooling-off period in strikes adjudged by the government to be serious. A new authority, the National Industrial Relations Court, was set up to deal with cases arising from the Act. One measure favourable to workers was included; the first of the Unfair Dismissal laws.

The Act was a total failure. It prompted more industrial action than any predecessor, and far more than it prevented. And it was rendered inoperative both by effective trade union opposition and by the employers' marked reluctance to use its provisions or to approach the new court, whose decisions provoked great alarm in the minds of professional company directors and managers. The court was only used by small employers and those who were not averse to industrial conflict. Whilst no new closed shop agreements could be made, major employers connived at the continuance of existing ones, and offered nearly universal co-operation to the unions in inserting escape clauses to nullify the legal enforceability of collective agreements. The state itself found that the Act backfired against it when it sought to impose a compulsory strike ballot on the railway workers, who voted a massive majority in support of their union, which had called for the continuation of an industrial action. The government never used this clause again, even though it was clearly designed to be deployed in the huge industrial crises of the miners' actions in 1972 and 1973. Finally, and most effectively, the unions, in almost complete conformity with TUC policy, did not register under the Act. This abstention caused them financial loss (through the adverse operation of tax immunity provisions) but effectively frustrated the government's design to incorporate them as agencies of the state, and to supervise their rulebooks. The AUEW (now the AEU) and the TGWU both suffered heavy fines for defiance of the NIRC, and five London dockers went to jail for refusing to call off an industrial action. They were hurriedly released, without any attempt by the court to extract a purging of their contempt, when the country approached the verge of a general strike against the imprisonment. By 1973, the Act was virtually a dead letter. In destroying it, the trade unions displayed great tenacity and strategic good sense in the defence of their fundamental corporate interests. They were, moreover, stimulated by the whole experience to re-evaluate, at least to some degree, their estimate of the uses of law. For they quickly set to work, through the TUC–Labour Party Liaison Committee, to elaborate a programme of positive rights legislation to be implemented by an in-coming Labour government. This programme became part of the 'social contract' which was intended to bind the two wings of Labour in an alliance which would preclude any repetition of the collision over *In Place of Strife*.

Between 1974 and 1976, Labour in office repealed the Industrial Relations Act, and set about the fulfilment of the social contract. In the Trade Union and Labour Relations Act 1974 (amended in 1976) the repeal provisions did not embrace the unfair dismissal clauses which were retained and strengthened. The 1974 Act restored the immunities laws as they had been under the 1875 and 1906 Acts. The 1976 amending law extended immunity to cover 'secondary boycotts' such as blacking of goods and firms, and sympathetic actions by workers not directly involved in the dispute, including disputes originating overseas. The full restoration of legality to the closed shop was achieved only in the 1976 Act, which provided that where a union membership agreement existed, an employer could fairly dismiss a non-unionist except where the latter could prove a religious objection to union membership. Trade union status was restored to its pre-1971 position. Unions could now claim independent status on application for a certificate from a Certification Officer, who had to satisfy himself that the union was truly free from outside influence, or control, particularly by an employer. Dismissal for trade union membership or activity was made expressly unfair and therefore actionable, as was dismissal for refusing to join a non-independent union, such as an employer-run staff association, or company union in American terms. Collective agreements were once again assumed to be non-enforceable, unless the parties jointly and expressly provided for legal enforcement. Some legal intervention in union affairs was retained in the 1974 Act, giving protection against arbitrary and unreasonable discrimination by unions against individual members, but the unions' opposition to these clauses prevailed, and they were repealed in 1976. In their place, the TUC was to act through an independent review body to hear appeals by members against exclusion or expulsion by their union.

The Employment Protection Act 1975 aimed to encourage collective bargaining and to extend the rights of individual workers. In pursuit of the first aim, it laid down a procedure for obtaining trade union recognition from an employer, and provided for disclosure of information relevant to collective bargaining by employers to trade unions. It further strengthened earlier provision for enforcing the 'going rate' on a recalcitrant employer, gave unions rights to advance notice of redundancies, allowed Wages Councils to be transformed into Joint Industrial Councils. More: it gave statutory rights to trade union representatives to time off work for industrial relations functions and for training, and established ACAS as an independent, tripartite body to undertake mediation, conciliation and arbitration.

Individual workers' rights in the Act included the right to written notice of terms of employment, the right to trade union membership and activity, the right to time off work for general trade union and public office duties, the right to an itemized pay statement, the right to a written statement of reasons for dismissal, the right to pay when suspended on medical grounds, guaranteed pay during short-time or lay-offs, certain rights to payment in the event of the employer's insolvency, and the right to maternity leave and pay.

The Act constituted nothing like a comprehensive workers' charter, being essentially piecemeal and tentative in its approach. The clauses on disclosure and recognition, moreover, were to be enforced by way of an arbitration award, not for disclosure or recognition, but by action for enhanced wages or conditions. In this way, government displayed a fatal unwillingness to invade, by law, the powers and prerogatives of companies. Consequently the clauses on recognition have proved particularly difficult to enforce.

The Health and Safety at Work Act 1974, a comprehensive statute covering all employees, provided for the appointment of trade union safety representatives, for their training, and for their right to consultation with, and information from, the employer.

The Equal Pay Act of 1970 came into full operation only in 1975, and the Sex Discrimination Act of this later year reinforced the state's intervention in this field. The application and enforcement of both Acts has proved very difficult in the face of social attitudes, employers' interests, and the indifference of some male trade unionists.

During the years of their apparent sovereignty, from 1975 to

1980, TULRA and the EPA did not escape 'creative interpretations' by the judges, who made clear their non-acceptance of the restored generality of the immunity principle. They displayed great imagination in limiting the definition of a trade dispute. If an action fails to qualify *in the judges' view* as a trade dispute, those taking action lose all immunity from the law. Secondary actions and blackings became especially vulnerable through judge-made law between 1976 and 1979, and the right to picket was heavily circumscribed in the Shrewsbury building workers' case of 1975–6, which led to heavy prison sentences, as well as by new methods of mass policing as witnessed in the Grunwick strike of 1977. Moreover, the government itself legislated to make resistance to redundancies liable to criminal charges when, in the Criminal Law Act 1977, it made trespass a criminal offence. This was clearly intended to discourage factory occupations, which occurred more frequently precisely at this time to combat numerous threats of plant closures.

The testing of the new laws on individual workers' rights during the years of their operation covered too short a period to allow dogmatic assertions about their efficacy. But even before their repeal or amendment by the Conservative governments of the 1980s, it was clear that their tentative and piecemeal nature was such that they would require extensive amendment and strengthening before they could qualify as a 'workers' charter'. The law on disclosure of information, for example, was limited by protecting the employer from disclosing original documents, or indeed any data which would cause 'substantial injury' to his business. It is not hard to intuit how judges would be inclined to interpret such a reservation, or the provision that employers were not obliged to produce information which would cost a 'disproportionate amount of time or expense'. Even the law on unfair dismissal, possibly the most significant of the new rights, had serious limitations. These were partly due to the statute itself, which fell short of compelling reinstatement as a remedy for unfair dismissal (extra financial compensation was the substitute), and which did not apply to workers with less than six months' service. Case law established by a new court, the

Employment Appeal Tribunal, made it progressively less likely that workers would win their claims before it. Already by 1977, a study observed that 'It is still possible for an employee to win an unfair dismissal case, but it is now a lot more difficult than it used to be.'[9] But a 1978 study also found that the law had had a big impact on management, prompting them to reform and formalize discipline procedures, and that it had reduced the rate of dismissals.

In the case of the new laws on strikes, the evidence, as we have seen, very soon demonstrated that the return to the old concept of immunities, unsupported by positive rights, rendered them vulnerable to a new wave of common law dilutions. The Health and Safety at Work Act, by affording real if limited rights to trade union representatives, stimulated a genuine advance in self-help trade union activity in this field, at least until the climate of mass unemployment and judge-made limitations on the safety representatives' rights to information undermined its effects in the 1980s.

The Conservative governments of the 1980s have acted partly through direct legislative change, and partly (even mainly) by removing all restraint on the judges' powers to make their own laws. Together, such actions have wrought a transformation of labour law, to the point where the immunities attached to strikes or other industrial action have been diminished to minimal proportions. Now, in any case, these are exclusively confined within the enterprise of the strikers. Trade unions' own internal affairs are now subject to extensive state and judicial interference, and individual workers' rights have been pared away by wholesale amendments and repeals. Fundamentally, the state no longer acts in its traditional role to support and reinforce collective bargaining as the norm. On the contrary, its interventions are solely concerned to produce the opposite condition of a fragmented and increasingly individualistic labour market. The courts have discovered new means of enforcement, including sequestration of union assets, and receivership, which have devastated union security in industrial disputes. Picketing has become ever more hazardous, as police powers and methods have developed to alarming proportions. We may now reasonably characterize British law on disputes as a condition of legal harassment of strikers, the like of which has not been experienced since the early nineteenth century, and which, in its degree, is unknown on the continent of Europe. At the same time, individual workers' rights are less secure, and more attenuated, than anywhere else in the Western world. We must first summarize the legal changes which have produced this condition, before attempting an explanation for its severity.

Conservative Legislation

The changes in statute law introduced since 1979 are contained in two Orders of 1979, the Employment Acts of 1980 and 1982, and the Trade Union Act of 1984. Judges' law has extended the impact of these Acts far beyond their apparent scope.

Concerning industrial action, which had been given substantial immunity in TULRA, the 1982 Act restricted the definition of a trade dispute to conflicts between workers and their own employer, whereas previously they could exist with any employer. A dispute must now also relate 'wholly or mainly' to a specified list of employment issues. Previously it need only be 'connected with' these matters. This change led the judges in the case of the Communication Union's campaign against the job losses threatened by the privatization of British Telecom to declare that it was their function to identify the 'predominant purpose' of a dispute, and that in this case, the union's industrial action was 'in substantial degree a political and ideological campaign' against privatization. An injunction was granted to stop planned strikes and a blacking campaign. 'This interpretation puts in question the very concept of "trade dispute" itself in major strikes . . . In a few words, parliament changed disputes which had for decades been "trade disputes" into "political disputes". There was no complaint from the judges.'[10]

These restrictions on what constitutes a trade dispute are not the summit of judicial creativity during the 1980s. A new doctrine, of 'economic duress' (first appearing in modern form in a 1976 case), has been imported from commercial law into the labour law field. This tort is committed by a 'threat to break a contract unless money is paid . . . causing the victim's intentional submission arising from the realization that there is no other practical choice open to him', according to the judge in a 1984 commercial case. It had already been applied to a labour dispute, however, in 1983 (*Tankships Inc. of Monrovia v ITWF*), in which the ITWF blacked a flag-of-convenience ship to help the crew to extract back wages and enforce minimum international standards, before the ship sailed. The company paid up, the ship sailed, and the company immediately issued a writ alleging economic duress and reclaiming the moneys paid out. The effect of this case is uncertain, since the union's counsel conceded the substance of the claim. But the pronouncements of the Law Lords in the case have led Lord Wedderburn to comment:

> We may yet see an employer claiming back a wage increase forced out of him by the duress in what is normal industrial pressure for acts that further a trade dispute and receive 'immunity' seen as a tort.[11]

Even the highly restricted immunity, now closed within the individual enterprise, which still survives the 1982 Act and its interpretation, would, in that event, disappear, and no strike whatsoever could be called with any certainty of its legality.

The fragmentation of labour is already reinforced to an extreme degree by the 'corporate veil' which, as we have seen, conceals the fact that an 'individual' employer may be part of a superstructure of companies under unified ownership and control. The effect of this restriction extends upwards to the apex of the trade union movement. Calls for sympathetic action, in the mining and printing disputes of the 1980s, to be led by the TUC, were met with rebuff by the General Council, in part because of its fear of being hauled before the courts. A general strike, it need hardly be added, would now be profoundly illegal.[12]

The 1982 Act reduced an employer's liability for unfair dismissal in strikes.

He may still not discriminate against some of the strikers at the plant of a claimant worker, but if he dismisses them all, and staggers dismissals in different plants over a time, he is immune from any claims.

Section 17 of the 1980 Act removes protection from what is called 'secondary action', that is, action against an employer who is not party to the dispute. In these cases, action leading to interference with a commercial contract, that is, action affecting supplies due under contract from one company to another, is as vulnerable as that affecting employment contracts. Blacking campaigns which cross company boundaries are thus rendered illegal, even when the companies in question are in fact jointly controlled. It is necessary to stress that employers have made use of this to render normal industrial action artificially illegal by deliberately setting up 'buffer' companies against which action by workers becomes secondary or tertiary. This device was pioneered by TBF Printers, one of whose owners (Pole-Carew) advised the News International Group on the same method in the much more extensive Wapping print workers' dispute.

Industrial action designed to compel an employer to extend recognition or negotiating rights to groups of workers other than those involved in the action are now devoid of immunity (1982 Act). Moreover, commercial contracts may no longer legally contain clauses requiring 'union labour only' or requiring that one party recognize or negotiate with a trade union. Industrial action to procure these ends is also unlawful. These provisions totally reverse previously well-established state policy of promoting collective bargaining through such contract clauses.

Picketing that takes place anywhere other than at the pickets' own place of work has lost immunity from the charge of procuring a breach of contract (1980 Act). The illegality of 'secondary picketing' now complements that of 'secondary action'. Again we can see at work the purpose of confining action within the enterprise.

A further, far-reaching obstacle to legal strike action was included in the 1984 Act. This requires that, to qualify for immunity, all official strikes or other industrial actions must be preceded by a ballot of the union members to be involved. The ballot must be held according to rules laid down in the Act, and is not protected against outside interference by, for example, the employer.

Consistent with its overall philosophy of undermining collective bargaining, in 1980 the government repealed the powers of the CAC to enforce the 'going rate' upon an employer in an industry covered by a collective agreement (a power reaching back to the 1940s). In the same year, the ACAS authority to require an employer to recognize a trade union was repealed, even though this section of the EPA 1975 had not proved very effective. The Fair Wages Resolution was rescinded in 1982, and in 1986, Wages Council jurisdiction over young workers' minimum wages was removed as part of a more general limitation of Wages Council powers. (They are now limited to fixing minimum wages: they used to determine holiday entitlements also.) The wages inspectorate which enforces Councils' decisions has been reduced from 150 in 1978 to 120 in 1986. Flying in the face of much careful research, the government claimed that these steps would promote employment in the Wages Councils industries, because wages there were too high, and because the Councils were a 'restrictive burden' on the employers. To enable it to limit their role, the government had to withdraw British ratification from an ILO Convention, a step also necessary when it cancelled the Fair Wages Resolution. In all these measures, the government intent was the replacement of collective bargaining supports by a 'free' labour market.

The protection of trade union funds from damages awards had been state policy since the 1906 Act, although this had been modified during the existence of the 1971 Act. It was decisively removed by the 1982 Act, which, however, sets limits to the amount of damages which can be extracted in any one hearing (£10,000 for unions of up to 5,000 members, up to £250,000 for unions over 100,000). Yet these limits are waived where a breach of duty occurs connected with ownership, occupation, control or use of property. In addition to these new threats to their funds in tort, unions face a militant judiciary very ready with injunctions, the defiance of which leads to unlimited fines, sequestration of union property and the imposition of a receiver to administer union funds – all in punishment for contempt of court. In 1984, over a strike at Austin-Rover, the TGWU was fined £200,000 for its contempt in defying an injunction, even though the strike had collapsed a week earlier!

The use by employers (and in cases such as the miners' strike, also by union members) of the procedure of the injunction has played the major part in bringing unions to court in recent years. The device works as follows. When a union takes, or proposes to take, an industrial action which the employer wishes to prevent or terminate, and which he estimates may fall outside the scope of immunity, he prepares evidence and submits it to the High Court in a written affidavit. The union receives a few days' notice at most of the application's hearing. The judge hears the evidence and, if the union is represented, also its defence of the industrial action. (But in an *ex parte* injunction, no defence is heard.) He then decides whether there is a case to answer, which should go forward to full trial. If he so decides, it is in his discretion to grant the employer's application for an injunction ordering the industrial action to be deferred, or to cease, in order, as the official description of court practice has it, to 'preserve the status quo until the rights of the parties have been determined' at the full trial. The courts are notorious, in the eyes of trade unions, for the built-in bias which they bring to this decision, because they tend to regard the employers' potential loss from the continuation of the industrial action as the most important question. Thus, employers' interests are likely to be defended by the granting of the injunction. This means that if the union feels unable to defy the injunction (and incur penalties for contempt) it will be forced to switch off its whole industrial pressure. This may have been built up over time, or may have been spontaneously generated. In either case, commonly, after what amounts to a forced 'cooling-off period', industrial action is extremely difficult to resume, especially as any full trial may be months away. The employer's objective is usually confined to the obtaining of the injunction; he rarely intends or needs to proceed to trial. The judges are his natural allies, since they recognize his immediate loss as an 'individual' facing a collective act. The loss to the individual workers within the collective, from abandoning the strike's initiative and impetus, does not enter into courtroom calculations.

Under the 1982 Act, unions are now liable for the actions of their senior officers, or for any other officers having authority in their rules, or indeed any officer not expressly denied authority. These liabilities aim to force unions into exercising restraint over the actions of their representatives, in order to protect themselves from damages. Any Orders issued by the courts which are defied can lead also to personal liability of the officials or union trustees.

The closed shop, or the union membership agreement, attracted the special hostility of a government wedded to the right of the individual to decide whether or not to join a union. Action to compel another employer to enforce a closed shop became liable in tort under the 1982 Act. Dismissal of a non-unionist is almost wholly outlawed; anyone claiming a 'deeply held personal conviction' against membership is protected by the 1980 Act. Moreover, the only closed shops which are recognized even to this marginal extent are those supported by a new ballot in which either 80 per cent of the workforce affected, or 85 per cent of those voting, support it. Any dismissal for non-unionism outside a closed shop is now automatically unfair, and is afforded specially enhanced compensation rights. Non-unionists who claim unfair dismissal may 'join' the union with the employer in the tribunal hearings, in the claim for compensation.

The 1984 Act introduces substantial state intervention in the internal government of unions, in rule-making and in decision-making processes. Part I requires that the principal executive committee of every union should be elected, not less frequently than every three years, in a ballot which must place all members of the committee directly into their seats. In the evolution of trade union government (see Chapter 2), many unions have traditionally provided for indirect representation via elections from regional or trade group committees, on to their top executive. A direct postal ballot is favoured in the Act, although a workplace ballot is permitted. Ballots at branch meetings are not permitted. Unions may claim financial subsidy from the state towards the costs of balloting their members, an issue which has seriously divided unions within the TUC. The EETPU and the AEU led the way in defying TUC policy on this question by applying for funds, and the TUC was unable to prevent them. More unions are being impelled, by the large costs involved, in the same direction. The new law on ballots contravenes an ILO Convention on Freedom of Association which stipulates that workers' organizations should have full freedom to make their own rules and elect their representatives without outside interference.

Part III of the 1984 Act deals with ballots for political funds. It requires that unions must hold ballots to establish or to continue a political fund every ten years, and that new ballots under this law had to be held within one year of the Act, for all funds more than nine years old. The definition of what constitutes political action was also widened by the Act, to cover not only affiliation to and other financial support for political parties, but also trade union campaigns against government policies, such as cuts in public services, privatization and the like. The unions provide over 80 per cent of the income of the Labour Party and the constitutional implications of the new law are profound. In the event, a series of ballots in 1985 by unions with Labour Party affiliation resulted in large majorities in favour of continuing the funds, and some unions which had hitherto not had a fund decided to institute ballots to establish one; this was particularly true in the civil service unions. This element in the Act undoubtedly back-fired in the government's face; it was intended to attack Labour Party viability as the chief party of the Parliamentary opposition. In fact, this Act contributed to a unique and healthy politicization of union members, and a new dialogue between leaders and members, at least during the ballot campaigns.

This chapter is principally concerned with law as applied to collective rights. But, in order to assess the full impact of the legal changes of the 1980s, we need a summary of measures taken against the employment rights of individuals. We have seen that unfair dismissal rights have been seriously eroded, as have maternity rights in employment (although a new right to time off for antenatal care has been introduced). Unfair dismissal claims were available under previous laws for workers with six months' service; in 1979 this restriction was extended to one year. In 1980 it was extended to two years for workers in small businesses, and in 1985, to two years for *all* newly employed workers. Guaranteed pay during short-time was reduced, and supplementary benefit deductions for striking workers' families has been deducted on the commonly unreal assumption that the strikers receive strike pay from the union.

To this summary account must be added the unmeasurable but cumulative impact of the increased frequency and severity of judicial intervention in labour law-making, which was unleashed by the new Acts. Of course, the government may disclaim formal responsibility for this effect (although it is far from ashamed of it). For, unlike the 1971 Act, the government gave to itself few formal new powers, and set up no novel labour court. Instead, it simply widened the scope for court actions by limiting immunities in the ways we have described. But this means that a third party is required to act before the new dispensation can influence events. In the 1980s more and more employers, and not always the small firms, have felt motivated to go to court. This is quite unlike their reactions to the 1971 Act. A number of factors have contributed to this change of employers' attitude to the law.

A Change in Status

The slump in employment has so weakened trade union influence in industrial relations that the employers' former concern to maintain pluralistic bargaining or corporate good relations with the unions has dwindled, although it is by no means extinct. (Some new gains, after all, flow for the employer from good relations with unions compelled into, or volunteering for, compliant and subordinate roles in slump-ridden Britain.) The government itself has set an extreme example of aggressive management and anti-union behaviour, which must have fostered previously dormant instincts for combat in employers' minds. This is true, for example, in its appointment of, and support for, aggressive managers in the Steel Corporation, the Coal Board and British Leyland. The government's willingness, indeed eagerness, to take on and 'beat' the miners in 1984–5, including their massive subsidization of the billions of costs involved in that strike, and their promotion of a unique and overwhelming police operation, provided a further extreme example of a new employer attitude. The government's disrespect for very basic trade union rights was also exemplified in its ban on membership at the intelligence-gathering centre (GCHQ) in Cheltenham, in 1984. In this measure, it received the support of the courts, who found no breach of the law or of ILO Conventions on freedom of association, because the action was the prerogative of the state, undertaken for reasons of 'national security'. This judgement, and the ban which gave rise to it, stigmatize the very act of joining a trade union as potentially subversive. It was consistent with the Prime Minister's description of the British miners on strike as 'the enemy within'. Finally, the employers are bound to note that the judges are most prone to find in their favour these days. All in all, there is quite simply no penalty, no deterrent, facing an employer contemplating legal proceedings. At first sight, it may even seem surprising that there has not been a greater rush to the courts by employers. The actual volume of applications for injunctions and damages has not increased dramatically. The reason is obvious: a few spectacular cases which produce devastating results for unions, strikers, their communities and individual workers are enough of a deterrent (reinforced by unemployment) to induce further docility amongst most other employees, so that the necessity for repetition of injunctions and suits does not arise. It is not necessary to rely on intuitive assumptions to reach this conclusion; the decline in the rate of strikes (see Chapter 8) provides all the supporting evidence required.

We live now under a government which pursues a systematic

and consistent view of society as a unitary organism in which subordinate collective action is seen as disorderly and illegitimate, an undermining of society's assumed unity of interest and purpose. Its economic doctrine is in harmony with this 'sociology', assuming that individual contracts and relationships are both fair and efficient, as means to regulate employment relations in a labour market which should be as 'free' from restrictions, state norms, or bargained standards, as is the market in potatoes in a peasant village.

Ranked behind the government stands a judiciary which can be relied upon resolutely to apply the same values. A harder line of reinforcement lies behind the courts, in the shape of a police force mobilized and trained in the most sophisticated forms of mass deployment against picketing, and against mass demonstrations, whether these are actually or incipiently violent or not. We have seen this at work in the miners' strikes, the Shah dispute, and at Wapping. The Public Order Act, which came into force in April 1987, gives the police wide new powers to limit the activities of strikers, pickets and demonstrators. Professor Peter Wallington of Lancaster University, an authority on the policing of industrial disputes, has written that 'In an area of great importance to the police, this means the opportunity and temptation to act injudiciously has been increased.' Further, he argues that the courts will not abandon their traditional reluctance to interfere with police operational decisions, and that juries will – given the wording of the Act – be less inhibited in convicting for the offences of riot, violent disorder and affray.[13] One employer at least, Mr Rupert Murdoch, at his new purpose-built plant at Wapping, has used industrial architecture itself to underline the psychology, as well as the physiology, of paramilitary confrontation which awaits workers who have the temerity to act against the new Order.

These dramatic developments have made irresistible material for media coverage. The visual impact of workers in conflict with policemen, and the whole language of illegality, reinforce each other to make a powerful message about the apparent connection between trade unionism and disorder, which suits the government's case very well, even though television presentation cannot avoid other impressions, particularly about police behaviour. But in the miners' strike at least, since almost all the court action stemmed from the common law, contested in the 'ordinary' courts, and not from statutes, the public impression was created of unions in conflict with legality itself, and not with an ideologically motivated government. Lord Stockton, however, was not misled by this appearance. His valedictory speech in the House of Lords raised the ghost of an earlier consensus now dead.

The government claims that it has achieved low inflation and social peace (a low strike level) through these and through complementary economic policies. It has not, however, established a unitary society in reality, unless by force of law. A true description of social reality must include a recognition of the wide disparities present within it, which have been exacerbated by recent trends and policies in the economy. Social reality is vastly more complex than the Conservative government has been able to recognize from behind its blinkers.

For those with open eyes, Britain in the eighties has been riven with overt conflict (as in the miners' strike) while it has suffered the unreal 'peace' which comes of repression and subordination, in much of industry, in many of the inner city communities, in the long dole queues everywhere, and in the rejection of a whole generation from constructive involvement in production. One measure of a kind of social peace may be sought by government in terms of strike statistics. But in Britain, under mass unemployment, the previous high levels recorded in that series have been displaced into other figures: those for crime, dereliction and urban violence. And here, in crowded prisons, in tense and sometimes psychotic police actions, on explosive terraces in the football stadiums, and in the inner city ghettoes, social conflict re-emerges, not as a collective, peaceful and purposive challenge to inequity and state authority, as it normally has been in pluralistic trade union activity, which has now been seriously curtailed, but as the raw rage of the dispossessed against all that oppressive world which has excluded them.

These outbursts of discontent now take forms which not only justify further recourse to 'law' and 'order' but do not require authority to defend itself rationally in any politically controlled dispute with a legitimate alternative. There are always, it now appears, 'enemies within', and it is not accidental that Mrs Thatcher is prone to associate, in a single sentence, football hooligans and strikers. Those 'enemies' are victims. The true enemy within is poverty, enforced idleness, xenophobia and loss of hope. It is everything that diminishes men and women and erodes their respect for one another. The more difficult the law makes it to mobilize against this enemy, the more intractable will Britain's crisis become.

The weakening of trade unions is the perfect weapon for those who wish that enemy to prevail. This may produce 'success', but it is illusory and is bound to be temporary. The repression of political pluralism will fail to establish a permanent new legal structure, capable of regulating industrial relations harmoniously. It will also fail in its wider social ambition, because it is both morally unacceptable and intellectually disreputable. Monetarism is not a valid account of the working of a modern capitalist economy, and the repudiation of pluralism is not founded on a reputable political sociology. Neither do our common law assumptions about contract, immunity and the 'individual' rights of employers correspond to social reality.

Britain may still formally be governed by a parliamentary majority elected by universal suffrage. But when that majority, fully intending the consequences, hands over its responsibilities in the crucial field of labour law to an unaccountable, unreformed and socially partial judiciary, which proceeds to make law to strengthen the already strong, and weaken the already weak, British pluralist democracy itself is at risk.

Monetarism has been abandoned by its protagonists as a coherent and realistic theoretical bolster for their policy prescriptions, leaving behind only the theology of individualism, which is itself founded on an unreal transposition of eighteenth-century laissez-faire doctrine derived from Adam Smith, into the world of conglomerate multinational capital of the late twentieth century. In this modern world there are no 'free' markets, and individual freedom, for those who are not in control, really depends on collective protections. The application of the mythic rigmarole of individualism in the law courts produces only injustice. The trade unions need a fundamental reassessment of their attitude to law, which must go to the roots of the legal system, and demand reform of its structures, forms, procedures and norms. Justice requires its own future accountability to the whole community.

NOTES

1. Otto Kahn-Freund, *Labour and the Law*, second edition, Stephens, 1977. Labour law changes frequently, as this chapter demonstrates. At the time of its publication, Professor Kahn-Freund's work was the most authoritative account of its subject.
2. In 1983–4, the NGA tried to maintain its closed shop, by industrial action, in a group of newspaper companies, the Messenger Newspapers group, all owned by Mr Eddie Shah. But action at one plant constituted pressure on a 'different' employer to adopt a closed shop at another plant, since each plant was a 'separate' employer. The industrial actions, the court proceedings which were initiated by Mr Shah, and the contempt incurred by the union for defiance of court orders, led to the sequestration of the union's assets.
3. This statement has been more quoted than any other on the question, in many texts on labour law.
4. P. Wintour, *Guardian*, 12 February 1986. Quoted in Lord Wedderburn, *The Worker and the Law*, third (completely revised) edition, Pelican Books, 1986, p. 93. The extended acknowledgement which we made to the work of Otto Kahn-Freund in the first edition of this book must be replaced with an even more substantial tribute to Bill Wedderburn's new edition of an earlier standard work (which first appeared in 1965). He has here achieved a monumental synthesis of law, politics, sociology, historical and comparative knowledge, which is quite indispensable for students of society, as well as of trade unionism. In this chapter, we draw heavily on his work.
5. Wedderburn, *op. cit.*, p. 93.
6. *Ibid*, p. 94.
7. Clive Jenkins and J. E. Mortimer, *The Kind of Laws the Unions Ought to Want*, Pergamon, 1968.
8. Otto Kahn-Freund, *op. cit.*
9. *Industrial Relations Review and Report*, no. 89, 25 May 1977.
10. Wedderburn, *op. cit.*, pp. 73–4.
11. *Ibid.*, p. 653.
12. For a discussion of the concept of the general strike, its theory and history, and the general strike implications of the 1984–5 miners' strike, see Ken Coates and

Tony Topham, *Trade Unions and Politics*, Basil Blackwell, 1986, Chapter 7, 'Class politics and the General Strike which will not come', pp. 197–226. Whilst no statutory ban on a general strike has been attempted by the 1980s governments, they would clearly regard it as coercive, and unconstitutional. In view of the judges' assumptions of wide unaccountable powers, the unions might well ask in response: 'What constitution?'

13. *Guardian*, 1 April 1987.

APPENDIX: PROPOSALS FOR FUTURE LEGISLATION

In preparation for the June 1987 General Election the government had already announced plans for further legislation to be implemented during the third term of the Thatcher administration. The Labour Party also published extensive plans for legal change, whilst it was still hoping to become the ruling Party. We therefore summarize both sets of proposals.

Conservative Plans

These were incorporated in a Green Paper[1] published by the government in February 1987. This proposed:

— The creation of a Special Commissioner for Trade Union Affairs, who would 'provide advice and support to individual union members who need to make a complaint and perhaps take legal action against a union and its officials who may be failing to comply with statutory duties. The Green Paper suggests that at present individual trade union members may be deterred from taking their union to court because of the difficulty of pursuing cases.'[2]

— Removing the (remaining) legal immunity from strikes called to enforce the closed shop.

— Taking away the remaining legal protection for the closed shop.

— Requiring secret postal ballots under independent supervision for the election of members of union executive bodies.

— Election by secret postal ballot under independent supervision of union Presidents and General Secretaries and every other member of the union executive whether or not they have a vote on that executive.

— An effective right to choose to go to work or cross a picket line despite a strike call.

— The right of union members to access to the union's financial records.

In their commenting on these proposals in the House of Commons, government Ministers of Employment said:

— '. . . We are proposing to end completely the use of the law in any circumstances to sustain the closed shop.'

— 'A large number of trade unions have retained workplace ballots and the conduct of such ballots continues to give rise to controversy. Now is the time to act against these abuses. When we legislated in1984, many trade unions did not have lists of membership of sufficient quality to serve as electoral rolls. Since 1984 they have been required to have such lists and they have now had the time and opportunity to draw them up. There is therefore no longer any reason why we should not move to the most secure method of balloting available – the secret postal vote under independent supervision.'

— 'The right to choose to go to work during industrial action is an essential freedom. We believe that union members are entitled to vote on whether their union should call them out on strike. We also believe that they are entitled to continue to go to work and honour their contract of employment if they disagree with their union's call.'

— 'Recent events have thrown light on the unusual ways in which some unions run their financial affairs. Union members ought to be seriously concerned about some of the manoeuvres which have been used to evade or circumvent the jurisdiction of the courts when unions find themselves in conflict with the law.'[3]

Although it is not mentioned in the Green Paper, a further possible restriction on strikes which won wide support in government circles was the proposal to outlaw strikes in 'essential public services'. It is not possible at the time of writing to say whether this will feature in future legislation.

Labour Plans

The Labour Party and TUC spent much time and effort between 1983 and 1987 seeking to agree on a legislative programme for trade unions and industrial relations. Differences of opinion amongst the participants in this debate centred around whether to return to the abstentionist tradition by restoring and reinforcing the legal immunities in industrial action, and wherever possible withdrawing legal intervention in union and industrial affairs, or instead to emphasize a 'positive rights' approach. In the second option workers and trade unions would be given defined legal rights by statute.[4]

The Labour Party's provisional proposals, emerging from that debate, are contained in a Working Group document of September 1985.[5] The principles and proposals which it contains are summarized as follows:

— Basic Principles; 'We want to extend workers' rights in a positive industrial relations framework, bringing democratic accountability into the workplace itself.'

— 'Instead of placing workers in a legal straitjacket . . . the aim is to widen the bargaining agenda beyond wages to include the whole range of company decisions . . . The next Labour government must introduce legislation which enables working people to play a constructive and responsible role in economic management.'

— Statutory support for collective bargaining will be restored and extended in minimum pay legislation.

— 'Labour intends to repeal all the Tory government's anti-trade union legislation passed since 1979. This will not be sufficient, however, to restore the rights of workers to the previous position, let alone to extend them. Nor will it be sufficient merely to re-enact the 1970s legislation conferring an immunity for workers in trade disputes, which was narrowly interpreted by the courts . . . It is time for a more positive framework . . . The positive framework of rights which the Labour government gave in the 1970s legislation is not totally independent of court interpretation and limitations.'

— 'The next Labour government should introduce a Workers' Rights Act.'

— 'There are two main issues which need to be discussed. We could restore the immunities form of protection for trade unions or create positive rights to organize industrial action. It will be essential to reduce the scope for interference by the courts in developing new rights to information, consultation and representation in companies.'

— 'We should consider the possibility of new rights to arbitration whose purpose would be to support collective bargaining and its extension into new areas.'

NOTES TO THE APPENDIX

1. *Trade Unions and Their Members*, Cmnd 95, HMSO, 24 February 1987.
2. Press Release, Department of Employment, 24 February 1987.
3. *Ibid.*
4. The pros and cons of this controversy are fully presented in contributions by Jim Mortimer, Andrew Wilson and Roy Green, in Ken Coates (ed.), *Freedom and Fairness*, Spokesman, 1986.
5. *Planning for Full Employment: Options for a Modern Employment Strategy*. Parliamentary Spokesmen Working Group, September 1985, Section 5. 'A Positive Industrial Relations Framework.'

CHAPTER 11

Trade Unions and the Labour Party

The Scope of Political Action

The decision which effectively launched the Labour Party was taken at the Trades Union Congress of 1899: 'to ensure that working-class opinion should be represented in the House of Commons by men sympathetic with the aims and demands of the Labour Movement, and whose candidatures are promoted by one or other of the organized movements'.[1] The resultant conference, in 1900, established the Labour Representation Committee, a federation of 41 trade unions and 3 socialist societies, together with 7 constituency associations.[2] One of the socialist societies promptly left for doctrinal reasons, but the number of unions rose to 65, to 127, and then to 165, all within the first four years of the new committee. Affiliated membership passed the million mark in 1907, by which time the 1906 election had seen the spectacular return of 29 Labour members to Parliament.

Rocketing success though this now seems, the unions nonetheless trod very cautiously and defensively into political organization. The 1902 LRC report states this, rather plainly: 'Menaced on every hand in workshop, court of law, and press, Trade Unionism has no refuge except the ballot box and Labour Representation.'[3] In this tentative way, the unions arrived in the House of Commons as a substantial interest before they announced themselves as a Party, and duly renamed their Representation Committee.

It has often been remarked that the British Labour Party's federal emergence from the unions is quite different from the common continental experience, in which trade unions themselves have often been established from scratch by a pre-existing political party. Socialist parties have been by no means the only innovators in this respect: some of the most successful trade union federations of the post-Second World War period were originally established decades earlier by Catholic parties, as a part of the consolidation of their mass influence. Not infrequently, the doctrine of such unions has been modified, through time, to diverge quite sharply from that of their parent bodies.[4]

The experimental and tentative way in which British unions groped towards a political voice does mean that British labour politics is perhaps less crystalline, less doctrinaire, and maybe even less 'principled' than some schools of continental socialism. Nonetheless, once political organization began, argument moved back and forth, and influences were by no means one-directional. More and more trade unions began to reconsider and amend their formal objectives.[5] Before the Labour Party itself was ready to embrace its explicitly socialist constitution of 1918, various major trade union bodies had preceded it. Up to 1918, the Party constitution stated its sole object as being

> to organize and maintain in Parliament and the country a political Labour Party.[6]

This was then replaced by a more elaborate set of aims including the famous clause IV:

> to secure for the producers by hand or by brain the full fruits of their industry, and the most equitable distribution thereof that may be possible, upon the basis of the common ownership of the means of production, and the best obtainable system of popular administration and control of each industry or service.[7]

Much later, when the political leaders of the Labour Party, following electoral defeat in 1959, tried to revise its constitution by deleting that clause, their moves were checked precisely by the resistance of the unions.[8]

The extent of union commitment to socialist objectives does vary through the years, of course: and more significantly, ideas about the main strategic socialist options have changed, and will continue to change, with alterations in the overall political economy which provokes their challenge.

We have discussed these processes in other works,[9] and will excuse ourselves from pursuing them here. But it is necessary to point up one key distinction which helps explain working-class responses to the political problems which confront trade unions. This is the distinction, first established in clarity by Antonio Gramsci, and later popularized in England by Perry Anderson,[10] between 'corporate' and 'hegemonic' attitudes and forms of thought. 'Corporate' thinking seeks to defend the perceived interests of working people against 'unfair' actions, or to protect trade unions from employer offensives or judicial interventions, and it leads precisely to the kind of defensive statements made by the LRC during its 1902 Conference, as it prepared to rally support against a variety of hostile 'menaces'. Essentially, such thinking is defensive rather than passive, seeking to prevent adverse changes, and marching behind the banner 'hands off' something or other. It is perfectly possible to be very 'militant' within such a perspective, and often people are.

On the other hand, 'hegemonic' thinking identifies a potential in labour to become the ruling social force, and seeks to challenge all acceptance of subordination whatsoever. In the classic words which Karl Marx used to reproach the unions of his day, it calls upon the unions 'instead of the *conservative* motto: "a fair day's wages for a fair day's work" . . . to inscribe upon their banners the *revolutionary* watchword "for the abolition of the wages system"!' This appeal takes widely different forms: sometimes, as in the words of the guild socialists, it is seen as an ethical denunciation of 'the bondage of wagery'. At other moments, it emerges as a call for the establishment of full co-operative self-management, annulling forever the social status of 'employee', and establishing a world in which labour employs capital, rather than the present upside-down state in which things lord it over people.

What is plain is that, however staunchly men and women seek to protect their 'corporate' interests, powerful economic forces are constantly undermining all such efforts. Pushed by such a realization, successive generations of trade unionists seek means of passing beyond the restrictions of defensive politics, into sweeping overall reform of the political-economic structure itself. 'Hegemonic' politics takes different forms, but is to be found in embryo wherever workers' organizations seek to control developments for themselves.

Yet no such imaginative leaps are possible unless labour organization has developed to the point where ordinary men and women can recognize their own vast collective social power, and this means therefore that unions must become capable of defending their 'corporate' interests before labour movements can develop an awareness of alternative possibilities. How has this process unwound?

Labour Representatives in Parliament

If we take the General Elections from 1900 to 1983, we find that the Labour Party has moved from a capacity to field 15 candidates to a regular expectation that it should contest all Parliamentary seats. When we examine the proportion of direct trade union candidates to those from other sources, however, we find that in 1906 35 out of 50 Labour candidates were directly sponsored by their unions, while by 1983 only 153 out of 633 were so sponsored.

In 1910, 95 per cent of all Labour MPs were directly put forward by unions. The proportion has now fallen to 54 per cent, although this itself represents a rise since 1945, when Labour's greatest victory was based upon a considerable influx of new MPs, but when only 30 per cent of the enlarged total had been put forward by the unions. One figure, however, indicates that unions tend to pick safe-ish seats from which to press their claims: 91 per cent of their nominees got home in the October 1974 election: and as much as 96 per cent of their 1945 team was in fact elected. In 1979, a bad year, 83 per cent were returned and the losses included not only long-established MPs, but also ministers. In the most severe defeat of 1983, three-quarters of union candidates were successful in spite of the ill-fortune which befell so many of their colleagues who were not directly sponsored.

Table 11.1
Union-sponsored MPs, 1900–87*

Election	Candidates: All Labour Party	Candidates: All union sponsored	MPs: All Labour Party	MPs: All union sponsored	Union sponsored MPs as % of all Labour Party MPs	Union sponsored MPs as % of all Labour sponsored candidates
1900	15	?	2	1	50.0	?
1906	50	35	30	21	70.0	60
1910	78	?	40	38	95.0	?
1910	56	?	42	39	92.8	?
1918	361	163	57	49	85.9	31
1922	414	?	142	86	60.6	?
1923	427	?	191	102	53.4	?
1924	514	?	151	88	58.2	?
1929	569	139	287	115	40.1	83
1931	491	132	46	32	69.5	24
1935	552	128	154	79	51.3	62
1945	603	126	393	121	30.8	96
1950	617	140	315	110	34.9	79
1951	617	137	295	105	35.6	77
1955	620	129	277	96	34.6	75
1959	621	129	258	93	36.0	72
1964	628	138	317	120	37.9	86
1966	622	138	364	132	36.3	95
1970	624	137	287	114	39.7	83
1974	627	155	301	127	42.2	82.7
1974	626	141	319	129	40.1	91
1979	622	159	268	132	49.5	83
1983	633	153	209	114	54.5	75
1987	633	146	229	130	56.8	89

* There is occasional disagreement among various authorities for the actual number of candidates supported by the Labour Party or sponsored by a trade union. This problem is especially acute for the years prior to 1929.
Source: W. D. Muller, *The Kept Men*, Harvester, 1977. For 1979 and thereafter sources are the Labour Party's press releases and the Labour Research Department.[11]

Not much union money, we may conclude, goes into intentionally contesting marginal seats, and still less into hopeless ones.

Direct trade union sponsorship takes a variety of forms. Its classic shape is to be found in the declining numbers of safe mining seats, in which the NUM (or before that, the MFGB) used to be able to boast that they could weigh the votes necessary to secure their victories. Other occupational concentrations explain how some unions are able to secure representation in particular areas. But more and more union nominees have to win selection as prospective Parliamentary candidates in open contests with a whole variety of other people, and cannot depend upon a built-in preponderance of their own supporters. The actual membership of the most recent Parliaments included the following union-sponsored detachments:[12]

Table 11.2

Individual union sponsorships, October 1974, 1979, 1983 and 1987

	Total				Elected			
	1974	1979	1983	1987	1974	1979	1983	1987
TGWU	23	27	29	34	22	20	24	31
AUEW	23	16	17	13	21	15	12	12
NUM	20	17	14	13	18	16	14	13
GMBATU	13	14	14	13	13	14	11	13
ASTMS	13	12	11	9	12	8	10	8
NUPE	7	8	10	12	6	7	4	9
APEX	6	6	3	4	6	5	3	4
NUR	6	11	12	8	6	10	10	8
USDAW	5	5	2	9	5	5	2	8
TSSA	4	3	1	2	3	3	—	2
UCW	4	4	1	1	2	2	1	1
UCATT	3	4	2	1	3	2	1	1
EETPU	3	4	7	3	3	4	3	2
TASS	—	—	—	6	—	—	—	5
Total, including other unions	141	159	153	146	129	132	114	130
Co-operative Party	24	25	17	18	16	16	14	10
All sponsored candidates	161	184	170	164	142	148	128	140

Whilst it is clear that there are mining constituencies, and may once have been 'railway' constituencies, or 'engineering' towns, it is doubtful whether there are ASTMS cities, or NUPE counties. These substantial groups of MPs have been adopted in an open process of choice, by constituency organizations which have usually included a wide variety of contending interests. Changes in the Labour Party's federal constitution have reinforced this openness: until the 1960s, local trade unions could send any member who paid into the union's own political fund as a delegate to his or her local Party organization. Now only persons who pay individual Party membership contributions as well as corporate affiliation tolls are eligible to serve as delegates to Party management committees. This means that the 'selectorate' which chooses Parliamentary candidates is now more restricted. Under the old dispensation, Mr Morgan Phillips, then General Secretary of the Party, sought nomination for the mining area of North-East Derbyshire. NUM delegates came from far and wide to prevent this happening, and instead the local miners' spokesman, Tom Swain, was chosen by a bone-crushing majority. Under the new dispensation, in the area of Ashfield, which is very much a pitmen's enclave, an NUM nominee was passed over in 1977 because only a handful of miners were eligible, as individual members of the Party, to participate in the selection conference. Subsequently, the non-miner who was chosen was rather spectacularly defeated, and the NUM then regained the nomination, but only after it had undertaken a major drive to recruit, from the mining community, numbers of new individual Party members who were willing to participate in the work of the management committee. The Political Committee of the Nottingham Area of the NUM even went so far as to offer to defray the costs of their own members' membership subscriptions to the Labour Party, in order to ensure adequate representation on the vital selection conference. This new system of affiliation will certainly change the pattern of trade union representation in Parliament, since it will tend to shrink the power of such traditional lobbies as the miners', while increasing the competition among contending groupings. There is a time-lag in this process.

For all the moral weight of their 130 MPs, the unions' political influence is certainly not restricted to their impact on the legislature. Indeed, it is arguable that a more direct and powerful influence is that which is exerted over Labour as a political Party, in determining policy and staffing the national, regional and local machinery of that Party. At national level, unions participate in the Labour Party Conference, at which they cast votes in accordance with their affiliated numbers.[13] At local level, unions may also send delegates to constituency management committees, which arrange the day-to-day local organization of the Party in addition to controlling the selection of Parliamentary candidates.

Affiliation to the Labour Party

Such local affiliation is based upon the number of trade union branch members paying political contributions and resident within a particular constituency area. Fees are payable to the constituency organization at rates varying between 3 and 6 pence per member per annum. Since many trade union branches organize people resident in different areas, it is perfectly possible for one trade union branch to be represented in several nearby constituency management committees, and this complicates the problem of allocating local resources from the unions' political funds.

At intermediate levels, unions are strongly represented in the Party's regional organization, and have, within the constitution, some fixed quota of representation in county and other policy-forming bodies. In order to qualify for all these lower levels of participation, a union has to be affiliated nationally.

This turns out to be expensive, the current rate involving a payment to national Labour Party funds of 60 pence per affiliated member per annum, in addition to local or regional payments and, of course, regardless of special contributions to national election appeals or building funds. Forty-seven unions were so affiliated in 1983,[14] and this brought 6.1 million 'members' into the Party. But these unions had 7.9 million

Table 11.3

Political fund contributions and Labour Party affiliations, 1984

Union	Total members	Contributing to General Fund	Paying political levy: No.	Paying political levy: % of total	Paying political levy: % of General Fund payers	Labour Party affiliations: No.	Labour Party affiliations: % paying levy	Labour Party affiliations: % 1982 levy payers
Bakers, Food and Allied	37,487	37,487	36,558	98	98	36,000	98	(98)
Ceramic and Allied Trades	28,873	28,873	28,496	99	99	28,000	98	(98)
NACODS	17,079	17,079	16,856	99	99	18,000	107	(102)
Communication Workers	196,426	196,426	183,325	93	93	187,000	102	(100)
UCATT	259,873	259,873	171,000	66	66	171,000	100	(100)
EETPU	405,041	383,829	295,254	73	77	180,000	61	(50)
AUEW (Constructional)	23,856	23,856	17,268	72	72	15,000	87	(82)
AUEW (Engineering)	943,538	735,960	542,584	58	74	850,000	157	(130)
(Foundry)	41,287	41,287	19,230	47	47	27,000	140	(100)
AUEW (TASS)	215,052	182,795	113,000	53	62	[a]143,000	127	(93)
Fire Brigades	43,405	43,405	26,999	62	62	16,000	59	(63)
Footwear, Leather and Allied Trades	41,897	38,115	36,879	88	97	39,000	106	(100)
FTAT	58,244	51,788	35,529	61	69	32,000	90	(86)
GMBATU	875,187	875,187	759,856	87	87	[b]725,000	95	(84)
SOGAT	216,639	193,710	121,176	56	63	76,000	63	(60)
NGA	133,949	113,619	59,457	44	52	31,000	52	(55)
COHSE	222,8695	222,869	203,730	91	91	200,000	98	(94)
ISTC	93,175	44,296	40,165	43	91	70,000	174	(142)

Union	Total members	Contributing to General Fund	Paying political levy			Labour Party affiliations		
			No.	% of total	% of General Fund payers	No.	% paying levy	% 1982 levy payers
ASLEF	23,589	23,589	21,954	93	93	24,000	109	(104)
Metal Mechanics	29,076	27,076	24,078	83	89	16,000	66	(73)
NUM	318,084	208,051	200,453	63	96	237,000	118	(107)
POEU	129,950	129,950	98,451	76	76	95,000	96	(94)
APEX	100,177	100,177	68,868	69	69	85,000	123	(111)
NUPE	689,046	689,046	670,736	97	97	600,000	89	(88)
NUR	143,404	143,404	138,529	97	97	151,000	109	(104)
NUS	28,511	28,511	22,523	79	79	23,000	102	(98)
USDAW	403,446	403,446	369,547	92	92	385,000	104	(100)
Tailors and Garment Workers	76,130	76,130	67,247	88	88	55,000	82	(81)
Textile Workers	15,273	15,273	14,540	95	95	17,000	117	(93)
TGWU	1,547,443	1,547,443	1,517,782	98	98	[c]1,361,000	90	(85)
TSSA	56,476	56,476	46,648	83	83	48,000	103	(96)
TOTALS	7,414,482	6,939,026	5,968,718	81	86	5,941,000	100	(94)

Table does not include unions with less than 10,000 affiliates to the Labour Party; ASTMS, whose membership shows a static 410,000 and who affiliate on 132,000 members (no political fund figures available from the Certification Officer since 1980).
Certain unions, recently amalgamated, do continue to affiliate separately to the Labour Party, but their membership is not shown separately by the Certification Officer.
[a]TASS includes 42,000 affiliates from Sheet Metal Workers.
[b]GMBATU includes 75,000 affiliates from Sheet Metal Workers.
[c]TGWU includes 75,000 affiliates from Agricultural Workers and 36,000 from Dyers and Bleachers.
Source: All figures are from *Report of the Certification Officer, 1984* except numbers of Labour Party affiliates, for which source is the Labour Party Annual Report, 1984.

members between them, of whom 6.5 million contributed to their political funds.

Table 11.4

Percentage of total membership contributing to political funds and affiliated to the Labour Party, 1976–86

	1976	1980	1981	1982	1983	1986
No. of unions with political funds[a]	81	69	68	63	58	44
No. of unions affiliated to Labour Party[b]	59	54	54	50	47	44
No. of members	9.4m	9.5m	8.9m	8.0m	7.9m	7.5m*
No. of members contributing to political funds[c]	7.6m	7.7m	7.2m	6.5m	6.5m	6.9m*
No. of members affiliated to Labour Party[d]	5.8m	6.4m	6.3m	6.2m	6.1m	5.8m*
Members contributing to political funds (%)[e]	81	81	81	81	82	n.a.
Members affiliated to Labour Party (%)	62	67	71	77	77	n.a.
Fund contributors affiliated to Labour Party (%)	76	83	87	95	94	n.a.

[a]Includes returns separately for four areas of NACODS and four areas of NUM as well as NACODS and NUM national returns.

[b]Some unions register political funds more than once, as local federated unions also file returns. (See[a].) The decline in numbers of unions affiliated otherwise reflects mergers between unions. *Source*: Labour Party Report, 1984, p. 104.

[c]For 1982 and 1983 numbers do not include ASTMS, which made no returns.

[d]*Source*: Labour Party Report, 1984.

[e]The 81–82 per cent figure is consistent and reaches back over the whole period of Certification Officer returns.

*These figures, from the *Report of the Certification Officer, 1986*, are the latest available at the time of writing. They pertain to 1985, so are an inappropriate base for the calculation of the following percentages.

Source: Except where otherwise stated, the source of these figures is the *Report of the Certification Officer, 1984*.

As will be seen, this list reveals very great discrepancies in the extent of the commitment of the different unions. Only slightly over half of NGA members are affiliated, and only 61 per cent of the Electricians. On the other hand, surprisingly, 157 per cent of the Engineers, and 174 per cent of those ISTC members who paid into their political funds were affiliated. There are three explanations which account for such surprising statistics.

First, there is the problem of 'fiscal drag', in which different accounting years produce a hangover of book representation, after actual membership has declined. Secondly, some unions have special categories of membership, like pensioners, who still pay political contributions after their industrial membership fees have been reduced to half or below. Thirdly, the last explanation is that in some cases these figures seem to be quite arbitrary. Taking the unions which nowadays affiliate on more than 100,000 members, we can see this quite plainly. Some unions affiliate on the same round number year after year, and it is quite evident that this is a convenient fiction. Others have systematically affiliated below their true strength. More recently some have over-affiliated. We have analysed these cases in greater detail elsewhere.[15] The global result always reflects under-affiliation, as can be seen in Table 11.4. But where a large union affiliates on too high a total, this can give rise to the accusation that it is 'buying votes' to which it is not truly entitled.

The situation is complicated by the fact that there is no standard rate of political levy, and that there is no standard rate of success in collecting it. Table 11.5 gives the 1985 levels in major unions, and they will be seen to vary between 70 pence and £3. In a study by Martin Linton it was revealed that in 1977 the NUR only collected an average of 60 pence per member out of the agreed levy of £1 per head. The NUGMW (now GMBATU) got in 35 pence out of the required 60 pence. Trade unions are voluntary organizations, and these figures remind us that whatever leading committees may rule, activists have then to persuade their colleagues actually to pay up, which is not always a simple matter.

Table 11.5

The rate of political levy in Britain's largest unions, 1985

Union	Rate per annum (£)
AUEW (Engineering)	1.00
(TASS)	1.56
APEX	1.04
ASTMS	3.00 (some still pay only £1.20 old rate)
COHSE	1.56
EETPU (skilled)	0.70
(unskilled)	0.55 (represents one week's full union sub)
GMBATU	2.40 (represents 3 weeks' full union subs)
NGA	2.60
NUM	2.88 (represents 4 weeks' full union subs)
NUPE	2.00
NUR	2.60
POEU	1.56
SOGAT	1.56
TGWU	1.56
UCW	1.56
UCATT	0.80
USDAW	1.04

Legislation on Political Fund Ballots

During the Thatcher administration which began in 1979, a number of events converged to put a question mark over the very existence of political funds. As we have seen, the 1984 Trade Union Act legislated, amongst other things, to impose regular decennial ballots as a precondition for the continuation of such funds. We shall consider the effect of this law in a moment, but first it is necessary to ask why the trade unions have established separate funds, instead of meeting their political expenditures from their ordinary funds, in the same way that companies and other private institutions freely make donations for political purposes.

The formation of the Labour Party followed the extension of

the franchise to male working-class voters. The Taff Vale decision of 1901, which obliged the Amalgamated Society of Railway Servants to pay damages to their employer in order to compensate him for the effects of their strike action, effectively nullified the right to strike, and thus compelled trade unions to seek legislation by which it could be restored. The resultant politicization brought a quick access of strength to the Labour Representation Committee, as we have already seen. But it also alarmed employers into a variety of counter-offensives.

The new Labour Party had been financed, from the beginning, by a compulsory levy of affiliated unions for what was called a Parliamentary Representation Fund. This quickly became the object of adverse attention from the opponents of Labour representation. In 1904 the Chief Registrar of Friendly Societies officially reported that such objects as Labour representation did not fall within the scope laid down by the legal definition of a trade union, established in the Act of 1876. Shortly afterwards, Mr Osborne of the Railway Servants Amalgamation took legal action to prevent his union from financing the Labour Party. Upon appeal, the case went through to the House of Lords, which upheld the judgement in Osborne's favour after lengthy litigation financed by a body called the Trade Union Political Freedom League. Now it was necessary for the trade unions to secure further statutory protection if they were to continue to act on the political plane. After considerable discussion, the 1913 Trade Union Act established a Parliamentary compromise under which trade unions could continue to pay for political actions, if they had previously agreed to establish an appropriate political fund, in a ballot of their members. Since such eminent Parliamentarians as Winston Churchill had defended the rights of trade unions to engage in free political activity without any such restriction, the new law was seen as an interim measure, and most trade unionists regarded it as restrictive. But subsequently almost every union which balloted itself was successful in establishing such a fund, and since such a fund, once agreed, remained in existence in perpetuity, the controversy soon subsided.

The next crisis in this area arose after the 1926 General Strike, when the government legislated to change the basis of political funds. Previously, once political funds had been agreed by a majority vote, they then applied to everyone who did not specifically withdraw or, in the jargon, 'contract-out': but henceforth they would only involve those who specifically insisted that they chose to 'contract-in'. The result was a substantial decline in fund revenue, and one of the very first actions of the 1945 Labour government was to restore the original terms of the 1913 Act.

It was not until the advent of Mrs Thatcher's government that this position was challenged. We have documented the arguments involved in some considerable detail elsewhere.[16] In a nutshell, the Conservative government began by proposing to reimpose the principle that trade unionists must 'contract-in', by a deliberate individual choice, before any monies could be collected from them for political purposes. A Green Paper to this effect was published. But the General Election of 1983 shortly followed, and in it the proportion of trade unionists voting for the Labour Party dropped substantially, by 26 percentage points, to its lowest recorded level of 29 per cent. There can be little doubt that this disastrous level was partly the result of the defection of the Social Democrats from the Labour Party, and partly the result of public conflicts between those who remained loyal to the Labour movement. But it was also affected by increased xenophobia (the 'Falklands Factor'), and by recollections of major conflicts between the unions and the last Labour government. As we saw in Chapter 6, the 'social contract' had eroded differentials and provoked a mutiny among skilled engineering workers, especially in the Midlands. Compounding this misfortune, the Labour government had then been compelled to impose policies of high austerity, bringing on the 1978 'Winter of Discontent', during which there was a ferocious rebellion by many of the very lowest paid workers, strangling in runaway inflation.

Whatever the explanation for the Labour Party's declining popularity, the Conservatives saw their opportunity. By the time that their draft for the 1984 Trade Union Act had been prepared, proposals to interfere with the political fund had been wholly radicalized. Instead of imposing 'contracting-in', ministers entered token negotiations with the TUC on this question. But from now on, the stakes were very much higher: the very existence of political funds was to be made subject to a regular affirmative ballot. It must have seemed to the Parliamentary draftsmen that most unions would have registered substantial votes against continuing their funds. Even the TULV's own private polls were far from encouraging. In the spring of 1984, MORI had reported that only three of the fifteen most important unions polled a majority to affiliate or give money to the Labour Party.[17] The disconnection of the trade unions from the Labour Party seemed to be a goal within reach. Had it been secured, Mrs Thatcher's government would have accomplished a major constitutional transformation in Britain.

But the unions rallied themselves, if not a moment too soon. The forty-seven unions which were affiliated to the Labour Party selected fourteen General Secretaries to a Trade Union Coordinating Committee which was staffed by Graham Allen under the chairmanship of Bill Keys. The TUC elaborated a careful strategy within which to campaign for a 'yes' vote in the ballots. It was agreed to stagger the ballots over the full period of time which was allowed, in order to create a bandwagon effect. The campaign 'Say Yes to a Voice' was very much a trade union campaign, and it represented a major effort of consultation and participatory involvement. It is doubtful whether there has ever been a more systematic campaign within British trade unions. Branches and workshops were linked by campaign co-ordinators, who were carefully briefed. The emphasis was placed on explanation, and the result was both a dramatic confirmation of the political funds, and the first important political defeat to be inflicted on Mrs Thatcher since 1979. Not only did every one of the unions register a significant majority in favour of the funds, but there followed a succession of ballots by unions which hitherto had never established political funds. These, too, obtained positive decisions.

If the trade unions, by their own actions, had succeeded in defending their political space, at any rate for the time being, there remained continuing problems. The day-to-day operation

Table 11.6

The Labour Party and TUC membership, 1906–86

Year	TUC Affiliations		Labour Party Affiliations		Labour Party	Labour Party	Labour Party	% of TUC membership affiliated to Labour Party
	No. Unions	Membership	No. Unions	Membership	Individual membership	Socialist & Co-operative membership	Total membership	
1906	226	1,555,000	176	975,182	—	20,885	998,338	—
1907	236	1,700,000	181	1,049,673	—	22,267	1,072,413	61.7
1912	201	2,001,633	130	1,858,178	—	31,237	1,895,498	92.8
1917	235	3,082,352	123	2,415,383	—	47,140	2,465,131	78.4
1922	206	5,128,648	102	3,279,276	—	31,760	3,311,036	63.9
1927	204	4,163,994	97	3,238,939	—	54,676	3,293,615	77.8
1928	196	3,874,842	91	2,025,139	214,970	52,060	2,292,169	52.3
1932	209	3,613,273	75	1,960,269	371,607	39,911	2,371,787	54.3
1937	214	4,008,647	70	2,037,071	447,150	43,451	2,527,672	50.8
1942	232	5,432,644	69	2,206,209	218,783	28,940	2,453,932	40.6
1947	187	7,540,397	73	4,386,074	609,487	45,738	5,040,299	58.2
1952	183	8,020,079	84	5,071,935	1,014,524	21,200	6,107,659	63.2
1957	185	8,304,709	87	5,644,012	912,987	25,550	6,582,549	68.0
1962	182	8,312,875	86	5,502,773	767,459	25,475	6,295,707	66.2
1967	169	8,787,282	75	5,539,562	733,932	21,120	6,294,614	63.0
1972	132	9,894,881	62	5,425,327	703,030	40,415	6,168,772	54.8

Year	TUC Affiliations		Labour Party Affiliations		Labour Party	Labour Party Socialist &	Labour Party	% of TUC
	No. Unions	Membership	No. Unions	Membership	Individual membership	Co-operative membership	Total membership	membership affiliated to Labour Party
1977	115	11,515,920	59	5,913,159	659,737	43,375	6,616,271	51.3
1978	112	11,865,390	59	6,259,595	675,946	54,623	6,990,164	52.8
1979	112	12,128,078	59	6,511,179	666,091	58,328	7,235,598	53.7
1980	109	12,172,508	54	6,406,914	348,156	56,200	6,811,270	52.6
1981	108	11,601,413	54	6,273,292	276,692	57,606	6,607,590	54.1
1982	105	11,005,894	50	6,185,063	273,803	57,131	6,515,997	56.2
1983	102	10,510,157	47	6,101,438	295,344	58,955	6,455,737	58.1
1984	98	10,082,144	46	5,843,586	323,292	60,163	6,227,041	58.0
1985	91	9,855,204	44	5,827,479	313,099	59,581	6,200,159	59.1
1986	88	9,585,729	44	5,778,184	297,364	57,762	6,133,310	60.3

of the Labour Party has never been easy. At every level it has a federal structure, although the principles governing the federation have been seriously modified from time to time. It is much easier for unions to relate at the top level than it is to maintain adequate involvement at the bottom, where things may always be more hit and miss. Further, of course, there is the problem of relations between the trade union movement as a whole and Labour governments, about which volumes have already been written.

Trade Union Participation in Labour Party Management

The part played by unions in the actual management of the Labour Party depends first of all on their national participation in its Annual Conference, and secondly on their influence on the election of its National Executive Committee (NEC). The relationship between union contingents at the Conference and the constituency organizations is made plain in Table 11.6. With a combined total of 313,099 members affiliated, the constituencies taken together cannot match the votes of either the TGWU, the GMBATU, NUPE or the AEU, taken singly.[18] If the issues debates at Conference find the unions agreed upon what should be done, then further argument is pointless, even if it may be undiminished for all that. Commonly, of course, unions are not agreed, and argument is then unavoidable.

The continuing work of the Labour Party between Conferences is controlled by its NEC. This, although federally structured, gives the major influence to the unions. Directly, they place twelve members on the Executive in their own right. One member is appointed by a handful of socialist societies such as the Fabians. Seven are elected by the constituency parties, representing all the individual members of the Party. A further five, the women's section, are chosen in a general ballot in which the unions have the preponderant influence. Finally, the treasurer is similarly chosen. In this way, allowing for the fact that the leader and deputy leader are, up to now, appointees of the Party's Parliamentary caucus, the unions can determine the occupancy of eighteen of the twenty-eight places on the ruling executive.

As far as the direct trade union contingent is concerned, this is generally chosen from a fairly restricted number of organizations. Only seventeen unions provided the necessary dozen victorious candidates during the last decade.[19]

Seventeen organizations is an exaggerated total: the Scottish Motormen joined the TGWU in the middle of this period, so that its candidate then became a TGWU nominee. The AEU, TASS and the Foundryworkers having conditionally merged, the total was reduced (to the extent that they in fact co-operated) by a further three. This left us with a situation in which, during a decade, a cabal of not more than thirteen organizations were involved in filling twelve places. When NUPE underwent an explosive membership growth in the following local government reorganization, it became one of the four largest organizations in the Party. Nonetheless, it took quite some time to break into the ring of NEC-represented bodies. For several years, the NUPE candidate was passed over by agreement among the other big battalions.

Although the five women's nominees are normally put forward by constituencies, in fact they each derive consistent support from particular unions, and some of them have very clear associations with those unions. Joan Maynard, MP, for instance, is a former vice-president of the Agricultural Workers' Union, while an unsuccessful runner-up for the women's section, Audrey Wise, had been a presidential candidate inside the Shopworkers' Union, USDAW.

In recent years, the treasurer has been chosen from direct union nominees. Norman Atkinson was an AEU Member of Parliament, and he was succeeded by Sam McCluskie of the National Union of Seamen.

Dissatisfaction with their Parliamentary leadership led Labour Party activists to press insistent demands for their Conference to play a greater role in the determination and application of policy, and to invest the Executive with greater authority. After the

Winter of Discontent, union delegations to the Party Conference were also disaffected, with the result that some years of argument were brought to a conclusion at the 1980 Conference and a related Special Conference in February 1981, in a series of important constitutional changes. These were intended to heighten the degree of accountability of Parliamentarians to the Party membership, and to ensure that the Party in the country (and not simply in Parliament) elected its leader and deputy leader. The regular reselection of Parliamentary candidates was fiercely contested, but finally brought into force. From 1980 onwards every MP had to face a constituency selection conference before he could be chosen to contest the next election; and from 1981 the leader and his deputy were appointed by an electoral college in which every constituency, affiliated union and MP had a vote. The proportion of votes in this college were divided 40 per cent to the unions, with the remainder equally split between constituencies and Labour MPs.

The Problem of the Block Vote

It is impossible, in this connection, to ignore the difficulties which are developing with the block vote. This system was inherited, for very good reasons, from the nonconformist churches, and it is in some circumstances an ideal method of regulating the affairs of a confederal organization. Each affiliate of such a federation votes according to its own input of money and members, and this simultaneously guarantees that the government of the organization is felt to be representative and fair, and that those whose efforts and contributions are greatest will receive due recognition of that fact. The federal structure of the Labour Party is a valued resource, since it enables a close, continuing political relationship with the trade unions which is thought to offer a guarantee that the Party must remain close to the people it seeks to organize and represent. But this structure obviously needs to be adapted to changing times, if it is to maintain its resilience and relevance.

In the formative years of the Labour Party, the federation consisted of up to 181 different trade unions, most of them small to medium-sized, so that the million-odd people associated in them were divided into many relatively equal groupings. The growth of trade unionism has been hastened by the concentration of capital, however, which has in turn enforced considerable concentration in the trade union movement itself. At the level of joint negotiations unions need to range over wider fields as companies eat one another up and managements bestride larger and larger colossi. Meantime, the greater complexity of industrial relations legislation, the growth of specialization in trade union offices, the burgeoning of new services which call for highly trained staff: all these pressures make small unions more and more difficult to maintain, and give the advantage to the vast amalgamations which dominate the modern TUC.

Yet, if concentration has been rapid in the past few years, high unemployment and industrial mergers, taken together, will accelerate it still further in the future.

Since 1951, the trend to larger and larger unions has been quite unmistakable. If this progression merely continues, without allowing for sharp speed-up in its tempo, we shall see a qualitative change in the resultant pattern.

From 1968 to 1977 the unions in the TUC (in spite of the gain of several important new affiliations) merged themselves down from 160 to 115. This trend extrapolated would have given us 83 unions in 1986, and maybe 75 in 1990. In fact, we had 88 unions in the TUC by 1986, so the trend has been somewhat slowed. But it remains more likely that mergers and takeovers might accelerate than that they will follow the existing trend line. Within the Labour Party, these processes of amalgamation have shrunk the number of affiliated unions from 59 in 1977 to 44 in 1985. This is not because organizations have resigned, but because they have fused. (See Table 11.6.) Talks have already gone on between the EETPU and the GMBATU, the AEU, and UCATT. Sooner or later one or another initiative will be successful. It would be a brave person who ruled out other marriages among the big league: NALGO and

NUPE, or either of these bodies with others, or a confederation of the general unions themselves: all seem at least thinkable. But whether these speculations are justifiable or not, union concentration poses a vast problem for the traditional procedures of the Labour Party. No longer are a large number of middle-sized bodies influential in decision-making: now everything turns on a handful of giants. Unlike the congregations of the independent churches which were roughly equivalent in size, now Labour Conferences are a league of whales and minnows. The whales are very big unions. The minnows are very little constituency organizations. This fact is now transparent, as can be seen in Table 11.6. Since 1980, changed proceedings in the recording of Party individual membership have recorded actual levels, instead of fictional assumptions that each constituency had a minimum of 1,000 adherents. But if those small constituency bodies don't swim, the whales will be sunk, when elections come around.

Worse: at the same time that the logic of the concentration of the block vote causes concern, so the individual members of the Labour Party, organized in their constituencies, find themselves called upon to assume greater financial and other responsibilities, in spite of their weaker voting power. After 1979 individual members were paying ten times the subscriptions levied upon affiliated members, and this might well prove a key lever for restructuring the Party: since it might seem reasonable to afford such contributors the equivalent, in trade union terms, of a 'financial vote'. An easier and more workable principle, derived from this example, would be to afford the constituency section parity with the trade union section, in the major forums in which policy is deliberated. This proposal was, in fact, canvassed from the union side, by Jack Jones in the late sixties, and repeated in modified terms by his colleague, Alex Kitson, in the eighties.

Determining Conference Arrangements

Even more spectacular than their heavy presence in the Conference at large and in the NEC has been the union near-monopoly of the Conference Arrangements Committee (CAC), which determines the agenda at the Party's Annual Conference. The capacity to steer the complex compositing of motions, and the order in which they are called, has often influenced the outcome of debates. In particular, during the strong chairmanship of Sir Harry Crane of the GMW, this small committee was widely credited with much responsibility for distorting the shape of debates by artificially encouraging extremely worded motions, to the discredit and possible defeat of milder ones. Conference management may be a fine art as well as a key to democratic development, and sometimes the artistry may have exceeded the democracy by a not inconsiderable factor.

The powers of the Conference Arrangements Committee, which is independent of the National Executive, are wide. First, it may exercise the option of applying the 'three-year rule', under which any matters already discussed during the two most recent Conferences may be kept off the agenda. Much depends on the stringency of definition, when such a rule is brought into force. Secondly, Labour Conferences normally involve several hundred resolutions, and an equivalent flood of amendments, which have to be composited into a reasonable number of representative motions. A key part of this work is done under the guidance of the CAC. Lewis Minkin cites an example of the pitfalls involved in this process, from the memoirs of Hugh Dalton, who used to dream of

> moving a resolution to nationalize the Solar System. This was regarded as a brilliant idea, but towards the close of the debate a Socialist Leaguer got up . . . and moved an amendment to add the words 'and the Milky Way'.[20]

A conservative CAC can make lethal use of the demand for social justice in the Milky Way, by encouraging it to be composited into every embarrassing proposal, whether for changes in foreign policy or for reform of the schools. It is therefore noteworthy that constituency representatives were never chosen for this function until the constitutional rebellion which culminated after 1979, and that even then they only secured one representative who was, of course, always outnumbered by his union colleagues.

Conclusion

Having thus amassed support on the Labour Party's leading committee, carrying an overwhelming preponderance of votes at its Conference, and maintaining a substantial presence in the Parliamentary Labour Party, how effective are British trade unions in politics? If one follows reports in the popular press, it seems that the unions rule. But if one examines the actual movement of political events, one may well form a sharply different impression.

However precisely unions may develop their industrial policies, they are ill-adapted organs for the refinement of detailed political strategies, with a result that they tend to find themselves reacting to the initiatives of others, rather than assuming any overall innovative role.

Without entering a long discussion of the meaning of day-to-day political issues, which would not be relevant to our present purposes, it seems clear that such major recent events as the formal abandonment of the priority commitment to full employment arose within the Labour government in response to Treasury pressures, and then to direct intervention by the International Monetary Fund, with only the most tardy of responses coming up from the unions.[21] Short of undertaking a detailed analysis of the fate of trade union-supported programmatic commitments, and of trade union legislation (or proposed legislation), we must, however, note that the political development of the unions by no means reflects the uninterrupted growth of support for Labour. In fact, the relative strength of TUC support for Labour declined from a little short of 70 per cent of the total membership in 1957 to just over 50 per cent in 1977. In 1985 it stood at 59 per cent, but the 'rise' merely reflects the fact that the numbers affiliated have been maintained while overall membership has been shrinking, so little encouragement can be drawn from it by Labour's organizers.

Of course, during those years, trade unionism grew continually until 1979: more unions, including white-collar giants such as NALGO and the NUT, joined forces with the TUC, thus to some degree diluting its erstwhile political linkages, while, as we have seen, Labour Party member-unions themselves sometimes shrank their proportional rates of affiliation. To this extent, unionateness seemed to have suffered a certain type of decline, at the same time that union densities were increasing. But mass unemployment was joined, after 1979, by declining union membership, declining densities, and, more significantly from this viewpoint, by a declining Labour vote. The one contrary trend shows a rising proportion of those union members eligible to affiliate to the Party, actually doing so. But it is a deceptive indicator, because it reflects declining membership totals in the real world. As these rolls shrink, they sink closer to the artificially lower levels of affiliation payments which had been established in palmier days.

It is at this point that the distinction between corporate and hegemonic forms of class consciousness, to which we referred earlier, has considerable relevance, since it can help us to appreciate the meaning of these events. If the Labour Party had proved able to adequately represent the corporate interests of working people, the least result we might have expected would have been a regular increase in percentage rates of membership affiliation, a serious argument among new or recent TUC affiliates raising the question that they might also wish to adhere to the Labour Party; and a certain rise in, or at any rate stability in, the Labour vote. In point of fact, since the Colliery Deputies and the Post Office Engineers decided to join the Party, none of the TUC's more recent major recruitment successes have generated any enthusiasm or even much bureaucratic pressure for additional political affiliations. Such decisions could not be taken without first achieving agreement by a majority in a membership ballot, and could normally be taken by the relevant leading committees. Even so, they had often not been taken. Now the figures have come more into line, but by shrinkage, not by expansion.

As for the popular vote, it has moved adversely:[22]

Table 11.7

Trends in Labour voting among trade unionists, 1964–87

Election year	Trade unionists voting Labour No.	(%)	Trade unionists affiliated to Labour No.
1964	6,077,980	73	5,502,001
1974	5,501,100	55	5,787,467
1979	6,185,280	51	6,511,179
1983	4,098,900	39	6,101,438
1987	n.a.	43	5,778,184*

* 1986 figure from Labour Party *Report*, 1987.

It is therefore an unavoidable conclusion that the unions have not only not been holding their ground politically, but actually losing out. If the membership had felt that their defensive needs were being met, it seems likely that some, if not all these indicators would have moved differently. In fact, by the time of the October 1974 election the Labour Party 'seemed to make no advance with trade union members', while, although both parties were more dependent than ever 'on their traditional class vote', nonetheless, because of the growth of minor parties, 'diminishing proportions of the working and middle class are voting for their "natural" party'.[23] Fifty-five per cent of union members voted Labour, the remainder dividing more or less equally between the Conservatives (23 per cent) and the minor parties (22 per cent altogether). Dismal though those figures were from the point of view of Labour loyalists among the union leaderships, in

1979 they got worse: 51 per cent of trade unionists voted Labour, and 31 per cent Conservative. As we have already seen, in 1983 union Labour loyalist voters were actually a minority.

Quite clearly, the defensive concerns of the unions were not adequately upheld by recent Labour governments. Far from moving over to some form of 'hegemonic' politics, involving, as Tony Benn put it at Labour's 1973 Conference, 'a fundamental shift in the balance of wealth and power in the direction of working people and their families', the 1974 Labour administration saw officially recognized unemployment pass the 1,400,000 mark, and whole legions of trade unionists subsequently found themselves in heated conflict with a Labour government about the most rudimentary questions of wages. Without oversimplifying these crucial and sometimes complex issues, it was clear that even as the trade unions readied themselves to enter the period of Conservative administration, they already had a lot of political thinking to do.

A number of urgent questions can, after seven years of the Thatcher era, no long be postponed, now that a profound and prolonged crisis undermines and crumbles away the last remnants of the postwar British welfare consensus.

How do the rather chaotic organizations of British labour match and outmanoeuvre the great transnational companies? What kinds of reform do the unions need in their internal structures (combine committees, industrial liaisons) and in their international relations? What joint arrangements can be evolved to control the ill-effects of new technologies and confront mass unemployment on a continental scale? What detailed programmes of self-defence are involved in meeting the hostile actions of governments and their judiciaries, and what positive strategies of advance will assure the defence of welfare and development of industrial democracy? Above all, what steps are needed to ensure that the British trade unions develop a political voice which can address these difficult issues, and the political weight to resolve them?

The unions may have come nearer to finding answers to such questions, through what they have learned in their successes in the political fund ballots. But they will not be likely to win out until they evolve very much more co-ordinated political campaigns on a variety of industrial questions, to recover on the political plane powers which unemployment has largely eroded on the industrial front.

NOTES

1. Margaret Stewart, *Protest or Power?* Allen and Unwin, 1974, p. 54.
2. Labour Party, *Report of the 45th Annual Conference*, p. 35.
3. R. T. McKenzie, *British Political Parties*, Heinemann, 1955, p. 386.
4. Cf. Anthony Carew, *Democracy and Government in European Trade Unions*, Allen and Unwin, 1976; Bonety *et al.*, *La CFDT*, Seuil, Paris, 1971; K. Coates (ed.), *A Trade Union Strategy in the Common Market*, Spokesman, 1971.
5. Documentation on this process may be found in W. Milne-Bailey, *Trade Union Documents*, G. Bell & Sons, 1929, Part 1, pp. 43–76.
6. R. T. McKenzie, *op. cit.*, p. 479.
7. Labour Party, Constitution and Standing Orders, Clause IV, subsection 4.
8. Cf. Mark Jenkins, *Bevanism*, Spokesman, 1979.
9. *The New Unionism*, Penguin Books, 1974.
10. P. Anderson and R. Blackburn, *Towards Socialism*, Fontana, 1964, pp. 221–90. Also see Anderson's 'The Antinomies of Antonio Gramsci', *New Left Review*, no. 100, 1976/7.
11. W. D. Muller, *The Kept Men*, Harvester, 1977, pp. 29–31. Table 11.1, with the exception of 1979 and 1987 figures, is to be found on page 30. Mr Muller cites the following sources:

    Except where otherwise noted, the above table is based on data derived from: F. W. Craig (ed), *British Parliamentary Election Statistics, 1918–1968* (Glasgow: Political Reference Publications, 1968), p. 54.

    [a] H. A. Clegg, Alan Fox and A. F. Thompson, *A History of British Trade Unions Since 1889*, vol. 1: *1889–1910* (Oxford: Clarendon Press, 1964), pp. 384, 387, 420–2.

    [b] David Butler and Jennie Freeman (eds.), *British Political Facts, 1900–1967* (Second edition; Macmillan, 1968), pp. 141–4.

    [c] Labour Party, Annual Conference Reports (1970 and 1974).

    [d] Based on correspondence with the Labour Party and detailed analysis of the information given in the Annual Report of the Labour Party for 1974.

    [e] The figure given by the Labour Party's Information Office for 1979 is 149, but this omits 4 NUM sponsorships, 2 AUEW sponsorships, 1 from the GMW, and 1 from the T & GWU, among others.
12. Butler and Kavanagh provide the 1974 figures in *The British General Election of October 1974*, Macmillan, 1975, p. 217, Table 6. Figures for 1979 from the Labour Research Dept.
13. Their behaviour is best documented in Lewis Minkin, *The Labour Party Conference*, Allen Lane, 1978. See also the dated but useful book by Martin Harrison, *Trade Unions and the Labour Party*, Macmillan, 1960.

14. *Labour Party Diary*, 1984.
15. Ken Coates and Tony Topham, *Trade Unions and Politics*, Blackwell, 1986.
16. *Ibid.*
17. Peter Hain, 'An Unhappy Marriage? The Labour Union Link', *Marxism Today*, November 1984, p. 12.
18. This becomes an important issue when union leaders do not evidently respect their own internal decision-making processes in deploying these huge votes. Cf. Martin Harrison, *op. cit.*; Lewis Minkin, *op. cit.*; Edelstein and Warner, *Comparative Union Democracy,* Allen and Unwin, 1975. Also K. Coates, *The Crisis of British Socialism,* Spokesman, 1971, Ch. XII; and Bulletin of the IWC, December 1978, pp. 2–4.
19. Martin Harrison, *op. cit.*, shows that twenty-two unions between them provided all the members of the NEC between 1935 and 1959. Fifteen of these were represented fairly continuously, the rest extremely infrequently, and briefly at that (p. 309).
20. Lewis Minkin, *op. cit.*, pp. 141–2. Cf. his Chapter V, on 'Agenda Politics'.
21. The best short account of these developments is Tom Forester, 'How Labour's Industrial Policy Got the Chop', in *New Society*, vol. 45, no. 822. This shows that the TUC 'either, because they were intimidated by the crisis atmosphere, felt that somehow it was an internal party or government row, had other priorities, or genuinely regarded the policy as a less immediate . . . matter, . . . didn't make its abandonment a central issue in their negotiations with the government.'
22. D. Butler and D. Kavanagh, *op. cit.*, p. 294.
23. *Ibid*, pp. 277–9.

CHAPTER 12

International Affiliations

TUC International Links

British trade unions maintain formal connections with a variety of international organizations, and the TUC as a whole is currently affiliated to four major bodies. These are the International Confederation of Free Trade Unions (ICFTU); the European Trades Union Confederation (ETUC); the Trade Union Advisory Committee to the Organization for Economic Co-operation and Development (TUAC OECD); and the Commonwealth Trade Union Council (CTUC). This network of affiliations is costly, and in 1985 the TUC spent £565,000 on its membership of the ICFTU alone. Membership of the other organizations does not come cheaply, either. In 1986, affiliation fees to the ETUC ran at £169,000, to the TUAC at £41,000, and even the CTUC was scheduled to cost £18,000 during the financial year beginning in mid-1986. These large sums of money would have been larger still if trade unions nationally had not been going through hard times and restricting the activities of their international organizations. In fact, a decade earlier, the TUC had spent almost 30 per cent of its total budget on overseas affiliation fees during the year 1977. The percentage has steadily declined to a little over 12 per cent but the commitment is still an important and costly one. Overseas expenditure is not restricted to outlays on such affiliation fees. There is a full-fledged International Department at Congress House, and although its costs are not separately itemized in TUC accounts, we calculated in 1977 that they ran at a figure of some £68,000. They have not diminished since. During that year there were also various grants to international causes, which brought the total expenditure on international relations to 34 per cent of TUC revenue.

Table 12.1

TUC international expenditure as a percentage of total revenue, 1960–84

Year	TUC (a) Recorded total expenditure £	(b) Recorded affiliations international expenditure (ICFTU, ISF, ERO, EFTA TU Ctee, TUAC OECD, ETUC) *not* including delegation costs, or costs of TUC International Committee £	% increase/ decrease	% (b) of (a) % of total income
1960	328,278	80,741		24.6
1962	387,584	83,700	+ 3.66	21.6
1964	532,250	164,449	+96.47	30.9
1966	592,507	169,942	+ 3.34	28.7
1968	784,947	195,151	+14.83	24.9
1970	841,875	207,028	+ 6.09	24.6
1972	999,181	214,334	+ 3.53	21.5
1974	1,282,425	334,657	+56.14	26.1
1976	1,917,941	564,389	+68.65	29.4
1978	2,422,858	544,000	− 3.61	22.5
1980	3,609,975	601,221	+10.52	16.7
1982	4,435,227	666,784	+10.90	15.0
1984	5,283,696	651,844	− 2.24	12.3

Source: TUC, *Annual Reports*.

We have already argued that the rocketing growth of the largest transnational companies makes necessary closer and closer association between workpeople in many different countries. Doesn't this need justify such a large investment? Have we not continually complained that multinational companies are becoming more and more powerful, and that they exercise a vast influence, not only over the British economy? For all that, it is unfortunately rather clear that little of the present international work of the unions is at all effective in controlling and rendering more accountable this colossal concentration of power.

Of course, the TUC acts as a national centre, and represents all its affiliated bodies: but this does not prevent individual unions from creating their own international linkages, which they do through International Trade Secretariats, some of which remain important and relevant bodies.

But whoever does it, international work can be extremely expensive. Not only are transport costs high, but telephone bills shoot out of sight. In addition, unless the movement is very fortunate in its recruitment of qualified linguists, translation costs can be truly astronomical. The idea that international expenditure covers junketing before all else is not true, even if the odd occasion may encourage gossips to think so. The fact is, the unions are committed to a level of activity in this area which is bound, in its nature, to be expensive.

Compared with earlier days, this kind of commitment is truly breathtaking. Back in 1909 there were no comparable trade union international organizations: the total expenditure of the TUC was £7,379 16s 7d, and, raking through its detailed accounts, we find £323 10s 7d allocated to international purposes. This amounts to 4.4 per cent of the total.

By the time that the interwar International Federation of Trade Unions had been reborn, the TUC could spend nearly as much on international work alone as it had received in total income a little more than a decade earlier. This emerges very clearly from a look at the figures during the first half of the 1920s:

Table 12.2

TUC expenditure on international work as a percentage of total, 1923–5

	Total	International	%
1923	£142,792	£6,474	4.5
1924	£107,727	£6,705	6.2
1925	£ 75,908	£7,353	9.7

These totals vary sharply, but the percentages of expenditure on all foreign relations work remained throughout that period very much lower than they were subsequently to become. During that time a major burden on TUC revenues was the maintenance of the *Daily Herald*, which, of course, provided a constant source of information on foreign affairs for all trade unionists, in addition to its domestic coverage. Perhaps such a commitment to the provision of relevant information to a wide audience is a precondition for any effective democratic trade union 'foreign policy'.

After the Second World War, trade union international links became a most complex affair, because of the outbreak of cold war, in which vast efforts were made, first by the Soviet and then by the American governments, to influence opinion-forming social organizations of all kinds. Much of the influence concerned was undertaken covertly, and a pattern of active intervention in union affairs was established which had very large consequences. It was in this context that trade union expenditures on international affiliations rose to unprecedented levels. Of course, these outgoings reflect a complicated mixture of idealism and genuine solidarity, together with other motives.

Throughout the 1960s and 1970s, leaving out of account altogether the costs of the International Department itself, a vastly distended budget was laid out in this field. This was at a time when there was no provision of mass-information by the TUC, and the only democratic control over foreign policy consisted of intermittent (and sometimes perfunctory) debates in Congress. The figures are nonetheless very large.

How far do TUC representatives control this large disbursement? It is difficult, from outside, to be sure, but it certainly looks as if the answer is 'not as far as might be expected'. To explore this question we have no alternative but to take a brief look at the chequered story of international trade unionism.

The International Organizations

International organization of trade unions began as a practical process, for limited purposes. People wanted help for various reasons: to stop strike-breaking by employers who were exporting jobs or importing workpeople, to secure information and support, to move up with or jump in front of adverse technologies. After the initial experiment of the International Working Men's Association, which struggled on for nine years with the active help of Karl Marx, it was not surprising that socialist parties were keen to repeat the same formula: and it is clear that the Second International, the socialist movement which dominated the Labour organizations of the earliest years of the twentieth century, played a major role in encouraging international trade union link-ups.

In 1886 the Scandinavian unions began a federation, to help each other out in strikes. Three years later, the first specialized standing association – or International Trade Secretariat – of printers, was set up. In 1890 the miners followed on by creating their own international body. Congresses of the Socialist International provided a regular meeting-place at which trade unions could make contact with one another, and in 1903 there was created an international secretariat of trade union national centres. This grew rather quickly, to embrace fourteen countries with 2½ million members in 1904 and 3½ million members in 1906. In 1909 the American Federation of Labor joined in, and the secretariat changed its name, to become the International Federation of Trade Unions. By 1913 this had sixteen members in thirty countries.

Meantime, an International Secretariat of Christian Trade Unions had been formed in 1908. Both of these centres appealed for solidarity funds in support of particular actions, but both were pre-eminently concerned with the exchange of information, and the circulation of reports. The political coloration of the IFTU was, at this time, complex. The socialist Germans found themselves joined up alongside French syndicalists and American craft unionists. How these trends of thought would have lived together given time is difficult to predict: but in the event they were wrenched apart by the 1914 war, which wrecked international labour co-operation whilst millions of trade union members put on uniforms and slaughtered one another. In 1917 the Russian Revolution brought the Bolsheviks to power, so that the rebirth of trade union internationalism after the restoration of peace saw the emergence of two federations. The IFTU opened up again, and in 1920 it included twenty-one centres with 23 million members. The Soviets, once they were sufficiently firmly grounded, began a rival Red International of Labour Unions (RILU) in 1921. Although this had a significant propaganda influence, it never gained any really permanent mass basis outside the USSR. However, the existence of two such bodies encouraged others, and the interwar years saw a marked fragmentation of international trade union efforts. Only after Hitler came to power in Germany were minds concentrated in other European countries: and there was, between 1933 and the outbreak of the Second World War, a certain convergence of forces. In particular, unsuccessful communist breakaways made their peace with their parent organizations, and in Scotland, France and Canada the IFTU affiliates were restored to sufficient unity to hold unchallenged preponderance over the unions in their countries. Communist influence had been large in Germany and Italy, but all independent unions were crushed by the Nazi and fascist governments. In Britain (apart from Scotland) separate communist unions had been the merest shadow,[1] quickly past, and there was never any very serious opposition to trade union unity.

Partly because the RILU was in these terms largely a failure, and, after the early thirties, no big threat to the (mainly) socialist-based trade union centres: and partly because the Second World War created a considerable sense of unity among the allies, so that trade union unity became for a time quite thinkable even though there were undoubtedly very great differences of function between the Soviet and West European labour organizations, there emerged, in 1945, a new body, the World Federation of Trade Unions.

This was established in two international conferences, the first of which (in London) agreed on a drafting committee to prepare a constitution, while the second (in Paris, in October) actually launched the new organization. Sir Walter Citrine, of the British TUC, played a major role in this work, and became the founding chairman. He has left an interesting description of what happened during the formation of the WFTU in his memoirs.[2] All the major national trade union centres then existing were represented, but there was no participation by workers from the defeated powers, Germany and Japan.

A festival atmosphere was understandable. The war was over, Labour was united, all over Europe socialists and communists were either sharing power in coalition governments, or governing alone, as in England. Trade unions had arrived, it seemed, at the threshold of a new society. But it was not to last. In a very short time the cold war had assumed such intensity that conflict raged in every inclusive international organization, not excluding the WFTU.

Communist-led federations now represented not only the Soviet and East European organizations, but also those of France and Italy. The argument which broke out between 1947 and 1949 was bitter and destructive, because there was no natural mediating influence, and the result was a direct East–West division. This became an irreconcilable split in 1949, and late that year those of the Western unions which were not under communist influence met in London to establish the International Confederation of Free Trade Unions (ICFTU). This set up its headquarters in Brussels.[3]

The formation of a separate international organization became an occasion for bitter faction fights in some of the national centres. In particular, the French CGT was split, and a breakaway body, Force Ouvrière (FO), became a founding constituent of the ICFTU. Within the fields of interest of individual trade unions, the International Trade Secretariats, which were continuing in spite of the inheritance of dislocation during the war, to provide functional contacts between unions in particular sectors, had, almost from the beginning, found their relationship with the WFTU imprecise and unsatisfactory. They had no wish to become subordinate desks of WFTU departments, and in addition they began to develop serious political disagreements with the overall international organization. When they withdrew from the WFTU in 1949, they quickly arrived at an agreement with the founders of the ICFTU, and whilst they remained technically autonomous, they agreed without difficulty to work within broad policy lines determined by the breakaway international. Today there are sixteen different International Trade Secretariats: their membership is something over 45 million, and thus is still within reach of being comparable with the claimed membership of the ICFTU itself. At the time of the split in the WFTU, these secretariats had even greater importance, because they represented functional international machinery whilst quarrelling international conferences represented only verbiage, and much of that remained unedifying. Even so, there was an important non-trade union influence at work in the split, and this has dogged the footsteps of trade union internationalism ever since.

During the wartime alliance which had made possible the launching of the WFTU, Stalin had unilaterally dissolved the Communist International, as a concession to the allied governments. Undoubtedly this had impressed many socialists and trade union spokesmen as well. After the war, with the increase of East–West tension, a new communist international body (embracing parties in East Europe as well as the French and Italian organizations) was quickly launched: it became known in the West as the 'Cominform'. Some of the prewar devices of communist international activity were thus resumed with greater intensity after the Americans launched the Marshall Plan.

It was in this context that the Americans developed a massive counter-offensive under the auspices of the CIA (Central Intelligence Agency). In the words of one English critic, this came to carry out 'at a more sophisticated level, exactly the same sort of organized subversion as Stalin's Comintern in its heyday'.[4] Although the whole story is by no means completely clear, it is quite apparent that the CIA played an important role in orchestrating the argument which created the ICFTU. In the words of one ex-employee of the Agency who subsequently defected:

> Agency labour operations came into being . . . as a reaction against the continuation of pre-World War II CPSU policy and expansion through the international united fronts. In 1945 with the support and participation of the British Trade Unions Congress (TUC), the American Congress of Industrial Organizations (CIO) and the Soviet Trade Unions Council, the World Federation of Trade Unions (WFTU) was formed in Paris. Differences within the WFTU between communist trade-union leaders, who were anxious to use the WFTU for anti-capitalist propaganda, and free-world leaders who insisted on keeping the WFTU focused on economic issues, finally came to a head in 1949 over whether the WFTU should support the Marshall Plan. When the communists, who included French, Italian and Latin American leaders as well as the Soviets refused to allow the WFTU to endorse the Marshall Plan, the TUC and CIO withdrew, and later the same year the International Confederation of Free Trade Unions (ICFTU) was founded as a non-communist alternative to the WFTU, with participation by the TUC, CIO, American Federation of Labor (AFL) and other national centres. Agency operations were responsible in part for the expulsion of the WFTU headquarters from Paris in 1951 when it moved to the Soviet sector of Vienna. Later, in 1956, it was forced to move from Vienna to Prague.
>
> The ICFTU established regional organizations for Europe, the Far East, Africa and the Western Hemisphere, which brought together the non-communist national trade-union centres. Support and guidance by the Agency was, and still is, exercised on the three levels: ICFTU, regional and national centres. At the highest level, Agency labour operations are effected through George Meany, President of the AFL, Jay Lovestone, Foreign Affairs Chief of the AFL and Irving Brown, AFL representative in Europe – all of whom are effective and witting collaborators. Direct

> Agency control is also exercised on the regional level. Serafino Romualdi, AFL Latin American representative, for example, directs the Inter-American Regional Labor Organization (ORIT) located in Mexico City. On the national level, particularly in underdeveloped countries, CIA field stations engage in operations to support and guide national labour centres. Its headquarters, support, guidance and control of all labour operations is centralized in the labour branch of the International Organizations Division.[5]

Jay Lovestone, who himself played a major role in the history of American communism (he had been national chairman of the CPUSA in 1929), was intimately familiar with Comintern behaviour and therefore well able to set up a most elaborate countering political organization. It is not, therefore, surprising that this apparatus bore a marked resemblance to the oppositional machine against which it was ranged. But, whilst in 1949 it is possible that some members of the British Labour movement might not, had they known of them, have objected very strongly to Mr Lovestone's activities, it is anything but likely that many people in British unions would have favoured the subsequent continuous manipulation of the ICFTU regional organizations for intelligence purposes and 'counter-insurgency'. It has become clear and undeniable that the CIA has not restricted its use of what it engagingly calls 'dirty tricks' to dictatorships, but has, to the contrary, been particularly active in destabilizing democratic regimes in which radical reformers have come to office.[6] The Agency's labour desk has not spared the unions their often unwitting involvement in this process. It is claimed, for instance, that

> A fourth CIA approach to labour operations is through the International Trade Secretariats (ITS), which represent the interests of workers in a particular industry as opposed to the national centres that unite workers of different industries. Because the ITS system is more specialized, and often more effective, it is at times more appropriate for

Agency purposes than the ICFTU with its regional and national structure. Control and guidance is exercised through officers of a particular ITS who are called upon to assist labour operations directed against the workers of a particular industry. Very often the CIA agents in an ITS are the American labour leaders who represent the US affiliate of the ITS, since the ITS would usually receive its principal support from the pertinent US industrial union. Thus the American Federation of State, County and Municipal Employees serves as a channel for CIA operations in the Public Service International, which is the ITS for government employees headquartered in London. And the Retail Clerks International Association, which is the US union of white-collar employees, gives access to the International Federation of Clerical and Technical Employees, which is the white-collar ITS. Similarly, the Communications Workers of America is used to control the Post, Telegraph and Telephone Workers International (PTTI) which is the ITS for communications workers. In the case of the petroleum industry the Agency actually set up the ITS, the International Federation of Petroleum and Chemical Workers (IFPCW) through the US union of petroleum workers, the Oil Workers International Union. Particularly in underdeveloped countries, station labour operations may be given cover as a local programme of an ITS.[7]

This matter was raised by Jim Mortimer, then the Draughtsmen's representative, at the TUC in 1967.

There is, . . . one issue . . . upon which I should like to suggest to Congress and to the General Council it would be most helpful if they could offer us their observations. I refer to the very detailed and specific revelations during the past twelve months of the channelling of millions of pounds from the Central Intelligence Agency of the United States Government under the cover of the international trade union movement. I am not saying anything about any other trade union.

We ourselves are in this problem. We are affiliated to an ITS against which very detailed charges have been made in United States newspapers. I know there are many other unions here in the same position. There are charges that some of the officials of the ICFTU are CIA agents, I cannot comment on whether those charges are correct or incorrect, but I think it reasonable that the General Council should have a look at the matter and should offer us their observations.

May I just make this point: that the charges have been very detailed indeed and they have come not only from American newspapers, like the *New York Times* and the *Washington Post,* but also from a number of American trade unionists themselves. The *Washington Post* said that the total amount of money channelled from CIA into the trade union movement and used for the purposes of the American Government was amounting now to 100 million dollars a year. One of our trade unionists who came to Britain only a few years ago – I remember his fraternal address, but I will not mention his name on this occasion – has, according to reports I have read in the *Washington Post*, confirmed that for six years his union acted as cover for CIA money being poured into an international trade secretariat with headquarters in London.

The UAW – the United Automobile Workers – in February this year withdrew all their officers from the American Federation of Labor and Congress of Industrial Organizations. They issued a detailed administration letter, a copy of which I have with me at this Congress, and one of the charges made by the UAW is that money has been used through the AFL–CIO for the purpose of the Central Intelligence Agency of the United States Government. Victor Reuther, the international representative of UAW, said that there is a very big story on the financial and policy relationship between the AFL–CIO and the CIA . . .

Very briefly, the way in which this money has been

> channelled into the trade union movement, according to the charges made, has been that the CIA has set up a number of dummy charitable foundations – about fifty are named in the *Washington Post* – and then those foundations have passed the money to American trade unions, which have used the money, mainly through the international trade secretariats but partly through the ICFTU, to carry out the policies of the American Government. I hope the General Council will agree that this is a matter that concerns many unions in this Congress and that it is one on which we look to them for their observations.[8]

There was no debate upon this cogent statement, but George Woodcock, the then General Secretary of the TUC, replied in a brief intervention.

> Mr George Woodcock (*General Secretary*): Let there be no assumption in this Congress that the TUC in any way has had money from any source whatsoever but from the affiliated bodies to Congress. I cannot speak for the trade secretariats; they are not within the control of the General Council of the TUC. We have examined the information from the ICFTU and there is no evidence whatever that any money has been received by the ICFTU from any source other than a trade union source. I do not want it to be thought that the TUC has anything here to hide at all. We have stood firmly, and always will stand firmly, to the view that we are quite capable of doing our own job and paying our own way.[9]

Whether the General Council really approved this rather laconic reply, or not, it is beyond reasonable doubt that this kind of revelation has been extremely unhelpful to the ICFTU as a whole.

The membership of the Confederation may be measured by three yardsticks. First, how many countries are represented within it? Second, how many national centres are affiliated? This can produce a different answer from the first question, because in some countries there exist several national trade union centres.

Table 12.3
ICFTU membership trends, 1949–86

Year	Number of countries and territories	Number of organizations	Number of individual members represented by affiliates
1949	51	67	48,000,000
1951	59	76	50,500,000
1953	59	97	53,200,000
1955	75	109	54,300,000
1957	88	124	53,800,000
1959	97	137	56,000,000
1962	106	137	56,000,000
1965	96	121	60,300,000
1969	95	123	63,000,000
1972	91	115	48,600,000
1975	88	118	51,800,000
1977	88	120	55,500,000
1978	88	122	59,000,000
1979	88	123	59,000,000
1980	89	127	70,000,000
1981	93	130	70,000,000
1982	93	132	84,000,000
1983	96	136	85,000,000
1984	95	136	83,000,000
1985	99	144	82,000,000
1986	99	144	80,000,000

Source: J. F. Windmuller, *op. cit.*,[10] and TUC, *Annual Reports*, 1978–86.

Thirdly, how many individual members are enrolled in the affiliated membership? The answers to these questions are given in Table 12.3.

Not all of these unions are strictly comparable, of course. While some are obviously widely representative, others are little more than propaganda desks, sometimes owing very much to the direct support of their governments, or as we have seen, to outside sponsorship.

Table 12.4
ICFTU membership by region, 1965 and 1975

	1965 Number (000s)	%	1975 Number (000s)	%
Europe	26,551	44.0	29,973	57.9
Africa	908	1.5	908	1.8
Asia (Far East and South Asia)	5,618	9.3	9,669	18.7
Near East	1,547	2.6	1,434	2.8
Australia and New Zealand	1,050	1.7	1,643	3.2
North America	14,139	23.5	1,516	2.9
Latin America and Caribbean	10,461	17.4	6,605	12.7
Total	60,274	100.0	51,748	100.0

Source: J. F. Windmuller, *op. cit.* [11]

When these figures are broken down for the different regions covered, however, a more precise picture emerges (see Table 12.4).

From both these tables, it is clear that ICFTU affiliates as a whole doubled in number between 1949 and 1962, and individual membership rose to a peak in 1969; they then shrivelled back to a point they had already passed twenty years earlier. During that time, in the advanced European countries, memberships were growing and this was reflected in the regional figures. Further overall growth set in in the eighties, with the reaffiliation of estranged American centres, and the restoration of democracy in many Latin American states. Subsequently, of course, the slump reduced union strengths in Europe itself, as we have continually stressed. But membership decline in such circumstances is quite a different matter from that involved in these other regional bodies. In Africa, for instance, nothing moved. One reason is that various African governments (sometimes for honest and quite understandable reasons, and sometimes solely in order to subordinate the unions to their own wishes) have outlawed both the ICFTU and the WFTU, on the (not altogether unreasonable) grounds that they 'were merely a clever disguise for penetration by one of the major power blocs'. As the Nigerian government reported:

> Both the ICFTU and the AALC supported the United Labour Congress of Nigeria (ULCN) regarded as the main counterbalance to the rival Communist-led Nigeria Trade Union Congress (NTUC). From a 1977 report of a government tribunal of inquiry into the activities of the trade unions, the following emerged:
>
> 1. So considerable was the ICFTU and US funding to the ULCN that most of the centre's affiliates didn't bother to pay dues to it. Leadership of unions which did pay expected in return financial and other rewards. Money was used to try and bribe union leaders to affiliate their unions with the ULCN.
> 2. The President of the ULCN had information that the AALC was connected with the CIA. He wrote to two of the AALC staff in Nigeria asking for an explanation. None was forthcoming.
> 3. In the early seventies the ICFTU paid out money for ULCN-run welfare schemes. The inquiry reported: 'The projects were established, but with (one) exception they were allowed to fizzle out largely because of lack of supervision of the personnel directly responsible for their operation by the Congress Secretariat. No member of the Congress Secretariat could tell us what had become of the projects – they just did not know. This led us to conclude that they had adopted a carefree attitude to the projects because the funding went through external sources.'
> 4. In 1973 the ULCN was able to get an additional 10,000 dollars from the ICFTU by pretending it was about to launch an organizational campaign. The inquiry said it 'was a specious cover to induce the ICFTU to part with its money'.

5. The ICFTU (which prides itself on a non-colonial relationship with affiliated Third World unions) along with the AALC 'had a free hand in the running of the affairs of the Congress'. Representatives of both took part in policy making meetings.
6. The inquiry found that because of the flow of money and material aid from the ICFTU and the US 'there appeared to be a tacit understanding among the officers of Congress of adopting a policy of "what you have you hold". The result was that each officer kept to himself/herself what came to him/her be it money, car or scooter and provided he acknowledged receipt of it to the donating organization, that virtually ended the matter.'[12]

In Latin America, where the CIA depredations were the most blatant and offensive,[13] membership dropped right back from 10½ to 6½ million in 1975. It is assumed by informed observers that all these figures are somewhat fictional: but it is certainly no fiction that ORIT, the Confederation's Latin American organization, to which Philip Agee refers above, has, as he claims, been heavily involved in CIA-funded operations. This no doubt accounts for the success of the more independent Christian federation in the region. Of course, ORIT operates on the doorstep of the American unions. The overseas work of the AFL-CIO, whilst it is mainly financed by the United States government, is also funded by an impressive list of companies: see Table 12.5. Small wonder that the veteran American labour leader, George Meany, preached a form of mirror-image Marxism:

> You can't dictate to a country from any angle at all unless you control the means of production. If you don't control the means of production, you can't dictate. Whether you control them through ideological methods or control them by brute force, you must control them.[15]

This kind of intervention makes it rather difficult to evaluate the real significance of the different pieces of international machinery. On the one side, virtually none of the rank-and-file

Table 12.5

Some companies which finance AFL-CIO's overseas work

W. R. Grace & Company	Brazilian Light & Power
Rockefeller Brothers Fund	First National Bank of Boston
International Telephone and Telegraph	United Fruit Company
Pan American World Airways	Anglo-Lautaro Nitrate Corporation
The United Corporation	IBM World Trade Corporation
David Rockefeller	International Basic Economy Corporation
Kennecott Copper Corporation	Sinclair Oil
Standard Oil Co. of New Jersey	Max Ascoli Fund Inc.
Koppers Company	International Mining Corporation
Gillette	Carrier Corporation
Shell Petroleum	Coca-Cola Export Corporation
Crown Zellerbach	Container Corporation of America
The Anaconda Company	Stauffer Chemical Company
ACFE (Venezuela)	American-Standard
King Ranch	International Packers
Sterling Drug, Inc.	Olin
General Foods Corporation	Standard Oil of California
Loeb Rhoades & Company	Warner-Lambard
Owens-Illinois Glass	Corning Glass
Union Carbide Corporation	Eli Lilly & Company
Ebasco Industries	J. Henry Schroeder Banking Corporation
Reader's Digest	United Shoe Machinery
Monsanto	Celanese Corporation
Southern Peru Copper Corporation	Bacardi Corporation
Merck	Schering Foundation
Pfizer International	Bankers Trust Company
Otis Elevator Company	Bristol Myers
Industrias Kaiser Argentina	Chase Manhattan Bank
American Cyanamid	Kimberly-Clark
First National City Bank	Upjohn Company
International Paper Company	Insurance Company of North America
Mobil Oil Company	3M Company
Standard Fruit Company	American International Oil Company
American Telephone & Telegraph	Combustion Engineering
Corn Products	Sheraton Corporation of America
Council for Latin America	Chemetron Corporation
Johnson & Johnson	Motion Picture Association of America
St. Regis Paper Company	Deltec
American Can Company	

Source: AIFLD, Senate Hearing, 1968, p. 21, cited in D. Thomson and R. Larson, *op. cit.*[14]

Note: In 1977 an AFL-CIO spokesman confirmed that companies still financed part of their overseas programme.

affiliated members, either of the ICFTU or the ITS networks, would endorse the diplomatic objectives of the intelligence operatives, leave alone their 'dirty tricks'. On the other side, the fact that bodies like ORIT have been compromised means that the international body lacks effective organs in a key zone of activity. In political terms the meaning of the ICFTU is complex: in spite of all the abuses of trust, it retains a degree of strong support from key union centres which are nobody's catspaws. So much is this the case that, when the American AFL-CIO walked out, they reproached it for being 'soft' on détente.[16] In industrial terms, the political alienation of some of the more dynamic and independent union centres in the third world means a severe restriction of capacity to deal with the practical problems involved in facing up to the multinational companies.

The Growth of Regionalism

All this has pushed the TUC and other European bodies in the direction of greater reliance upon regional organization.[17] To some extent this development has been a global one, with similar bodies gaining strength in both African and Arab regions.

The European Trade Union Confederation was set up at a founding Congress held at the beginning of 1973 by eighteen of the ICFTU's European affiliates, including all the relevant centres in all the nine EEC countries, except Ireland, together with those of Austria, Finland (2), Iceland, Norway, Sweden (2), Switzerland and Spain. (The additional centre comes from Italy, where, at the time, both the CISL and the UIL were affiliated to the Brussels international office.)

The ETUC knit together previous co-ordinating groups for both the EEC and EFTA: and it specifically set out to mark and pace the growth of transnational companies, at the same time as it sought representation in relevant EEC committees. In May 1974 at an extraordinary Congress in Copenhagen, the Confederation took all the major National Christian Trade Union Centres into membership, and also the radical French centre, the

CFDT, together with the Irish Congress of Trade Unions. Within a few weeks the Italian CGIL (which is a joint communist-socialist federation, formerly affiliated to the WFTU, but now independent) was also accepted into membership. By 1976 the second (London) ETUC Congress had representation from thirty organizations with 37 million members.

This left outside only the French, Spanish and Portuguese communist centres (the CGT, Commisiones Obreras and Intersyndical), the first and last of which maintained links with the WFTU, not without certain developing frictions, but which also in France and Spain faced the intransigent hostility of old rivals, such as Force Ouvrière, or the UGT. Applications for membership from the Commisiones Obreras which, because it remained independent of the WFTU, was never strictly ineligible, were hotly debated during 1985 and 1986, in a long-running hassle. The TUC in particular was keen to enable the dissident Spaniards to join the Confederation. The point of the Confederation, they argued, was to establish representative institutions on the most inclusive possible basis. Ideological considerations did not, therefore, come into consideration. But the Spanish UGT did not share this measure of toleration. The CCOO, they argued, were opposed to the Spanish Socialist government, and thus beyond the pale. The TUC and its co-thinkers rejected this line of reasoning on the grounds that perfectly representative trade unions might be quite agnostic about the actions of governments, even when they felt themselves to be in general sympathy with those governments. There is no short answer to such questions, because ideological commitments are deeply significant to the organizations which uphold them. But the spokesmen of the TUC are surely right in their insistence that the most important question about a trade union must remain, 'How representative is it?' To put together a European network, which can be useful to rank-and-file trade unionists, whatever their political colour, one needs to aim at the broadest and most comprehensive inclusiveness. A useful trade union network should perhaps be compared to a telephone exchange: it should enable people to get in touch with one

Table 12.6
ETUC national affiliates

Country	Initials	Organization
Austria	ÖGB	Österreichischer Gewerkschaftsbund
Belgium	FGTB	Fédération Générale du Travail de Belgique
Belgium	CSC	Confédération des Syndicats Chrétiens
Cyprus	SEK	Cyprus Workers Confederation
Cyprus	TURK-SEN	Cyprus Turkish Trade Unions Federation
Denmark	LO	Landsorganisationen i Danmark
Denmark	FTF	Fällesrädet for Danske Tjenestemandsoj Fünktionärorganisationer
Finland	TVK	Toimihenkilö- ja Virkamiesjäjestöjen Keskusliitto
Finland	SAK	Suomen Ammattiliittojen Keskusjärjesto
FR Germany	DGB	Deutscher Gewerkschaftsbund
France	CGT-FO	Confédération Générale du Travail – Force Ouvrière
France	CFDT	Confédération Française Démocratique du Travail
Great Britain	TUC	Trades Union Congress
Greece	GGCL	Greek General Confederation of Labour
Iceland	ASI	Althydusamband Islands
Iceland	BSRB	Bandalag Starfsmanna Rikis og Baeja
Ireland	ICTU	Irish Congress of Trade Unions
Italy	CISL	Confederazione Italiana Sindacati Lavoratori
Italy	CGIL	Confederazione Generale Italiane del Lavoro
Italy	UIL	Unione Italiana del Lavoro
Luxembourg	CGT-L	Confédération Générale du Travail de Luxembourg
Luxembourg	LCGB	Letzbuerger Chrëstleche Gewerkschaftsbond
Malta	GWU	General Workers Union
Malta	CMTU	Confederation of Trade Unions
Netherlands	FNV	Federatie Nederlandse Vakbeweging
Netherlands	CNV	Christelijk Nationaal Vakverbond
Norway	LO	Landsorganisasjonen I Norge
Portugal	UGT	Uniao Geral de Trabalhadores
Spain	UGT	Union General de Trabajadores de Espana
Spain	STV-ELA	Solidaridad de Trabajadores Vascos
Sweden	LO	Landsorganisationen i Sverige
Sweden	TCO	Tjänstemännens Centralorganisation
Switzerland	SGB	Schweizerischer Gewerkschaftsbund
Switzerland	CGS	Christlichnationaler Gewerkschaftsbund der Schweiz
Turkey	DISK	

another, directly, whenever they need to do so. Too often, however, national union centres seek to establish political filters on the contacts which are possible. In doing so, they may well deprive their members of access which might be useful to them.

As of 1986, then, the ETUC comprised thirty-five organizations from twenty-one countries. The total membership of all these organizations was approximately 43 million.

Acting in concert, these thirty-five centres have agreed to create an apparatus of industry committees, eleven of which were functioning by 1986. These covered metalworkers, farmworkers, postal workers, commercial and clerical workers, miners, entertainment workers, transport workers, teachers, public servants, builders and workers in the food trades. No small amount of friction with the old-established International Trade Secretariats has resulted from the formation of these bodies, and the threat of formation of others.[18] The more that campaigns such as that for the thirty-five-hour week, or for five weeks' annual holiday, or for international action against unemployment, take on grass-roots support, the more real the ETUC as an institution will become, in distinction from both the ICFTU and, maybe, some of the Trade Secretariats.[19]

If the problem of admitting the last French, Spanish and Portuguese centres could be resolved, the ETUC would become an inclusive organization, with obvious representative functions, and with active commitments from such diverse bodies as the (part-communist, Italian) CGIL, the (radical former Christian, French) CFDT and the (socialist, Belgian) FGTB.

At first sight, such an alliance is infinitely more useful, and equally less morally suspect, than either of the established overall trade union internationals. But there is a limitation involved in a European regional link-up, which is that, by definition, it is incapable of developing, on its own account, direct associations with unions in the third world. If both existing comprehensively international bodies could be accused of frequently manipulating such unions in the past, and sometimes of very much worse behaviour, this does not lift from our shoulders the burden of need for some sort of open international framework which can knit together the efforts of trade unionists in the overdeveloped and the underdeveloped nations, and defend their common interests. The option of regionalization is perfectly understandable, given the infragrant scent left behind by cold war trade unionism: but regionalism is not enough. Multinationals will continue to shift their operations into ever newer territories, and, much as British unions will need closer contact with their European counterparts, they will also need to know who are their natural allies in South Korea, Taiwan, or the Philippines. To mark, and pace, the modern multinationals, fully international organization is desirable. Needless to say, it is also desirable that such organization should serve trade union purposes, and should not be unduly influenced, leave alone bankrolled, by governmental agencies of any power whatsoever.

The Commonwealth Trade Union Council

A new organization aimed at strengthening links between trade union centres in the Commonwealth came into being on 1 March 1980.

Membership of the Commonwealth Trade Union Council (CTUC) based in London, consists of the 25 million workers who belong to trade unions in over forty Commonwealth countries. The list of these at the time of the foundation of the CTUC was: Australia, The Bahamas, Bangladesh, Barbados, Botswana, Britain, Canada, Cyprus, Dominica, Fiji, The Gambia, Ghana, Grenada, Guyana, India, Jamaica, Kenya, Kiribati, Lesotho, Malawi, Malaysia, Malta, Mauritius, New Zealand, Nigeria, Papua New Guinea, St Lucia, Seychelles, Sierra Leone, Singapore, Solomon Islands, Sri Lanka, Swaziland, Tanzania, Tonga, Trinidad and Tobago, Tuvalu, Uganda, Western Samoa and Zambia. Announcing the launching of the new body, a press release reported:

> Close ties between Commonwealth trade union organizations have existed for many years and regular meetings have been held during the International Labour Conference each year in

Geneva. It was at the 1978 meeting that it was agreed in principle to establish a new Commonwealth trade union body and a special working party was set up to examine the form such a body should take. In 1979 the Commonwealth unions agreed to establish the new Council and at a meeting in Madrid in November Dennis McDermott, President of the Canadian Labour Congress, was elected President, and Carl Wright, formerly Secretary to the Economic and Social Committee of the International Confederation of Free Trade Unions, was appointed the full-time Director of the CTUC.

The aims of the CTUC are to promote the interests of workers in the Commonwealth through enhanced co-operation between national trade union centres; to influence Commonwealth institutions and decisions; and to promote acceptance of, and respect for, trade unionism and for the Commonwealth Declaration of Principles of 1971 which sets out the basic relationship between the Commonwealth countries.

The top priority for the new Council is to establish relations with Commonwealth institutions and governments (such contacts have been established, from the initiation of the CTUC, between its Director and the Commonwealth Secretary-General, Shridath S. Ramphal). These contacts are aimed at assessing how the CTUC can best be involved in the follow-up to the Lusaka Heads of Government Meeting and the Valetta Finance Ministers Meeting which took place in 1979, with a view to ensuring that trade union views are taken into account by Commonwealth governments and institutions.

Another priority is an examination of ways in which practical assistance can be given to trade unions in Commonwealth countries. This includes building up a register of needs of member organizations; approaching relevant aid-giving organizations and initiating specific projects, along with the development of procedures for controlling and reviewing such projects.

As the Commonwealth comprises approximately a third of the independent nations of the world, and contains people of different races, religions and cultures, it is uniquely placed to make a significant contribution towards the development of the

'North-South' dialogue and to promote better understanding between the developed and developing world. This is something which was highlighted in the 1980 report of the 'Brandt Commission'.

Central to its aims is the goal of achieving a fair world social and economic order and highlighting and supporting the role of trade unions in economic and social development.

The executive body of the CTUC is its Steering Sub-Committee, on which sit trade union leaders from the UK and Mediterranean, Canada, Africa, Asia, the Caribbean and Australasia and the Pacific. A general session will be held each year to maintain contacts between member centres and to allow an exchange of views. The first of these was held in Geneva in June 1980 during the International Labour Conference.

Some Criteria for International Organization

Difficult though it may be for the average trade unionist to follow the story of intrigue and high diplomacy which is knit into trade union internationalism, there remain a series of practical tasks which all trade union members will recognize as requiring a variety of forms of international action.

First, to bargain with a multinational, even on one's home base, one needs adequate information about what one's employer is up to elsewhere. A well-known company in the English Midlands has two foundries, one in Derby, one in Lincoln. For years work was switched back and forth along the railway line which passes both plants, to the frustration of shop stewards, first in one place, then the other. They found this capacity to move work to be a major resource, enabling the employer to offset many perfectly reasonable trade union pressures. Only effective combine organization could control such movement. How much more true is this of the great transnational companies, which possess footholds (and giant ones, sometimes) in several continents? If the workers at Imperial Typewriters had known what Litton Industries were planning overseas, at the time they were taken over, they could have developed an appropriate political and industrial campaign to defend and expand typewriter production.[20] As things went, Litton consolidated their hold over the English market while they were running down their newly acquired but aged plants in Leicester and Hull, and building up production in Germany. Then they shut their production shops in England at the moment that their distribution plans were advanced enough to allow this. A full flow of information, concerning what was happening at Litton's German plants, for instance, would have been no negligible resource, from the union viewpoint.

Second, beyond information flows, what contacts can be introduced to make bargaining company-wide? At shop steward level, various rank-and-file initiatives have been taken (by Ford workers, for instance). A serious and sustained attempt at co-ordination was that of the Dunlop-Pirelli joint committee, linking British and Italian stewards.[21]

At inter-union level, the TGWU and the AUEW commenced a series of international meetings with the (American) United Auto Workers. Attempts at company level to approach international collective bargaining, even in the broadest terms, have always been repudiated by the big car companies. This is true not only when joint union approaches are made[22] on an ad hoc basis, but also when the International Trade Secretariats are brought into the picture. Some ITSs have set up world company councils for the major transnational companies. In 1972, the Ford World Auto Union Council (convened under the auspices of the International Metalworkers' Federation, an ITS) asked to discuss the company's international investment policy. The company replied that it preferred to operate its labour relations on a country-by-country basis, 'because labour relations procedures differ'.[23] Slightly more success was obtained by the European Industry Committee for Philips, the Dutch-based electronic company. At the time, this employed 350,000 people round the world, 285,000 in Europe. At the time of the initial approach 150 European plants existed. For six years the company did talk with the European Committee for the Metal Trades, starting in 1967.

They broke relations with the ECMT in 1971, refusing to discuss investment programmes.

This is what the unions are up against. The multinationals reserve the right to operate from a tightly controlled centre, and to plan all their operations in an integrated way. But they will not discuss those overall plans, at the level at which they have been conceived, with appropriate matching union representation.

Perhaps the most significant response to this problem has come from an unexpected source: as unemployment has risen, so it has shaken a number of social agencies into concern and involvement. The rationalization of multinational operations has hit certain regions particularly hard, and it is for that reason that local authorities have begun to react. A notable example was set by the Greater London Council, whose Employment and Industry Branch set out to provide support to trade unionists when they opposed plant closures in the region. The GLC Industrial Development Unit created an 'early warning system' to help trade unionists identify signs which implied forthcoming threats to employment in their companies.[24] In addition, the Council established a Popular Planning Unit to research into the operations of multinational companies, to provide educational material and courses for trade unionists, and to assist three particular international combines of trade unions, in Ford, Kodak and Philips.

The GLC was pushed into this initiative by a phenomenal contraction in multinational involvement in manufacturing in the London area. London unemployment became a matter of profound concern. One group of workers after another found themselves condemned to redundancy by multinational employers: and frequently such workers found themselves to be last in line to learn about the closure of their workplaces.[25]

In June 1983, the European trade unions involved in Kodak's operations met in Paris to discuss the company's future, which was clearly in some jeopardy. Eastman-Kodak had decided to run down European production and research, so that the European companies would become 'marketing satellites of the

United States'. Conventional Labour movement responses to this threat were, in these circumstances, not very appropriate. Some trade unionists asked,'Why not nationalize Kodak?' But as Mike Ward, the GLC's leading spokesman on economic affairs, replied, such a demand would mean that the national authorities in different countries would have taken over the shadow of the company, without its substance. 'In Britain, we would find that we had nationalized a shed,' said Councillor Ward. The problem was to insist upon an adequate Research and Development commitment to guarantee a European capacity for involvement in all the significant new technologies. With the help of the Val de Marne Council in France and the GLC, Kodak workers were able to establish a standing conference of their European unions, in order to pursue the demand for European-level negotiations with the company as a whole. The newspaper *KViewfinder* disseminated the unions' arguments throughout the international workforce.[26]

In the same spirit, the GLC sponsored a conference of European Ford workers in February 1984,[27] and brought together workers from Ireland, Denmark, Portugal, Spain, France, West Germany, Belgium and the UK. Workers from outside Europe took part, bringing reports from as far afield as Brazil.

The problems involved in organizing such international meetings are not small. There is a major difficulty about interpretation. Simultaneous translation facilities are expensive to hire, and even more expensive to staff. The assistance of a friendly public authority in providing such facilities is therefore a priceless asset. It may well turn out to be the case that benevolent intervention of this kind becomes a major function of the European Parliament, or at any rate of the trade union members of that body.

This leads us to a third area of concern: appropriate legislation. If companies will not recognize adequate trade union rights voluntarily, how can they be constrained to do so? Legislation can be a matter for particular national governments, or for pressure upon and through intergovernmental agencies.

Reams of paper have been covered in the offensive to enlist aid from these agencies: but whilst national sovereignty retains any validity it is direct pressure on national governments which will remain the principal trade union approach. In Britain, this was reflected in the Employment Protection Act of 1975, which charged the Advisory, Conciliation and Arbitration Service with the obligation to prepare and publish codes of industrial relations practice, which naturally applied to the foreign-based subsidiaries of foreign multinationals in Britain no less than to domestic-based firms. (It did not, however, affect British-based overseas subsidiaries in any direct way.) The provisions of the 1975 Act covered not only recognition, but also disclosure questions, but its teeth were never very sharp. International solidarity action by unions received specific protection under the Trade Union and Labour Relations Act of 1976, which repealed the previous restriction, affording protection only to disputes in which it could be shown that those involved had a direct stake in the outcome. The most important legislation in Britain, however, was the Industry Act of 1975, which made it possible for the government to prohibit foreign takeovers in major industrial concerns, and specifically opened up the issue of investment decisions to tripartite discussion in the framework of planning agreements. Yet, as we saw in Chapter 8, planning agreements were a dead letter, because at the last moment the Prime Minister intervened to fillet the Act of the stipulation that they should be obligatory. The subsequent change of policy with the advent of the Thatcher administration liberated devastating transnational encroachments, and Westland Helicopters is only the most publicized example of these.

The other major components of the trade union offensive to come within reach of imposing accountability on multinationals was, of course, the demand for legislation on industrial democracy, which we have already discussed in Chapter 8. None of this was enacted. Undoubtedly, however, the agitation for such legal changes will continue, since the problem of multinational intervention in the British economy, and of British company involvement abroad, poses more acute difficulties for the unions each year.

If national legislation has taken small effect up to now, the resolutions and memoranda of the ICFTU, the ILO, and the OECD have taken less. The OECD Trade Union Advisory Committee has called for a package of internationally co-ordinated simultaneous legislation, which, though it is seen as hyper-moderate by many of the affiliated trade union centres, has not been taken up by the OECD states. Instead, they drew up guidelines for yet another code of (voluntary) conduct. The result of all those conferences, all those declarations, is not, to date, impressive. As the TUAC explained in November 1978:

> The trade unions judge the Guidelines from the point of view of their impact on the real world. Their existence created expectations among the unions who hoped that the climate for their relations with multinational enterprises would change for the better. Evidence of this, after almost three years of experience, still is not forthcoming. There is little to show that the world of the multinational enterprise has been changed. Furthermore, there is very little evidence that the present voluntary set of Guidelines is being vigorously pursued or that there is effective action to create a framework within which their implementation could be ensured. TUAC underlines that even if its involvement in the follow-up of the Guidelines so far has been active and will continue to be so, it is not primarily for the trade union movement to see to the functioning of the Guidelines. They were agreed upon by Governments, who took upon themselves the responsibility to address them to the multinational enterprises. Consequently, they should also ensure their implementation.
>
> Unless the Guidelines are really implemented, the trade union movement will have to seriously consider their usefulness and also any further support to them. As a compromise, TUAC accepted the Guidelines in 1976 as a first step. At that time, the trade unions clearly envisaged not only their implementation but also further development. If no change to the better has taken place in the real world due to the Guidelines, what was the use of the whole exercise?[28]

Table 12.7

The ILO Declaration obstacle race

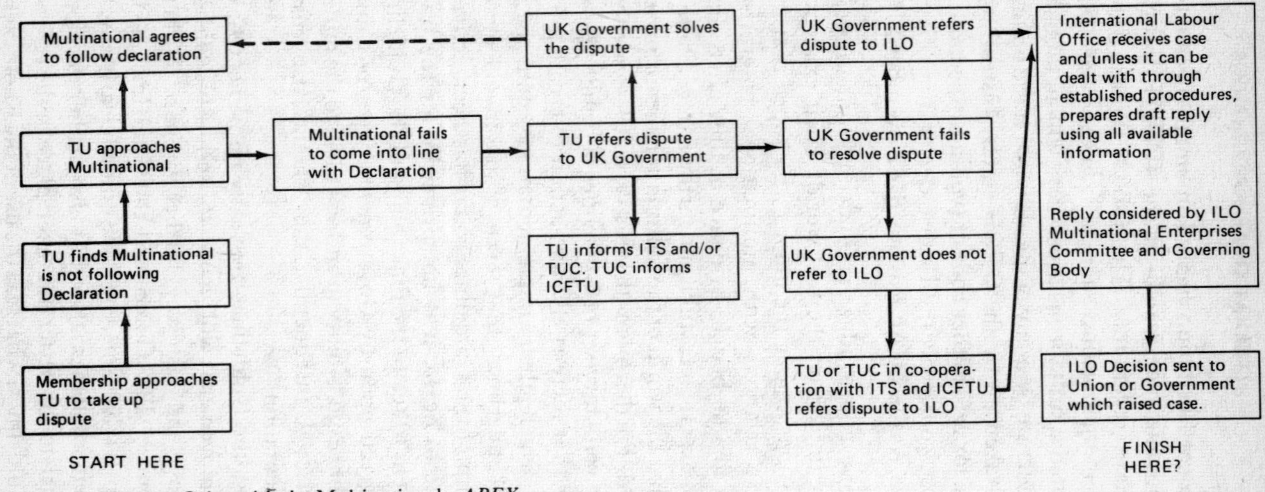
Multinational agrees to follow declaration
TU approaches Multinational
TU finds Multinational is not following Declaration
Membership approaches TU to take up dispute
START HERE
Multinational fails to come into line with Declaration
UK Government solves the dispute
TU refers dispute to UK Government
TU informs ITS and/or TUC. TUC informs ICFTU
UK Government refers dispute to ILO
UK Government fails to resolve dispute
UK Government does not refer to ILO
TU or TUC in co-operation with ITS and ICFTU refers dispute to ILO
International Labour Office receives case and unless it can be dealt with through established procedures, prepares draft reply using all available information
Reply considered by ILO Multinational Enterprises Committee and Governing Body
ILO Decision sent to Union or Government which raised case.
FINISH HERE?

Source: Getting to Grips with the Multinationals, *APEX*

We might be forgiven for thinking that there has been a veritable plague of guidelines. In addition to the OECD, there are extensive recommendations in the codes of the International Labour Organization (ILO). The ILO code condemns victimization of trade unionists and enjoins management to behave positively towards trade unions. The ILO also lays down desirable practices on health and safety, bargaining and the right to strike. A United Nations code of practice for multinational corporations is also under consideration. APEX provides its members with a diagram to show how the ILO code of conduct can be used by an aggrieved trade union (see Table 12.7).

Whilst every trade unionist will want to derive what support there may be from such general declarations, it is quite clear that all this paraphernalia will be cold comfort to any trade unionist who lacks the benefit of strong and self-reliant organization.

The issue remains urgent. Michael Barratt Brown puts it very clearly:

> Differences in trade union strength reflect national cultural and historical differences between the European countries. But the fact remains that in the countries where capitalism is strong the unions are weak: where capitalism is weak the unions are strong. One is bound to ask which is cause and which is effect. We began by suggesting that there were two new elements in recent capitalist development: the transnational company as the centre of capital accumulation; and the shop stewards committee as the expression of organized labour. In an important sense we are no longer looking only at national centres of capitalism – British, French, or Italian. These still exist. The City and the CBI are centres of financial and industrial power; the Bourse and the Patronat also. The interlinking of State and private finance is crucial to Italian industry. But, increasingly, national finance – private and state – are the servants of the giant transnational companies. These may have had their origins in Britain or Italy, West Germany or France, in the Netherlands or Belgium and a large number came from the United States; but their attitude to nation states is

increasingly opportunistic. National loyalties have been replaced by a hard headed commercial view of the costs and benefits of locating their multifarious activities in this country or that. As in the case of Dunlop and Pirelli, so it is with others. Minerals, oil and other raw materials attract investment to one area; for other areas it will be cheap labour for processing work, a pool of skilled workers for machine making, a docile labour force will all attract investment, while a country with low rates of tax will attract the headquarters and registered offices. Where goods are bulky and transport costs high, production, or at least the final assembly, will be located near the richest and largest markets.[29]

In Chapter 1 we called in evidence Karl Marx, who, it may be remembered, spoke with the voice of a prophet more than a hundred years ago:

> The battle of competition is fought by cheapening commodities. The cheapness of commodities depends, *ceteris paribus*, on the productivity of labour, and this again on the scale of production. Therefore, the larger capitals beat the smaller . . .

Now this centralization has become a vast and universal affair, a continental drift of the major economic forces, squeezing even nation-states until they crack, sometimes, in its minor movements. This huge thraldom is answerable to no democratic control, and pursues its own greedy interest across and beneath the frontiers of nations, law and morality, meeting no obstacle which may seriously restrain it in any of the territories over which it holds dominion.

Improbable though it may seem, and fiercely difficult though it will be to accomplish, the only imaginable counterforce upon which to base the future of democracy in the struggle against this unbridled power, is the trade union movement. The last years of the twentieth century will see a major contest in which these elemental economic powers are increasingly opposing and confronting every possibility of humane social development. They may dictate the terms upon which they operate: more and more commonly they buy deeply into newspapers and communications media: where necessary they do not scruple to remove governments. The hopes of far more than this generation may well depend upon the courage, the audacity and the intelligence of the answering response of today's trade unionists. The sooner they merge their resources, the better they will match this task.

NOTES

1. Cf. Shirley Lerner, *Breakaway Unions and the Small Trade Union*, Allen and Unwin, 1961, pp. 85 *et seq*.
2. Lord Citrine, *Two Careers*, Hutchinson, 1967, pp. 219 *et seq*. Soviet delegate Kuznetsov 'seemed to regard the invitation (to Buckingham Palace) with pleasure'.
3. Cf. TUC, *Free Trade Unions Leave the WFTU*, 1949. This document states the reasons for the withdrawal of the TUC, the CIO and the Dutch CFTU from the Executive Bureau of the WFTU in Paris. One sentiment in this report is prophetic: 'Our affiliated unions would not count the cost if real international Trade Unity were developing; but if the General Council have to answer whether the £15,000 now being paid annually by organizations affiliated to the British TUC is being spent profitably . . . the answer is assuredly "no".' Thirty times that sum now goes out annually, but the General Council does not receive many questions.
4. Richard Fletcher, *CIA and the Labour Movement*, Spokesman, 1977, p. 51.
5. Philip Agee, *Inside the Company – CIA Diary*, Penguin Books, 1975, pp. 74–5.
6. Cf. *The Pike Report*, Spokesman, 1977. Also V. Marchietti and J. D. Marks, *The CIA and the Cult of Intelligence*, Jonathan Cape, 1974, pp. 48 *et seq*.
7. Agee, *op. cit.*, p. 76.
8. TUC, *Annual Report*, 1967, pp. 487–8.
9. *Ibid*, p. 488.
10. J. F. Windmuller, 'Realignments in the ICFTU: the Impact of Detente', *BJIR*, XIV, 3, November 1976, p. 249.
11. *Ibid*.
12. This is the account of the findings of the Nigerian *Report of the Tribunal of Inquiry into the Trade Unions* (Federal Ministry of Information, Lagos, 1977) given by D. Thomson and R. Larson, *Where Were You, Brothers?*, War on Want, 1978, pp. 60–1.
13. Cf. Fred Hirsch, *CIA and the Labour Movement*, Spokesman, 1977. Also Cheddi Jagan, *The West on Trial*, Michael Joseph, 1966, pp. 170 *et seq*. pp. 296 *et seq*.
14. Thomson and Larson, *op. cit.*, p. 26.
15. George Meany speaking at the House of Representatives, Committee on Foreign Affairs: 'Winning the Cold War – the US ideological offensive.' 88th Congress, 1st Session, part two, 30 April 1963: cited Thomson and Larson, *op. cit*.
16. Cf. Windmuller, *op. cit.*, p. 258: 'The current outlook . . . is . . . one of realign-

ment on terms more rather than less favourable to the objectives of the Soviet Union . . .'

17. B. C. Roberts and Bruno Liebhaberg, 'The European Trade Union Confederation: Influence of Regionalism, Detente and Multinationals', *BJIR*, XIV, 3, November 1976, pp. 261 *et seq.*
18. *Ibid.*
19. We discuss these initiatives in greater detail in the penultimate chapter of our *Trade Unions and Politics*, Blackwell, 1986.
20. Cf. Institute for Workers' Control, *Why Imperial Typewriters Must Not Close*, no. 46.
21. For a discussion of this and other cases, see Michael Barratt Brown, 'Working Class Internationalism' in K. Coates and F. B. Singleton (eds.) *The Just Society*, Spokesman, 1977, p. 77.
22. John Gennard, *Multinationals: Industrial Relations and the Trade Union Response*, Occasional Papers in Industrial Relations, Universities of Leeds and Nottingham, 1976, p. 20.
23. Michael Barratt Brown, *op. cit.*, p. 77.
24. GLC, *Information Pack on The Greater London Enterprise Board*, which contains a paper describing the Industrial Development Departments' Early Warning System. Employees' Booklet, GLC Industrial Development Unit.
25. See the very strong analysis (by Robin Murray) in the Introduction to the GLC's *London Industrial Strategy*, 1985, and GLC, *Multinationals in London.*
26. *K Viewfinder*, Autumn 1983. See also Counter Information Services, *Striking Back*, 1983, pp. 13–14.
27. Cf. GLC Industry and Employment Branch, *The Ford Report*, 1986.
28. ICFTU, *Economic and Social Bulletin*, XXVII, no. 1, Jan–Mar. 1979, p. 15.
29. Michael Barratt Brown, *op. cit.*, p. 79.

Conclusion

We hope this book contains a fair representation of British trade unionism, warts and all, but not more wart than face. A portrait, however lovingly painted, is likely to upset various people. Sometimes, a sitter is scandalized. Sir Winston Churchill apparently resented the most faithful and insightful portrait that was ever painted of him. At other times, the sitter's antagonists are distressed. 'Where is all the villainy, the greed, the smugness, which we associated with this character?' they may ask.

Among ten million plus people there is a necessary quotient of selfishness, narrowmindedness, and gluttony. A vast newspaper industry ensures that these qualities are adequately advertised. But there is also a rich fund of generous concern, of human warmth, of solidarity; which virtues are not so widely noised about. The British trade union movement is the greatest single community resource of the British people. It stimulates a large and continuing voluntary effort, innumerable anonymous acts of self-sacrifice, and a major and vital part of the national commitment to ideals of justice and democracy. Who doubts this must leave reading books, and move among the people who have created the elaborate machinery which is inadequately outlined in these pages.

We have tried, in this book, to portray the British unions as they actually stand. When first we finished our picture, at the beginning of a new decade, the 1980s, things looked very different. In this revision, completed nearly seven years later than our original, we are bound to admit that its subject has aged disproportionately. The seven years which have elapsed have been lean ones indeed, and there is no reason to believe that things will improve in the very near future.

Back in 1980, we knew there was trouble in store. As we wrote then, trade unionism 'now faces a challenge such as few institutions in history have been able to survive. The economic crisis which generated successive governmental onslaughts on union rights and liberties, briefly documented above, now in 1980 takes on a convulsive form in which major industries are shivering on the edge of collapse.

'During the late 1970s a sombre debate began on the question of "de-industrialization". The rickety competitive position of British manufacturing industry had become steadily more disadvantageous, as British entry to the European Economic Community created an acute imbalance in trade in manufactures. Instead of improving investment in this manufacturing industry, the oil boom undermined it: by maintaining a grossly inappropriate rate of exchange, the oil revenues contributed to the throttling of marginal enterprises in one sector after another. By the beginning of the 1980s, unemployment was already fixed at around the one and a half million mark. However, all reputable economic forecasters anticipated an early rise to two million or more.' In fact, it levelled off at three million in heavily massaged official counts, with a million or more other people lost in the shadows behind them. Our 1980 conclusion continued:

'With widespread unemployment, poverty, already endemic, became more and more acute.

'In this context, all the principal achievements in the field of welfare provision and humane social organization, established during the decades following the Second World War, became objects of bitter contention. The postwar decades had previously been marked by a consensus. This broad social agreement assumed continuous improvement in living standards; growing social provision in the fields of education, housing and health; and greater involvement by trade unions in the regulation of an increasingly liberal society. The architects of this consensus would be dismayed by the Britain of 1980. Marked authoritarianism, increasingly obtrusive and arbitrary police powers, surveillance, and frenetic preparations for an impossible war: all marked an end to the postwar settlement, whose dreams had turned into nightmares.'

The governments of 1979 and 1983 kept their pledges. In consequence, as we have seen, a whole rain of blows fell on the unions. Their previous legal underpinning was lasered out by hostile law reform. Set loose among the scant mercies of unfriendly judges now unrestrained by traditional immunities, trade unionists soon found other predators ravening around them. Transnational companies began to impose new patterns of work and organization to their calculated detriment. These included the devices of single-union and 'no-strike' agreements, within a framework of 'flexibility' in which all the give came from one side and all the take from the other. Newly privatized public services began to study such examples and inventively applied their lessons. While the unions themselves lost members, the corporations gathered greater economic force and influence, and began to orchestrate internationally concerted industrial relations policies. 'Divide' became the watchword of the corporate empires, and internecine labour troubles were not slow to follow its ruthless application. These have often taken the form of inter-union disputes, with which the Trades Union Congress has been unable to cope at all adequately. But they have not spared individual unions, in which, all too often, one section has been set against another.

In this new edition of our study, we have sought to trace the course of each of these nightmares. Although there is abundant evidence, our account is incomplete, because the pace of change always outruns the record of its effects.

In 1987, the Thatcher administration gained a third term of office in the June General Election. Further legal encroachments into trade union power were thus guaranteed, alongside continued attrition of welfare, and privatization of virtually every remaining asset of public enterprise. But all these promises are held out against a background of gathering menance.

The world's Stock Exchanges have seen a chain reaction of crashes. The United States economy, beset by deficits in its budget and its overseas payments at the same time, appears all too likely to retrench us into a global recession. There is a worldwide crisis of debt: a time bomb, which, were it to explode, could devastate the banking and financial systems. None of these horrors will bring any comfort to trade unionists, who may certainly expect to suffer for the miscalculations of their employers and political leaders.

International crisis demands an international response. For the trade unions, this is a difficult challenge. Old answers, partial and sectoral, may appear more 'practical' than the utopian project of political unity and action across frontiers. To create an international network of support and solidarity may seem an arduous and unheroic labour, for which the decades of consensus and partial corporatism have ill-prepared trade union structures. Yet linkages are emerging, and these will become firmer with adversity.

A hundred years ago, the task of *national* co-ordination would have seemed equally remote.

Few observers in the early 1880s imagined that the victims of East End sweatshops, starting with the matchgirls, would soon light a flare able to show all the most suffering labourers, living in the margins of starvation, and enduring cruel exploitation, how to associate themselves and insist upon a human status. Soon we shall celebrate the centenary of the great dock strike, which began a new unionism that brought the dispossessed into the political world, pioneering forms of organization which were at once comprehensive, more radical, and more powerful than any available to working people in all the fraught decades of earlier struggle.

Today, an agenda of co-operation on a European and wider scale faces employees whose companies already straddle the world. Long years of struggle for political and economic emancipation have perfected various national instruments of democracy which are now grossly inadequate to match or pace, leave alone control or direct, what has become a global economy. Perhaps our contemporary matchgirls are preparing, even while we survey the immensity of the necessary project ahead of us.

If they are, they will raise their cries for help in a world which can transmit them by satellite, or fax them by telephone to the other side of the world. Such a world is, materially, far beyond the carniverous universe with which Adam Smith did so much to contend, in the age of waterwheels and little steam engines. Our age has seen improvement in everything except the expectations of its peoples.

The real crisis of capitalism is one which will not be overcome within it. The greater the material and social powers it bestows and concentrates, the smaller the space it affords to the remnants of the cardinal human virtues, of love and of hope.

In the dawn of the world, while transport technologies were determined by what could, and what could not, be accomplished by a horse, philosophers and others could dream of universal brotherhood. Now we have people working in vast teams to send rockets to Mars and beyond. Yet such people quite commonly experience a terror of being alone, and some of them can only cope with the miseries of life by recourse to valium and chemical addictions. Even while we are probing the mysteries of Uranus and Neptune, bending genes and enslaving light to work in wires, we still remain members of one another.

For this reason, we do not believe that the closing words of our first edition have become inappropriate.

'If anyone remains free to write an updated version of this book in 1990, it will very possibly record events which have hitherto been unthinkable. No one can with certainty predict the outcome of the desperate period into which we are entered: and we do not wish to end this book on a note of vapid optimism. But if the British trade unions still need an expositor at the end of the trials which are about to be encountered, then there will remain a real hope that the goals of liberal civilization, of brotherhood, sisterhood and mutual support, may yet prevail.

'If, however, the unions were in fact to be powdered between the pitiless grindstones of official repression and economic ruin, those who dared remember them at all would remember also the democratic promise which they held out, and the large freedoms which were always rooted in their ample support. Books would be burnt, and witches soon after them, on the evil day when the British trade unions were compelled to close their offices.

'Educated working people may be relied upon to make all these most dire events quite difficult to achieve.'

ACKNOWLEDGEMENTS

We prepared this book to meet the needs of our students, and in the hope that it might be helpful to others who wished to understand the complex structure of the trade union movement. No doubt there remain some errors in our text, but there would have been many more were it not for the generous advice which these students have given us.

We are also extremely grateful to many academic colleagues for their assistance and advice. We must particularly mention Michael Barratt Brown, who has been a constant inspiration; Michael Somerton, who gave us the benefit of a most careful examination of an early draft of the whole work and who assisted greatly in our discussion of low pay. Graham Winch and Daniel Vulliamy read parts of the work, and helped us to avoid various mistakes; the late Don Thomson gave advice on the chapter on International Trade Unionism which was extremely helpful. The scholars whose work we have consulted and reported are listed in a bibliographic index, and our debt to them is quite apparent.

Much of the information recorded in this book is the result of direct enquiries at trade union offices. We wish to thank every research officer who endured our inquisitive questions, and responded to our questionnaires together with all the other numerous officials who have given so much time to answering us. We are most grateful to our colleagues at the Institute for Workers' Control, all of whom provided us with valued advice.

Above all, we wish to thank Ken Fleet, who was an unfailing source of encouragement as well as practical assistance, and Rita Maskery, whose vast patience and unremitting hard work enabled this text to be retyped more times than she or any of us care to remember.

ABBREVIATIONS

International trade unions are included here but British trade unions are listed separately (page 427).

AALC	African American Labor Centre
ACAS	Advisory, Conciliation and Arbitration Service
AFL	American Federation of Labor
BDC	Biennial Delegate Conference (TGWU)
CAC	Central Arbitration Committee
CBI	Confederation of British Industries
CCOO	Commissiones Obreras
CFDT*	French, formerly Christian, Trade Union Federation
CGIL*	Italian Communist and Socialist Trade Union Federation
CGT*	French Communist Trade Union Federation
CIA	Central Intelligence Agency
CPSU	Communist Party of the Soviet Union
CPSUA	Communist Party of the United States of America
CTUC	Commonwealth Trade Union Council
EAT	Employment Appeal Tribunal
ECMT	European Committee for the Metal Trades
EEC	European Economic Community
EEF	Engineering Employers' Federation
EFTA	European Free Trade Association
EPA	Employment Protection Act
ETUC	European Trade Union Confederation
FGIB*	Belgian Socialist Trade Union Federation
FO*	French Trade Union Federation
GCHQ	Government Communications Headquarters
GLC	Greater London Council
GLEB	Greater London Enterprise Board

ICFTU	International Confederation of Free Trade Unions
IFTU	International Federation of Trade Unions
ILO	International Labour Organization
ISF	International Solidarity Fund (of ICFTU)
ITS	International Trade Secretariat
ITWF	International Transport Workers' Federation
IWC	Institute for Workers' Control
JCC	Joint Consultative Committee
JIC	Joint Industrial Committee (or Council)
JRC	Joint Representation Committee
LO*	Swedish Trade Union Federation
LRC	Labour Representation Committee
MDW	Measured Day Work
MSC	Manpower Services Commission
NEC	National Executive Committee (Labour Party)
NEDC	National Economic Development Council
NIC	National Incomes Commission
NIRC	National Industrial Relations Court
OECD	Organization for Economic Co-operation and Development
ORIT	(American Regional Labour Organization)
PBR	Payment by Results
Quango	Quasi-Autonomous National Governmental Organization
RILU	Red International of Labour Unions
TBF	T. Bailey Forman (printers)
TULRA	Trade Union and Labour Relations Act
TUAC	Trade Union Advisory Committee (of OECD)
UAW	United Automobile Workers
ULCN	United Labour Congress of Nigeria
UMA	Union Membership Agreement
WEA	Workers' Educational Association
WFTU	World Federation of Trade Unions
WMEB	West Midlands Enterprise Board

*For an exact rendering of these initials, see Table 12.6.

BIBLIOGRAPHY AND INDEX OF WORKS CITED

Numbers in bold refer to pages in the text, where there has been direct citation.

I. BOOKS AND PAMPHLETS

Agee, Philip, *Inside the Company – CIA Diary*, Penguin, 1975. **397**

Allen, V. L., *Power in Trade Unions*, Longmans, 1954. **94, 106**

Allen, V. L., *Trade Union Militancy*, Merlin Press, 1966. **262**

Allen, V. L., *The Sociology of Industrial Relations*, Longmans, 1971. **39, 142**

Anderson, P. and Blackburn, R., *Towards Socialism*, Fontana, 1964. **362**

Arnison, J., *The Million Pound Strike*, Lawrence and Wishart, 1970. **264**

Ascher, K., *The Politics of Privatisation*, Macmillan, 1987. **298**

Bain, G. S. (ed.), *Industrial Relations in Great Britain*, Blackwell, 1983. **59**

Barratt Brown, Michael, *From Labourism to Socialism*, Spokesman, 1972. **28, 39**

Barratt Brown, Michael, *Study Packs 1–6*, Greater London Council Industry and Employment Branch, 1983–5. **298, 398**

Barratt Brown, Michael, 'Working Class Internationalism', in K. Coates and F. B. Singleton (eds), *The Just Society*, Spokesman, 1977. **397**

Barratt Brown, Michael, 'The Growth and Distribution of the National Income', in K. Coates (ed.), *What Went Wrong*, Spokesman, 1979. **221**

Barratt Brown, M., Coates, K., Fleet, K. and Hughes, J., *Full Employment*, Spokesman, 1978. **39**

Bassett, P., *Strike-Free: New Industrial Relations in Britain*, Macmillan, 1986. **188, 212**

Batstone, Eric, *Working Order: Workplace Industrial Relations over Two Decades*, Blackwell, 1984. **212**

Batstone, E., Boraston, I. and Frenkel, S., *Shop Stewards in Action*, Blackwell, 1977. **170, 171**

Batstone, E., Boraston, I. and Frenkel, S., *The Social Organisation of Strikes*, Blackwell, 1978. **262, 264**

BBC, *Democracy at Work: Trade Union Studies.* **106**

Beck, Tony, *The Fine Tubes Strike*, Stage 1, 1974. **264**

Blackburn, R. M., *Union Character and Social Class*, Batsford, 1967. **11–12, 39**

Bodington, Steve, *Computers and Socialism*, Spokesman, 1973. **297**

Bonety, R., *et al.*, *La CFDT*, Seuil, Paris, 1971. **362**

Boraston, I., Clegg, H. A. and Rimmer, M., *Workplace and Union*, Heinemann, 1975. **171**

Brannen, P., Batstone, E., Fatchett, D., and White, P., *The Worker Directors*, Hutchinson, 1976. **298**

Bristol Aircraft Workers, *A New Approach to Public Ownership*, IWC pamphlet no. 43, 1974. **298**

Brown, G., *Sabotage*, Spokesman, 1977. **262**

Butler, D. and Kavanagh, D., *The British General Election of October 1974*, Macmillan, 1975. **362**

Bye, Basil and Doyle, Mel, *European Trade Union Co-operation*, WEA, n.d. **384**

Carew, Anthony, *Democracy and Government in European Trade Unions*, Allen and Unwin, 1976. **362**

Citrine, Lord, *Two Careers*, Hutchinson, 1967. **397**

Citrine, N.A., *Trade Union Law*, Stevens, 1950. **39**

Clegg, H. A. *The System of Industrial Relations in Great Britain*, Blackwell, 1970. **57, 142, 169**

Clegg, H. A. and Adams, R., *The Employers' Challenge*, Blackwell, 1957. **263**

Clegg, H. A., Fox, A. and Thompson, E.F., *A History of British Trade Unions since 1889: Vol. 1, 1889–1910*, Clarendon, 1964. **169, 362**

Clegg, H. A., Killick, A. J. and Adams, R., *Trade Union Officers*, Blackwell, 1960. **105, 169**

Clements, Richard, *Glory Without Power*, Barker, 1959.

Coates, Ken, *The Crisis of British Socialism*, Spokesman, 1971. **336**

Coates, Ken, *Democracy in the Labour Party*, Spokesman, 1977. **356**

Coates, Ken (ed.), *Freedom and Fairness*, Spokesman, 1986. **142, 212**

Coates, Ken, *Work-ins, Sit-ins and Industrial Democracy*, Spokesman, 1980. **39, 297**

Coates, Ken (ed.), *A Trade Union Strategy in the Common Market* (Programme of the Belgian FGTB), Spokesman, 1971. **362**

Coates, Ken (ed.), 'What Happened at Leeds', in *British Labour and the Russian Revolution*, Spokesman, 1972. **294**

Coates, Ken (ed.), *The New Worker Co-operatives*, Spokesman for IWC, 1976. **39, 298**

Coates, Ken, (ed.), *The Right to Useful Work*, Spokesman, 1978. **171, 297**

Coates, Ken and Topham, Tony, *Workers' Control*, Panther, 1970. **40**

Coates, Ken and Topham, Tony, *The New Unionism*, Penguin, 1974. **264, 297**

Coates, Ken and Topham, Tony, *Industrial Democracy in Great Britain*, Vols 1–4, Spokesman, 1975. **40, 211, 296, 298**

Coates, Ken and Topham, Tony, *A Shop Stewards' Guide to the Bullock Report*, Spokesman, 1977. **297**

Coates, Ken and Topham, Tony, *Trade Unions and Politics*, Blackwell, 1986. **105, 142, 263, 328, 363, 397**

Cole, G. D. H. and Mellor, W., *The Meaning of Industrial Freedom*, Allen and Unwin, n.d. **296**

Cole, G. D. H., *British Trade Unionism: Problems and Policy*, Labour Research Department, 1925. **74, 104**

Conboy, Bill, *Pay at Work*, Arrow in association with the Society of Industrial Tutors, 1976.

Connolly, James, *Socialism Made Easy*, Irish TGWU various dates. **266**

Cooley, Mike, 'Design, Technology and Production for Social Needs' in Coates, K. (ed.), *The Right to Useful Work*, Spokesman, 1978. **297**

The Conservative Party, *The Right Approach*, October, 1976. **105**

Counter-Information Services, *Report: The New Technology*, Anti-Report no. 23, 1979. **297**

Counter-Information Services, *Striking Back*, 1983. **398**

Coventry Workshop, *Crisis in Engineering: Machine Tool Workers Fight for Jobs*, IWC, June, 1979. **171**

Daniel, W., *Wage Determination in Industry*, PEP, 1976.

Daniel, W., *Workplace Industrial Relations and Technical Change*, Frances Pinter with PSI, 1987. **212**

De Tocqueville, Alexis, *Journeys to England and Ireland* (ed. J. P. Mayer), Faber, 1958. **40**

De Tocqueville, Alexis, *Democracy in America (1835)*, OUP, World's Classics, 1946. **32, 39**

Docks Workers' Control Group, *The Dockers Next Step*, IWC pamphlet no. 12, 1969.

Drulovic, Milojko, *Self-management on Trial*, Spokesman, 1978. **262, 297**

Durkin, Tom, *Grunwick: Bravery and Betrayal*, Brent Trades Council, 1978. **264**

Edelstein, J. D. and Warner, M., *Comparative Union Democracy*, Allen and Unwin, 1975. **105, 106, 363**

Edmonds, John, 'Uniting the Fragments', in Ken Coates (ed.), *Freedom and Fairness*, Spokesman, 1986. **212**

Eldridge, J. E. T., *Industrial Disputes*, Routledge and Kegan Paul, 1968. **262**

Elliott, John, *Conflict or Co-operation*, Kogan Page, 1978. **298**

Evans, E. W. and Creigh, S., *Industrial Conflict in Britain*, Frank Cass, 1977. **262**

Flanders, Allan, *Trade Unions*, Hutchinson, 1957. **296**

Fletcher, Richard, 'Trade Union Democracy – Structural Factors', in *Trade Union Register, 2*, Spokesman, 1970. **106**

Fletcher, Richard, 'Trade Union Democracy: the Case of the AUEW Rule Book', in *Trade Union Register, 3*, Spokesman, 1973. **93, 106**

Fletcher, Richard, *CIA and the Labour Movement*, Spokesman, 1977. **397**

Florence, P. Sargant, *The Logic of British and American Industry*, Routledge, 1953. **297**

Forester, Tom, 'The Neutralisation of the Industrial Strategy', in Coates, Ken (ed.) *What Went Wrong*, Spokesman, 1979. **297, 363**

Fox, Alan, 'The Social Origins of Present Forms and Methods in Britain and Germany', in *Industrial Democracy: International Views*, SSRC, 1978. **211**

Fraser, Ronald, *Work*, vols 1 and 2, Penguin Books, 1968, 1969. **40, 297**

Friedman, Henry, *Multi-Plant Working and Trade Union Organisation*, WEA, 1976. **171**

Fryer, R. H., *Redundancy, Values and Public Policy*, Warwick University, November, 1972.

Fryer, Bob, Fairclough, Andy and Manson, Tom, *Organisation and Change in the National Union of Public Employees*, University of Warwick, 1974. **78–9, 105**

Gardner, Jim, *Key Questions for Trade Unionists*, Lawrence and Wishart, 1960. **105**

George, M. and Levie, H., *Japanese Competition and the British Workplace*, CAITS, 1984. **212**

Gennard, John, *Multi-nationals: Industrial Relations and the Trade Union Response*, Occasional Papers in Industrial Relations, Universities of Leeds and Nottingham, 1976. **397**

Gill, C., Morris, R. and Eaton, J., *Industrial Relations in the Chemical Industry*, Saxon House, 1978.

Goldstein, J., *The Government of British Trade Unions*, Allen and Unwin, 1952. **105**

Goldthorpe, J. H., *et al.*, *The Affluent Worker*, CUP, 1968–9. **105**

Goodman, J. E. B. and Whittingham, T., *Shop Stewards in British Industry*, McGraw-Hill, 1969. **171**

Gorz, André, *The Division of Labour*, Harvester Press, 1976. **39**

Gowan, Doug, 'The Bargaining System' in *Industrial Studies 2: The Bargaining Context*, ed. E. Coker and G. Stuttard, Arrow in association with the Society of Industrial Tutors, 1976.

Graubard, S. R., *British Labour and the Russian Revolution*, OUP, 1956. **296**

Harrison, Martin, *Trade Unions and the Labour Party*, Macmillan, 1960. **362**

Harman, Chris, *Is a Machine After Your Job? New Technology and the Struggle for Socialism*, Socialist Workers' Party, 1979. **297**

Hawkins, Kevin, *The Management of Industrial Relations*, Pelican, 1978.

Heath, R. H., 'The National Power Loading Agreement in the Coal Industry and Some Aspects of Workers' Control', in *Trade Union Register, 1969*, Merlin Press, 1969. **263**

Hemingway, J., *Conflict and Democracy: Studies in Trade Union Government*, OUP, 1978. **96, 106, 262**

Hirsch, Fred, *CIA and the Labour Movement*, Spokesman, 1977. **397**

Holland, Stuart, *Strategy for Socialism*, Spokesman, 1975. **27, 39**

Holton, Bob, *British Syndicalism*, Pluto Press, 1977.

Hughes, John, *Trade Union Structure and Government, Part 1*, Donovan Commission Research Paper no. 5, HMSO, 1967. **72**

Hughes, John and Moore, Roy, *A Special Case?*, Penguin, 1972. **263**

Humberside County Council, *A Low Pay Strategy*, 1987. **212**

Hunter, R., *The Road to Brighton Pier*, Arthur Barker, 1959. **106**

Hyman, Richard, *Marxism and the Sociology of Trade Unionism*, Pluto Press, 1971. **105**

Hyman, Richard, *Disputes Procedure in Action*, Heinemann, 1972.

Hyman, Richard, *Industrial Relations – A Marxist Introduction*, Macmillan, 1975. **35, 40**

Hyman, Richard, *Strikes*, Fontana, 2nd edition, 1977. **262**

Ingham, G. K., *Strikes and Industrial Conflict*, Macmillan, 1974. **264**

International Labour Reports: Educational Packs for Trade Unionists, *The Auto Industry*, 1986. **212**

IWC Motors Group, *A Workers' Inquiry into the Motor Industry*, CSE, 1978. **171**

IWC, *Why Imperial Typewriters Must Not Close*, IWC pamphlet no. 46, 1975.

Jackson, M. P., *Industrial Relations*, Croom Helm, 1977. **262**

Jagan, Cheddi, *The West on Trial*, Michael Joseph, 1966. **397**

Jenkins, Clive and Mortimer, J. E., *The Kind of Laws the Unions Ought to Want*, Pergamon, 1968. **328**

Jenkins, Clive and Sherman, Barrie, *The Collapse of Work*, Eyre Methuen, 1979. **298**

Jenkins, Mark, *Bevanism: Labour's High Tide*, Spokesman, 1979. **106**

Jones, Jack, *Union Man: an Autobiography*, Collins, 1986. **61, 72, 169**

Jones, R., Halstead, J. and Barratt Brown, M. (unpublished), *Report on Sheffield Engineering Shop Stewards 1977.* **169, 170**

Kahn-Freund, Otto, *Labour and the Law*, Stevens, 1972, 2nd edition, 1977. **40, 328**

Kerr, Clark and Siegel, A., 'The Inter Industry Propensity to Strike – an International Comparison', in Kornhauser, A., Dubin, R. and Ross, A. (eds.), *Industrial Conflict*, McGraw-Hill, 1954. **263**

Knowles, K. G. J. C., *Strikes: a Study in Industrial Conflict*, Blackwell, 1952. **262**

Knowles, K. G. J. C., 'Strike Proneness and its Determinants' in Galenson, W. and Wiley, S. M. (eds.), *Labour and Trade Unionism*, Wiley, 1960. **263**

Labour Party, *Report of 45th Annual Conference*, 1946.

Labour Research Department, Bargaining Report, *Facilities for Shop Stewards*, 1986. **170**

Labour Research Department, Bargaining Report, no. 5, 1979. **170**

Lane, T. and Roberts, K., *Strike at Pilkingtons*, Fontana, 1971. **263**

Leeson, R. A. (ed.), *Strike: A Live History 1887–1971*, Allen and Unwin, 1973. **263**

Lerner, Shirley, *Breakaway Unions and the Small Trade Union*, Allen and Unwin, 1961. **397**

Linn, Ian, *Single Union Deals, a Case Study of the Norsk-Hydro Plant at Immingham, Humerside*, TGWU Region 10, 1986.

Lucas Shop Stewards Committee, *Lucas, an Alternative Plan*, IWC, 1977. **297**

Mackintosh, M. and Wainwright, H., *A Taste of Power*, Verso, 1987. **298**

Marchietti, V. and Marks, J. D., *The CIA and the Cult of Intelligence*, Jonathan Cape, 1974. **397**

Marglin, Stephen, 'What do Bosses Do?' in A. Gorz, *The Division of Labour*, Harvester, 1976. **39**

Marsh, Arthur, *Trade Union Handbook*, Gower Press, 1979.

Marsh, A. I., Evans, E. O. and Garcia, P., *Workplace Industrial Relations in Engineering*, Research Paper 4, Engineering Employers' Federation, 1971. **262**

Marsh, A. I. and McCarthy, W. E. J., *Disputes Procedures in British Industry*, Research Paper no. 2, Part 2, Donovan Royal Commission, HMSO, 1966.

Marx, Karl, *Capital*. **26, 39, 221**

McAuley, Mary, *Labour Disputes in Soviet Russia, 1957–65*, Clarendon, 1969. **262**

McCarthy, W. E. J., *The Role of Shop Stewards in British Industrial Relations*, Research Paper no. 1, Donovan Royal Commission, HMSO, 1966. **169, 170**

McCarthy, W. E. J. and Parker, S. R., *Shop Stewards and Workplace Relations*, Research Paper no. 10, Donovan Royal Commission, HMSO, 1968. **169, 170**

McKenzie, R. T., *British Political Parties*, Heinemann, 1955. **362**

McMullen, Jeremy, *Rights at Work*, Pluto Press, 1978.

Minkin, Lewis, *The Labour Party Conference*, Allen Lane, 1978. **362**

Michels, Roberto, *Political Parties*, Constable/Dover, 1950. **81, 105**

Millward, N. and Stevens, M., *British Workplace Industrial Relations 1980–4*, Gower, 1986. **169, 170, 212**

Milne-Bailey, W., *Trade Union Documents*, Bell, 1929. **40, 362**

Morrison, Herbert, *Socialisation and Transport*, Constable, 1933. **296**

Muller, W. D., *The Kept Man*, Harvester, 1977. **362**

O'Higgins, Paul, *Workers' Rights*, Arrow in association with the Society of Industrial Tutors, 1976.

Parker, S. R., *Workplace Industrial Relations*, 1972, HMSO, 1974. **169**

Parker, S. R., *Workplace Industrial Relations*, 1973, HMSO, 1975. **169, 170, 171**

Parsons, Talcott, 'Communism and the West' in *Social Change* (eds. A. and E. Etzioni), Glencoe Ill., 1964. **262**

Partridge, B., *Towards an Action Theory of Workplace Industrial Relations*, Aston University Management Centre, working paper no. 50, 1976. **171**

Passingham, Bernie and Connor, Danny, *Ford Shop Stewards on Industrial Democracy*, IWC pamphlet no. 54, 1977. **171**

C. A. Parsons Shop Stewards Committee: (1) 'C. A. Parsons Unions Explain', IWC *Bulletin*, 1977, no. 36: (2) 'An Alternative Strategy for Power Engineering', IWC *Bulletin*, New Series, 1978, no. 1. **297**

Pearce, Brian, 'Some Rank-and-File Movements', *Labour Review*, 1959. **105**

PEP, *British Trade Unionism*, 1948. **105**

The Pike Report, Spokesman, 1977. **397**

Postgate, Raymond, *The Bolshevik Theory*, Grant Richards, 1920. **296**

Ralph, C., *The Picket and the Law*, Fabian Research Series no. 331, 1977.

Roberts, B. C., *Trade Union Government and Administration in Great Britain*, Bell, 1956. **105, 106**

Roberts, B.C., *The Trades Union Congress 1968–1921*, Allen and Unwin, 1958. **142**

Roberts, B.C., 'United Kingdom' in J. P. Windmuller *et al.*, *Collective Bargaining in Industrialised Economies: a Re-appraisal*, International Labour Office, 1987. **213**

Rolph, C. H., *All Those in Favour – the ETU Trial*, Andre Deutsch, 1962. **106**

Ross, A. M. and Hartman, P. T., *Changing Patterns of Industrial Conflict*, Wiley, 1960. **263**

Sayles, L. R., *Behaviour of Industrial Workgroups: Predictions and Control*, Chapman and Hall, 1958. **171**

Singleton, Norman, *Industrial Relations Procedures*, Department of Employment Manpower Papers no. 14, HMSO, 1975.

Smith, Adam, *The Wealth of Nations* (1776), Everyman Library. **19, 32, 39**

Somerton, M. F., *Fair Pay or Foul Play: Survey of Low Pay on Humberside*, Low Pay Unit, 1987. **212**

Somerton, M. F., 'The Proposals for Changes in the Engineering Procedural Agreement', *Trade Union Register, 2*, Spokesman, 1970.

Somerton, M. F., *Trade Unions and Industrial Relations in Local Government*, WEA, 1978.

Stewart, Margaret, *Protest or Power?* Allen and Unwin, 1974. **362**

Sweet, T. G. and Jackson, D., *The World Strike Wave 1969–7?* Aston University Management Centre, working paper no. 63, 1977.

Tayor, Robert, *The Fifth Estate – Britain's Unions in the Seventies*, Routledge and Kegan Paul, 1978. **105, 106, 142, 170**

Taylor, Mike, 'The Machine-Minder', in R. Fraser (ed.), *Work, vol. 2*, Penguin, 1969.

Thomson, Don and Larson, Rodney, *Where Were You Brothers?* War on Want, 1978. **397**

Topham, Tony, *Planning the Planners*, IWC/Spokesman, 1983. **298**

Topham, Tony, 'New Types of Bargaining', in *The Incompatibles: Trade Union Militancy and the Consensus*, Penguin, 1967.

Topham, Tony, *The Organised Worker*, Arrow in association with the Society of Industrial Tutors, 1975. **212**

Trade Union Research Unit, Ruskin College, *Nowt for Nowt*, Economic Appraisal no. 41, December, 1985. **170**

Turner, H. A., *Trade Union Growth, Structure and Policy*, Allen and Unwin, 1962. **54, 72**

Turner, H. A., *The Trend of Strikes*, Leeds University Press, 1963. **263**

Turner, H. A., *Is Britain Really Strike Prone?*, CUP, 1969. **262**

Turner, H. A., Clack, G. and Roberts, G., *Labour Relations in the Motor Industry*, Allen and Unwin, 1967. **171, 262**

Turner, H. A., Roberts, G. and Roberts, D., *Management Characteristics and Labour Conflict*, CUP, 1977. **264**

Urwin, Harry, *Plant and Productivity Bargaining*, TGWU, 3rd edition, 1972.

Useem, M., *The Inner Circle*, Oxford University Press, 1986. **298**

Vickers National Combine Shop Stewards Committee: (1) *Building the Chieftain Tank and the Alternative*, 1978; (2) *Alternative Employment for Naval Shipbuilding Workers*, 1978; (3) *Economic Audit on Vickers Scotswood*, 1979. **297**

Wainwright, H. and Elliott, D., *The Lucas Plan*, Allison and Busby, 1982. **298**

Webb, S. and B., *History of Trade Unionism*, London, 1894, WEA edition, 1920. **15, 39, 105**

Webb, S. and B., *Industrial Democracy* (1897), 1913 edition, WEA, 1926 edition, Longman, Green **72, 172, 211, 221, 296**

Westergaard, John, and Resler, Henrietta, *Class in a Capitalist Society*, Pelican, 1976.

Wedderburn, K. W., *The Worker and the Law*, Penguin, 1965. New, completely revised edition, 1986. **328**

Weiner, Norbert, *The Human Use of Human Beings*, Boston, 1950. **39**

Wells, H. G., *The Time Machine*. **34, 40**

Wigham, E., *Strikes and the Government 1893–1974*, Macmillan, 1976. **263**

Windmuller, J. P., *Collective Bargaining in Industrialised Market Economies*, ILO, 1987. **213**

II. ARTICLES FROM JOURNALS

Anderson, P., 'The Antinomies of Antonio Gramsci', *New Left Review*, no. 100, 1976/7. **362**

Brown, W., 'A Consideration of Custom and Practice', *British Journal of Industrial Relations*, vol. X, no. 1, March 1972.

Brown, W., Ebsworth, R. and Terry, M., 'Factors Shaping Shop Steward Organization in Britain', *British Journal of Industrial Relations*, vol. XVI, no. 2, July 1978. **170, 171**

Brown, W. and Sissons, K., 'Industrial Relations in the Next Decade', *Industrial Relations Journal*, XIV, 1, 1983. **186, 187, 212, 213**

Brown, W. and Terry, M., 'The Future of Collective Bargaining', *New Society*, 23 March, 1978. **171**

Carter, Peter, 'New Technology: the Challenge which the Unions Must Face', *Tribune*, 31 October, 1986. **212**

Child, J., Loveridge, M. and Warner, M., 'Towards an Organisational Study of Trade Unions', *Sociology*, vol. 7, no. 1. **40**

Daniel, W. W., 'The Effects of Employment Protection Law in Manufacturing Industry', *Department of Employment Gazette*, June, 1978.

Durcan, J. W. and McCarthy, W. E. J., 'The State Subsidy Theory of Strikes: an Examination of the Statistical Data for the Period 1956–70', *British Journal of Industrial Relations*, vol. XII, no. 1, March 1974. **264**

Forester, Tom, 'How Labour's Industrial Policy Got the Chop', *New Society*, vol. 45, no. 822. **297, 363**

Gennard, J. and Lasko, R. J., 'The Individual and the Strike', *British Journal of Industrial Relations*, vol. XIII, no. 3, November 1975. **264**

Goodman, J. F. B., 'Strikes in the UK', in *International Labour Review*, vol. 95, 1967. **263**

Hughes, John, 'The Rise of the Militants', *Trade Union Affairs*, no. 1, 1960–1. **264**

Hunter, L. C., 'The State Subsidy Theory of Strikes: A Reconsideration', *British Journal of Industrial Relations*, vol. XII, no. 3, November, 1974. **264**

Hyman, Richard, 'The Politics of Workplace Trade Unionism: Recent Tendencies and Some Problems for Theory', *Capital and Class*, vol. 8, Summer 1979. **171**

Incomes Data Services, *Focus*, July, 1976.

Incomes Data Service, *International Report*, *95*, April, 1979.

Industrial Relations Review and Report, no. 370, 1986. **212**

IWC, 'Chrysler: The Workers Answer', *Workers Control Bulletin*, no. 32, May–June, 1976.

IWC, *Workers Control Bulletin*, no. 37, 1977. **297**.

IWC, *Workers Control Bulletin*, new series, nos. 3 and 4, 1979. **106**.

Knee, Fred, 'The Revolt of Labour', *Social Democrat*, 1910. **173, 211**

Knight, K. G., 'Strikes and Wage Inflation in British Manufacturing Industry 1950–68', *Bulletin of the Oxford Institute of Economics and Statistics*, vol. 34, 1972. **262**

Lewis, Roy, 'The Historical Development of Labour Law', *British Journal of Industrial Relations*, vol. XIV, no. 1. March 1976.

Linton, Martin, 'Together We Stand', *Labour Weekly*, 8th June, 1979. **345**

LRD, 'Micro-Electronics: the Trade Union Response', *Labour Research*, June 1979.

McCarthy, W. E. J., 'The Nature of Britain's Strike Problem', *British Journal of Industrial Relations*, vol. VIII, 1970. **262.**

Martin, Roderick, 'The Quiet Triumph of the New Realism', *The Times Higher Education Supplement*, 30 January 1987. **170**

Nicholson, N., 'The Role of the Shop Steward: an Empirical Case Study', *Industrial Relations Journal*, vol. 7, no. 1, 1976. **170, 171**

Nicholson, N. and Ursell, G., 'The NALGO Activists' in *New Society*, 15 December 1977. **170**

Partridge, B., 'The Activities of Shop Stewards', *Industrial Relations Journal*, vol. 8, no. 4, 1977–8. **170**

Price, R. and Bain, G. S., 'Union Growth in Britain: Retrospect and Prospect', *British Journal of Industrial Relations*, XXL. **31, 59**

Rideout, R. W., 'The Content of Trade Union Disciplinary Rules', *British Journal of Industrial Relations*, vol. 3, 1965. **106**

Roberts, B. C. and Liebhaberg, Bruno, 'The European Trade Union Confederation: Influence of Regionalism, Detente and Multi-nationals', *British Journal of Industrial Relations*, vol. XIV, no. 3. November 1976. **397**

Sunday Times, 'The Truth About Britain's Strikes', 29 October 1978, and 'The Awful Truth About Strife in our Factories', 12 November 1978.

Silver, M., 'Recent Strike Trends: a Factual Analysis', *British Journal of Industrial Relations*, vol. XI, no. 1, 1973. **262, 263**

Scargill, Arthur, 'The Case Against Workers' Control', *Workers*

Control, Bulletin of IWC, no. 37, 1977. **296**

Smart, M., 'Performance Management Reaches County Hall', *Manpower Policy and Practice*, vol. 1, no. 1, 1985, Institute of Manpower Studies, Gower, 1985. **212**

Sullivan, Terry, 'Is There a Cycle in Labour Law?', *The Law Teacher*, April 1977.

Sullivan, Terry, 'Some Comments on Current Labour Law', *Personnel Review*, vol. 7, no. 1, 1978.

Sullivan, Terry, 'Collective Bargaining and Disclosure of Information: a View from Labour Economics', *Personnel Review*, vol. 7, no. 3, Summer, 1978.

Thomson, W. J., Mulvey, C. and Farbman, M., 'Bargaining Structure and Relative Earnings in Great Britain', *British Journal of Industrial Relations*, July 1977. **212**

Turner, H. A., 'Trade Union Structure: A New Approach', *British Journal of Industrial Relations*, vol. II, no. 2, July 1964.

Undy, Roger, 'The Devolution of Bargaining Levels and Responsibilities in the TGWU, 1965–75', in *Industrial Relations Journal*, vol. 9, no. 3. **105, 106**

Wilders, M. G. and Parker, S. R., 'Changes in Workplace Industrial Relations 1966–72', *British Journal of Industrial Relations*, vol. 13, 1975. **169, 171**

Winch, Graham, 'Shop Steward Turnover and Workplace Relations', *Industrial Relations Journal*, 1980. **170**

Windmiller, J. F. 'Re-alignments in the ICFTU: the Impact of Detente', *British Journal of Industrial Relations*, vol. XIV, no. 3, November 1976. **397**

Wintour, Patrick, 'The TUC's Foreign Policy', *New Statesman*, 2 March 1979.

Woods, Sir J., 'Last Offer Arbitration', *British Journal of Industrial Relations*, vol. 23, no. 3, 1985. **189, 212**

III. OFFICIAL REPORTS

ACAS, *Annual Report*, 1978 and 1979, HMSO. **213**

Bullock, Lord (Chairman), *Report of the Committee of Inquiry on Industrial Democracy*, HMSO, Cmnd, 6706, January 1977. **29, 39**

Central Arbitration Committee (CAC), *Annual Reports*. **213**

Certification Officer, *Annual Reports*.

Commission on Industrial Relations, Study no. 2, *Industrial Relations at Establishment Level: A Statistical Survey*, HMSO, 1973. **169**

Devlin, Lord (Chairman), *Final Report of the Committee of Inquiry under the Rt. Hon. Lord Devlin into Certain Matters Concerning the Port Transport Industry*, HMSO, Cmnd 2734, August 1965. **72**

Donovan, Lord (Chairman), *Report of the Royal Commission on Trade Unions and Employers Association*, HMSO, Cmnd 3623, 1968. **16, 39, 211, 263**

GLC, *The Ford Report*, 1986. **398**

GLEB, *Corporate Plan*, 1984. **298**

HMSO, *The Regeneration of British Industry* (White Paper), HMSO, August 1974.

HMSO, White Papers on Incomes Policy: (1) Cmnd 5125, November 1972; (2) Cmnd 5205, 5206, January 1973; (3) Cmnd 5267, March 1973; (4) Cmnd 5444, and 5446, October 1973; (5) Cmnd 6151, July, 1975; (6) Cmnd 6507, July 1976; (7) Cmnd 6883, July 1977; (8) Cmnd 7293, July 1978. **213**

HMSO, *Industrial Democracy*, Cmnd 7231, May 1978. **122, 142**

Labour, Ministry of, *Industrial Relations Handbook*, HMSO, 1964. **212, 213**

Labour, Ministry of, *Written Evidence* to the Donovan Royal Commission, HMSO, 1965.

Nigerian Ministry of Information, Report of the Tribunal of Inquiry into the Trade Unions, 1977. **397**

OECD, Economic Survey, *United Kingdom, 1984/5*. **298**

Registrar of Friendly Societies, *Report*, 1974.

West Midlands county Council, *Action in the Local Economy*, 1984. **298**

IV. TRADE UNION PUBLICATIONS

AEF, *Structure and Functions of the Union*, 1969. **106**

AEU, *Trade Unions and the Contemporary Scene*, (evidence to the Royal Commission on Trade Unions and Employers' Associations), 1965. **77–8, 164**

APEX, *Office Technology: the Trade Union Response*, 1979. **298**

ASTMS, *Discussion Document: Technological Change and Collective Bargaining*, 1979. **298**

AUEW/TASS, *Computer Technology and Employment*, 1978. **298**

DATA, *Evidence to the Royal Commission on Trade Unions and Employers Associations*, 1965.

ETU, *Submission of Evidence to the Royal Commission on Trade Unions and Employers Associations*. **76, 104**.

GMWU, *The General and Municipal Workers' Union – its History, Structure, Policy, Benefits and Services*, 1975. **76–7, 104**.

ICFTU, *Economic and Social Bulletin*, vol. XXVII, no. 1, Jan .–Mar. 1979. **398**

NUJ, *Journalists and New Technology*, 1978. **298**

POEU, *The Modernisation of Telecommunications*, 1979. **298**

TGWU, *Training Manual*, 1960. **77, 104**

TGWU, *Minutes of Evidence to the Donovan Commission*, 1966. **24, 39**

TGWU, *A Positive Employment Programme for ICI*, 1971. **297**

TGWU, *Report and Balance Sheet*, 1972.

TGWU, *The Ford Wage Claim*, 1977.

TGWU, *Micro-Electronics: New Technology, Old Problems, New Opportunities*, 1979. **298**

TGWU, *Record*, July 1979

TGWU, *Link-up Campaign*, 1987. **212**

TUC, *Free Trade Unions Leave the WFTU*, 1949. **397**

TUC, *Annual Reports. Various years as cited.*

TUC, *Trade Unionism*, TUC, 1966. **18, 39, 211**

TUC, *Post-Donovan Conferences: Collective Bargaining and Trade Union Development in the Private Sector*, 1969.

TUC, *Good Industrial Relations: a Guide for Negotiators*, 1971.

TUC, *Industrial Democracy*, TUC, 1974, (2nd edition, 1977, 3rd and revised edition, 1979). **297**

TUC, *Bargaining in Privatised Companies*, 1986. **170, 212**

TUC, *Collective Bargaining and the Social Contract*, June 1974. **213**

TUC, *Strategy of Technology Agreements*, 1979. **212**

TUC, *Fair Wages Strategy: National Minimum Wage*, April 1986. **212**

TUC, *Economic Review*, annually.

TUC, *Employment and Technology*, 1979. **298**

USDAW, *Introducing USDAW, The Structure, Government and Administration of the Union*, 1972. **74–5, 104**

LIST AND INDEX OF BRITISH TRADE UNIONS

Not every organization listed is discussed in the text, but where necessary a page reference is given. Alphabetization follows the practice of the TUC. Initials of organizations are listed so that readers can decode them.

GENERAL INDEX